Designing Effective Work Groups

*Paul S. Goodman
and Associates*

Designing Effective Work Groups

Jossey-Bass Publishers

San Francisco • London • 1986

DESIGNING EFFECTIVE WORK GROUPS
by Paul S. Goodman and Associates

Copyright © 1986 by: Jossey-Bass Inc., Publishers
433 California Street
San Francisco, California 94104
&
Jossey-Bass Limited
28 Banner Street
London EC1Y 8QE

Library of Congress Cataloging-in-Publication Data

Goodman, Paul S.
  Designing effective work groups.

  (The Jossey-Bass management series)
  (The Jossey-Bass social and behavioral science
series)
  Includes bibliographies and indexes.
  1. Work groups—Addresses, essays, lectures.
I. Title. II. Series. III. Series: Jossey-Bass social
and behavioral science series.
HD66.C66   1986   658.4'02   85-45903
ISBN 0-87589-680-4 (alk. paper)

Manufactured in the United States of America

The paper in this book meets the guidelines for
permanence and durability of the Committee on
Production Guidelines for Book Longevity of the
Council on Library Resources.

JACKET DESIGN BY WILLI BAUM

FIRST EDITION

Code 8611

A joint publication in
The Jossey-Bass Management Series
and
The Jossey-Bass
Social and Behavioral Science Series

Preface

This book is about groups in organizations. It provides a new set of theoretical perspectives about how to better understand and to design effective groups. The chapters explore determinants of work group effectiveness and strategies for designing effective groups.

Groups are exciting phenomena; they pervade our very existence. In our world of work, much of our time is spent in groups. Policy committees, coordinating committees, staff meetings, loan committees, new product committees, labor management committees, quality circles, and advisory groups are only a few of the group assignments people find themselves in in organizations. Such groups serve as mechanisms for political representation, information sharing, involvement opportunities, or as areas for handling grievances. We all have participated in and experienced the excitement, enthusiasm, and power of groups. We also have spent lots of unproductive time in groups. One simple rationale for this book is that groups are a pervasive phenomenon; they dramatically affect our lives in both positive and negative ways, and we need to learn more about groups and to understand how to make them more effective.

Another rationale for this book is that the literature on groups does not provide the intellectual guidance or models for understanding theoretically or practically how to design and maintain effective work groups. In this set of chapters, new models are presented on leadership in groups, technology and group performance, intergroup relations, and so on.

The third rationale is that there has been a renewed interest in groups in organizations. The projects on quality of work and work innovation that have emerged in the last ten years provide a unique arena for studying groups in organizations. Quality circles, labor-management participation teams, and autonomous work groups are a few examples of the types of groups that have proliferated in organizations over the past few years. Although these group mechanisms were introduced out of practical concerns for improving productivity, quality, and labor-management relations, they have provided abundant experience in the realm of designing and managing groups. Given the renewed interest in groups from the perspectives of practice and research, it seems appropriate to review where we are, note the intellectual dilemmas in understanding groups in organizations, and chart out new ways for designing and managing effective work groups.

Our strategy is to limit this book to groups in organizations. The particular focus is on performance groups—those that produce some identifiable good or service. These might range from production groups (for example, coal-mining crews) to decision-making groups (for example, loan committees). Also, our interest is in permanent as opposed to temporary groups. *Permanent* groups reflect the importance of historical and social context. The boundaries for this book are established to make our task manageable and to produce a focused product. Our interest in groups in organizations does not exclude acknowledging the vast body of literature on groups and selectively using that literature in the following chapters.

All of us who have contributed to this book hope it will stimulate new avenues of theoretical research and management practice. While researchers are one primary audience, we also want to influence the ways senior line and staff managers and consultants think about groups. Our strategy is to delineate the fundamental issues about groups in organizations and to reorient both the theory and the practice of managing groups in organizations.

Overview of Contents

In the first chapter, Paul S. Goodman, Elizabeth C. Ravlin, and Linda Argote explore the current status of our knowledge about performance groups in organizations. The chapters that follow the introductory one try to increase our understanding of designing effective work groups. Some of the chapters focus directly on work groups or on determinants of work group effectiveness. Others draw from other research on groups that can increase our understanding of groups in organizations.

Richard A. Guzzo, in the second chapter, examines two major lines of research about groups in organizations. The first line of research focuses on decision-making groups; the second concerns performance groups. Typically, work on decision making and that on models of group performance have been relatively independent. Guzzo's contribution links some of the ideas from the models of group performance with models of group decision making.

J. Richard Hackman and Richard E. Walton present a new theory of leadership in task-oriented groups in Chapter Three. The theory is built around three general ingredients that are critical to group performance: clear engaging direction, an enabling performance situation, and adequate material resources. The conceptualization of leadership functions is built from these three factors.

In Chapter Four, Paul S. Goodman provides a new perspective on understanding the meaning of task and technology on group performance. Limitations of current usages of task and technology are identified, and then a new interdisciplinary perspective is provided.

Richard E. Walton and J. Richard Hackman, in Chapter Five, distinguish between organizational contexts that are characterized by control and by commitment. The authors explore the differences between the types of groups and the functions of groups within these two organizational contexts. Of particular interest in this chapter is the treatment of formal and informal groups and new perspectives on the critical functions of groups within organizations.

A different level of analysis—intergroup relations—is

undertaken in Chapter Six, by Jeanne M. Brett and Jorn Kjell Rognes. Although previous chapters have focused on the group as the key unit of analysis, it is clear that groups in organizations are linked together. This chapter begins by examining the nature of intergroup relations, causes of differences among groups, and ways to improve intergroup relationships.

The next three chapters are designed to provide different disciplinary views about groups. In the first five chapters we focus specifically on groups in organizations. In the next three, we wanted to step back to see how some different disciplinary perspectives might contribute to our understanding of groups. Helen B. Schwartzman provides an anthropological view of groups in organizations in Chapter Seven. She demonstrates that cultural biases can shape the way we think about work group effectiveness and shows how such biases have influenced research in this area. Schwartzman also develops some alternative methodological and theoretical ways of understanding groups.

Chapters Eight and Nine provide two different social psychology perspectives for viewing groups in organizations. Bibb Latané, in Chapter Eight, examines the relevance of a large body of literature in social psychology, to which he has contributed, that deals with phenomena such as social loafing and social facilitation. James H. Davis and Norbert L. Kerr, in Chapter Nine, focus on a distinguished body of research on group decision making, particularly on how methodology used in that research might apply to work on groups in organizations.

The final two chapters provide both reviews of and comments on critical issues about groups in organizations. In Chapter Ten, L. L. Cummings focuses on themes and "disturbing contributions" in the chapters of this book. Joseph E. McGrath, in Chapter Eleven, examines ten critical needs for the study of groups at work.

Genesis of the Book

The unique feature of this book is the caliber of contributors. Linda Argote, Jeanne M. Brett, L. L. Cummings, James H. Davis, Richard A. Guzzo, J. Richard Hackman, Norbert L.

Kerr, Bibb Latané, Joseph E. McGrath, Elizabeth C. Ravlin, Jorn Kjell Rognes, Helen B. Schwartzman, and Richard E. Walton have produced significant contributions to the field.

It is important for the reader to understand the process by which this book was completed. We organized the book by "people" rather than by content. That is, we tried to identify people who have made important contributions to research on groups with particular emphasis on groups in organizations. However, we did not want the focus to be too narrow, so we also invited people who have contributed to the literature of research on groups in areas that bear on groups in organizations. We contracted with each author or team of authors for an original chapter—one that would extend our thinking about theory and practice. When the initial drafts were completed, they were circulated to all contributors. We then met at Carnegie-Mellon University for two days of intensive discussion to generate new ideas on each chapter. Tapes of the workshop discussions were given to the contributors to use in revising their chapters.

The intellectual effectiveness of the workshop format in generating new ideas was based on our work with a group of faculty members from Carnegie-Mellon University and the University of Pittsburgh, who served as "provocateurs" for the discussion of the chapters. The group included Linda Argote, Robert Atkin, Jack Brittain, Lance Kurke, John Levine, Daniel Levinthal, and Richard Moreland.

The major support for this endeavor came through a contract with the U.S. Bureau of Mines. The contract is part of a larger research program called the Carnegie-Mellon Coal Research Program, which is involved in investigations of absenteeism, group productivity, and safety. We appreciate the interest and support of our project officers, James Peay and Robert Peters. Marilyn Samples Hersh, the administrative assistant of the Coal Project, was responsible for all administrative aspects relevant to the workshop and completion of this book.

Pittsburgh, Pennsylvania   Paul S. Goodman
February 1986

Contents

The Authors

Paul S. Goodman is professor of industrial administration and psychology at the Graduate School of Industrial Administration, Carnegie-Mellon University, Pittsburgh. Previously he was on the faculty at the Graduate School of Business at the University of Chicago and was a visiting professor at Cornell University. He was educated at Trinity College (Hartford, Connecticut), where he received a B.A. degree in economics in 1959. His master's work was done at the Amos Tuck School at Dartmouth College in 1961, and he received his Ph.D. degree from Cornell University in organizational psychology in 1966.

Goodman's main professional interests are in research on work motivation and attitudes, organizational design, productivity, and organizational effectiveness. Some of this research has concerned the effects of pay inequity on performance, motivation of scientists and engineers, designing organizations to retain disadvantaged workers, and the effects of new forms of work organizations on organizational effectiveness. His research has been published in many professional journals, including the *Journal of Applied Psychology, Organizational Behavior and Human Performance,* and *Human Relations.* Recent books include *Assessing Organizational Change, Change in Organizations* and *Absenteeism: New Approaches to Understanding, Measuring, and Managing Employee Absence.*

Goodman is on the editorial board of *Organizational Behavior and Human Performance* and he also serves in a consulting capacity for private industry and the government. His research includes a large-scale study on group productivity and absenteeism, new forms of work organizations, the impact of robotics on the work force, and organizational effectiveness. He is currently director of the Center for the Management of Technology and Information in Organizations at Carnegie-Mellon, which concerns itself with the introduction and impact of technology on the work force.

Linda Argote is assistant professor of industrial administration, Graduate School of Industrial Administration, Carnegie-Mellon University.

Jeanne M. Brett is professor of organizational behavior, Kellogg Graduate School of Management, Northwestern University.

L. L. Cummings is Kellogg Distinguished Professor of Organizational Behavior, Graduate School of Management, Northwestern University.

James H. Davis is professor of psychology, Psychology Department, University of Illinois.

Richard A. Guzzo is associate professor, Department of Psychology, New York University.

J. Richard Hackman is professor of organizational behavior and of psychology, School of Organization and Management, Yale University.

Norbert L. Kerr is associate professor of psychology, Department of Psychology, Michigan State University.

Bibb Latané is professor of psychology and director of the Institute for Research in Social Science, University of North Carolina.

Joseph E. McGrath is professor of psychology, Psychology Department, University of Illinois.

Elizabeth C. Ravlin is assistant professor of organizational behavior, College of Business Administration, University of South Carolina.

Jorn Kjell Rognes is a doctoral candidate in organizational behavior, Kellogg Graduate School of Management, Northwestern University and Norwegian School of Economics and Business Administration.

Helen B. Schwartzman is associate professor, Department of Anthropology, Northwestern University.

Richard E. Walton is a Jessee Isidor Straus Professor of Business Administration, Harvard University.

Designing Effective Work Groups

1

Current Thinking About Groups: Setting the Stage for New Ideas

Paul S. Goodman
Elizabeth C. Ravlin
Linda Argote

A brief review of the literature on groups in organizations should prepare you for what follows in this book. This chapter will provide a brief status report of what we know and do not know, focusing on where we are now while the other chapters focus on new perspectives for thinking about groups in organizations.

Our review is selective and thematic. For example, we review models of group performance. Our intention is not to enumerate all possible models of group performance and the corollary empirical evidence related to these models. Rather, we will select some representative models and then extract the basic themes and issues that characterize these models. We also review some of the empirical studies relevant to groups in organizations. Our strategy is to illustrate areas of empirical interest rather than to give a detailed cataloguing of findings. We focus primarily on literature on groups and groups in organizations

Note: Support for this paper was sponsored by Bureau of Mines Contracts J0100069, J0328033, and J0123040.

1

over the last five years, making use of recent reviews (McGrath and Kravitz, 1982; Zander, 1979; McGrath, 1984). However, given the dearth of information about permanent groups in organizations, we also selected influential research pieces from prior time periods.

The review is organized into two parts. The first part examines some current models of group performance. The second part provides a brief review of some empirical evidence about groups in organizations. The basic strategy is to capture how we currently think about groups. This will set the stage for new directions in thinking about groups in organizations. That is the role of the subsequent chapters.

Groups in Organizations: Current Models

In reviewing several current and/or influential models of group performance in organizations, our choice of models is illustrative rather than comprehensive. The models are presented, compared, and finally explored with a set of critical issues in the development and specification of these models.

Team Performance Model. A model by Nieva, Fleishman, and Rieck (1978) was selected because it was part of a well-constructed review of the performance of groups, and it develops some strategies for a taxonomy of team performance. The basic thesis of their model (see Figure 1-1) is that team performance is a function of four variables: external conditions, member resources, team characteristics, and task characteristics and demands. *Performance* is divided into task behaviors by individuals and task-related behaviors at the team level. The individual performance functions refer to specific job behaviors performed by an individual (for example, pushing a lever, monitoring a machine). Task-related team function requires interaction and coordination among members. Individual task behavior and team behaviors determine the group's performance. In some tasks (for example, additive tasks), the role of individual task behaviors may be more important than team task behaviors in affecting performance. In other tasks, team behaviors may be crucial in determining team performance.

Figure 1-1. Nieva, Fleishman, and Rieck's Conceptual Model
of Team Performance.

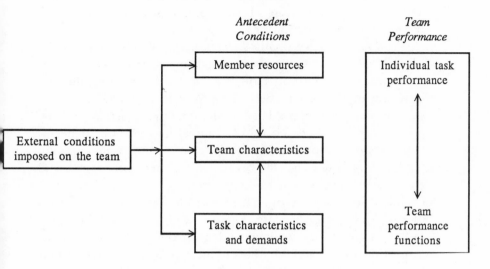

Source: Nieva, Fleishman, and Rieck, 1978.

External conditions simply acknowledge that most groups
are part of a larger social system. This larger social system determines to a large extent the membership in the group, the structure of the group, and the procedures by which the group carries out its function. *Member resources* refer to the ability,
motivations, and personality characteristics of the member.
Team characteristics refer to the structural aspects of the group.
Size, communication patterns, team climate, and authority
structure are all examples of team characteristics that bear on
performance. The arrows in Figure 1-1 indicate that team characteristics are affected by members' resources. For example,
member characteristics can affect the degree of homogeneity in
the group or the communication pattern. Task characteristics
and external conditions also affect team characteristics. Team
characteristics, in turn, can affect either individual task performance or team task behaviors. For example, group size will affect coordination (a team task behavior). *Task characteristics*

and demands specify the kinds of activities that are permitted. That is, task characteristics determine individual task behaviors and team task behaviors. Task characteristics in turn are affected by external conditions.

   Model of Task Group Effectiveness. We selected a model of task group effectiveness by Gladstein (1984) because it is representative of current models on groups in organizations and it is one of the few models to be formally tested with a large sample of work groups. The initial model by Gladstein (see Figure 1-2) is a revised version of a model by McGrath. It begins with a series of inputs: *group composition,* which is measured in terms of variables such as organizational and job tenure, and *group structure,* which includes group roles, size, leadership characteristics, and so on. These variables affect a second class of variables—*group process.* Figure 1-2 illustrates the interrelationships among the variables. Most of the group-level and organizational-level variables have a direct effect on effectiveness and an indirect effect through group process. The group task variable plays a different role. It moderates the relationship between the process variable and effectiveness. Organizational structure is predicted to affect group structure.

   The Gladstein model is one of the few in this literature that have been formally tested. Using a sample of approximately a hundred sales groups, a variety of sophisticated multivariate procedures were used to test aspects of the model. As is often the case, the tests of complicated models such as this one are inconclusive. Some of the findings indicate group process was not related to actual sales and the moderating effect of task on the process-effectiveness relationship was not supported, two results contrary to other studies on groups. The effect of group structure on process relationships, however, was supported.

   Sociotechnical Model. The sociotechnical framework is a major intellectual perspective for understanding groups in organizations. Trist and Bamforth's (1951) well-known studies of coal mines articulated the importance of designing groups in a way to reflect the optimum fit between technology and social characteristics and set the stage for new forms of work groups in organizations, particularly autonomous work groups or self-

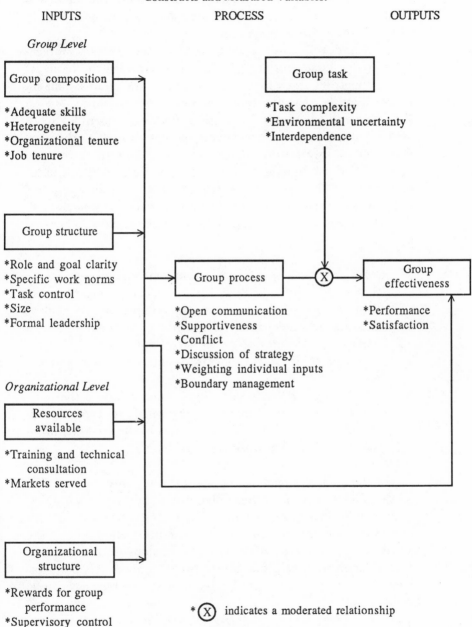

Figure 1-2. Gladstein Model of Group Behavior:
Constructs and Measured Variables.

INPUTS   PROCESS   OUTPUTS

Group Level

Group composition

*Adequate skills
*Heterogeneity
*Organizational tenure
*Job tenure

Group task

*Task complexity
*Environmental uncertainty
*Interdependence

Group structure

*Role and goal clarity
*Specific work norms
*Task control
*Size
*Formal leadership

Group process

*Open communication
*Supportiveness
*Conflict
*Discussion of strategy
*Weighting individual inputs
*Boundary management

Group effectiveness

*Performance
*Satisfaction

Organizational Level

Resources available

*Training and technical
   consultation
*Markets served

Organizational structure

*Rewards for group
   performance
*Supervisory control

* X indicates a moderated relationship

Source: Gladstein, 1984.

designing teams. In a nice piece of research by Kolodny and Kiggundu (1980), a more differentiated model of the sociotechnical approach to groups is presented and employed in a study of work groups harvesting timber.

Figure 1-3 captures the basic elements of this sociotechnical model. *Organizational arrangements* concern the basic organizational decisions that constrain the work groups. This includes number of shifts, the schedules of hours worked, group size, patterns of rotation, machines used, assignment of work areas, transportation arrangements, policies about work interdependence, interaction, and so on. *Task conditions* refer to the physical environment of work. Harvesting of wood is affected by weather, terrain, density of trees, and other physical factors. *Group characteristics* refer to the demographic and cultural background of group members. These variables, in turn, affect:

1. *Group interaction,* referring to the pattern and work activity among group members. In wood harvesting, there are strong interdependencies between certain members such as operators and mechanics. The character of this interaction pattern is a predictor of group effectiveness.
2. *Technical skills* of the operators, mechanics and supervisors.
3. *Supervision and leadership.* Supervision refers to the quality of supervisory functions performed by formally appointed individuals. Leadership refers to the informal influence pattern among work group members.

The critical aspect of the model is not only the selection of variables but also the interrelationship among the variables. Task conditions, group characteristics, and organizational arrangements determine the nature of the interaction among the variables within the rectangle. The relationships among technical skills, leadership, and group interaction determine group performance. The group outcome or effectiveness variables have direct feedback effects on the variables in the model and leadership and supervision, which in turn affects organizational arrangements.

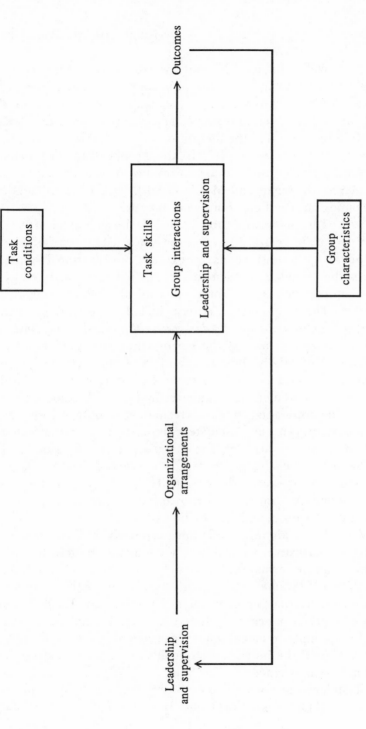

Figure 1-3. A Sociotechnical Systems Model and Its Key Variables.

Source: Adapted from Kolodny and Kiggundu, 1980.

While this model is not formally tested, it is used to explain variation in work group performance. The concepts provide a nice way to organize some complex phenomena and shed light on some determinants of group performance that are not often recognized in the literature.

A Normative Model. Hackman is one of the major current researchers on groups in organizations. A number of his papers, such as Hackman and Morris (1975), have been influential in shaping our thinking about work groups.

The main structure of the Hackman model (1983) appears in Figure 1-4. *Effectiveness* is defined in terms of whether the group output meets or exceeds organizational standards, whether member needs are more satisfied than frustrated by the group experience, and the propensity of members to work over time. The intermediate criteria includes the *level of member effort, amount of knowledge and skill applied to the task,* and *the appropriateness of the performance strategies* used by the group. The relative importance of these three criteria on group effectiveness depends in part on the nature of the material resource requirements. In some technologies, all three are important determinants; in other technologies only effort may be important. The intermediate criteria, in turn, are affected by two classes of variables. The *design* aspects of the group include the nature of the group task, the composition of the group (homogeneity versus heterogeneity), and group norms about performance strategies. The *organizational context* includes reward, education, and information system.

Other Models. While our purpose is to illustrate and not to be exhaustive, we will briefly enumerate some other models of group performance. We would be remiss in not noting Steiner's work (Steiner, 1972). His book is one of the more significant intellectual pieces in the groups literature. His basic model views performance as a function of task demands, resources (for example, member knowledge and abilities), and processes (that is, all the individual and collective actions of people who have been assigned a task). Shiflett (1979) has expanded some of Steiner's notions into more formal mathematical representations. Cummings (1981) and Herold (1978) have developed

Figure 1-4. Hackman's Overview of the Normative Model of Group Effectiveness.

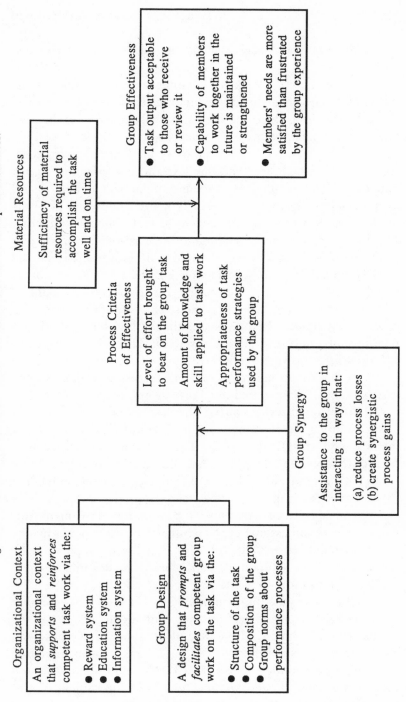

Source: Hackman, 1983.

group performance models that parallel the four models we discussed earlier.

Comparison of Models. Our understanding of the current status of groups in organizations may be sharpened by comparing and evaluating these models. This analysis provides the context and rationale for the other chapters in this book. A cursory review of Figures 1-1 to 1-4 indicates marked commonalities. All the models embrace the same levels of analysis—that is, we understand groups in terms of the group, individual, and organizational levels of analysis. There are many similarities in terms of the specific variables. Antecedent variables such as task characteristics, group composition, and organization factors appear in the models. Group process variables are important in all the models but more explicit in Figures 1-2 and 1-3. All the models describe a general concept of group effectiveness that should be relevant for different types of groups. The form of these models is also very similar. In one sense, they "flowchart" the interrelationships among a set of variables. The relationships are specified in terms of direction (that is, with arrows) rather than in terms of functional form or weights among variables. The variables, also, are specified in a fairly aggregate form.

Commonalities far outweigh differences, but some contrasts are apparent. Hackman (Figure 1-4) introduces the idea of intermediate and final criteria. The other models focus on a final criterion. The Nieva, Fleishman, and Rieck model (Figure 1-1) pays more attention to the differences between individual performance in a group setting and team performance in a group and specifically develops a taxonomy of team performance. We would assume the "architects" of these performance models acknowledge that there are feedback loops in their frameworks. The Kolodny and Kiggundu model makes these feedback loops more explicit.

While it is possible to point out other divergences among these models of group performance, our judgment is that the models are very similar. The source of the similarity comes from similar training experiences of the "architects," the influence of a few dominant models such as McGrath's, and the fact that the class of variables in these models have been the subject of empirical investigation over the last twenty to thirty years.

Issues in Model Development and Specification. Our account of the group performance models has been very descriptive. These models depict the current state of art in theorizing about groups in organizations. In this section we take a more critical stance by identifying some of the critical problems or issues with these models that should point to new directions or strategies for research and theorizing about groups.

Most of the current theoretical work generates heuristic models. These are useful for presenting a conceptual mapping of variables, but they are not in a form that allows for identifying the critical variables or understanding the interrelationships among these variables. Heuristic models need to be recast into more fine-grained models if we are to extend our understanding of groups. At minimum that would mean both identifying the relevant variables and specifying the functional relationships among these variables to the criterion variables.

The reason for moving toward a more fine-grained analysis is threefold. First, it will help uncover nonobvious, interesting relationships. For example, in one study (Goodman, 1979) we found the relationship between number of workers and labor productivity to be in the form of an inverted *U*. Within a certain range, variation in crew size was not related to productivity. After a point, increasing the crew reduced the productivity of the marginal workers. In another analysis in the same study, the impact of crew cohesiveness on productivity appeared under conditions of high process uncertainty. That is, on a day-to-day basis, cohesive groups that were positively disposed toward the company did not produce more, on average, than groups low in cohesiveness. However, when there were conditions of high production uncertainty brought about by environmental factors, productivity of the cohesive groups was higher. The point of these examples is to show that there were some unique interaction effects among variables that may explain productivity differences. One can uncover these relationships by more carefully examining the functional relationships among the variables.

The second reason for pushing toward a more fine-grained analysis is that it will sharpen our construct specification. Most constructs in the models we discussed are very broad in nature.

Organizational arrangements include a whole host of variables. Skill or knowledge is available in most group performance models. In the abstract it is hard to know how to use that variable. Are we talking about general education, job experience, or a specific set of activities? In a study by Kolodny and Kiggundu (1980), one factor in distinguishing between high- and low-productivity crews was the skill of the operator in sensing possible breakdowns, diagnosing the problem, and being able to override automatic controls. Skill was not then the general capacity to operate the machines. Rather, skill as it related to productivity was a unique package of skills relevant to a particular condition of uncertainty. To identify the appropriate meaning of skill requires, among other things, an intimate knowledge of the production process.

Third, in their current form, it is difficult to assess the confirmability or disconfirmability of any of the models. For example, Gladstein reports that group process variables were not related to an effectiveness measure scale. However, almost all group performance models assert that group process is related to effectiveness. What does this result say about the model? It is always possible to generate reasons (for example, bad measures) for the absence of an expected empirical relationship, but listing the reasons is unlikely to tell us about the goodness of the model. Our position is that the very general specification of these models precludes assessing the models' validity, whether the empirical relationships appear as predicted or not.

A second issue in current models of group performance concerns the criterion variables. The models seem to either specify a general construct of effectiveness (for example, Figure 1-4) or specify some dimensions of effectiveness. The former position is not very viable since effectiveness per se is not a very clear concept. The dimensional approach, as illustrated in Hackman's model, appears to be a more useful approach in that it attempts to delineate what effectiveness means. The critical issue in the dimensional approach is whether the different dimensions are all explained by the same model. For example, is the model that explains individual performance the same as the one that explains task performance, or are the variables that explain group performance the same variables that explain member satisfaction? Findings from some of the communication net studies indicate the group structures that covary with satisfaction do not necessarily predict performance variation (Shaw, 1976). The point is that we probably need a more differentiated set of models as we delineate the concept of effectiveness.

The third issue concerns the generalizability of the models. Generalizability here refers to explanatory and predictability of the models across different types of groups. The Kolodny and Kiggundu model (Figure 1-3) was derived from a wood-harvesting group production task. Gladstein's model focuses on sales teams. In the former group, the nature of the machinery, technological arrangements, and physical environment dominate the group process, while in the latter group, the labor component is probably more important. An issue is whether we can construct models that are generalizable across different settings (for example, harvesting as opposed to sales) and within a setting across different forms of group activities. For example, within any given setting, a group may be involved in a production task (for example, mining coal) or in a decision-making task (for example, deciding where to mine coal or how). The question still remains whether the model that is useful in explaining performance tasks fits a decision-making task, within the same technology.

The last issue concerns the role of time in any of these models. We do not expect the explanatory variables to have an instantaneous effect on performance. A refined model of group performance should tell us something about the lagged structure among variables. Basically we need to learn more about dynamic processes in groups in organizations. We need to do more than indicate that there may be feedback loops.

The basic thrust of this argument is that (1) there are a set of viable current models of group performance in organizations, which provide a useful way to organize our thinking about how groups operate in organizations, and (2) there is a need to improve on these models. Improvement can come in a number of ways: better understandings of the set of critical variables that affect performance, better conceptualization of

these variables, better understanding about the functional relationship among variables, more concern for stating models in a
way that allows for confirmability or disconfirmability, more
recognition of the role of level of analysis in understanding
group performance, and a more careful consideration of the
generalizability of models across different settings.

While the chapters in this book do not resolve all these
problems, they provide new directions for resolving some of the
theoretical issues enumerated above. For example, some of the
chapters move from general models of groups performance to
focusing on critical variables (for example, in Chapter Three by
Hackman and Walton on leadership). This movement toward
more "middle-range" theorizing seems promising in that we
should have a more detailed view of the phenomena in question.
Other chapters (for example, Goodman's Chapter Four) focus
on the issue of the generalizability of models of group performance and approaches to develop models that are confirmable
or disconfirmable.

We also recognize that theoretical developments about
groups in organizations should come from people not solely involved in research about groups in organizations. So Latané in
Chapter Eight and Davis and Kerr in Chapter Nine provide a different social psychological perspective on groups. Similarly,
Schwartzman in Chapter Seven provides an anthropological perspective.

Group Effectiveness: Empirical Evidence

In reviewing some of the empirical work on groups, our
goal is to provide a brief status report on the empirical research
related to group performance in organizations in order to set
the stage for the other chapters in this book. The focus is more
on identifying areas that have been researched and summarizing
what we know rather than critiquing specific studies. We will,
however, provide a brief commentary on that research literature.

The review covers research on group performance published since 1979.[1] Studies are included if they measure group-level outcomes (for example, performance) of groups with interdependent tasks. Therefore, this review does not examine studies in which outcomes of performance, satisfaction, or absenteeism are measured at the individual level or studies of coacting groups (for example, Kerr and Bruun, 1981). This approach eliminates most attitude studies and many studies on participation that did not utilize the group level of analysis (for example, Jackson, 1983). The interest here is in research related to group outcomes; thus literature that focuses on process considerations without measuring effectiveness indicators is also omitted (for example, Stasser and Davis, 1981). Other literature related to groups in organizations was selectively reviewed. The review is organized around the following variables that have dominated much of the literature on group performance: group composition, size, leadership, group cohesiveness, communication, group decision techniques, coordination and technology, and interventions in group performance.

Group Composition. Previous research on group composition has focused on homogeneity of traits and attitudes or abilities of group members. Past studies (Nieva, Fleishman, and Rieck, 1978) indicated that heterogeneity of member characteristics contributed positively to group performance when task requirements were diverse. Heterogeneity of abilities has a general positive effect. There is nothing in our current review (Birnbaum, 1981; Stumpf, Freedman, and Zand, 1979; Crosbie, 1979; Hawley and Heinen, 1979; Hendrick, 1979; Tziner and Eden, 1985) that would contradict this basic finding on the importance of the homogeneity of members' characteristics, given certain task requirements on group performance. Some changes in the current studies on member composition include a re-

1. The specific journals reviewed include _Academy of Management Journal, Administrative Science Quarterly, American Journal of Sociology, American Review of Sociology, Human Relations, Journal of Applied Behavioral Science, Journal of Applied Psychology, Journal of Applied Social Psychology, Journal of Experimental Social Psychology, Journal of Personality and Social Psychology, Journal of Psychology, Organizational Behavior and Human Performance, Personality and Social Psychology Bulletin,_ and _Social Psychology Quarterly._

focusing on variables such as organizational and role affiliation and sex in addition to the more traditional composition variables of personality and ability (Stumpf, Freedman, and Zand, 1979; Nutt, 1979; Wood, Polek, and Aiken, 1985). Also, there seems to be a decline in the relative number of studies examining the effect of group composition.

Size. Past research (Nieva, Fleishman, and Rieck, 1978) has indicated an inverted *U*-shaped relationship between size and performance, depending to some degree on task diversity and coordination requirements. As task coordination becomes increasingly difficult through addition of new members, performance begins to decline with size. Some recent laboratory studies and simulations (Yetton and Bottger, 1982; Grofman, Feld, and Owen, 1984) seem to be consistent with past research. A field study by Goodman (1979) demonstrated the decreasing marginal productivity of adding extra workers in mining crews. A study on navy crews (Dean and others, 1979) indicated that manning levels were related to safety criteria, while utilization of manpower related to other performance criteria such as maintenance and efficiency. The results from the field studies suggest that organizations do not operate without some minimal numbers to perform the task. Above that point there may be a range of sizes that do not impact on performance. However, when size is incongruent with task requirements, we would expect a diminishing return for additional workers. In general, the task requirements determine the degree to which size affects performance or other criteria.

The relationship between group size and absenteeism rates has also been examined during the period covered by the review (Markham, Dansereau, and Alutto, 1982). No relationship was found when size was examined between groups. When size was conceptualized as the change a group experiences in number of members over time, individual groups showed either a linear or curvilinear relationship between size and absenteeism.

Leadership. Past research (Nieva, Fleishman, and Rieck, 1978) on leadership has indicated that situational factors are important in determining the effectiveness of a leader and that participative leadership tends to be more effective than authoritarian leadership. Current research indicates that task structure and group characteristics play an important role in determining just what effects leadership has on the group. One set of studies (Saha, 1979; Konar-Goldband, Rice, and Monkarsh, 1979; Rice and others, 1982), using the least-preferred co-worker (LPC) approach to leadership effectiveness, found moderate support for this contingency view of leader effects on performance. Another line of current research (Rice, Bender, and Vitters, 1980; Schneier and Bartol, 1980; Drory and Gluskinos, 1980) examined the effects of leader traits (for example, sex, personality characteristics) on group performance. Performance effects found in these studies are inconclusive. An additional group of studies examined the effect of leader behavior on group effectiveness (Vecchio, 1982; Curtis, Smith, and Smoll, 1979; Ruzicka and others, 1979). Unfortunately, the studies look at different types of behavior so we do not find a consistent body of information supporting one kind of behavior over another. However, one observation we can make is that behaviors such as sanctioning (O'Reilly and Weitz, 1980), developing orientation, coordination, and planning (see Lord and Rowzee, 1979, or Tziner and Vardi, 1982) seem to affect group performance, and their effect is generally moderated by some group or situational variable. Research on participative behavior in groups, however, seems to have declined; therefore, no new insights into the effects of this type of leader behavior on group performance can be derived from these studies. The issue of causality of relationships between performance and leader behavior is beginning to be noted, and findings indicate that leader behavior must be considered as a dependent variable as well as an independent variable if researchers are to understand the broader system of group performance effects.

  Group Cohesiveness. Little research has been done recently that treats cohesiveness as an independent variable. Past reviews (Nieva, Fleishman, and Rieck, 1978) have concluded that effects of group cohesiveness are mediated by performance-related norms. A review by Zander (1979) provides a useful discussion on some of the determinants of cohesiveness. The few recent studies (Fodor and Smith, 1982; Manz and Sims, 1982) were done within the context of the groupthink phenomena but they are not conclusive on the relationship among cohesiveness, groupthink, and quality of decision outcomes. Another body of new literature concerning the design of autonomous work groups is related to cohesiveness and will be discussed under "interventions in group performance."

Communication. Past reviews (Nieva, Fleishman, and Rieck, 1978) suggest that the effects of the amount of communication on performance are dependent on the type of task and performance measure used. For example, measures of quantity and quality are positively related to amount of communication on structured but not on unstructured tasks. Vigilance-monitoring task performance is negatively affected by increases in the amount of communication.

Our review of recent research uncovered a small number of studies on the impact of task information requirements of the task on communication and process aspects of group communication. The most relevant research for the focus of this book is a series of studies on communication patterns in R&D groups by Tushman and Katz (Tushman, 1979a, 1979b; Katz and Tushman, 1979; Katz, 1982). These researchers focus on variables of communication type and amount, project (task) type, longevity of the project, task environment, and intra- and extradepartmental interdependence. It is not within the scope of this chapter to review all the results from this research program. One basic theme in their findings is that group effectiveness is influenced by the match between communication pattern and the nature of the group's task. High-performing groups exhibited a match between characteristics of their tasks (that is, routineness) and communication structure, while less effective groups did not. Findings on the effect of the environmental variability communication structure match on group performance were mixed. Differences in task type appeared to influence the manner in which the high-performing group dealt with external concerns, but not in ways completely consistent with a structural contingency approach to understanding effectiveness. Another theme focused on group longevity and levels of communication both within and outside of project groups. A

study by Katz (1982) indicated that longevity is related to diminished levels of communication for tasks requiring different
types of communication. Lack of this communication will lead
to decreased effectiveness. In a replication of some of Tushman's work in a different setting (Morrow, 1981), no support
was found for the proposition that subunit effectiveness can be
increased by matching the communication practice to the level
of uncertainty faced by the subunit.

The other communication studies we reviewed focused
on communication content and process. Guzzo and Waters
(1982) examined the content of communication, Kaplan (1979)
studied the effects of expressions of affect on performance, and
Casey and others (1984) studied the differential impact of social and informational components of interaction. Other studies
explored variations in communication processes. Research has
examined the effect of time pressure on member speaking time
(Isenberg, 1981), the relationship between how long a member
speaks to perceived influence on the final group decision (Bottger, 1984), and the patterns of interaction on a brainstorming
task (Ruback, Dabbs, and Hopper, 1984). Additionally, Zimbardo and Linsenmeier (1983) examined the impact of dispositional factors, gender, and roles on communication. As a whole,
these studies suggest that individual characteristics, situational
factors, and content of communication all affect both process
and performance.

Group Decision Techniques. As knowledge concerning
group decision processes has developed, researchers have developed specific techniques to improve group decision making. We
found a number of studies in this tradition as we reviewed the
literature relevant to groups in organizations. The techniques in
these studies include the nominal approach (Miner, 1979; Rohrbaugh, 1981), disaggregation of the decision task (Grofman,
1985), the delphi process (Miner, 1979; Spinelli, 1983; Rohrbaugh, 1979) problem-centered leadership (Miner, 1979), social
judgment analysis (Rohrbaugh, 1979, 1981), multiattribute
utility analysis (Eils and John, 1980), and alternative group voting strategies (Tjosvold and Field, 1983). A general conclusion
drawn from these studies is that many of these procedures are

more effective than simply using implicit or intuitive processes for group decision making, but there is no dominant technique.

Coordination and Technology. Past research on coordination in groups has been based on contingency theory. That is, methods of coordination must match the environment or technology with which the group must cope. Current research on coordination has continued in that tradition. The effects of technology on group performance have been in the past primarily considered under the domain of sociotechnical systems theories. Since most of the current research on technology in groups focuses on contingency theory, we have combined our analysis of both these areas.

The results of recent studies we reviewed at the group level provide mixed support for contingency theory (Cheng, 1984; Meadows, 1980; Middlemist and Hitt, 1981). Argote (1982) in a study of emergency rooms in a hospital found an interaction effect between models of coordination and environmental uncertainty. In general, programmed modes of coordination were more effective when uncertainty was low than when it was high, while the opposite was the case for nonprogrammed modes. Schoonhoven (1981) looked at the role of technology in operating room teams. A basic finding was that the relationships of technology and structure to effectiveness were more complex than posited by contingency theory. Fry and Slocum (1984) studied teams in a police department and did not find support for the contingency theory hypothesis concerning the effect on uncertainty and group structure on group effectiveness. A more thorough analysis of this type of research will be found later in this book (Chapter Four).

Other studies have focused on coordination as a main effect (Kabanoff and O'Brien, 1979a, 1979b; Gillespie and Birnbaum, 1980; Sutton and Ford, 1982; Rosenbaum and others, 1980; and Cheng, 1983). The findings from this work represent isolated findings; there is no cumulative body of results primarily because widely varying definitions of coordination prevent integration of the studies.

Interventions in Group Performance. Action research studies, in which researchers create change in order to understand how groups function, can also enhance our understanding of groups in organizations. Most of the studies we reviewed above come from the traditional research literature where the focus is on understanding the interrelationship among variables rather than creating change to make groups more effective.

A variety of different intervention techniques appear in studies of groups over the last five to six years. Koch (1979) examined the effects of goal setting and performance feedback (see also DeNisi, Randolph, and Blencoe, 1983) on product quality, quantity, and group cohesion. Nadler, Cammann, and Mirvis (1980) report on a sophisticated program to use survey feedback to improve group functioning. The use of team building (Woodman and Sherwood, 1980; Eden, 1985; Porras and Wilkins, 1980) and participative decision making (Koopman and others, 1981) appears in other studies.

The reader should also pay attention to the broad literature on quality of working life (QWL) projects (Goodman, 1979). Many of these interventions are at the group level of analysis. The proliferation of quality circles and labor-management participation teams illustrates the growing emphasis on finding new group arrangements to enhance organizational effectiveness. One of the most elaborate types of intervention is the creation of autonomous work groups or self-designing teams. These groups represent major departures from traditional work groups in organizations in terms of the communication, reward systems, and authority arrangements (Cummings and Molloy, 1977). An example of the introduction of autonomous work groups is the Rushton quality of working life experiment. Accounts of this and other autonomous work group interventions can be found in Trist, Susman, and Brown, 1977; Goodman, 1979; and Blumberg and Pringle, 1983.

Other Critical Issues. In this section we have provided a status report of the current literature relevant to group performance in organizations. Our goal has not been to be comprehensive but, rather, to highlight types of empirical research on groups. Additional areas the reader might find of interest are the group as opposed to individual research (Laughlin and Shippy, 1983; Laughlin and Futoran, 1985; Nichols and Day,

1982; Yetton and Bottger, 1982) and research on psychological states of group members (for example, Bray and Sugarman, 1980; Baumeister and Steinhilber, 1984; Kindler, 1979). The categories we used to organize the literature provide a fairly good picture of major thrusts of current empirical work. In examining the research on group performance that has been done over the last five years, we can identify some similarities and some shifts in the type of studies being executed. Of the group performance studies reviewed here, roughly half came from the laboratory and half from field studies. There does seem to be an increase in the amount of research performed in actual, ongoing task groups. Overall, for such a broad and important topic of research, the number of group performance studies is relatively small, limited to an average of about twelve studies per year. Trends in what variables are studied are changing. Whereas in the past most studies focused on group-level variables such as composition, cohesiveness, leadership, and size, we now see many more studies dealing with variables such as technology and task, and communication both within and between groups.

Some of the paths that group performance research appears to be following are very promising for progress in the field, while others are less promising. On the positive side, greater consideration of the organizational environment is reflected in many studies through use of contingency theory approaches, field data, or focus on contextual variables. The recognition that environmental contingencies are central to an understanding of group performance necessitates research of these contingencies, rather than the study of group-level variables alone.

A second trend that is very hopeful for the future of groups research is the increase in the number of multiple-variable and system studies (Gladstein, 1984). When groups in existing organizations are studied, a broader range of interacting variables must be accounted for to understand the results. Complex relationships between variables exist in the real world, and the only way to get at these complexities is to study systems of variables, rather than two or three variables at one time.

Less positive trends in group performance research also

can be identified. As concepts and relationships become more complex, there appears to be a trend toward less conceptual clarity. If coordination and technology are not adequately specified, as constructs they lose their explanatory power. It is especially clear from the research reviewed here that coordination in particular has no generally accepted meaning. Such disagreement is indicative of the existence of multiple dimensions of a particular construct that are probably important to understanding performance and that require multiple conceptualizations and operationalizations in research.

When conceptualizations are less than clear, measures of concepts are in turn generally poor and inadequate in themselves. Multimethod operationalizations are not used frequently, and noncomparability of measures across studies is a major problem for progress of the research area.

An additional problem with some research is a lack of attention to the appropriate level of analysis. For example, some studies conceptualize a concept at the group level but measure it at the individual level. In fact, in defining our search set for the review, studies that measured performance at a level inappropriate to their conceptual design were not considered. Variables such as technology, structure, and coordination must be identified at different levels, and we may well wish to develop differential hypotheses based on interrelationships *within* these variables at different levels of analysis.

While much of the research reviewed above is contingency theory based, there are also many studies that have virtually no theory associated with their variable choice and hypothesized relationships. Additionally, contingency theory appears, from some of the negative findings reviewed above, to be too broad to make correct predictions for specific situations. Other theories that are applied to groups also are quite general. They are more heuristic models that generally map out a set of relationships rather than clearly specify a set of variables to be analyzed.

The absence of clearly specified models affects the quality of data analytic procedures. Many of the studies we reviewed acknowledge the importance of multiple variables for

understanding group performance, the multidirectional relationships among these variables, and possible nonlinear effects. Few,
however, bring to bear the appropriate analytic techniques to
tease out these relationships.

We noted above that there is an increasing amount of research that focuses on systems rather than isolated variables.
These studies generally recognize the importance of multidirectional relationships between variables. Unfortunately, multidirectional relationships are ignored or neglected in many studies that seem especially subject to such effects. Correlational
studies must explicitly examine the possibility of these complex
relationships among variables to be useful in the progress of
groups research.

Another issue is that most of the current empirical work
we reviewed is not connected to the current models of groups in
organizations. The empirical literature seems to be driven by a
consideration of variables and not by the models of group performance we discussed earlier in this chapter. It is unfortunate
that this divergence exists between the empirical and theoretical
literature on groups in organizations.

Design of This Book

Our review of current models of group performance and
of the current empirical literature provides a brief status report
of the literature on groups. The review indicates that we have
made progress and that there are gaps, dilemmas, and problems
in our knowledge of group phenomena. The goal of this book is
to provide new perspectives, concepts, theories, and language to
think about groups in organizational contexts.

The following chapters try to expand our understanding
of groups in organizations. The book, of course, does not end
with a simple prescription of how to create effective work
groups. That may be desirable, but not likely, given the complexity of groups and the current state of knowledge about
groups. The strategy in selecting chapter topics was based more
on the person than on a grand design of some ideal set of topics
that fit our conceptualization of effective work groups.

We first identified people who have made major contributions to the groups literature and who are innovative and then asked them to extend our knowledge about groups in organizations. While some contributors are directly involved in research on groups in organizations, others are main figures in the groups literature but not in an organizational context. In addition, we tried to introduce different disciplinary perspectives as well as people who differentially emphasize research to develop theory as opposed to research to improve practice.

References

Argote, L. "Input Uncertainty and Organizational Coordination in Hospital Emergency Units." *Administrative Science Quarterly,* 1982, *27,* 420-434.

Baumeister, R. F., and Steinhilber, A. "Paradoxical Effects of Supportive Audiences on Performance Under Pressure: The Home Field Disadvantage in Sports Championships." *Journal of Personality and Social Psychology,* 1984, *47* (1), 85-93.

Birnbaum, P. H. "Integration and Specialization in Academic Research." *Academy of Management Journal,* 1981, *24* (3), 487-503.

Blumberg, M., and Pringle, C. D. "How Control Groups Can Cause Loss of Control in Action Research: The Case of Rushton Coal Mine." *Journal of Applied Behavioral Science,* 1983, *19* (4), 409-425.

Bottger, P. C. "Expertise and Air Time as Bases of Actual and Perceived Influence in Problem-Solving Groups." *Journal of Applied Psychology,* 1984, *69* (2), 214-221.

Bray, R. M., and Sugarman, R. "Social Facilitation Among Interacting Groups: Evidence for the Evaluation-Apprehension Hypothesis." *Personality and Social Psychology Bulletin,* 1980, *6* (1), 137-142.

Casey, J. T., and others. "A Partition of Small Group Predecision Performance into Informational and Social Components." *Organizational Behavior and Human Performance,* 1984, *34,* 112-139.

Cheng, J. L. C. "Interdependence and Coordination in Organizations: A Role-System Analysis." *Academy of Management Journal*, 1983, *26* (1), 156-162.

Cheng, J. L. C. "Organizational Coordination, Uncertainty, and Performance: An Integrative Study." *Human Relations*, 1984, *37* (10), 829-851.

Crosbie, P. V. "Effects of Status Inconsistency: Negative Evidence from Small Groups." *Social Psychology Quarterly*, 1979, *42* (2), 110-125.

Cummings, T. "Designing Effective Work Groups." In P. C. Nystrom, III and W. H. Starbuck, *Handbook of Organizational Design*. Vol. 2: *Remodeling Organizations and Their Environments*. New York: Oxford University Press, 1981.

Cummings, T., and Molloy, E. S. *Improving Productivity and the Quality of Work Life*. New York: Praeger, 1977.

Curtis, B., Smith, R. E., and Smoll, F. L. "Scrutinizing the Skipper: A Study of Leadership Behaviors in the Dugout." *Journal of Applied Psychology*, 1979, *64* (4), 391-400.

Dean, L. M., and others. "Manning Levels, Organizational Effectiveness, and Health." *Human Relations*, 1979, *32* (3), 237-246.

DeNisi, A. S., Randolph, W. A., and Blencoe, A. G. "Potential Problems with Peer Ratings." *Academy of Management Journal*, 1983, *26* (3), 457-464.

Drory, A., and Gluskinos, U. M. "Machiavellianism and Leadership." *Journal of Applied Psychology*, 1980, *65* (1), 81-86.

Eden, D. "Team Development: A True Field Experiment at Three Levels of Rigor." *Journal of Applied Psychology*, 1985, *70* (1), 94-100.

Eils, L. C., and John, R. S. "A Criterion Validation of Multi-Attribute Utility Analysis and of Group Communication Strategy." *Organizational Behavior and Human Performance*, 1980, *25* (2), 268-288.

Fodor, E. M., and Smith, T. "The Power Motive as an Influence on Group Decision-Making." *Journal of Personality and Social Psychology*, 1982, *41* (1), 178-185.

Fry, L. W., and Slocum, J. W., Jr. "Technology, Structure and Workgroup Effectiveness: A Test of a Contingency Model." *Academy of Management Journal*, 1984, *27* (2), 221-246.

Gillespie, D. F., and Birnbaum, P. H. "Status Concordance, Coordination, and Success in Interdisciplinary Research Teams." *Human Relations,* 1980, *33* (1), 41–56.

Gladstein, D. "Groups in Context: A Model of Task Group Effectiveness." *Administrative Science Quarterly,* 1984, *29* (4), 499–517.

Goodman, P. S. *Assessing Organizational Change: The Rushton Quality of Work Experiment.* New York: Wiley-Interscience, 1979.

Grofman, B. "Research Note: The Accuracy of Group Majorities for Disjunctive and Conjunctive Decision Tasks." *Organizational Behavior and Human Decision Processing,* 1985, *35* (1), 119–123.

Grofman, B., Feld, S. L., and Owen, G. "Group Size and the Performance of a Composite Group Majority: Statistical Truths and Empirical Results." *Organizational Behavior and Human Performance,* 1984, *33,* 350–359.

Guzzo, R. A., and Waters, J. A. "The Expression of Affect and the Performance of Decision-Making Groups." *Journal of Applied Psychology,* 1982, *67* (1), 67–74.

Hackman, J. R. "Group Influences on Individuals." In M. D. Dunnette (ed.), *Handbook of Industrial and Organizational Psychology.* Skokie, Ill.: Rand McNally, 1976.

Hackman, J. R. "A Normative Model of Work Team Effectiveness." Technical Report No. 2, Research Program on Group Effectiveness, Yale School of Organization and Management, 1983.

Hackman, J. R., and Morris, C. G. "Group Tasks, Group Interaction Process and Group Performance Effectiveness: A Review and Proposed Integration." In L. Berkowitz (ed.), *Advances in Experimental Social Psychology.* Orlando, Fla.: Academic Press, 1975.

Hawley, K. E., and Heinen, J. S. "Compatibility and Task Group Performance." *Human Relations,* 1979, *32* (7), 579–590.

Hendrick, H. W. "Differences in Group Problem-Solving Behavior and Effectiveness as a Function of Abstractness." *Journal of Applied Psychology,* 1979, *64* (5), 518–525.

Herold, D. M. "Improving the Performance Effectiveness of Groups Through a Task-Contingent Selection of Intervention Strategies." *Academy of Management Review,* 1978, *3* (2), 315-325.

Isenberg, D. S. "Some Effects of Time-Pressure on Vertical Structure and Decision-Making Accuracy in Small Groups." *Organizational Behavior and Human Performance,* 1981, *27,* 119-134.

Jackson, S. E. "Participation in Decision Making as a Strategy for Reducing Job-Related Strain." *Journal of Applied Psychology,* 1983, *68* (1), 3-19.

Kabanoff, B., and O'Brien, G. E. "Cooperation Structure and the Relationships of Leader and Member Ability to Group Performance." *Journal of Applied Psychology,* 1979a, *64,* 526-532.

Kabanoff, B., and O'Brien, G. E. "The Effects of Task Type and Cooperation upon Group Products and Performance." *Organizational Behavior and Human Performance,* 1979b, *23* (2), 163-181.

Kaplan, R. E. "The Utility of Maintaining Work Relationships Openly: An Experimental Study." *Journal of Applied Behavioral Science,* 1979, *15* (1), 41-59.

Katz, D., and Tushman, M. "Communication Patterns, Project Performance, and Task Characteristics: An Empirical Evaluation and Integration in an R&D Setting." *Organizational Behavior and Human Performance,* 1979, *23* (2), 139-162.

Katz, R. "The Effects of Group Longevity on Project Communication and Performance." *Administrative Science Quarterly,* 1982, *27,* 81-104.

Kerr, N. L., and Bruun, S. E. "Ringelmann Revisited: Alternative Explanations for the Social Loafing Effect." *Personality and Social Psychology Bulletin,* 1981, *1* (2), 224-231.

Kindler, H. S. "The Influence of a Meditation-Relaxation Technique on Group Problem-Solving Effectiveness." *Journal of Applied Behavioral Science,* 1979, *15* (4), 527-533.

Koch, J. L. "Effects of Goal Specificity and Performance Feedback to Work Groups on Peer Leadership, Performance, and Attitudes." *Human Relations,* 1979, *32* (10), 819-840.

Kolodny, H., and Kiggundu, M. "Towards the Development of a Sociotechnical Systems Model in Woodlands Mechanical Harvesting." *Human Relations,* 1980, *33,* 623–645.

Konar-Goldband, E., Rice, R. W., and Monkarsh, W. "Time Phased Interrelationships of Group Atmosphere, Group Performance, and Leader Style." *Journal of Applied Psychology,* 1979, *64* (4), 401–409.

Koopman, P. D., and others. "Content, Process, and Effects of Participative Decision-Making on the Shop Floor: Three Cases." *Human Relations,* 1981, *34* (8), 657–676.

Laughlin, P. R., and Futoran, G. C. "Collective Induction: Social Combination and Sequential Transition." *Journal of Personality and Social Psychology,* 1985, *48* (3), 608–613.

Laughlin, P. R., and Shippy, T. A. "Collective Induction." *Journal of Personality and Social Psychology,* 1983, *45* (1), 94–100.

Lord, R. G., and Rowzee, M. "Task Interdependence, Temporal Phase, and Cognitive Heterogeneity as Determinants of Leadership Behavior and Behavior-Performance Relations." *Organizational Behavior and Human Performance,* 1979, *23,* 182–200.

McGrath, J. E. *Social Psychology: A Brief Introduction.* New York: Holt, Rinehart & Winston, 1984.

McGrath, J. E., and Kravitz, D. A. "Group Research." *Annual Review of Psychology,* 1982, *33,* 195–230.

Manz, C. C., and Sims, H. P. "The Potential for 'Groupthink' in Autonomous Work Groups." *Human Relations,* 1982, *35* (9), 773–784.

Markham, S. E., Dansereau, F., Jr., and Alutto, J. A. "Group Size and Absenteeism Rates: A Longitudinal Analysis." *Academy of Management Journal,* 1982, *25* (4), 921–927.

Meadows, I. S. G. "Organic Structure and Innovation in Small Work Groups." *Human Relations,* 1980, *33* (6), 369–382.

Middlemist, R. D., and Hitt, M. A. "Technology as a Moderator of the Relationship Between Perceived Work Environment and Subunit Effectiveness." *Human Relations,* 1981, *34* (6), 517–532.

Miner, F. C., Jr. "A Comparative Analysis of Three Diverse

Group Decision-Making Approaches." *Academy of Management Journal,* 1979, *22* (1), 81-93.

Morrow, P. C. "Work-Related Communication, Environmental Uncertainty, and Subunit Effectiveness: A Second Look at the Information Processing Approach to Subunit Communication." *Academy of Management Journal,* 1981, *24* (4), 851-858.

Nadler, D. A., Cammann, C., and Mirvis, P. H. "Developing a Feedback System for Work Units: A Field Experiment in Structural Change." *Journal of Applied Behavioral Science,* 1980, *16* (1), 41-62.

Nichols, M. L., and Day, V. E. "A Comparison of Moral Reasoning of Groups and Individuals on the 'Defining' Issues Test." *Academy of Management Journal,* 1982, *25* (4), 201-208.

Nieva, V. F., Fleishman, E. A., and Rieck, A. "Team Dimensions: Their Identity, Their Measurement, and Their Relationships." Final Technical Report for Contract No. DAHC19-78-C-0001. Washington, D.C.: Advanced Research Resources Organizations, 1978.

Nutt, P. C. "On the Quality and Acceptance of Plans Drawn by a Consortium." *Journal of Applied Behavioral Science,* 1979, *15* (1), 7-21.

O'Reilly, C. A., III and Weitz, B. A. "Managing Marginal Employees: The Use of Warnings and Dismissals." *Administrative Science Quarterly,* 1980, *25* (3), 467-484.

Porras, J. I., and Wilkins, A. "Organization Development in a Large System: An Empirical Assessment." *Journal of Applied Behavioral Science,* 1980, *16* (4), 506-534.

Rice, R. W., Bender, L. R., and Vitters, A. G. "Leader Sex, Follower Attitudes Towards Women, and Leadership Effectiveness: A Laboratory Experiment." *Organizational Behavior and Human Performance,* 1980, *25,* 46-78.

Rice, R. W., and others. "Task Performance and Satisfaction: Least Preferred Coworkers as a Moderator." *Personality and Social Psychology Bulletin,* 1982, *8* (3), 534-541.

Rohrbaugh, J. "Improving the Quality of Group Judgment: Social Judgment Analysis and the Delphi Technique." *Organizational Behavior and Human Performance,* 1979, *24* (1), 73-92.

Rohrbaugh, J. "Improving the Quality of Group Judgment: Social Judgment Analysis and the Nominal Group Technique." *Organizational Behavior and Human Performance,* 1981, *28* (2), 272-288.

Rosenbaum, M. E., and others. "Group Productivity and Process: Pure and Mixed Reward Structures and Task Interdependence." *Journal of Personality and Social Psychology,* 1980, *39* (4), 626-642.

Ruback, R. B., Dabbs, J. M., Jr., and Hopper, C. H. "The Process of Brainstorming: An Analysis with Individual and Group Vocal Parameters." *Journal of Personality and Social Psychology,* 1984, *47* (3), 558-567.

Ruzicka, M. F., and others. "The Relation of Perceptions by Leaders and Members to Create Group Behavior." *Journal of Psychology,* 1979, *103,* 95-101.

Saha, S. K. "Contingency Theory of Leadership: A Study." *Human Relations,* 1979, *32* (4), 313-322.

Schneier, C. E., and Bartol, K. M. "Sex Effects in Emergent Leadership." *Journal of Applied Psychology,* 1980, *65* (3), 341-345.

Schoonhoven, C. B. "Problems with Contingency Theory: Testing Assumptions Hidden Within the Language of Contingency 'Theory.' " *Administrative Science Quarterly,* 1981, *26,* 349-377.

Shaw, M. E. *Group Dynamics: The Psychology of Small Group Behavior.* (2nd ed.) New York: McGraw-Hill, 1976.

Shiflett, S. "Toward a General Model of Small Group Productivity." *Psychological Bulletin,* 1979, *86* (1), 67-79.

Spinelli, T. "The Delphi Decision-Making Process." *Journal of Psychology,* 1983, *113,* 73-80.

Stasser, G., and Davis, J. H. "Group Decision Making and Social Influence: A Social Interaction Sequence Model." *Psychological Review,* 1981, *88* (6), 523-551.

Steiner, I. D. *Group Process and Productivity.* Orlando, Fla.: Academic Press, 1972.

Stumpf, S. A., Freedman, R. D., and Zand, D. E. "Judgmental Decisions: A Study of Interactions Among Group Membership, Group Functioning, and the Decision Situation." *Academy of Management Journal,* 1979, *22* (4), 765-782.

Sutton, R. I., and Ford, L. H. "Problem Solving Adequacy in Hospital Subunits." *Human Relations,* 1982, *35* (8), 675–701.

Tjosvold, D., and Field, R. H. G. "Effects of Social Context on Consensus and Majority Vote Decision Making." *Academy of Management Journal,* 1983, *26* (3), 500–506.

Trist, E. L., and Bamforth, K. W. "Some Social and Psychological Consequences of the Long-Wall Methods of Coal-Getting." *Human Relations,* 1951, *4,* 3–38.

Trist, E. L., Susman, G. I., and Brown, G. R. "An Experiment in Autonomous Working in an American Underground Coal Mine." *Human Relations,* 1977, *4,* 175–185.

Tushman, M. L. "Impacts of Perceived Environmental Variability on Patterns of Work Related Communication." *Academy of Management Journal,* 1979a, *22* (3), 482–500.

Tushman, M. L. "Work Characteristics and Subunit Communication Structure: A Contingency Analysis." *Administrative Science Quarterly,* 1979b, *24,* 82–98.

Tziner, A., and Eden, D. "Effects of Crew Composition on Crew Performance: Does the Whole Equal the Sum of Its Parts?" *Journal of Applied Psychology,* 1985, *70* (1), 85–93.

Tziner, A., and Vardi, Y. "Effects of Command Style and Group Cohesiveness on the Performance Effectiveness of Self-Selected Tank Crews." *Journal of Applied Psychology,* 1982, *67* (6), 769–775.

Vecchio, R. A. "A Further Test of Leadership Effects Due to Between-Group Variation and Within-Group Variation." *Journal of Applied Psychology,* 1982, *67* (6), 769–775.

Wood, W., Polek, D., and Aiken, C. "Sex Differences in Group Task Performance." *Journal of Personality and Social Psychology,* 1985, *48* (1), 63–71.

Woodman, R., and Sherwood, J. "Effects of Team Development Intervention: A Field Experiment." *Journal of Applied Behavioral Science,* 1980, *16,* 211–227.

Yetton, P. W., and Bottger, P. C. "Individual Versus Group Problem Solving: An Empirical Test of a Best-Member Strategy." *Organizational Behavior and Human Performance,* 1982, *29,* 307–321.

Zander, A. F. "The Psychology of Small Group Processes." *Annual Review of Psychology,* 1979, *30,* 417–451.

Zimbardo, P. G., and Linsenmeier, J. A. W. "The Influence of Personal, Social, and System Factors on Team Problem Solving." Final Report Z–83–01. Department of Psychology, Stanford University, 1983.

2

Group Decision Making and Group Effectiveness in Organizations

Richard A. Guzzo

Bridges are popular metaphors. We hear how a political candidate is a bridge between the liberal and conservative factions of a political party, for example, or how an airline's frequent flights create an air bridge between two cities. I, too, will use a bridge metaphor to introduce the content and aims of this chapter. In particular, a suspension bridge serves as a useful metaphor. A suspension bridge is a structure that connects distinct areas by hanging a platform (such as a roadway) from two or more cables that stretch beyond the platform itself. With the platform secured we can get to places we otherwise would have difficulty reaching.

This chapter seeks to construct a platform, not of concrete and steel but of ideas and concepts useful for getting us to new places in theory, research, and practice with regard to decision-making groups in organizations. The two cables supporting the platform are the bodies of research and theory on (1) group decision making and (2) group effectiveness in organizations. As is true for a suspension bridge, the value of the platform depends on the strength of the supporting cables. And those cables are not unchanging entities: They rise, fall, sway, and stretch. Thus, changes in research findings or theory can be accommodated. That the cables outdistance the platform itself suggests that these bodies of theory and research have a history and future that surpass the life of the ideas presented in this chapter.

A final comment about a suspension bridge as a metaphor for the work of this chapter is necessary. One meaning of the word *suspension* refers to keeping something fixed to await the information and consideration needed to evaluate it. This chapter will present some ideas and propositions that, although derived from prior knowledge, are not yet tested. Thus, they hang suspended until further data are collected.

Presented first in this chapter is the meaning of decision making and implications of its definition for understanding groups in organizations as decision-making bodies. Next, various issues about the nature of group decision making in organizations are illustrated through an examination of some typical decision-making groups in organizations, quality circles. Existing theoretical frameworks of group effectiveness are then reviewed for their relevance to the understanding of group decision making, leading to a consideration of conditions that improve the effectiveness of decision-making groups in organizations. Last, some thoughts on impending areas of concern to research and theory are offered.

Decision Making Defined

Decisions are commitments to action, and decision making is defined here the way Herbert A. Simon, winner of a Nobel prize for his work on decision processes in organizations, defines it. According to Simon (1977), decision making is made up of four kinds of activity: intelligence, design, choice, and review. Simon's is a realistic, broad definition of decision making that provides the opportunity to learn a great deal about the effect of various factors on group decision making and sources of effectiveness.

The intelligence phase of decision making is concerned with recognizing occasions calling for a decision. The term *intelligence* is used here in the military sense of monitoring and gathering information that can be analyzed for its meaningfulness. In organizations, occasions calling for decision might be routine and familiar or dramatic and unpredicted. Routinely, for example, decisions are made about matters such as allocating employees to jobs and the purchase of a vendor's goods. Suddenly appearing occasions calling for a decision might be a competitor's marketing a new product or a rapid deviation from quality standards in a production process.

There are infinite numbers of occasions calling for decisions, some more easily recognizable than others. Few people fail to recognize the need for decision making when a crisis occurs, and most are well aware of chronic problems that interfere with work and call for some decision to be made to alleviate those problems. Perhaps the most difficult-to-recognize occasions for decision are what Mintzberg, Raisinghani, and Theoret (1976) call opportunities. These are situations that permit decisions to be made when there is no threat or trouble, decisions that can improve an already satisfactory state of affairs. For example, circumstances may arise that call for a decision to change compensation practices in an organization, not because of a crisis (for example, a strike) or a problem (for example, unwanted turnover), but because a change in rulings by the Internal Revenue Service make new means of compensation preferable to old for both the organization and individual employees. The intelligence phase of decision making involves determining when decisions ought to be made in response to a wide variety of circumstances.

The second phase of decision making, design, is concerned with creating, developing, and assessing possible courses of action. Design activities yield alternative courses of action for consideration. In some instances of decision making the time spent on design may be brief because the alternatives are limited, such as go or no go. In other instances, though, this phase may be quite extensive, such as when designing alternative solutions to unfamiliar problems. Once alternative courses of action are identified, the third phase of decision making, choice, becomes operative.

Choice activities refer to the process of selecting one course of action from those specified in the design phase. It is this phase of decision making that has received the greatest amount of research attention. In fact, many investigators define decision making in terms of choice only (Nutt, 1976) and others offer multiple descriptions of and prescriptions for making choices, especially by individuals (Einhorn and Hogarth, 1981; Svenson, 1979). Choice is but one phase of decision making in organizations, and it is the third of four phases described by Simon (1977).

The fourth phase of decision making is review. Activities in this phase involve monitoring past choices both to see if chosen courses of action are properly implemented and to determine if new decisions must be made. Review activities close the cycle of phases in decision making: Reviewing past choices is, in part, a reinitiation of the intelligence activities that are a part of all decision-making episodes in organizations. Note, though, that not all intelligence activities are prompted by the review of past choices.

Relations Among Phases of Decision Making. The phases of decision making are discernible but loosely bounded. Designing alternative courses of action may go on at the same time that data-gathering intelligence activities occur, for example, and examination of available courses of action in the choice phase may bring about an awareness that new alternatives must be formulated. Although in a general way intelligence precedes design and design precedes choice (all of which precede review), there exists neither a necessarily orderly progression through the stages nor a set of markers that differentiate one phase from the next (Alexander, 1979; Simon, 1977). Further, each phase also can be thought of as a microcosm of the complete episode of decision making. Decision-making episodes are often best thought of as wheels within wheels within wheels (Simon, 1977), such as when decisions are made during the intelligence phase about what facts are to be regarded as important. Decision-making episodes in organizations must therefore be regarded as complex, even messy, however difficult such regard makes the task of studying decision making.

It is now widely accepted that most organizational decisions are not made in a perfectly rational way. That is, incomplete information search, imperfect logic in the design of alternatives, and nonoptimal selections among alternatives occur. The definition of decision making presented here in no way implies that decisions are truly rational.

Decision Making as a Group Task. The variety of tasks worked on by groups has long received attention in social psychological research on group performance effectiveness. Most of this research has not directly concerned groups in organizational settings.

An excellent overview of theory and research on group tasks is provided by McGrath (1984). As McGrath recounts, early distinctions among group tasks were relatively straightforward, such as distinctions between intellectual and motor tasks and between simple and complex tasks. As time passed, distinctions became more detailed and varied. For example, Carter, Haythorn, and Howell (1950) discussed six types of group tasks: clerical, discussion, intellectual construction, mechanical assembly, motor coordination, and reasoning. Shaw (1973), through a multidimensional scaling analysis, identified six dimensions on which group tasks vary: intellective as opposed to manipulative requirements, task difficulty, intrinsic interest, population familiarity, solution multiplicity, and cooperation requirements. Hackman (1968) also adopted an empirical approach to the description of "thinking" tasks and identified three types—production, discussion, and problem solving—for which solutions were seen to vary in identifiable ways, such as in originality and action orientation. An often-cited typology of group tasks is Steiner's (1972) distinction between unitary tasks (those that require the combination of group members' outputs into a single product) and tasks that can be divided among members. Unitary tasks were further described as being disjunctive (the task can be completed by any one member of a group), conjunctive (the task can be completed only by having all members of a group perform it), additive (members' contributions are summed to fulfill the task), and discretionary (the task can be solved through a variety of ways of combining members' inputs). A final example of the analysis of group tasks is Laughlin's (1980) classification of intellective and decision tasks for groups whose members pursue the same goal as opposed to competitive and bargaining type tasks for groups whose members pursue divergent goals.

From the lengthy list of existing descriptions of group tasks a few organizing principles were distilled by McGrath (1984). McGrath suggested that two basic dimensions of group tasks underlie existing descriptions. One dimension is the presence of conceptual, as opposed to behavioral, demands of tasks, or "thinking" as opposed to "doing." The second dimension is the degree to which a task induces conflict as opposed to cooperation among group members. Further, McGrath suggested that four general categories of action (or group process) occur during the performance of a task: generating, choosing, negotiating, and executing. From these organizing principles, McGrath classified descriptions of group tasks into eight types and used these types to review and discuss results of research on group performance.

I believe that McGrath's account is an accurate portrayal of most existing descriptions of group tasks but that it does not adequately describe group tasks as they occur in organizations. The reason concerns how group tasks and task performance typically have been studied: The predominant research method has been laboratory investigation. This method of investigation limits in many ways the nature of tasks open to investigation, such as restricting tasks to those of short duration, comparatively low complexity, and one-shot as opposed to cyclical performance requirements.

The complete task of decision making, for example, is rarely captured in laboratory studies. Most such studies examine what transpires after a group has been told that a decision must be made, precluding from study the intelligence phase of decision making. Similarly, laboratory studies of decision making often end abruptly once a choice among alternatives is made, giving little attention to the role of review in decision making. (For an example of a laboratory study of decision making that ignores intelligence and review activities, see Guzzo and Waters, 1982). Consequently, typologies of tasks derived from the laboratory study of groups are not fully applicable as descriptions of group tasks in organizations because of the comparatively greater variety in tasks performed by groups at work.

In no way are the comments made here to be construed as a general argument against the value of laboratory research on group task performance. On the whole, laboratory research has given considerable insight into several aspects of group task performance, including insight into two of the four phases of decision making. However, descriptions of group tasks based on what groups do in research laboratories are likely to be impoverished when applied to groups in organizations.

Quality Circles:
An Illustration of Group Decision Making

It is useful to examine group decision making in organizations in concrete terms. While there are many ways in which to do this, an examination of quality circles (also known as quality control circles) as decision-making groups is especially instructive because of the highly visible, systematic manner in which their decision making occurs.

Quality circles are an innovation in workplace practices that emphasize groups as important units in organizations. Interest in quality circles in American organizations began in the mid to late 1970s, partly in response to what was widely believed to be the instrumental role played by quality circles in making Japanese organizations successful. It is ironic that quality circles were in fact an American invention that found domestic acceptance only after another country implemented them on a large scale (Cole, 1979).

Quality circles generally are groups of five to ten workers who perform similar jobs. Membership in the quality circle group often is voluntary and group meetings are held regularly. The meetings may take place during or after work hours. A leader is usually designated for each quality circle, typically the first-level supervisor, although in some quality circles the leadership role is rotated among members or may be filled by nonsupervisory personnel. The leadership role is a special one, requiring skills as a discussion moderator and facilitator of meetings.

There are many objectives to be served by the establishment of quality circles, such as increasing workers' commitment to the organization and job satisfaction. A principle objective, as the name suggests, is to resolve problems that concern the quality of production or service in an organization, although problems of quantity of output, safety, and other matters also are addressed in quality circles. To aid these groups in their work as quality circles, members are trained in a method of tracking information through devices such as Pareto diagrams, cause-and-effect diagrams, graphs, histograms, scatter diagrams, and other statistical displays. Members also receive training in communication skills and brainstorming techniques.

Organizations invest in quality circles significant responsibility to make and implement decisions about work procedures that have a bearing on productivity. Whereas the responsibility for such decision making might previously have resided with the quality control department in an organization or levels of management above the workers, the use of quality circles moves that responsibility to groups of workers who themselves perform the basic tasks of the organization. While many interesting issues can be raised concerning the impact of quality circles, for present purposes they are discussed to illustrate dynamics of group decision making.

Much time in quality circle meetings is spent in the intelligence phase of decision making. Training in statistical analysis and display of information facilitates the group's work in this phase as the group seeks to identify those circumstances calling for a decision. Most often those circumstances are in the form of problems (of wasted resources, defective products, time inefficiencies), but the group also has the capacity to recognize opportunities for new actions that may help performance without necessarily solving a prior problem. Through quantitative and diagnostic displays of patterns of defects, scrap rates, quantity of output, accidents, and other data, quality circle procedures make explicit much of the information needed by a group to determine whether the next phases of decision making, designing alternative courses of action and choosing among them, need to be initiated.

The design phase of decision making in quality circles is a direct extension of the intelligence phase. In design, group members construct alternative ways of solving an identified problem, for example, or implementing a new idea. Brainstorming procedures often are used during this phase as a means of developing a broad range of alternatives. Proponents of quality circles suggest that the real value of quality circles is to be found in the design phase of decision making because the people who know best how to solve problems on the workfloor are those closest to the work: the workers themselves, not management or a removed quality control staff. Said another way, quality circles have the proper group composition for generating solutions to a problem.

The third phase of decision making, choice, is less patterned than design or intelligence. That is, quality circles are not necessarily instructed that their selections among alternative actions must reflect unanimous consent, majority opinion, or any other means of committing the group to an action. Variability among quality circles exists in *how* choices are made. Choices made by quality circles may or may not require the approval of management prior to implementation.

The final phase of decision making in organizations is review. In quality circles this phase is facilitated by the regularity of meetings and standardized methods of tracking and displaying performance information. In fact, in quality circles the activities of review blend easily with those of intelligence.

This account of quality circles is presented to illustrate how the four phases of decision making apply to groups as decision makers in organizations, although the account undoubtedly presents decision making in groups in too orderly a fashion. Most quality circles are likely to jump from one decision problem to another, to be interrupted, to cycle back and forth between phases of decision making, to undergo changes in membership, and to experience any number of things that make the decision process more complex. Further, quality circles are not *just* decision-making groups. They are groups that, in McGrath's (1984) terms, execute. That is, they physically apply themselves toward the completion of the duties inherent to their jobs in the organization. Quality circles might also serve as a vehicle for socializing individuals in organizations. While quality circles are good arenas to examine group decision making, it is important to recognize that their decision processes occur in a busy context.

In addition to quality circles, there are many other quarters in organizations in which group decision making occurs. These include committees, task forces, top management teams, flight crews (Foushee, 1984), and the highest levels of policy making in government (Janis, 1982). Janis provided a number of case studies of defective decision making attributable to what he termed "groupthink," a syndrome characterized by a deterioration of thinking and judgment among group members. The symptoms of groupthink and its consequential defective decision making include poor information search, incomplete survey of alternatives, and failure to examine the risks associated with the preferred alternative. These symptoms are interpretable as errors occurring within the framework of the intelligence, design, and choice phases of decision making.

General Models of Group Performance

Thus far decision making has been considered as a group task, one of many tasks that groups perform. Past research and theorizing has generated a number of models of group task effectiveness meant to apply to groups performing all sorts of tasks, such as laying pipe, delivering health care, or playing basketball. Consideration of such general models of group performance effectiveness can help identify causes of effectiveness specific to the task of decision making. The following section reviews some general models of group effectiveness in order to draw from them an understanding of determinants of effective group decision making.

Steiner's Work. Steiner's (1972) model of group performance integrated much previous social psychological research on group effectiveness. There is a deceptively simple quality to the model's assertion that actual group productivity equals its potential productivity minus losses due to faulty group process. The true complexity of the model stems from the role played by Steiner's group task typology described earlier.

Potential productivity refers to the maximum level of competence on a task that can be expressed by a group when the group possesses, and can apply, the resources required to complete the task. Depending on the situation, maximal competence might be defined according to speed, accuracy, or some other criterion. Resources include information, experience, skills, and tools available to group members. Note that the distinction between available and applied resources indicates that although a group may have the capacity to perform well, it will not necessarily utilize those resources appropriately. Inappropriate utilization of resources, in Steiner's model, is due to process losses. Process refers to all possible behaviors occurring in a task-performing group, including both task-oriented and purely social behaviors, and some group process may prevent the optimal combination of a group's resources for task completion.

How a group's resources *should be* combined is determined by the nature of the task, according to Steiner's model. For example, a task may demand that members' resources be summed for maximal performance (as in a group pulling a heavy object), or a task may demand that no more than one member's resources need be applied to the task (as in a group solving a riddle). The former is an example of an additive task, the latter a disjunctive task. Process losses, the impediments to maximal group competence that prevent the group from combining its resources for optimal task performance, arise from two kinds of deficits, those of motivation and coordination. Group members' motivation to perform is influenced by group size and systems of allocating among group members the rewards for performance. Coordination deficits are seen to occur in association with greater group size and dissimilarity of dispositional qualities among group members.

Steiner's model stimulated a great deal of subsequent research, especially on the relationship of group size to performance for various types of tasks and on differences between individual and group performance on various tasks. The model is often cited as a useful conceptual framework for organizational research on group performance. The task typology, however, has found little use in the description of jobs. Steiner's model raises issues of great concern to organizations, though, such as the impact of staffing and reward practices on group performance.

Shiflett (1979) proposed a representational framework for depicting the determinants of group productivity that subsumes Steiner's and related models. This generalized mathematical formulation depicts group productivity as a function of resources in the group and the constraints operating in a situation that hinder the transformation of group resources into productive output. These constraints include motivation and coordination deficits as well as a host of other factors that affect how resources are utilized. In organizations, these other factors might concern such things as leadership style.

Hackman's Work. Hackman (1982) provided a different perspective on group effectiveness in organizations. This model reveals an evolution in theory development, especially from the model of group performance stated by Hackman and Morris (1975) to that by Hackman and Oldham (1980) to the more recent version. Several features survived over time, and the most recent statement of the model is the most complex.

A starting point in Hackman's model of group effectiveness is the organizational context in which groups perform. Critical aspects of the context are how groups are rewarded, the extent to which the organization provides education and training bearing on group performance, and the extent to which the organization makes available to the group performance-related information, such as feedback and organizational standards. A second category of variables affecting performance pertains to what Hackman calls the design of the group. Issues of concern here are group norms as they pertain to task performance, composition of the group, and the nature of the group task. The nature of the group task is depicted by Hackman in terms quite different from those of Steiner (1972), McGrath (1984), and others. Hackman's concern is not only with the formal requirements of the task but also with how task characteristics motivate group members. Motivating task characteristics include the amount of autonomy inherent in a task and the task's meaningfulness. A third category of variables determining group performance in Hackman's model concerns the availability of assistance and interventions that can be implemented to aid a group at work. In organizations, managers or consultants can be sources of such help.

An interesting distinction is made by Hackman between intermediate indicators and ultimate indicators of group effectiveness. Ultimate effectiveness is defined by group outputs, member satisfaction, and healthy social interaction. Intermediate effectiveness pertains to the quality of the group interaction process as it performs the task at hand. Indicators of the effectiveness of group interaction process in Hackman's model include assessments of the level of member effort, the extent to which resources are applied toward task accomplishment, and the appropriateness of the strategies used by a group to accomplish its task.

The distinction between intermediate and ultimate effectiveness is useful. It suggests that the connection between effective process and outcomes is less than certain for groups. Nowhere is this more apparent than in organizational decision making. Groups can blunder about as they consider few alternatives and misread data yet make a choice that, when implemented, proves to be a beneficial one. Likewise, groups with a careful, meticulous decision process can adopt alternatives that prove inferior. Janis and Mann (1977) discuss this often tenuous link between decision process and outcome. Hackman's model also recognizes that the link between intermediate (or process) and ultimate effectiveness for task-performing groups in general is influenced by a variety of environmental factors, such as technological constraints.

Socio-Technical Work. The socio-technical framework (Cummings, 1978; Trist, 1981) offers another perspective on work group effectiveness in organizational settings. According to this framework, effectiveness is the joint optimization of task and social ends in the workplace. That is, effective groups are those that fulfill not only the task requirements imposed on them by the organization but also the social needs and goals of group members.

From the socio-technical perspective, effectiveness is achieved through the creation of self-regulating work groups (Cummings, 1978). The conditions for creating such groups involve task differentiation, boundary control, and task control. Task differentiation refers to the extent to which the group's task is a complete, meaningful whole and is distinct from the tasks of other groups. Boundary control refers to the degree to which group members exert influence over the physical space in which the group works and its membership, as well as the degree of its independence from outsiders. Groups with strong control over their social and spatial boundaries can thus determine autonomously who belongs, who influences, where the group resides, and other matters of importance. Task control refers to a group's capability to determine its own work methods and goals. Socio-technical theory does not emphasize the demands of a task on group process as determinants of performance (as does Steiner's model, for example). Rather, it stresses that groups determine the processes engaged in to complete the task. When both boundary and task control are high and task differentiation exists, groups are said to be self-regulating and, hence, likely to jointly optimize social and task objectives.

Self-regulating work groups pose a set of conditions not customarily found in organizations, although certain similarities between quality circles and self-regulating work groups can be observed. For example, quality circles are given some degree of task and boundary control. Further, the tasks of quality circle members may often be at least moderately differentiated from the tasks of others. Socio-technical principles constitute a significant departure from usual organizational practices regarding the management of group performance, and evidence exists that their application can lead to effective task performance (Trist, 1981).

A New Approach. Shea and Guzzo (1984) have developed a theoretical model of work group effectiveness that differs from earlier models. Their model, shown in Figure 2-1, cites three variables as primary causes of work group effectiveness: task interdependence, outcome interdependence, and potency. These variables are said to influence effectiveness through their

Figure 2-1. A Model of Group Task Effectiveness.

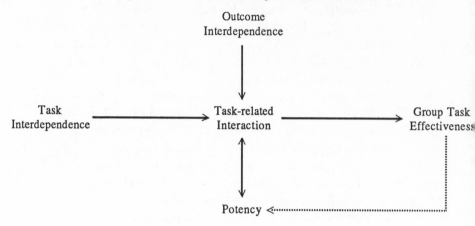

Source: Shea and Guzzo, 1984.

impact on the task-related interaction of a work group. Effectiveness is defined in terms of accomplishment of that which it is chartered to do.

Task interdependence refers to the degree of task-required cooperation in a group. When task interdependence is low, group members can carry out their roles relatively independently of other members. When task interdependence is high, however, group members must closely coordinate their actions and share resources for attaining task completion. Thus, group tasks differ in their demands for coordinated action among group members. Too little or too much orchestration of action among group members can bring about ineffectiveness. Task interdependence also influences effectiveness by moderating the impact of outcome interdependence.

Outcome interdependence refers to the degree to which important rewards are contingent on group performance. The more valuable rewards (for example, pay) are made available on the basis of group accomplishments, the greater the degree of outcome interdependence among group members. The model assumes that some minimal amount of outcome interdependence is necessary for groups to sustain effective performance.

Not only is the degree of outcome interdependence important to the model but also important is the way in which outcomes are distributed to group members. Based on the work of Miller and Hamblin (1963), Johnson and others (1981), Rosenbaum (1980), and others, it is predicted that effectiveness is hindered when, if task interdependence is high, outcomes earned by a group are distributed in a competitive way to group members. Noncompetitively distributed outcomes in conditions of high task interdependence, however, are predicted to facilitate effectiveness. Competitively distributed rewards may impede the cooperation vital to task accomplishment when task interdependence is high. When task interdependence is low, outcomes distributed either competitively or cooperatively can be expected to enhance effectiveness.

The third major explanatory variable, potency, is motivational in nature. Potency refers to the collective belief in a group that it can be effective. It is similar to Bandura's (1982) concept of self-efficacy, but potency refers to a collective phenomenon. The theory holds that a minimal amount of potency must characterize a group before it can perform tasks effectively, and the greater the potency the greater the effectiveness of a group. It is possible to speculate, however, that too strong a belief in group effectiveness may be detrimental. Janis (1982) reports cases of poor decision-making performance by groups that held unduly favorable self-regard.

Potency is determined by a number of factors. These include perceptions by members of the level of skill and knowledge within the group, the support given the group by leaders and others in an organization, and the availability of resources (tools, information, time) needed to complete a task. As the model in Figure 2-1 shows, a major determinant is performance feedback: Knowledge of past effectiveness is an influential force in shaping beliefs about future effectiveness. The development of the concept of potency owes much to Sayles's (1958) study of the behavior of work groups in organizations. He found different types of groups to exist, differentiated by how powerful each saw itself in solving problems and producing changes in the organization. In the terms of the model in Figure 2-1, some types of groups in Sayles's study experienced greater potency than others.

According to the model in Figure 2-1, task interdependence, outcome interdependence, and potency combine to shape the task-related interaction in groups. As used in that figure, task interaction process refers specifically to those behaviors and exchanges among group members that, directly or indirectly, affect task accomplishment. A great deal of interaction takes place among members of any task-performing group, some of which is relevant to doing a task and some not. Behavior in a group that affects things other than task accomplishment (such as friendship among members) is not incorporated into the model.

On the Meaning of Effectiveness. The ultimate interest of each of the above models is the effectiveness of groups performing tasks. The models based on Hackman's (1982) work and socio-technical theory (Trist, 1981) provide two similar definitions of effectiveness. According to each model, effectiveness is indicated not only by the adequacy of group outputs but also by the extent to which members experience satisfying interpersonal relations. By comparison, Steiner's (1972) account of effectiveness (productivity, in his terms) is content-free. Steiner's model is concerned with groups doing as well as they are able, but the model does not identify any criteria with which to judge whether a group is maximally effective. The model of Shea and Guzzo (1984) is similar to Steiner's in that it does not identify specific attributes of effectiveness. However, Shea and Guzzo assert that effectiveness must be defined situationally in terms of the extent to which a group fulfills its charter. If a group is established to make a decision, then effectiveness for that group would be gauged in terms of the merits of the decision produced by the group; if a quality circle exists to raise the quality of production, its effectiveness would be gauged in terms of the gains in quality it yields. Note, though, that if a quality circle is established to raise production quality *and* to provide members with satisfying interpersonal relations, then effectiveness for that group would be assessed in terms of both aspects of its charter, according to this model.

Recent research on the link between group interaction process and task effectiveness raises essential questions about the meaning and causes of task effectiveness in groups. Gladstein (1984), for example, reports data that, although group members perceived "good" interaction to be related to high task performance, an objective measure of group effectiveness (sales) in an organization was in fact unrelated to the reported nature of the interaction among group members. Guzzo and others (forthcoming) report data that effective groups, in terms of task accomplishment, are perceived to be characterized by favorable interaction among members and groups with poorer task accomplishment are seen as characterized by poorer interaction process. Similar data were reported by Staw (1975). Further, Guzzo and others (forthcoming) found that groups with favorable interaction process had their task accomplishment evaluated more positively than groups with less favorable interaction process, even though there was no objective difference in the task accomplishment of groups.

These findings indicate that people hold an implicit belief about groups that task accomplishment and quality of social interaction are related (Gladstein, 1984; Guzzo and others, forthcoming; Staw, 1975). Consequently, groups effective in terms of task accomplishment are often groundlessly perceived as having desirable interaction process characteristics and groups with desirable interaction are often erroneously perceived to be effective in task accomplishment. Researchers who define group effectiveness (in part) in terms of favorable social interaction may themselves be expressing this same implicit belief. Task accomplishment and satisfactory social interaction may be separate and independent. If so, perhaps they should not be mixed together as ingredients of effectiveness.

Determinants of Effective Group Decision Making

What can be learned from these general models of group performance that relates to group decision-making effectiveness? What do they say about organizational conditions and properties of groups that facilitate effective decision making in groups? Based on these models, I suggest the following five points are essential considerations.

The Task. The properties of the task confronting a group

play an important role in determining group effectiveness, a point recognized by all the models reviewed. The task is important in at least two respects. First, the nature of the task has clear implications for the appropriateness of various performance strategies adopted by groups at work. A performance strategy is a set of norms and procedures operating in a group to guide task accomplishment. Depending on the task, certain performance strategies are likely to be more effective than others. Steiner's (1972) discussion of group productivity recognized this point explicitly, although the concern there was not with differences among decision tasks per se but rather with differences among all tasks that groups perform. The discussion of task interdependence also concerned the fit between demands of cooperation imposed by the task and actual cooperation among group members as a determinant of group effectiveness. Socio-technical theory suggests that effectiveness is enhanced to the degree that a group has a task that is differentiated from the tasks of other groups.

In regard to decision-making groups, greater attention needs to be given to differences among the various decision tasks encountered and the implications of those differences for the use of various strategies for making decisions in groups. Performance strategies for group decision making are examined more thoroughly below.

A second reason why the task is an important consideration in group decision-making effectiveness is its motivational properties. High motivation means high effort. Hackman's work (Hackman and Oldham, 1980; Hackman, 1982) strongly suggests that group member motivation is affected by factors such as the importance of the group task and the extent to which groups engage in whole tasks. Socio-technical theory, too, emphasizes the importance of meaningful, whole tasks to group effectiveness.

For decision-making groups, then, the implication is that motivation will be high when important issues are addressed and when decision-making groups are engaged in all four phases of decision making: intelligence, design, choice, and review. A common practice in organizations is for groups to become involved in decision making only in the choice phase, such as when a meeting of managers is called to approve one of several alternative courses of action brought to them by subordinates. In this case the decision-making task is fractionated—those engaged in intelligence and design are not those who engage in choice. Breaking up in this way the work of decision making may affect motivation. The nature of organizations and information is such that it is impossible (and undesirable) always to have a single group of people complete a whole decision-making task from intelligence to review, but it is useful to think about exploiting opportunities for groups to complete whole decision-making tasks because of the apparent motivational benefits of doing so.

One caveat about the motivational properties of important, whole decision-making tasks is based on work by Janis (1982; Janis and Mann, 1977). Janis suggests that important decisions, those with substantial consequences, can be stressful, and that this stress may lead decision-making groups to make poor decisions if they cope with the stress inadequately. It may be, then, that an optimal level of motivation exists for decision tasks, and that optimal level is generated either by the task itself or by techniques for managing motivation when it is below or above that optimum.

Rewards. It is hardly surprising that rewards are important determinants of group effectiveness. Of concern here are rewards attainable by the group on the basis of the group's task completion and goal attainment. In the models reviewed, the importance of rewards to group performance is recognized by the work of Hackman (1982), Steiner (1972), and Shea and Guzzo (1984).

Rewards for group achievements can affect both the effort and coordination of a group. Effort, of course, is affected through the incentive value of the rewards. Rewards that an organization can provide groups include pay, recognition, and time off. Coordination, on the other hand, is affected by the way rewards earned by the group are distributed. As discussed earlier, distributions that induce competition among group members (for example, the "best" individual receives the entire reward) may be dysfunctional when tasks demand a high level of coordination. As is true for other tasks, the proper administration of rewards for group performance can be expected to facilitate effectiveness in decision making.

Unfortunately, rewards for group performance generally are not very common in organizations. For example, incentive pay plans that reward group performance are used very infrequently in comparison to those that reward individual or organization-wide performance (Nash and Carroll, 1975). The establishment of quality circles, though, has brought attention to the need to build into organizations ways of rewarding group performance (Munchus, 1983; Thompson, 1982). Some organizations, especially Japanese firms, reward quality circles with money and recognition (Cole, 1979; Munchus, 1983; Thompson, 1982). These rewards are, in part, based on excellence in the decisions made and implemented by quality circles. It may be problematic, however, to reward decision-making groups other than quality circles for their performance (Murnighan, 1982). Decision-making groups such as committees and task forces often form and disband in relatively short periods of time, and other decision-making groups may be made up of people from various quarters of the organization who meet informally only for the time necessary to make a particular decision. Thus, it may be that rewarding such intact, long-term groups as quality circles for their decision-making performance is more easily accomplished than rewarding the many other kinds of groups engaged in decision making in organizations.

Resources. It is indisputable that effectiveness depends on the resources embedded in the composition of a group. Insufficient skill, expertise, or strength for a task doom a group to failure. And as pointed out by Shiflett (1979) and others, the mere presence of the right resources does not guarantee effectiveness. Effectiveness also depends on the manner in which those resources are converted into group products through the group's interaction.

Apart from membership resources, resources in the organizational environment also appear to be an important determinant of group effectiveness. Groups that are able to tap an organizational environment rich in resources are more likely to be effective than those that are unable to do so. In Hackman's model of effectiveness, resources that an organization can provide include training and development for group members, advice, and planned interventions (for example, team-building experiences) that can change the group in the interest of greater effectiveness. Organizational resources also play a role in affecting a group's sense of potency, according to Shea and Guzzo (1984). Potency refers to the collective belief by a group that it can be effective, and an important influence on that belief is the extent to which the organization makes available to a group the support the group needs to accomplish its work. Teams in retail stores, for example, will need on different occasions display racks, accounting forms, adequate floor space, training in product knowledge, and other goods or support services that relate to the task of selling. Thus, the availability of resources from the environment in which groups perform tasks is a determinant of effectiveness.

The performance of decision-making groups can be aided through the existence of decision support systems in organizations. Decision support systems may involve computerized information processing that helps groups manage the data on which decisions are based, such as by aggregating and displaying information in new ways and easing the difficulties of estimating consequences of proposed alternatives. Computers also can help resolve conflict in decision-making groups (Cook and Hammond, 1982), as discussed more thoroughly below. Computers as resources hold great potential for enhancing the effectiveness of decision-making groups, although few demonstrations of their favorable impact on organizational decision making exist (Bass, 1983).

Autonomy. Two theoretical perspectives on group effectiveness emphasize autonomy as an essential ingredient in successful group performance. Hackman's (1982) model regards autonomy as a necessary element in the design of the group and its task because autonomy is viewed as stimulating effort, the use of member skills and abilities, and the adoption of an appropriate task performance strategy. The socio-technical perspective regards autonomy as crucial to the creation of truly effective work groups because autonomy enables the group to control its own task performance procedures and boundary transactions.

Investing autonomy in a decision-making group empowers it in a number of ways. With autonomy, groups can determine their membership, rules for meetings, division of labor, rules for selecting one alternative over another, and methods of reviewing past choices. Returning to the example of quality circles as decision-making groups, it can be seen that these groups experience considerable autonomy in selecting the problems they address. Autonomy in a decision-making group, however, does not always coincide with responsibility for decisions. A work group may have autonomy in specifying problems and devising solutions, but a decision may require approval from a different level in the organization before it can be implemented. Thus, responsibility for implementing the chosen course of action resides outside that group.

Appropriate Performance Strategies. A fifth stimulus to group decision-making effectiveness that can be derived from the general models reviewed is the importance of the appropriateness of the group's performance strategy for fulfilling the demands of its task. The general models of both Steiner (1972) and Hackman (1982) state that, for groups to be effective, they must adopt performance strategies that are consistent with the performance requirements of the task. With regard to decision-making groups, there is little systematic analysis of the fit between available performance strategies and the demands of decision making, which I will explore in the next section.

Performance Strategies for Group Decision Making

Various performance strategies available to groups are discussed here as those strategies pertain to the distinct demands of the four phases of decision making.

Intelligence Phase. The intelligence of decision making is concerned with identifying circumstances calling for a decision. Those circumstances include crises, the resolution of problems, and opportunities for new and innovative actions. Intelligence (and review) activities are not nearly as well understood as design and choice activities (Edwards, 1954), and thus it is difficult to specify appropriate norms and procedures for decision-making groups to adopt when performing intelligence activities. Some possibilities, though, are described below.

Strategies for identifying problems in need of resolution through decision making adhere to a basic principle of detecting a discrepancy between *what is* and *what should be* (Bass, 1983; Taylor, 1984). *What should be* is a standard or goal against which to evaluate a present state of affairs, and a description of what should be is predicated on agreement about goals and goal clarity. Often in organizations goal agreement and clarity exist, but sometimes they do not, leading to differences of opinion about whether or not decisions need to be made.

When objectives are clear, deviations from them can be assessed through systematic analysis of the source and magnitude of the discrepancy. Kepner and Tregoe's (1965) approach to discovering problems relies on the use of a series of structured questions pertaining to the nature of and reasons for a discrepancy from goals. A similar technique for organizing information about a problem is force field analysis (Ulschak, Nathanson, and Gillan, 1981). When applied to groups, it first requires them to define as precisely as possible the discrepancy between present and desired conditions. Next, force field analysis calls for specification of the "driving" and "restraining" forces as they pertain to achieving desired conditions. Driving forces are those things that help bring about the desired end; restraining forces are those that prevent it. To illustrate, assume a decision-making group is formed to determine how to reduce turnover among part-time employees in an organization. The desired state is, say, 5 percent turnover per month while the present state is 15 percent monthly turnover. Forces that prevent the desired state might include low wages, poor working hours, and a mismatch between work force skills and job demands. Forces that help achieve the desired state might include a favorable organizational climate, skillful management, and a work force dominated by students and others who typically seek part-time employment. After identification of driving and re-straining forces, force field analysis calls for the assessment of their relative strengths. Which forces are the most powerful in preventing the desired state? Which are most powerful in help-ing to achieve the desired state? Following this step, the group can move on to the design phase of decision making to create alternative courses of action that would solve the problem with-out weakening the favorable driving forces while eliminating the most powerful restraining forces acting to prevent attainment of the desired state.

Force field analysis is simply a way of organizing infor-mation in a group that helps to identify problems calling for a decision. It is neither jazzy nor technologically advanced, yet it does provide a performance strategy for groups to adopt in the intelligence phase of decision making.

A different strategy for use by groups in intelligence ac-tivities is brainstorming. Brainstorming is, as mentioned earlier, a technique often used in quality circles to generate alternative courses of action. It is a technique that also can be used in the intelligence phase of decision making to identify problems and opportunities for decision making.

Brainstorming is a strategy that relies on four essential rules to govern a group meeting (Stein, 1975). The rules are (1) criticism is ruled out, (2) freewheeling is welcomed (that is, any idea is acceptable to report), (3) as many ideas as possible should be stated, and (4) combining and improving already stated ideas is desired. The concern of brainstorming is the gen-eration of ideas in a nonevaluative atmosphere. It is predicated on assumptions that the best ideas appear when they are not subject to immediate evaluation and when dominant, relatively common ideas have already been released (hence the emphasis on quantity and combination).

Considerable controversy exists in the research literature regarding the merits of brainstorming as a performance strategy for groups, in part because some studies compared the perfor-mance of brainstorming groups to nonbrainstorming groups while other studies compared the performance of brainstorming groups to that of individuals. When compared to individuals, brainstorming groups are not superior; when compared to other groups, however, brainstorming groups appear superior (McGrath, 1984). Thus, brainstorming appears to have value as a strategy for managing the intelligence and design activities of groups.

Design Phase. A number of performance strategies exist for use in the design phase of decision making. Brainstorming, just described, is one technique applicable when alternative courses of action must be devised. Other techniques for generating novel ideas are described by Stein (1975) and Maier (1970). A technique that has enjoyed a measure of popularity in organizations is the nominal group technique (NGT) (Delbecq, Van de Ven, and Gustafson, 1975).

NGT imposes a sequence of steps that control the interaction among group members during decision making. The steps of NGT actually extend into the choice phase of decision making. The first step calls for group members to work silently in generating their own lists of alternative solutions. The second step then requires group members to report in round-robin fashion the alternatives each generated during the prior step. These are recorded publicly on a master list, and the members are given sufficient opportunity to exhaust their private lists of alternatives. Discussion among members during this stage is not permitted; talking is permissible only to report an alternative from one's list. The third step permits discussion but restricts it to issues of clarification and brief comment on the alternatives on the master list. The objective of this stage is to ensure that all group members understand each alternative and to provide each alternative limited exposure to evaluative comments. At the conclusion of this step in the NGT, the last step is one of selecting a single alternative through voting.

NGT imposes structure and limits discussion in the interest of effective decision making. The procedure, in effect, attempts to reduce process losses due to social interaction and lack of task orientation in groups. Evidence of favorable effects of NGT exists (for example, Delbecq, Van de Ven, and Gustafson, 1975), although that evidence is best construed as showing that groups using NGT tend to produce greater *numbers* of alternative solutions than groups not using NGT, but the *quality* of alternatives generated by NGT is not necessarily greater than the quality of alternatives generated by groups not using NGT (Guzzo, forthcoming).

The application of computers, in the manner described by Cook and Hammond (1982), to aid decision process in groups provides a unique performance strategy for facilitating design activities. Cook and Hammond argue that a common obstacle to effective group decision making is conflict, especially in the expression of divergent points of view by group members. They suggest, in fact, that people are relatively poor communicators of their own thinking on a decision issue and that much ineffectual verbal debating ensues in groups because of this. To overcome this problem, Cook and Hammond describe a way of representing, through computer-based mathematics and graphics, each group member's "judgment policy."

A judgment policy refers to the manner in which an individual weighs the importance of different factors in a decision and combines those factors into a preference for one alternative over others. Since individuals are relatively ineffective at communicating judgment policies, a method of depicting differences among group members' judgment policies and communicating these differences may aid groups greatly. The method advocated by Cook and Hammond is multiple regression analysis of the relationship between preferences for alternatives and points of information relevant to the evaluation of alternatives. Applied to each group member, such analysis yields a statistical model of how each person weighs the importance of each pertinent factor for each alternative. For example, differences of opinion may reside in a group given responsibility for deciding what computer network system an organization should purchase. The opinion differences may concern many possible factors relevant to the purchase, such as cost, ease of implementation, service, expandability of the system, and so on. Policy capturing through multiple regression can provide the group with a picture, in objective terms, of exactly how group members disagree with regard to the importance each member gives to the various factors and, thus, why group members disagree about which alternative computer system to purchase.

The general applicability of the policy-capturing method described by Cook and Hammond is limited because of requirements of time to put it in place and accessibility to computers, but once established the method can be used repeatedly with relative ease. More details of the method are described by Cook and Hammond (1982). Of interest here is the usefulness of adopting the policy-capturing strategy to give members insights that might otherwise be unattainable. These insights can lead to the creation of other alternatives that satisfy all members' concerns for the factors to be considered in making a choice. Thus, policy capturing is a diagnostic device. It does not prescribe a way of choosing among alternatives but it does give a unique view for group members to think about existing alternatives and can lead to the development of new alternatives.

Choice. The process of choice, selecting one from among two or more alternatives, has been studied in a variety of ways. Many studies of choice in groups are descriptive. That is, they seek to describe how it is that groups arrive at a commitment to one alternative. Some but not all such descriptive studies lead to prescriptions for managing group interaction during the choice phase to enhance effectiveness. Other prescriptions for appropriate performance strategy during choice arise from research on individual decision making.

One line of research describing how groups make choices grew out of Davis's (1973) social decision schemes framework. This framework seeks to identify by what rule individual preferences become translated into group choices. Possible rules include unanimity (all individuals must agree) and majority rule. Most groups appear to operate on the basis of majority rule to make choices, although the strength of the majority required for choice and other aspects of choice processes have been found to vary according to group size, power differences among members, and other situational factors (McGrath, 1984; Murnighan, 1982).

A different descriptive approach is Hoffman's (1979, 1982) work on the relationship between the valence of alternatives and the selection among them by groups. According to Hoffman's model, valence is a force toward the adoption of an alternative. Each alternative acquires valence during group discussion. The strength of an alternative's positive valence is determined by the number of favorable and unfavorable comments made about it, and the likelihood of its adoption is directly related to the strength of its positive valence. Hoffman (1982) suggests that the accumulation of valence by an alternative is an implicit process, one that goes on out of the awareness of group members, and that the valence accumulated by alternatives is often unrelated to the quality of alternatives. Thus, the favored alternative in a group is not always the best. Hoffman (1982) discusses a number of implications of his model for improving the decision process of groups by preventing an alternative from being adopted too early or without adequate justification.

Techniques for making choices abound in the literature (Bass, 1983; Taylor, 1984), although these techniques are not necessarily targeted for use with groups and little evidence exists of their impact on group decision-making effectiveness. Examples of these techniques include the use of a decision matrix and multiattribute decision analysis. A decision matrix is a means of systematically arraying the alternatives under consideration and the attributes, positive and negative, of the alternatives. The matrix facilitates comparisons among alternatives and, thus, should facilitate the choice process. Multiattribute utility analysis is, in a sense, a refinement and extension of the use of a decision matrix. It calls for a display of alternatives and their attributes, but it also calls for each attribute to be assigned a value (for example, purchase cost) and a weight of importance. The values of each attribute are standardized, and the standardized values are then multiplied by the weight assigned to each attribute. Since each alternative course of action has multiple attributes, the means of arriving at a choice are to add the "scores" (that is, the products of the attribute weight times attribute value) for each alternative and to adopt the alternative with the most favorable score. Note that multiattribute utility analysis, however, says little about how to arrive at agreement among group members when they differ in their assessments of weights and values for attributes.

While no single best technique for choice has been identified for use with groups, a technique for *challenging* favored alternatives has been found useful in decision-making groups. That technique is performing the role of "devil's advocate." In the devil's advocate role a group member challenges the merits of an alternative favored by the majority of the group, airing arguments against the alternative and testing the wisdom of selecting it. The objective of the role, of course, is to prevent poor choices resulting from hurried or careless considerations. Evidence of the usefulness of the role in government decision-making groups is reported by Janis (1982) and George (1975). The usefulness of the role may depend heavily on the style with which it is carried out. Schwenk and Cosier (1980) found that a devil's advocate as a carping critic added little to decision-making effectiveness but an objective, nonemotional devil's advocate enhanced effectiveness.

Review. Owing to a dearth of research in this area, there are few performance strategies to be considered for use by groups during the review phase of decision making. However, there are interesting findings regarding postchoice experiences of individual decision makers that appear relevant to decision-making groups. These findings concern postchoice rationalization and escalating commitment to a choice.

Research on postchoice rationalization suggests that considerable energy is spent by individuals to justify a choice just made (Bass, 1983; Janis and Mann, 1977). This postchoice rationalization can be useful in that it can build commitment to the chosen alternative that may sustain efforts to implement it. On the other hand, justifying the choice can diminish the capacity to evaluate objectively the merits of its implementation. Thus, the need for a new decision making may be missed. Relatedly, research on escalating commitment shows that individuals tend to adhere too long to a chosen course of action in the face of mounting costs (Staw, 1976). In other words, once a line of action gets under way consistent with an initial choice, individual decision makers find it difficult to break away from it.

The extent to which the review activities of decision-making groups are subject to the influences of postchoice rationalization and escalating commitment to action is not clear at this time. Awareness of such phenomena, however, may prove useful to groups examining the consequences of choices they made.

Summary

Decision making is comprised of four types of activity: intelligence, design, choice, and review. These activities can be considered phases in a cycle, although the phases do not necessarily occur in a strict, orderly progression and each phase shares elements of the activities of the other phases. This definition of decision making subsumes a number of distinctions among group tasks made by other group researchers and adds a significant measure of complexity to the study of group decision making. Such a definition, however, provides a realistic account of the activities of decision-making groups in organizations and forces the consideration of multiple factors as determinants of decision-making effectiveness.

General theoretical frameworks of group performance give insight into determinants of effective decision making by groups in organizations. These determinants include (1) the nature of the decision task, both in terms of the demands it places on the group interaction process and its motivational properties, (2) the existence of rewards for task performance by groups and the distribution of those rewards in a way that facilitates the member interaction and effort needed to perform a task, (3) the availability to the group of those resources, found both within the group and in the group's environment, that facilitate task performance, (4) autonomy for groups in their work as decision-making units, and (5) the appropriateness of performance strategies for groups to implement when making decisions. Potential performance strategies for use by decision-making groups were reviewed for their relation to the four phases of decision making. In terms of managing groups for effective decision making, organizations can act to ensure effectiveness by managing the conditions in which groups make decisions and the procedures used to make them.

A Look Ahead

In this section I wish to suggest some directions for future research and theorizing that I believe will lead to significant advances for understanding and practice. The list of points below pertains to the study of decision-making groups in organizations and follows closely from many of the issues already discussed. By no means is the list exhaustive.

1. *Focus on all phases of decision making.* Past research and theory on group decision making has focused almost exclusively on the design and choice phases of decision making. As mentioned previously, the focus of past research is strongly tied to the predominance of a certain method of research. The neglected phases of decision making, intelligence and review, need to receive more research attention, and theories of group decision making that span the four phases stand to make substantial contributions. It was noted that much recent research on group decision making is descriptive in nature, aimed at uncovering the processes that go on "naturally" in decision-making groups. It may be worthwhile to develop normative theories of group decision making—that is, theories of how it should occur throughout its four phases—and then conduct research to test these theories. Much of Maier's (1970) early work on group decision making and creativity was normative in nature and generated many useful prescriptions for enhancing effectiveness.

2. *Field experiments are needed.* Although there is an appreciable body of literature on group decision making, relatively few research reports exist of experimentation with group decision making in field settings. Most experimental research to date has been with groups in laboratory settings, and most field research has been nonexperimental. Thus, a need for field experiments exists, especially with regard to the impact of various performance strategies on group decision-making effectiveness. Does the nominal group technique "work" when used repeatedly by decision-making groups in organizational settings? What are the conditions that make the devil's advocate role most successful in aiding decision-making quality (see George, 1975)?

How do changes in group membership affect the performance of a decision-making group? These and many other questions are answerable through controlled experimentation in field settings.

3. *Examine differences in decision tasks.* The intelligence phase can reveal many different kinds of occasions for decision making, and it will be fruitful to examine more closely the kinds of decision tasks addressed by groups. A gross but useful distinction of this sort already discussed was that of crises, problems, and opportunities made by Mintzberg, Raisinghani, and Theoret (1976). A more detailed analysis may find, for example, that within each of these categories there are identifiable differences among decision tasks that have implications for the appropriateness of various performance strategies. Decision tasks surely differ in the demands they place on each of the four phases of decision making, and the development of theory relating the demands of decision tasks to performance strategies for groups may prove very valuable.

4. *Consider the role of motivation in decision making.* General thories of group performance frequently cite the importance of motivation in determining performance, such as by citing the role of member effort or the effects of incentives in a group. Theories related to group decision making, however, seem not to focus on motivational factors. Instead, the focus tends to be on information processing or social interaction. If motivation is an important determinant of group performance in general, then it should also be so for group decision-making performance: Motivation may play a significant role in driving information search behaviors, creativity, and other components of group decision making. Many factors conceivably could influence motivation in decision-making groups, including incentives, the importance of the decision task, or the degree of involvement in all phases of decision making, and there is ample opportunity to explore the causes and consequences of motivation in decision-making groups.

5. *Assess resource needs.* Effective decision making by groups in organizations may often require many resources, and the resource needs of groups may change as groups pass through

the various stages of decision making. Research on group performance traditionally has given much attention to how groups make use of the resources within a group (especially as those resources reside in group members in the form of expertise) but comparatively little attention to understanding how groups make use of resources *outside* the group, such as resources provided by the organizations in which groups work. The transactions between a group and its environment, especially those through which a group draws from its environment the information, guidance, tools and other resources that aid group performance, should prove to be a worthwhile topic of investigation in the study of group decision making. The nature of those transactions may well vary with the phases of decision making.

6. *Prepare for the future.* There *is* a computer revolution going on, even if it is less sudden or sweeping than many prognosticators thought. The use of computers has many implications for group decision making, especially related to ways of processing information and interacting with fellow group members. Computer conferencing, for example, is a method by which a group can engage in decision making without meeting face-to-face. The impact of such technology on group decision making is an important area of research and theorizing (Kiesler, Siegel, and McGuire, 1984). Future research on this topic might want to consider not only what technology does to groups as decision makers but also examine how that technology can best be managed for raising the effectiveness of decision-making groups.

References

Alexander, E. R. "The Design of Alternatives in Organizational Contexts: A Pilot Study." *Administrative Science Quarterly,* 1979, *24*, 382–404.

Bandura, A. "Self-Efficacy Mechanism in Human Agency." *American Psychologist*, 1982, *37*, 122–147.

Bass, B. M. *Organizational Decision Making*. Homewood, Ill.: Richard D. Irwin, 1983.

Carter, L. F., Haythorn, W. W., and Howell, M. "A Further Investigation of the Criteria of Leadership." *Journal of Abnormal and Social Psychology,* 1950, *46,* 589–595.

Cole, R. E. *Work, Mobility, and Participation: A Comparative Study of American and Japanese Industry.* Berkeley: University of California Press, 1979.

Cook, R. L., and Hammond, K. R. "Interpersonal Learning and Interpersonal Conflict Resolution in Decision-Making Groups." In R. A. Guzzo (ed.), *Improving Group Decision Making in Organizations: Approaches from Theory and Research.* Orlando, Fla.: Academic Press, 1982.

Cummings, T. "Self-Regulating Work Groups: A Socio-Technical Synthesis." *Academy of Management Review,* 1978, *3,* 625–634.

Davis, J. H. "Group Decision and Social Interaction: A Theory of Social Decision Schemes." *Psychological Review,* 1973, *80,* 97–125.

Delbecq, A. L., Van de Ven, A. H., and Gustafson, D. H. *Group Techniques for Program Planning: A Guide to Nominal Group and Delphi Processes.* Glenview, Ill.: Scott, Foresman, 1975.

Einhorn, H. J., and Hogarth, R. M. "Behavioral Decision Theory: Processes of Judgment and Choice." In M. R. Rosenzweig and L. W. Porter (eds.), *Annual Review of Psychology.* Vol. 32. Palo Alto, Calif.: Annual Reviews, 1981.

Edwards, W. "The Theory of Decision Making." *Psychological Bulletin,* 1954, *51,* 380–417.

Foushee, H. C. "Dyads and Triads at 35,000 Feet: Factors Affecting Group Process and Aircrew Performance." *American Psychologist,* 1984, *39,* 885–893.

George, A. L. "Appendix D: The Use of Information." In *Commission on the Organization of Government for the Conduct of Foreign Policy.* Vol. 2. Washington, D.C.: U.S. Government Printing Office, 1975.

Gladstein, D. L. "Groups in Context: A Model of Task Group Effectiveness." *Administrative Science Quarterly,* 1984, *29,* 499–517.

Guzzo, R. A. *Managing Group Decision Making in Organizations.* Reading, Mass.: Addison-Wesley, forthcoming.

Guzzo, R. A., and Waters, J. A. "The Expression of Affect and the Performance of Decision Making Groups." *Journal of Applied Psychology*, 1982, *67*, 67–74.

Guzzo, R. A., and others. "Implicit Theories and the Evaluation of Group Process and Performance." *Organizational Behavior and Human Decision Processes*, forthcoming.

Hackman, J. R. "Effects of Task Characteristics on Group Products." *Journal of Experimental Social Psychology*, 1968, *4*, 162–187.

Hackman, J. R. "A Set of Methods for Research on Work Teams." Technical Report No. 1, School of Organization and Management, Yale University, 1982.

Hackman, J. R., and Morris, C. G. "Group Tasks, Group Interaction Process, and Group Performance Effectiveness: A Review and Proposed Integration." In L. Berkowitz (ed.), *Advances in Experimental Social Psychology*. Vol. 8. Orlando, Fla.: Academic Press, 1975.

Hackman, J. R., and Oldham, G. *Work Redesign*. Reading, Mass.: Addison-Wesley, 1980.

Hoffman, L. R. (ed.) *The Group Problem Solving Process: Studies of a Valence Model*. New York: Praeger, 1979.

Hoffman, L. R. "Improving the Problem-Solving Process in Managerial Groups." In R. A. Guzzo (ed.), *Improving Group Decision Making in Organizations: Approaches from Theory and Research*. Orlando, Fla.: Academic Press, 1982.

Janis, I. L. *Victims of Groupthink*. (2nd ed.) Boston: Houghton Mifflin, 1982.

Janis, I. L., and Mann, L. *Decision Making: A Psychological Analysis of Conflict, Choice, and Commitment*. New York: Free Press, 1977.

Johnson, D. W., and others. "Effects of Cooperative, Competitive, and Individualistic Goal Structures on Achievement: A Meta-Analysis." *Psychological Bulletin*, 1981, *89*, 47–62.

Kepner, C. H., and Tregoe, B. B. *The Rational Manager*. New York: McGraw-Hill, 1965.

Kiesler, S., Siegel, J., and McGuire, T. W. "Social Psychological Aspects of Computer-Mediated Communication." *American Psychologist*, 1984, *39*, 1123–1134.

Laughlin, P. R. "Social Combination Processes of Cooperative, Problem-Solving Groups as Verbal Intellective Tasks." In M. Fishbein (ed.), *Progress in Social Psychology.* Vol. 1. Hillsdale, N.J.: Erlbaum, 1980.

McGrath, J. E. *Groups: Interaction and Performance.* Englewood Cliffs, N.J.: Prentice-Hall, 1984.

Maier, N. R. F. *Problem Solving and Creativity: In Individuals and Groups.* Monterey, Calif.: Brooks/Cole, 1970.

Miller, L. K., and Hamblin, R. L. "Interdependence, Differential Rewarding, and Productivity." *American Sociological Review,* 1963, *28,* 768-778.

Mintzberg, H., Raisinghani, D., and Theoret, A. "The Structure of 'Unstructured' Decision Processes." *Administrative Science Quarterly,* 1976, *21,* 246-275.

Munchus, G. "Employer-Employee Based Quality Circles in Japan: Human Resource Policy Implications for American Firms." *Academy of Management Review,* 1983, *8,* 255-261.

Murnighan, J. K. "Game Theory and the Structure of Decision Making Groups." In R. A. Guzzo (ed.), *Improving Group Decision Making in Organizations: Approaches from Theory and Research.* Orlando, Fla.: Academic Press, 1982.

Nash, A. N., and Carroll, S. J. *The Management of Compensation.* Monterey, Calif.: Brooks/Cole, 1975.

Nutt, P. C. "Models for Decision Making in Organizations and Some Contextual Variables Which Stipulate Optimal Use." *Academy of Management Review,* 1976, *1,* 84-98.

Rosenbaum, M. E. "Cooperation and Competition." In P. B. Paulus (ed.), *Psychology of Group Influence.* Hillsdale, N.J.: Erlbaum, 1980.

Sayles, L. R. *The Behavior of Industrial Work Groups: Prediction and Control.* New York: Wiley, 1958.

Schwenk, C. R., and Cosier, R. A. "Effects of the Expert, Devil's Advocate, and Dialectical Inquiry Methods on Prediction Performance." *Organizational Behavior and Human Performance,* 1980, *26,* 409-424.

Shaw, M. E. "Scaling Group Tasks: A Method of Dimensional Analysis." Ms. No. 294. *JSAS Catalog of Selected Documents in Psychology,* 1973, *3,* 8.

Shea, G. P., and Guzzo, R. A. "A Theory of Work Group Effectiveness." Unpublished manuscript, The Wharton School, University of Pennsylvania, 1984.

Shiflett, S. "Toward a General Model of Small Group Productivity." *Psychological Bulletin,* 1979, *86,* 67–79.

Simon, H. A. *The New Science of Management Decision.* (Rev. ed.) Englewood Cliffs, N.J.: Prentice-Hall, 1977.

Staw, B. M. "Attribution of the 'Causes' of Performance: A General Alternative Interpretation of Cross-Sectional Research on Organizations." *Organizational Behavior and Human Performance,* 1975, *13,* 414–432.

Staw, B. M. "Knee-Deep in the Big Muddy: A Study of Escalating Commitment to a Chosen Course of Action." *Organizational Behavior and Human Performance,* 1976, *16,* 27–44.

Stein, M. I. *Stimulating Creativity.* Vol. 2: *Group Procedures.* Orlando, Fla.: Academic Press, 1975.

Steiner, I. D. *Group Process and Productivity.* Orlando, Fla.: Academic Press, 1972.

Svenson, O. "Process Descriptions of Decision Making." *Organizational Behavior and Human Performance,* 1979, *23,* 86–112.

Taylor, R. N. *Behavioral Decision Making.* Glenview, Ill.: Scott, Foresman, 1984.

Thompson, P. C. "Quality Circles at Martin Marietta Corporation Denver Aerospace/Michoud Division." In R. Zager and M. P. Rosow (eds.), *The Innovative Organization: Productivity Programs in Action.* Elmsford, N.Y.: Pergamon Press, 1982.

Trist, E. *The Evolution of Socio-Technical Systems: A Conceptual Framework and an Action Research Program.* Toronto, Canada: Ontario Quality of Working Life Centre, 1981.

Ulschak, F. L., Nathanson, L., and Gillan, P. G. *Small Group Problem Solving: An Aid to Organizational Effectiveness.* Reading, Mass.: Addison-Wesley, 1981.

3

Leading Groups in Organizations

J. Richard Hackman
Richard E. Walton

It's not that there are no theories of leadership around. There are theories of managerial leadership, from the classic statements of organization theorists such as Fayol ([1916] 1949), Gulick, and Urwick (Gulick and Urwick, 1937) to the sophisticated contemporary ideas of Bennis (Bennis and Nanus, 1985) and Drucker (1966). There are descriptive models of leader behavior that provide great insight into what leaders usually *do* (Mintzberg, 1973). There are psychological theories that focus on the traits of effective leaders (Fiedler, 1978), on their behavioral styles (Fleishman, 1973), and on the nature of "charismatic" leadership (Bass, 1985; House, 1977). There are social psychological models (Calder, 1977; Graen, 1976; Hollander and Julian, 1970) that examine the interactions and attributions that take place between leaders and the led. There are explicitly

Note: Prepared for a conference on groups in organizations held at Carnegie-Mellon University, September 16–18, 1984. Support for the first author's work on this chapter was provided in part by the Organizational Effectiveness Research Program, Office of Naval Research, through Contract N00014-80-C-0555 to Yale University. Support for the second author's work on this paper was provided by Lex Service PLC and the Division of Research, Harvard Graduate School of Business Administration. Helpful comments on an earlier draft of this paper were provided by the participants at the Carnegie-Mellon conference and by Connie Gersick.

normative theories that specify how a leader ought to act under various circumstances (Blake and Mouton, 1964; Hersey and Blanchard, 1982; Vroom and Yetton, 1973). And there are reviews on top of reviews attempting to make sense of the voluminous empirical and conceptual literature on leadership (Hollander, 1985; Stogdill, 1974).

It is arguable that the world has all the theories of leadership. it will need for some time to come. We will, nonetheless, sketch in this chapter the beginnings of yet another such theory —even though we are acutely aware of the risk of putting even more unrefined ore atop an already substantial conceptual pile. We justify the venture in two ways. First, so far we have not found among existing leadership theories one that deals to our satisfaction with the leadership of *task-performing groups in organizations,* a topic of special interest to both of us. And second, there is a way of thinking about leadership, the "functional" approach, whose potential for pushing forward understanding about group leadership is, in our view, both high and relatively unexploited.[1] With this chapter, we hope to help readers determine for themselves if the potential of a functional approach is as great we we believe it to be.

We seek a way of thinking about the leadership of groups that has the following attributes.

1. It would deal specifically with leadership phenomena that occur in bounded groups that do real work (ranging from making decisions to actually producing things) in purposive social systems. We have no particular interest in contributing to discussions about possible differences between "leadership" and "management," nor do we care which academic discipline traditionally has owned the concepts we use in our explorations. Instead, we seek power in understanding what can be done to improve the effectiveness of task-performing groups in organizations, and we will use whatever concepts turn out to be helpful in that endeavor. If what we come up with turns out to

---

1. Early functionalist thinking about management is found in the work of Barnard (1938) and Davis (1942). Signs of a resurgence of the approach are found in the recent work of Rauch and Behling (1984) on leadership and that of Peterson (1982) on interpersonal relationships.

be useful in gaining leverage on other leadership phenomena (for example, political leadership, the supervision of individuals, or the management of whole organizations) so much the better —but that will be serendipitous rather than by design.

2. It would focus on the person (or, in some cases, persons) who link a group with the larger social system of which it is a part. This person typically has special responsibility for how well the group performs and has access to information and resources that are less readily available to other group members. We will refer to him or her as the "leader" of the group (even though occasionally group leadership may be done by a team of leaders). We are not concerned at this point with how the leader came to occupy the role (that is, by appointment, election, or simple emergence) or with the organizational location of the role (that is, within the group, on its boundary, or outside). We prefer an approach that is not tied to a particular perch from which leadership is provided or to the path by which the occupant of that perch got there.

3. It would be normative and usable. It would focus specifically on what is required for a leader to help a group do its work effectively, and it would provide a cognitive model that leaders can use in designing, building, and maintaining effective groups in varying organizational circumstances. For example, it should provide ways of dealing with questions such as the following:

- What factors should leaders give special attention to when a group's performance is substandard or when members appear to be unable to work together competently?
- On what basis should people be selected for leadership roles, and how should they be trained to perform them effectively?
- When should organizational representatives appoint (or require that the group select) someone inside the group to serve as team leader? When might an internal team leader be unnecessary or redundant?
- What should be done differently in designing and staffing leadership roles for new as opposed to relatively mature groups, or for groups that operate in widely different task and organizational circumstances?

4. It would prompt research on leadership that is both of scholarly interest and practical use. While the approach we suggest in this chapter probably cannot be tested as an intact whole, it should generate numerous questions that *are* amenable to systematic research test—tests that, taken together, would provide an assessment of the validity and usefulness of the overall approach. It should be possible, for example, to demonstrate empirically both that the cognitive models leaders use to guide their behavior differ substantially (and in predictable ways) for effective as opposed to ineffective leaders and that effective leaders are more skilled at executing the behaviors called for by their models than are their less effective peers. And it should be possible to show that groups led by individuals who have been selected and trained in accord with our approach are more effective than groups led by individuals not so selected and trained.

The aspirations listed above are ambitious, and let us say at the outset that we do not adequately fulfill them in this chapter. We do hope, however, to provide some new ideas, and some directions for further development of those ideas, that may eventually contribute both to a better understanding of leadership in task-oriented groups and to an improved technology for helping group leaders perform their roles well.

Functional Approach to Leadership

The key assertion in the functional approach to leadership is that "[the leader's] main job is to do, or get done, whatever is not being adequately handled for group needs" (McGrath, 1962, p. 5). If a leader manages, by whatever means, to ensure that all functions critical to both task accomplishment and group maintenance are adequately taken care of, then the leader has done his or her job well.

What are the critical functions that must be fulfilled in a task-performing group? Roby (1961) identified nine functions key to group task accomplishment, ranging from scanning the environment to coordinated execution of the group's response.[2]

2. The full list is (1) vigilance, (2) storage, (3) transformation, (4) forecasting, (5) addressing, routing, and distributing, (6) action selection, (7) jurisdiction, (8) execution, and (9) phasing.

Schutz (1961), focusing on the maintenance of the group as a social system, described critical functions in three areas: the group's relations with other people and groups, members' relations with one another, and members' interdependent work toward some shared goal.[3]

Explicitly building on Roby's ideas about task functions and Schutz's ideas about group and interpersonal functions, McGrath (1962) developed a generalized statement of critical leadership functions, which he arrayed in a two-by-two matrix. One axis deals with the *type* of activity—specifically, monitoring or taking executive action. The other axis describes the *orientation* of the activity—whether it is internal or external to the group. The resulting cells describe key leadership functions that must be fulfilled if a group is to be effective (McGrath, 1962, p. 17):

1. Diagnosing group deficiencies (monitoring/internal)
2. Taking remedial action to correct deficiencies (executive action/internal)
3. Forecasting impending environmental changes (monitoring/external)
4. Preventing deleterious environmental changes or their effects (executive action/external)

Based on this framework, McGrath developed lists of the knowledge and the skills that a leader should have to fulfill these functions. For example, in the "diagnosis" cell, a leader needs *knowledge* of (1) what are and are not critical group functions, (2) their relative importance, (3) standards of adequacy for each of them, and (4) procedures for assessing their presence and absence. The leader also needs *skill* in observing critical

---

3. Examples include (taking one item from each of the three areas): ensuring sufficient involvement with outside groups to avoid isolation, but not so much that the group loses its privacy; ensuring sufficient control that members can influence one another, but not so much that individual contributions are lost; and finding ways to recognize and integrate the cognitive styles of group members.

group functions and inferring group deficiencies. McGrath does similar derivations for the other three cells and shows their implications for leadership training.

McGrath's paper (a mimeographed report written at the request of the U.S. Civil Service Commission) is virtually unknown, even to researchers in the leadership area, if frequency of citation is any indication. Yet it anticipates many of the currently promising developments in leadership research, in which the emphasis is not so much on what the leader *should do* as on what *needs to be done* for effective performance (compare House and Mitchell, 1974; Kerr and Jermier, 1978; Oldham, 1976). Because the functional approach leaves room for an indefinite number of specific ways to get a critical function accomplished, it avoids the need to delineate the specific behaviors that a leader should exhibit in given circumstances—a trap into which it is all too easy for leadership theorists to fall.

As formulated by McGrath, the functional approach is generic almost to a fault: It could apply to virtually anybody leading virtually anything. For our purposes, we must ask a more focused question: What are the critical functions that need to be fulfilled if a *work group in an organization* is to perform effectively? To answer that question requires that we know something about those aspects of the group and the situation that are particularly potent in determining how well organizational teams perform—those matters about which something may "need to be done" by group leaders.

Group Effectiveness

There are several factors that determine whether or not a team is an appropriate device for performing some piece of work—such as the degree to which the work requires interdependent activity for successful completion, whether the organization tilts toward a "control" or a "commitment" work force management strategy (see Chapter Five by Walton and Hackman), how feasible it is to create and support a team in the organizational culture, and so on. Rather than delve into such matters here, we will assume that a team *is* the performing unit of choice and proceed to explore what is required to foster its effectiveness.[4]

Group Effectiveness Defined. The overall effectiveness of a group, in our view, depends on its standing on the following three dimensions:

1. *The degree to which the group's productive output (that is, its product or service) meets the standards of quantity, quality, and timeliness of the people who receive, review, and/ or use that output.* If, for example, a group generated a product that was wholly unacceptable to its legitimate client, it would be hard to argue that the group was effective—no matter what the group's own evaluation of its product was or how the product scored on some objective performance index. While it is uncommon for group researchers to rely on system-defined (rather than objective) performance assessments, the fact is that reliable objective performance measures are rare in work organizations. Even when they do exist, what *happens* to a team usually depends far more on others' assessments of the output than it does on any objective performance measure.

2. *The degree to which the process of carrying out the work enhances the capability of members to work together interdependently in the future.* Some groups operate in ways that make it impossible for members to work together again (for example, mutual antagonism becomes so high that members would choose to accept collective failure rather than share knowledge and information with one another). In other groups, members become highly skilled at working together, resulting in a performing unit that becomes increasingly capable over time (for example, a string quartet or athletic team whose members become able to anticipate one another's next moves, initiating appropriate responses to those moves even as they occur). Even when a group is temporary (such as a one-shot task force), we would examine what has happened to the performance capability of the team *qua* team over its life in judging its overall effectiveness.

3. *The degree to which the group experience contributes*

---

4. The next two sections draw heavily on Hackman (forthcoming).

to the growth and personal well-being of team members. Some groups operate in ways that block the development of individual members and frustrate satisfaction of their personal needs; other groups provide their members with many opportunities for learning and need satisfaction. Even when the official purpose of a group has nothing to do with personal development, we would examine the impact of the group experience on individual members in assessing its overall effectiveness.

In sum, we maintain that there is no single, unidimensional criterion of team effectiveness; determining how well a team has performed always involves much more than simply counting outputs. Not only must social and personal criteria be considered, but even assessments of task performance are complex because they depend on system-specified (rather than researcher-specified) standards.

The relative weights one would assign to the three criterion dimensions vary across circumstances. If a temporary team were formed to perform a single task of extraordinary importance, for example, then the second and third dimensions would be of little relevance in judging the team's effectiveness. On the other hand, teams sometimes are formed primarily to help members gain experience, learn some things, and become competent as a performing unit. The task of such a group may be more an excuse for the team than the reason for it, and assessments of the team's effectiveness would depend far more on the second and third dimensions than on the first.

With this understanding of the three dimensions of team effectiveness, let us turn now to the conditions that, if present, increase the chances that a group will achieve a high standing on them. We will give relatively more attention to the task dimension than to the social and personal dimensions because it appears that one of the most powerful ways to help a team on the latter two dimensions is to foster its standing on the first. Indeed, it may be next to impossible for a group to achieve a high standing on the social and personal dimensions if it is failing on its task.

Conditions Required for Group Effectiveness. As scientists, we have been trained to look for the specific causes of phenomena in which we have interest. When a group performs particularly well (or poorly), for example, our tendency is to rule out as many possible explanations as we can and pin down the *true* causal agent. In studies of social system effectiveness our training can mislead us, for three reasons.

First, influences on group effectiveness do not come in separate, easily distinguishable packages. They come, instead, in complex tangles that often are as hard to straighten out as a backlash on a fishing reel. To try to partial out the effects of each possible determinant of team effectiveness can lead to the conclusion that *no* single factor has a very powerful effect—a conclusion reached by more than one reviewer of the group performance literature. Each possible cause loses its potency when studied in isolation from other conditions also in place for the groups under study. It appears that group effectiveness in organizations usually is overdetermined—that is, it is the product of multiple, nonindependent factors whose influence depends in part on the fact that they *are* redundant.

Second, there are many different ways a group can behave and still perform work well, and even more ways to be nonproductive. Systems theorists call this aspect of organized endeavor "equifinality" (Katz and Kahn, 1978, p. 30). According to this principle, a group can reach the same outcome from various initial conditions and by a variety of means. Equifinality encourages us to view the leadership of work teams as centrally involving the creation of conditions that amply support effective performance, but doing so in a way that leaves plenty of room for a group to develop and implement its own unique strategy for carrying out the task. There is no single strategy that will work equally well for different groups, even groups that have identical official tasks.

Third, groups (like any social system) develop and enact their own versions of reality—and then act in accord with the environment they have helped create (see Chapter Five for more discussion of this phenomenon). A team's redefinition of reality, which cannot be prevented, can either blunt or enhance the impact of specific actions taken by a researcher or manager to influence the group.

Together, these difficulties suggest that traditional cause-effect thinking about group effectiveness may have to give way to an alternative kind of theorizing, one that is more congruent with the facts of life in social systems. We describe below one such approach, which involves examining the *conditions* that are present in the performance setting where the group works.

Ingredients of Work Group Effectiveness

In this section, we will identify and discuss three general ingredients of team effectiveness. Our research (and that of others) suggests that when all three ingredients are present, the likelihood increases that a group will function in ways that promote effectiveness (as defined above); when one or more of them is absent, the likelihood of effectiveness diminishes. As will be seen, however, there are multiple ways each of the ingredients can be provided and a virtually unlimited number of ways groups can choose to behave when they are present.

Clear, Engaging Direction. In laboratory research on group effectiveness, it is rare for performance to suffer because members do not know what they are supposed to accomplish. Expert experimenters know that they should be clear about such matters, and invariably instructions to experimental groups are accompanied by rhetoric intended to convince subjects that the work they will do is important, something worth trying to do well.

In work organizations, on the other hand, questions of direction are considerably more problematic. Repeatedly we have observed a group formed and given a task to perform without any briefing about the purpose of the work or how it fits into overall organizational aspirations. Although ambiguity about direction is common in organizations, it is a mistake. We know of no group we would consider effective that did not have a clear sense of direction, and we have studied many groups that spent a great deal of their time wallowing around and being frustrated because they received confusing instructions about their purpose.

It is, of course, possible to have direction that is both

crystal clear and alienating (rather than engaging). What will engage a given team depends in part on members' personal interests and aspirations, and on the degree of motivational alignment between the team and the organization (see Chapter Five). Engagement also is enhanced when objectives have the following attributes:

- While the overall direction for performance is clear, details are not completely specified, so there is room for the team to "tailor" the objectives to fit with members' own inclinations.
- The aspirations sought will have visible and substantial effects on the psychological or physical well-being of other people.
- Seeking the aspirations will stretch team members and provide them with opportunities for personal learning and growth.
- Success or failure in achieving the aspirations will be directly consequential for the team and its members.

Sometimes it is argued that stating objectives clearly risks lowering the motivation of group members because they will react negatively to being told what to do. We have found the opposite: An engaging, authoritative statement of purpose orients and empowers teams (Walton, 1985). Having a clear sense of what is expected, and why it is important, appears to be a prerequisite condition for team effectiveness. Direction is not, however, the whole story: How the group's performance situation is structured can either undermine good direction or exploit its positive potential.

An Enabling Performance Situation. Groups that know where they are supposed to be going have three hurdles to surmount in order to get there. They must (1) exert sufficient *effort* to get the task accomplished at acceptable levels of performance, (2) bring adequate levels of *knowledge and skill* to bear on their task work, and (3) employ *task performance strategies* that are appropriate to the work and to the setting in which it is being performed (Hackman, forthcoming).

We refer to these hurdles as the *process criteria of effec-*

tiveness. They are not the ultimate test of how well a group has done (see above for our views about that), but they turn out to be of great use both in assessing how a group is doing as it proceeds with its work and in diagnosing the nature of the problem if things are not going well. One can readily ask, for example, whether a group is having difficulties because of an effort problem, a talent problem, or a strategy problem. And (as will be seen below) the answers that emerge can be useful in determining what a leader might do to help a group improve its effectiveness.

Although a high standing on the process criteria suggests that a group is performing well, it is not possible to achieve that by merely issuing an exhortation or ultimatum. Instead, we must probe a bit further and identify conditions that do increase the likelihood that a group's work will be characterized by sufficient effort, ample task-relevant knowledge and skill, and task-appropriate performance strategies. As we do that, we will identify three additional points of leverage for promoting team effectiveness.

1. *A group structure that promotes competent work on the task.* Some groups have difficulty getting anything done because they were not set up right in the first place. Our research suggests that particularly important structural features include the following:

- *Task structure.* The task should be clear, consistent with the direction of the group, and high on what Hackman and Oldham (1980) call motivating potential—that is, the team task is a meaningful piece of work, for which members share responsibility and accountability and which provides many opportunities for the team to learn how well it is doing.
- *Group composition.* There should be as few members as possible given the work that needs to be done, they should have among them the talents required by the task, and they should be balanced on homogeneity/heterogeneity (that is, members should be neither functional replicas of one another nor so different that they cannot learn from one another).
- *Core norms that regulate member behavior.* While it is per-

haps unusual to include group norms as an aspect of structure, research shows that expectations about behavior get established and enforced very early in the life of a group (Gersick, 1983). Moreover, these norms tend to remain in place until and unless something fairly dramatic occurs to force a rethinking about what is and is not appropriate behavior. To foster effective task performance, norms should, at minimum, provide for the efficient regulation of member behavior, thereby making coordinated action possible, and promote active scanning of the task and situation and proactive planning of group performance strategies.[5]

2. *An organizational context that supports and reinforces excellence.* While organizational supports may strike some as mundane, our research shows that their presence (or absence) can dramatically foster (or limit) team effectiveness. Specific features of the organizational context that are significant in creating conditions for team effectiveness include the following:

- The reward system. It should provide recognition and other positive consequences for excellent *team* performance. Rewards to individuals should never provide disincentives for task-oriented collaboration.
- The educational system. It should provide the group with technical assistance regarding any aspect of the task work for which members do not presently have adequate knowledge, skill, or experience.
- The information system. It should make available to group members the data and projections they need to invent or

5. Norms regulate many aspects of group life, not just the management of performance strategies. We emphasize norms about strategy because they are critical to the task-appropriateness of a team's way of proceeding with the work. Norms about other matters (for example, how members relate to one another or how much effort they expend on the task) tend to develop as a function of other aspects of the performance situation (such as the design of the task or the composition of the group). For additional discussion of the role of norms in task-performing teams, see Hackman (forthcoming).

select a task- and situation-appropriate strategy for proceeding with the work.

3. *Available, expert coaching and process assistance.* It is
not always easy for a team to take advantage of positive performance conditions, particularly if members have relatively little
(and relatively negative) experience working collaboratively.
Too often a task is tossed to group members with the assumption that "they'll work it out among themselves." And, too
often, members may not know how to do that. A leader or consultant can do much to promote team effectiveness by helping
team members learn *how* to work interdependently—although
this is probably a hopeless task if the group has an unsupportive
organizational context or was poorly structured in the first place.

The role of the help provider is not, of course, to dictate
to group members the "one right way" to go about their collab-
orative work. It is, instead, to help members learn how to minimize the "process losses" that invariably occur in groups (Steiner, 1972) and how they might work together in ways that
generate synergistic process *gains*. Specific kinds of help that
might be provided can be divided into three areas and may include the following:

1. Regarding *effort*: Helping members minimize coordination
   and motivation decrements (process losses that can waste effort) and helping members build commitment to the group
   and its task (a process gain that can build effort).
2. Regarding *knowledge and skill*: Helping members avoid inappropriate "weighting" of members' ideas and contributions (a process loss) and helping members share expertise
   and learn from one another (a process gain).
3. Regarding *performance strategies*: Avoiding flawed implementation of performance plans (a process loss) and developing inventive, creative ways of proceeding with the work
   (a process gain).

Table 3-1 summarizes our discussion of an enabling performance situation. It relates our initial list of three process cri-

Table 3-1. Points of Leverage for Creating Conditions
that Enhance Group Task Performance.

Process Criteria of Effectiveness	Points of Leverage		
	Group Structure	Organizational Context	Coaching and Consultation
Ample effort	Motivational structure of the group task	Organizational reward system	Remedying co-ordination problems and building group commitment
Sufficient knowledge and skill	Group composition	Organizational education system	Remedying inappropriate "weighting" of member inputs and fostering cross-training
Task-appropriate performance strategies	Group norms that regulate member behavior and foster scanning and planning	Organizational information system	Remedying implementation problems and fostering creativity in strategy development

teria of effectiveness—hurdles that must be surmounted if a group is to perform well—to the several points of leverage we identified for helping a group do well on the process criteria. For each of the process criteria, some aspect of the group structure, some feature of the organizational context, and some type of process assistance is identified as of particular relevance.

Thus, as shown in the table, for *effort*-related issues, one would consider the motivational structure of the group task, the reward system of the organization, and group dynamics having to do with coordination, motivation, and commitment. For *talent*-related issues, one would consider group composition, the educational system of the organization, and group dynamics having to do with how members weight each other's contributions and learn from one another. For *strategy*-related issues, one would consider group norms relevant to the management of performance processes, the information system of the organization (that is, whether the group gets the data it needs to design and implement an appropriate strategy), and group dynamics having to do with the invention and implementation of new ways of proceeding with the work.

Adequate Material Resources. The third generic condition required for effectiveness is having the wherewithal needed to do what needs to be done—such as money, space, staff time, tools, and so on. This condition is not terribly interesting conceptually, but it turns out to be a major roadblock to team effectiveness in many organizations we have studied. Even groups that have a clear and engaging direction, and who are ready to sail over the process hurdles, eventually will fail if they do not have (and cannot get) the resources they need to do their work. Indeed, among the saddest kinds of failures are those experienced by well-designed and well-supported groups with a clear sense of direction but who cannot obtain the resources they need to fulfill their promise.

Analyzing Group Effectiveness

In the preceding section, we have explored three generic ingredients that support team effectiveness and have broken the second one down into three components. The result is a list of five conditions that we believe to be key to the effectiveness of task-performing teams in organizations:

1. Clear, engaging direction
2. An enabling performance situation
   - A group structure that fosters competent task work
   - An organizational context that supports and reinforces excellence
   - Available, expert coaching and process assistance
3. Adequate material resources

These conditions, and the way they shape group behavior and effectiveness, can be illustrated in the two task forces formed by President John F. Kennedy to assist him in the development of U.S. strategy for the Bay of Pigs invasion and the Cuban missile crisis. (These two teams were selected for use here both because they are likely to be familiar to most readers and because they provide a relatively vivid illustration of favorable as opposed to unfavorable performance conditions.)

Briefly, in the Bay of Pigs a task force developed a plan for military action that, when executed, resulted in a military and foreign policy fiasco. The action was based on several distinct assumptions that were invalid—and that could easily have been known to be invalid before the action was executed. In the missile crisis, a task force produced recommendations that not only achieved their objectives (a fact also influenced by good fortune and autonomous actions taken by representatives of other governments), but that also appear to have anticipated what turned out to be critical variables in the unfolding crisis.

Table 3-2 provides an assessment of the performance conditions that were in place for the two task forces, based primarily on written accounts by Kennedy (1969) and Schlesinger (1965). The table shows that the Bay of Pigs task force operated under numerous unfavorable performance conditions, while the Cuban missile crisis task force enjoyed relatively favorable conditions. Some of these conditions were determined by the nature of the international situation in the two instances, but others were shaped by the president as he formed and managed the two task forces. Note, however, that there also are some conditions that did not differ substantially for the two teams (for example, highly significant objectives, available but unused educational support, and ample material resources), and that the conditions for both teams were mixed in significant ways (that is, not everything was favorable for the missile crisis task force, nor was everything unfavorable for the Bay of Pigs task force). The point, again, is that one cannot understand differences in effectiveness in terms of single variables; instead, multiple and often redundant conditions operate in concert to determine how well a team will be able to perform.

Critical Leadership Functions

How do we put a functional approach to leadership together with the conditions for team effectiveness just discussed?

The answer, we hope, is obvious: The critical leadership functions for a task-performing team in an organization are *those activities that contribute to the establishment and maintenance of favorable performance conditions.* Following McGrath's (1962) framework, this involves two types of behavior: *monitoring*— obtaining and interpreting data about performance conditions and events that might affect them—and *taking action* to create or maintain favorable performance conditions.

Monitoring. The team effectiveness model prompts a number of diagnostic questions. Does the team have clear and engaging direction? Is the team well structured? Does it have a supportive organizational context? Are ample coaching and process assistance available to the team? Does it have adequate material resources? While these questions are posed here in the present tense, the monitoring function includes not only assessments of the present state of affairs (diagnosis) but also projections about how things are changing and what deleterious or fortunate events may be about to occur (forecasting).

Taking Action. Based on assessments of the group and the situation, action can be taken to improve the present state of affairs, to exploit existing opportunities, or to head off impending problems. Again, the content of the actions will be to clarify direction, to strengthen the design of the group or its contextual supports, to provide coaching or process assistance to the group, or to ensure it has adequate material resources.

Sometimes the focus of such actions will be within the group (as when the leader works with members to help them understand the significance of their task or learn better ways of coordinating their activities). Other times external action will be required (as when the leader negotiates a change in the organization's compensation system to provide rewards for excellent team performance, or when he or she helps establish a relationship between the group and a consultant or trainer from elsewhere in the organization).

These critical leadership functions described can be arranged in a matrix, as in Figure 3-1. There are two types of functions (monitoring and action taking) for each of the five conditions (direction, structure, context, coaching, and re-

Table 3-2. Comparison of Bay of Pigs and Cuban Missile Crisis on Conditions for Team Effectiveness.

Conditions Fostering Effectiveness	Bay of Pigs	Cuban Missile Crisis
Clear, Engaging Direction	Unclear objectives, and conflicting objectives among members	Clear, shared objectives
	Engaging objectives (stakes high), but tolerance by president of mediocre task force work	Engaging objectives (stakes extremely high), insistence by president on highest-quality task force performance
Enabling Performance Situation		
Facilitative Group Structure		
Well-structured group task	High meaningfulness, less clear accountability, little regularized feedback about status of the work	High meaningfulness, clear accountability and assigned responsibility for outcomes, regular on-line feedback about status of the work
Well-composed group	Large, constantly changing membership, little familiarity and trust at outset	Smaller membership, stable, familiarity and trust among members at outset
	Diverse levels of knowledge and experience; some new to executive branch	All members experienced operators in the Kennedy administration
	Balance of perspectives, but imbalance in the relative power of military and intelligence representatives versus those from other agencies	Balance of perspectives, and relatively balanced power of different agencies
Norms that regulate behavior, foster active scanning and planning	Regulation: Advocacy acceptable, with members representing and defending their own agencies; unspoken suspicion of others' agendas, disagreements not aired or dealt with explicitly in group meetings	Regulation: Advocacy unacceptable, with support instead for problem identification and solution; "general management" perspective required, with turf protection unacceptable; mutual respect supported; members held accountable for expressing and dealing with differences in views

Supportive Organizational Context	Scanning and planning: Critical assumptions never challenged; nonsystematic and noncritical assessment of the situation; no support for active contingency planning	Scanning and planning: Constant questioning and testing of assumptions; ongoing, skeptical assessment of the situation; positive support for active contingency planning
Reward system	Absence of organizational rewards contingent on *team* (as opposed to individual) performance (the risks of personal embarrassment being more potent for members than possible team failure)	Strong organizational rewards contingent at the *team* level, supplemented by perception that team performance had consequences for national and personal survival (individual embarrassment therefore less salient)
Educational system	Ample educational and consultative resources available, generally not used	Ample educational and consultative resources available, generally not used
Information system	Ample support staff available for collecting and analyzing data, making projections of strategy implications; staff work not well used, and poor-quality staff work tolerated	Ample support staff available for working with information; insistence on quality staff work assessing the situation and devising (and testing) implementation and contingency plans
Available, Expert Coaching	Coaching neglected, except for that by the president himself (which confounded the roles of coach and client/authority, president not experienced in coaching role)	Coaching done by president's brother, who played a liaison and internal task force leadership role (which confounded coach and authority roles, given blood relation with the president)
Adequate Material Resources	Unlimited resources on call	Unlimited resources on call

Sources: Kennedy (1969), Schlesinger (1965).

Figure 3-1. Summary of Critical Leadership Functions.

Function Type

Conditions for Team Effectiveness	Monitoring		Taking Action	
Clear, Engaging Direction	Diagnosis	Forecasting	Internal	External
Facilitative Group Structure	D	F	I	E
Supportive Organizational Context	D	F	I	E
Available, Expert Coaching	D	F	I	E
Adequate Material Resources	D	F	I	E

sources). For monitoring functions, both diagnosis and forecasting are specified, and for action-taking functions, both internal and external targets are specified.

So far we have defined what we mean by group effectiveness, identified the conditions we believe to be most potent in promoting it, and specified a set of critical leadership functions based on that material. Now, continuing to work backwards, we turn to the behavior of group leaders. What is it, we ask, that a leader actually *does* to help a group perform as effectively as possible?

Appropriate Leadership Behaviors

To reiterate, our view is that the behavioral requirement for the leader is to ensure that critical functions are fulfilled. This does *not* mean that the leader must handle them personally. As a work team matures, group members often assume responsibility for an increasing number of leadership functions—a constructive development, but one that also poses some problems for the leader who finds that he or she is needed less and less (Walton and Schlesinger, 1979). What is important is that the critical leadership functions are fulfilled, not who fulfills them.

President Kennedy's Task Forces. Recall the comparison we made earlier between the Bay of Pigs and the Cuban missile crisis task forces. The behavior of the president was clearly different in the two instances. In the Bay of Pigs episode, President Kennedy was still new in his job, and he was dealing with an awkward fact his administration had inherited from the previous one—namely, the existence of a force of Cuban exiles who were being trained by the Central Intelligence Agency (CIA) and who had been assured that they would be supported by the United States in an invasion of Cuba. His first omission was in not providing direction for the advisory task group he formed; he never clarified whether the objectives were (1) to dispose of the political problem of the increasingly ready, impatient, and visible Cuban exile force or (2) to accomplish some foreign policy objective in relation to Cuba.

Table 3-2 summarizes a number of other deficiencies in the conditions under which this task force operated. From the perspective of effective leadership, the president:

- Failed to communicate to the task force an expectation that members were collectively accountable for the team's product
- Failed to diagnose and remedy the consequences of the large size of the group and its changing composition from meeting to meeting

- Failed to diagnose and deal with problems caused by the heterogeneity of the team, especially the fact that members representing one faction (the CIA and the military) were in possession of more information (and had a somewhat different foreign policy orientation) than other task force members
- Failed to specify roles, promote norms, and set standards that would encourage members to candidly express their own views and challenge assumptions made by others
- Failed to ensure that members of the task force other than himself took an overall national perspective (instead, each faction was allowed to advocate its own agenda throughout the life of the group)

In the Bay of Pigs case, the group product ultimately was judged poor by both the president and historians; moreover, the immediate effect of the group experience and the outcome was divisive for the group and demoralizing for individuals. Fortunately, however, President Kennedy and key members of his administration learned from the experience.

That learning paid off in the second (Cuban missile crisis) task force. In this case, the president took care to ensure that the purpose of the task force was clear and understood by all. In addition, he provided a structure for the team that was better —in the composition of the group, certainly, but perhaps most importantly in his communicated expectations about how the task force should operate, expectations that became translated into group norms that served the group well. The president also provided better organizational support for the team (specifically regarding the reward and information systems) but did little of which we are aware regarding the educational system or the provision of material resources (perhaps because those supports were more than ample already). Finally, the president kept himself out of the day-to-day deliberations of the task force, turning to his brother to fulfill the ongoing coaching function—activities that he had learned (perhaps in part from the Bay of Pigs experience) are not well performed by a president of the United States.

In sum, while the president ensured that the critical functions were taken care of, he did not attempt to handle all of them personally (that would almost certainly have been counterproductive), he apparently gave relatively little attention to functions that were already in relatively good shape (that would have been a waste of energy), and he focused on the design of the group and its organizational context, refraining from personal interventions into the group's internal processes. To the extent the reports available to us about President Kennedy's leadership of the Cuban missile crisis are accurate, he deserved excellent marks as the external leader of this task force—certainly higher marks than he would have been given for his leadership of the Bay of Pigs task force.

Leading a Group That Is Having Problems. Since few of us have the opportunity to help with crisis management teams in the White House, let us consider now a more typical leadership situation. A group is performing a piece of work in a business organization, its leader has some concern that all may not be well with the group and its performance, and he or she wants to figure out whether there is in fact a problem—and if so what might be done to remedy it.

Our overall approach suggests that remedial action would be initiated by a leader when he or she observes that a team is falling short on one or more of the three criteria of team effectiveness. It might be that the clients of the team's work are becoming increasingly less satisfied with its products. Or that the capability of team members to work interdependently is slipping. Or that individual members are finding their experiences in the team frustrating or alienating.

In such circumstances, the leader would begin by collecting diagnostic data and then take action to remedy problems revealed in the diagnosis. For clarity of presentation, we will discuss the leader's behavior in terms of an ordered set of questions, recognizing that in practice they may not be dealt with in this order. Indeed, some of them will be quickly dismissed as of little consequence for a given group, and attention will turn immediately to other issues that have greater significance for that team's effectiveness.

1. *Does the group have clear direction?* Are there signs

that members have oriented their work activities toward inappropriate ends, that there is disagreement among them about what they are actually supposed to be doing and why, or that members do not understand the significance of their work?

If direction is a problem, then the leader must do further diagnostic work to determine *why* it is a problem. It may be that direction has always been unclear, that the people who created the group were unsure just what it actually was supposed to accomplish. Or it may be that organizational representatives were clear about the direction of the group, but the word never got to the group (or was never understood by them). Or it may be that direction was communicated but not *accepted* by group members—that is, they redefined the task to fit better with their own interests and aspirations without much concern for organizational needs.

Obviously, the behaviors of a leader to solve a "direction problem" would depend significantly upon the answers to these diagnostic questions. In one case, the appropriate behavior might be to exercise influence outward or upward to get senior managers to be clearer about what they seek from the group. In another, it might be to spend time with group members, communicating and teaching the direction and its implications. In yet another, it might require the leader to exercise his or her *own* authority to insistently articulate organizational expectations of the group.

2. *Are performance conditions satisfactory?* To deal with this question, the leader would first examine how the group is doing on the three process criteria of effectiveness.

First, effort. Is sufficient effort being applied to the task? If this is a problem, then diagnostic questions continue. Is the group task unmotivating? Does the organization fail to provide positive consequences for *team* excellence (or, worse, are members competing for scarce rewards given out for individual performance)? Are members interacting in ways that result in coordination or motivation decrements, or in the alienation and withdrawal of individuals?

Second, knowledge and skill. Is sufficient talent being brought to bear on the work? If not, is the main difficulty with members' knowledge (that is, they do not know what they need to know to do the task) or with their skills (that is, they know what needs to be done, but they are not able to pull it off)? If there is a problem with knowledge or skill, what are its roots? Is it a composition issue (too many people, the wrong people, or the wrong mix of people)? Is it an organizational support problem (for example, the unavailability of task-related training or consultation needed by the group)? Is it a group dynamics problem (members weighting each others' contributions in accord with some task-irrelevant criterion, such as demographic attributes rather than task expertise, or failing to recognize and use nonobvious talents of individual members)?

And finally, performance strategies. Are the performance strategies being used by the group appropriate to the task and the situation? Or are members going about the work in a way that does not quite fit with what is required for effectiveness (for example, attempting to write a committee report by sitting around a table writing sentence after sentence by consensus)? Again, if this is a problem, the questions continue. Do norms discourage rather than encourage active scanning of the performance situation and planning of alternative ways for proceeding with the work? Does the group not have access to information that members need to develop performance strategies that fit with the realities of the task and situation? Are members interacting in ways that introduce "slippage" in the implementation of their performance strategies?

Obviously, the actions of a leader should depend on the answers to these diagnostic questions. Although one cannot state ahead of time what specific behaviors will be particularly useful in aiding team effectiveness, there is a preferred order to actions that might be taken. It is highly doubtful, for example, that attempts to work on group dynamics problems will be successful if the structure of the group, or its relation with the organizational context, are fundamentally flawed. And it is doubtful that an improvement in context supports will be of much help if the structure of the group itself is disabling. So, in general, one would attempt first to get the structure of the group in shape; that would be followed by attention to organizational supports, and attention to group dynamics issues would come last.

3. *Does the group have adequate resources?* As noted earlier, even a well-designed and well-supported group in which members are interacting competently will fail if the resources needed to accomplish the work are unavailable. Generally, inadequate resources are easy to discern and difficult to remedy: A search committee that discovers late in the game that it has no candidates to consider, for example, may be genuinely stuck. The same is true for a production team that cannot get the raw materials it needs because there is a worldwide scarcity of those materials. So the *forecasting* part of the diagnostic work is of special importance here—so that action can be taken before a resource crisis occurs to head it off or to redirect the work of the group when it hits. And, once again, the actions taken by a leader to remedy the problem may focus much more on exercising influence external to the group than on attempts to directly alter members' behaviors in relation to one another.

Leader Behaviors at Special Times. Certain leadership functions may be more appropriately fulfilled at certain times in a group's life and, indeed, may be impossible to fulfill at other times. Consider, for example, the period before a group is initially formed or convened. At this time, the leader has a unique opportunity to review in his or her own mind the direction for the team's work (and to clarify that direction with senior managers if need be) and to make sure that a team is an appropriate device for accomplishing that work. If this review affirms the choice of a team as the performing unit, then the leader would proceed to determine how much self-managing authority the team will have, to design the team task and determine the composition of the group, to arrange for needed organizational supports and resources, and to plan the first group meeting. These are key leadership functions, and they often can be accomplished more thoughtfully and efficiently before the group is convened than would be possible later, after the group has formed and is under way.

Timing also conditions the kinds of leader behaviors that are likely to "take" at various points in the life of a group. This is illustrated below for two very different types of groups: temporary task forces and permanent production teams.

Task Forces. In a study of the life cycles of temporary task forces in organizations, Gersick (1983, 1984) found that such groups do *not* proceed, serially and inexorably, from developmental stage to developmental stage as some textbook accounts would have us believe. Instead, each group studied (all of which had to prepare a product by some deadline) spent the first half of its life on whatever track was established in the first meeting of the team. That track was different for different groups, depending on the conditions in place when members first gathered; but in each case, what got established initially guided group behavior until almost exactly halfway through the time the team had to complete its work (in some cases that was a few days, in others over two months). At the midpoint, each group reengaged with the person in authority who had assigned the task and experienced a major transition in how members construed the work and went about performing it. In effect, each team redesigned itself at the midpoint. Then followed a period of relatively intense production work, culminating in a flurry of wrap-up activities just before the deadline for completing the group product.

In summarizing her findings, Gersick identifies five phases in the life of a group: (1) the first meeting, (2) Phase I, when the group is learning and exploring but may appear to be producing relatively little, (3) the midpoint transition, when the group has a major upheaval and redesigns itself, (4) Phase II, the major production period, and (5) completion.

1. *First meeting.* This meeting, when the theoretical design for the group becomes real, is an occasion when a knowledgeable leader can help fulfill a number of critical functions and lay the groundwork for fulfilling others. He or she can, for example, help the team with at least three start-up challenges members face: starting to come to terms with the *task* the team will perform, developing an appropriate *boundary* for the group, and beginning to develop the *norms* that will guide behavior in the group during the first part of its life (Hackman, forthcoming). In addition, the leader can educate team mem-

bers about the organizational supports that will be available to help them in their collective work and in the process can begin to collect diagnostic data about the kinds of problems and opportunities the group is likely to encounter as it gets under way.

2. *Phase I.* The time from the first meeting to the midpoint of a group's life cycle is relatively barren of opportunities for constructive intervention by external leaders. The group, in effect, has its head down and is doing the kind of internal exploring and trial-and-error learning that is most appropriately done on its own. It is not very receptive to interventions by outsiders during this period.

3. *Midpoint transition.* Because the group's readiness for assistance is particularly high during the transition, this period provides a unique leadership opportunity. It is, for example, a good time for diagnostic and forecasting work, to assess with the group what has happened thus far, where the group stands at the moment, and what problems or opportunities are likely to appear in the second half of the life cycle. These data may prompt a number of actions by the leader—such as helping the group reflect on (and consider doing something about) the process difficulties (and unexploited opportunities for synergy) it has encountered. In addition, the transition provides an opportunity to reaffirm (and potentially to renegotiate) the group's direction, to fine-tune the group's task (and perhaps even the composition of the group), to assess the appropriateness of the group norms that have guided behavior thus far, and to consider what organizational supports and resources may be needed for the next phase of the group's work.

4. *Phase II.* While the group is heavily involved in production work, the leader might appropriately focus his or her attention on two activities: first, monitoring the processes and progress of the group and providing coaching and process assistance as required, and second, running interference on behalf of the group with the larger organization, making sure that members have the supports and resources they need for smooth, competent task execution. The leader, in this phase, is much more a helper than a provider of direction or instruction.

5. *Completion.* Although group members may be tired

and have limited receptivity to reflection during the team's pre-deadline spurt of activity, the time immediately thereafter provides a good opportunity for a leader to encourage members to review the life and work of the group and to learn from those reflections. Recall that our definition of team effectiveness included not only acceptable group output but also gains in the competence of the team as a performing unit and the personal growth of individual members. The completion phase is a good time to consider how these personal and collective lessons can be consolidated and extended.

For clarity, the above account has been written as if the group were a temporary, time-bounded team performing a single task. Many work teams in organizations are ongoing entities, whose first meeting may have happened many months (or years) ago, whose composition has gradually changed over the team's life, and whose work is continuous rather than one-shot. How do timing questions apply to ongoing groups?

Permanent Task Teams. Walton's studies of ongoing production teams (Walton, 1980; Walton and Schlesinger, 1979) show that the timing of leader interventions also is critical for these groups. But because the life cycle of permanent teams differs substantially from that of temporary task forces, the requirements for leader behavior also differ.

The teams studied by Walton were production groups in new plants, where they constituted the fundamental building blocks of the plant task organization. They were, in addition, intended to serve as a major vehicle for transmitting organizational values (such as high standards of excellence, integration of business requirements and human needs, autonomy, participation, and egalitarianism). The organizational plan was for these groups to become as self-managing as possible.

At the time the groups were formed, members were new employees, only superficially acquainted with one another, with relatively little technical expertise. They had little or no prior experience working in self-managing teams and had only vague ideas about what the stated values of the organization might imply for their daily work activities.

The most effective leaders in this setting initially positioned themselves half in and half out of their groups. They were sufficiently involved that they could readily provide technical education on a daily basis; they were present to articulate organizational values at propitious times; and they could help members derive the implications of those values for group norms and performance strategies. But because the leaders also were partially outside the group, members could not count on their continuing guidance—and therefore they had to develop norms and processes for group *self*-management.

Over the first eighteen months, the effective leaders became increasingly removed from the daily activities of their groups. Many of the functions they had attended to earlier were either not required or were being supplied by one or more members (that is, emergent leaders) within the teams. The supervisors remained organizationally responsible for the productivity of the groups, their development, and the well-being of members; however, an increasing number of the ingredients for group effectiveness were monitored and adjusted by regular team members.

In this particular genre of teams, certain other leadership requirements tended to emerge and become acute at predictable times in the group life cycle. For example, after several months of intensive learning by individuals (and a growing sense of potency on the part of the teams), many groups developed expectations for increased compensation beyond that contemplated in the formal reward system created when the plant was begun. Supervisors who were effective leaders became actively involved with both the teams and organizational managers in dealing with this issue—understanding both perspectives and helping negotiate modifications of the reward system as appropriate.

In sum, both the *roles* of the leaders and the *issues* that required their attention changed over time in these production teams, in predictable ways, but quite different from what developed in the temporary task forces. In both cases, however, appropriate leader behavior depended on the waxing and waning of functions that needed to be fulfilled. The different imperatives for leaders arose because different kinds of teams require different supports at different times. These findings suggest that our understanding of team leadership could be furthered by research on what might at first seem to be a quite different topic—namely, mapping regularities in the life cycles of various types of task-performing teams and identifying the generic problems that appear at predictable times in teams' lives.

Summary

Clearly, there is no single set of leader behaviors that are always desirable and appropriate, nor will any single "style" of leadership be generally effective. Sometimes, for example, intense, involved coaching will be appropriate and helpful (as with Walton's production teams early in their lives); other times, external leaders should remain mostly in the background, leaving group members themselves to wrestle with the issues they face (as with Gersick's task forces in the period following the first meeting).

So what do we have here? Have we just sketched the beginnings of one of the most complex contingency tables ever constructed in behavioral science? We think not. Although the specific leader behaviors that are needed do indeed vary as a function of circumstances, what we have tried to do here is provide a relatively straightforward and theory-driven set of tests that a leader can use to guide his or her own behavior and to assess the likely impact of that behavior.

A summary of our approach, from the perspective of the leader, is provided in Figure 3-2. The figure reviews the performance-enhancing conditions we have been discussing; its main purpose, however, is to highlight the monitoring function of team leaders. It shows that a leader's first priority is to keep track of changes in a team's standing on the effectiveness dimensions. "How is the group doing?" the effective leader asks. "Are there signs of problems in the task work, in members' ability to work together interdependently, or in the quality of individuals' group experiences?" When problems, unexploited opportunities, or negative trends are noted, he or she would examine

Figure 3-2. Summary of the Team Leader's Monitoring Function.

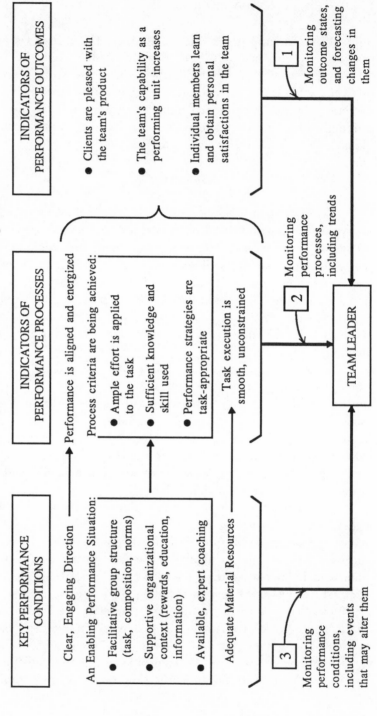

the process indicators in the center of the figure to learn more about what may be going on.

Then, guided by the answers to the diagnostic questions, a leader's attention would turn to the group and organizational conditions at the left of the figure. "Which performance conditions most need strengthening?" the leader continues. "How are we doing in direction, in structure, in context supports, in hands-on help, in resources?" If it turns out that things are not as great as they could be, the question then becomes one of inventing (the word is chosen deliberately) ways of behaving that may remedy a deficiency or exploit an unrealized opportunity. The five critical conditions we have identified and discussed, then, serve as criteria for evaluating alternative behaviors the leader has invented and is considering. That is a far more feasible activity than attempting to regulate one's behavior in accord with some contingency model that specifies exactly which behaviors should be exhibited in which particular circumstances.

Leaders always behave in accord with some model (even if implicit) that specifies what kinds of actions will yield what kinds of results. We have attempted to provide here a theory-based model that can be learned by a leader and used in his or her day-to-day work—a supplement to, or possibly a replacement for, whatever personal model a leader happens to have developed over time based on his or her own experience. Our hypothesis (and it is open to empirical test) is that leaders who are successful in helping task-performing groups become effective already have in their minds, and use in their work, models of action that emphasize monitoring and action-taking in relation to roughly the same five conditions (that is, direction, group structure, organizational context, hands-on coaching, and material resources) that we are discussing in this chapter.

Applications and Implications

In applying the functional approach to decisions about selecting leaders, training them, and designing their roles, we follow the same logic that we have used thus far: first identifying what is required for effectiveness, and then testing those inventions against the requirements of the situation. The only real difference is that this time the focus is on the person and role of the leader, not the group itself; the logic remains the same.

Training Team Leaders. Clearly, our approach to group leadership will not be comfortable to those who have a highly rationalistic view of leadership, to those who see leadership exclusively as an intuitive artistic activity, or to those who think that effective leadership has mainly to do with the style one uses in dealing with subordinates. We believe that leaders have to both *know* some things and know how to *do* some things. How, then, should one think about helping leaders obtain the knowledge and the skill they need to perform effectively?

Once again, we find McGrath's (1962) paper on critical leadership functions helpful. He suggests that one can develop a matrix, with the critical functions as rows and the knowledge and skills required to fulfill those functions as columns. Such a matrix for our leadership functions is shown in Exhibit 3-1.

Exhibit 3-1. Knowledge and Skills Required for Group Leadership.

Critical Leadership Functions	Required Knowledge	Required Skills
Monitoring and Taking Action Regarding:		
1. Setting Directions		
2. Designing the Group		
3. Tuning the Context		
4. Coaching and Assisting		
5. Providing Resources		

In designing a leadership training program, one would determine which among the functions are critical for the work to be done and proceed to fill in the cells with the actual knowledge and skills that would be required of the leader. To a considerable extent, that activity must be idiosyncratic to the organization in which the leaders will function, because the knowledge and skills that are critical will vary from setting to setting. In some organizations, for example, political skills will be needed to obtain organizational supports and resources; in others, those supports may be abundantly available or obtainable simply by asking—in which case political skills would be irrelevant to their acquisition. As another example, consider the help provided to a group through on-line coaching and process assistance. In some organizations, there will be great need for such help and no one available to provide it but the leader; in others, members may be experienced and expert in teamwork (and therefore less in need of such help) and, moreover, there may be a staff of organization development professionals on call to help out if asked. Obviously, the need for leader training in process skills will vary as a function of those circumstances.

There are, nonetheless, some generic knowledge and skills that we believe to be generally valuable in the leadership of teams, capabilities that almost any leader of a work team should have. We identify these below, separately for the two critical leadership functions, *monitoring* and *action taking*.

Monitoring. To effectively diagnose the state of a group and forecast future problems and opportunities that may arise, a leader most of all needs knowledge about what the key conditions for team effectiveness are. In addition, he or she needs knowledge of the relationships that link those conditions to the process criteria and to ultimate team effectiveness. We have attempted to provide some guidance about such matters in this chapter and suspect that it would be reasonably straightforward to develop a training course for team leaders based on this material.

In addition to general knowledge about the conditions for effectiveness, team leaders need some specific skills if they are to generate valid and reasonably complete diagnoses (or forecasts) about the state of a group and its performance situation. These include the following:

- Data-gathering skill. The ability to collect data about social systems that are reliable (trustworthy) and valid (the data mean what they appear to mean).

- Diagnostic and forecasting skill. The ability to apprehend complexity and make sense of it, drawing on both data and existing knowledge in shaping one's conclusions.
- Hypothesis-testing skill. The ability to use data to conduct assessments of the relative validity of alternative hypotheses about the state of a social system (or, for forecasting, about its likely future state).
- Learning skill. The ability to learn about leadership and management and to apply what is learned in understanding social systems and planning actions to change them.

Taking Action. In taking action to help a team perform well, a leader needs knowledge about both the key levers that are available (or can be made so) to improve the performance system and timing considerations that condition when various interventions are likely to "take" (as opposed to when they may fall on barren ground and have little effect). Again, we have tried in this chapter to provide some guidance about these matters.

Among the skills required for competent action taking may be the following:

- Envisioning skill. The ability to envision desired end states and to articulate and communicate them to others.
- Inventive skill. The ability to think of numerous nonobvious ways of getting something done.
- Negotiation skill. The ability to work persistently and constructively with peers and superiors to secure resources or assistance that are needed to support one's subordinates.
- Decision-making skill. The ability to choose among various courses of action under uncertainty, using all perspectives and data that can be efficiently obtained to inform the decision.
- Teaching skill. The ability to help others learn both experientially and didactically.
- Interpersonal skill. The ability to communicate, listen, confront, persuade, and generally to work constructively with other people, particularly in situations where people's anxieties may be high.
- Implementation skill. The ability to get things done. At its

simplest level, knowing how to make lists, attend to mundane details, check and recheck for omitted items or people, and follow plans through to completion. At a more sophisticated level, the ability to constructively and assertively manage power, political relationships, and symbols to get things accomplished in social systems.

We believe it is feasible to design and conduct training that will help team leaders develop the knowledge and skill they need to fulfill the critical leadership functions. Yet there are some individuals for whom such training would be a waste of time—individuals who, perhaps, should not be invited to serve as team leaders. With that possibility in mind, we turn now to the selection of people for team leadership roles.

Selecting Team Leaders. Are there general qualities (or "traits") that can be used to differentiate between people who are likely to develop into first-rate team leaders and those who will never be effective in such a role? Although we are mindful of the pessimistic conclusions that have emerged from decades of research on leadership effectiveness traits, we believe that relatively stable individual differences in leadership potential do exist and that these differences can be assessed.

Specific qualities needed for leading particular teams will, of course, vary from circumstance to circumstance—such as the need for certain technical skills to effectively lead a scientific team. We will pass over idiosyncracies such as these, pausing only to suggest that in many cases managers may weight technical or "subject matter" knowledge too heavily in selecting team leaders, that group-oriented monitoring and action-taking skills (such as those we listed in the previous section) may prove to be more critical to a leader's effectiveness, even for groups doing technical work.

We list below three qualities that might be assessed when people are being considered for team leader roles, qualities that are probably not trainable in the short term. People who have these qualities, we suspect, will be both better able to obtain the knowledge and skill they will need as team leaders and better able to use what they know in working with teams. These three qualities have little in common with those that have been studied in trait-oriented leadership research, and we offer them here in a speculative spirit:

- Courage. A willingness to buck the tide (and social norms) when necessary to create conditions required for effectiveness. To help a team address and modify dysfunctional group dynamics, a leader may need to challenge group norms and disrupt established routines—and may risk incurring the anger of group members in so doing. To improve a team's contextual supports or to increase the resources available to it, a leader may need to rock the organizational boat—and may risk a loss of esteem with his or her peers and superiors in so doing. Moreover, the leader may need to do both at the same time, running the risk of incurring nearly everyone's displeasure. Such behaviors require courage.
- Emotional maturity. The ability to move toward anxiety-arousing states of affairs in the interest of learning about them and doing something about them (rather than moving away to get the anxiety reduced as quickly as possible).
- Personal values. An internalized commitment to *both* economic effectiveness (or, for public sector and nonprofit entities, efficient and responsive service) and individual well-being (especially individuals' personal development). Without some well-understood sense of what is valued, leaders will find it difficult to choose among competing options for action. Values are, in this sense, the criterion used to assess the relative merit of alternative behaviors. While almost any clear value can serve this function, we believe that the specific values identified above are required for the effective leadership of teams. According to the theory set forth in this chapter, groups are judged effective based on both their task performance and their impact on individual well-being. Leaders who genuinely value both of these outcomes should be better able to detect and anticipate shortcomings on either dimension and be more likely to invent actions that promote the two values simultaneously.[6]

---

6. Groups also are judged on a third dimension (that is, how well they develop their capabilities as performing units), but this dimension

The above list may seem a bit strange to organizational scientists who typically do not deal with things such as courage, emotions, and values. But stranger still, perhaps, is the fact that excellent leaders we have studied in organizations tend to have many, if not all, of exactly these qualities. Can we devise a paper-and-pencil test to determine who has them? Probably not. Can we turn to past behavior to see if the qualities are present in a leader candidate? Sometimes, but not if the person has been in a work situation that has provided few opportunities to exhibit these qualities. Do we need to continue to think, as creatively as we can, about new ways to assess candidates for leadership positions on difficult-to-measure but potentially significant attributes such as those listed above? Certainly.

Designing the Leader Role. Should each task-performing team in an organization have a clearly identified internal leader? Or should internal leadership be informal, a matter to be worked out at the group's discretion, with an external leader available to assist the group? Or should there be both a designated internal leader (whether appointed or elected by group members) and an external leader (perhaps a manager with responsibility for several teams) who work together to guide and support the team? How much official power should people who hold such roles be given? Should they have full authority to deal with virtually anything that comes up in the team, or should their authority be limited so they have an incentive to work interdependently with others in the organization in providing direction and support to work teams?

We hope it is clear by now that in a functional approach to leadership such questions are derivative. There are no generally right or wrong answers to them, nor is there any contingency table that can specify which option to select in what circumstances. The *real* questions, following the line of thinking we have been developing here, are these: What are the resources

---

often is primarily instrumental and only weakly linked to fundamental values. We recognize, nonetheless, that for some individuals and organizations (for example, worker cooperatives) competent interdependent work is also an end-state value, something worth pursuing for its own sake. In such organizations, leaders who endorse that value should perform more effectively than those who do not, for the same reasons as outlined above.

the leader needs to fulfill the critical functions well? How should the leader role be designed to provide its occupant with access to those resources, thereby increasing the chances that he or she will be able to perform effectively?

The design strategy that derives from a functional approach is, once again, an "invent and test" methodology. That is, those responsible for leader role design in a given circumstance would first generate a number of alternative ways to structure leader roles for the group being considered. Then, with several alternatives on the table, each possibility would be assessed to determine which one shows the greatest promise for getting the critical leadership functions fulfilled for that particular group.

Considerations in making this judgment might include the following:

- From what perch would a leader be best able to provide direction to the group? Will he or she be *setting* direction or merely translating and communicating it? How much authority needs to be built into the role to legitimize and support the direction-setting function?
- How can the group be provided with the maximum amount of autonomy to manage its own affairs, given organization-specified directions and constraints? Would having a strong leader within the group assist in maintaining an appropriate balance between collective direction and team autonomy?
- How much external influence will the leader require? How can his or her role be designed to make it relatively easy to exercise that influence?
- To what extent will the leader need to coordinate his or her behavior and decisions with other leaders who have responsibility for other groups? How can the role be designed to foster such coordination?
- What are the key data and resources the leader will need to perform well? How can the role be designed to make it easy for the leader to obtain them?

Once questions such as these are reviewed, it is likely that one or another of the alternative designs under consideration will emerge as dominant (or, perhaps, a new and better alternative will come up in the testing process). The remaining design issue (which, in our view, should be addressed last) is the feasibility question—determining if the design of choice is actually possible, given organizational circumstances such as individuals' work loads, organizational politics, and the like. We have found that a good way to address the feasibility question is to ask "*How* can this design be implemented?" (rather than "*Can* this design be implemented?"). The former question invites a creative, problem-solving stance toward achieving what people have agreed is the preferred design alternative; the latter question invites objections and skepticism.

So, is there a generally correct design for team leader roles? The functional approach to leadership suggests not. Instead, as with the other aspects of leadership we have discussed in this chapter, the "right answer" is to have a device that will help *generate* an answer that is right for particular organizational circumstances.

Conclusion

The major proposition in the model of leadership we have developed in this chapter is this: Effective leadership is that which contributes to the provision of engaging direction, an enabling structure, a supportive context, coaching as needed, and adequate material resources. We suggest three elaborations of this general proposition:

- The conditions created should be robust enough that they can survive normal organizational turbulence and remain in place for a reasonable period of time (they should not, for example, be easily reversible as soon as the leader has put them in place).
- Redundant conditions are to be sought rather than avoided (as, for example, when the direction communicated to a team, the design of its task, the reward system of the organization, and the coaching provided by a leader all contribute

positively to high, task-focused effort). Redundancy lessens the vulnerability of the performance system to unexpected and unfortunate changes in any one condition (for example, senior managers unilaterally altering the reward system, or a new technology having unanticipated negative effects on team task design).

- The process by which the conditions are established should not undermine either the capability of team members to work together or the personal well-being of individual members.

A subordinate proposition is that behaviors intended to strengthen each of the conditions will be helpful only if (1) the condition is not already at a satisfactory level, (2) the present level of the condition, even if satisfactory, is below its potential, or (3) there is risk that the state will soon fall from its present satisfactory level because of impending changes in the organization or the environment. To use a mechanical metaphor, our model of leadership suggests that continuous monitoring of the state of the system and regular preventative maintenance often can preclude the need for expensive and difficult repair work later.

Finally, a number of derivative propositions also can be developed from the general model—for example, regarding what will be needed (and therefore the kinds of functions that should occupy a leader's attention) under specifiably different group and organizational circumstances, and the attributes of leaders who are likely to be relatively more and less effective in various kinds of settings.

We could close the chapter by formalizing these propositions and derivations and generating specific researchable hypotheses based on them. On reflection, it seems premature to do that. This chapter has been an explicitly exploratory venture by two scholars who heretofore have been farming adjacent fields, growing similar crops but cultivating them differently. We prefer to keep learning from one another for a while, and we hope to learn from readers of this chapter as well, before attempting to develop a more formal statement of our ideas.

Let us end the chapter, then, by attempting to summarize

our thoughts from a slightly different perspective than we have used throughout the chapter, in hopes that this alternative frame may provide readers with an additional perspective on our ideas or some new notions of their own. Specifically, we will state, as succinctly as we can, how our model looks when examined from the perspective of individuals who *occupy* positions of team leadership.

Individuals who provide leadership to task-performing teams in organizations behave in accord with some cognitive model that specifies what kinds of actions are likely to yield what kinds of results. Their assumptions about the links between actions and results have developed from their past experience and their formal training. These personal models often are implicit, they often are wrong, and they typically focus selectively on a limited set of variables. For example, one leader may be preoccupied with manipulating formal rewards, another with personally facilitating constructive group dynamics, and still another with obtaining material resources. Often a leader's selective attention to one or a few ingredients relates to his or her particular areas of personal competence and experience—and therefore helps the leader keep his or her performance anxieties under control.

Our approach posits that *effective* leaders are those who, first of all, have valid personal models of team effectiveness—models that specify desired outcome states, identify conditions that foster their attainment, and specify useful points of leverage for altering those conditions. The ability to work backward from outcomes (or anticipated outcomes) to implicate precursor conditions (such as a poorly designed task or a flawed reward system) requires both that leaders have trustworthy data about outcomes, processes, and conditions and that they have the analytic ability to draw inferences and test hypotheses about relationships among the various factors in their models.

Assuming that a leader does have a reasonably valid general model of team effectiveness and that he or she has trustworthy diagnostic insights into the conditions that are currently impeding team effectiveness, then the leader's effectiveness depends on whether he or she can competently generate and select among actions intended to deal with conditions that are serving as performance bottlenecks.[7] Ideally, the action actually selected would be influenced by two considerations: how potent it is—that is, how much leverage would likely be gained by altering a given condition—and how feasible it is to change the condition, taking account of the leader's own power and skill as one relevant factor. The more imaginative the leader is and the more options he or she considers, the greater the likelihood that inventive options can be developed that will have high potency, high feasibility, and, ultimately, constructive consequences for the work of the team, its capabilities as a performing unit, and the well-being of individual team members.

References

Barnard, C. I. *The Functions of the Executive.* Cambridge, Mass.: Harvard University Press, 1938.

Bass, B. M. "Leadership: Good, Better, Best." *Organizational Dynamics,* Winter 1985, pp. 26-40.

Bennis, W., and Nanus, B. *Leaders: The Strategies for Taking Charge.* New York: Harper & Row, 1985.

Blake, R. R., and Mouton, J. S. *The Managerial Grid.* Houston, Tex.: Gulf, 1964.

Calder, B. J. "An Attribution Theory of Leadership." In B. M. Staw and G. R. Salancik (eds.), *New Directions in Organizational Behavior.* Chicago: St. Clair Press, 1977.

Davis, R. C. *The Fundamentals of Top Management.* New York: Harper & Row, 1942.

7. Note that the major categories of enabling conditions in our model are comprised of successively more detailed subordinate conditions. For example, "an enabling performance situation" includes as a subordinate condition "a well-composed team," which includes as a subordinate condition "a balance between homogeneity and heterogeneity of member skills and interests," which in turn can be broken down even further. It is not necessary for a leader to keep all these subordinate conditions in mind. What *is* important is that the leader's model prompts and directs a search for subordinate conditions that are appropriate to the present situation and that it provide a criterion for testing the adequacy of ideas for actions that emerge.

Drucker, P. F. *The Effective Executive.* New York: Harper & Row, 1966.

Fayol, H. *General and Industrial Management.* (C. Storrs, trans.) London: Pitman, 1949. (Originally published 1916.)

Fiedler, F. E. "The Contingency Model and the Dynamics of the Leadership Process." In L. Berkowitz (ed.), *Advances in Experimental Social Psychology.* Vol. 11. Orlando, Fla.: Academic Press, 1978.

Fleishman, E. A. "Twenty Years of Consideration and Structure." In E. A. Fleishman and J. G. Hunt (eds.), *Current Developments in the Study of Leadership.* Carbondale: Southern Illinois University Press, 1973.

Gersick, C. J. G. "Life Cycles of Ad Hoc Groups." Technical Report No. 3. Group Effectiveness Research Project, School of Organization and Management, Yale University, 1983.

Gersick, C. J. G. "The Life Cycles of Ad Hoc Task Groups: Time, Transitions, and Learning in Teams." Unpublished doctoral dissertation, Yale University, 1984.

Graen, G. "Role-Making Processes Within Complex Organizations." In M. D. Dunnette (ed.), *Handbook of Industrial and Organizational Psychology.* Skokie, Ill.: Rand McNally, 1976.

Gulick, L., and Urwick, L. *Papers on the Science of Administration.* New York: Institute of Public Administration, 1937.

Hackman, J. R. "The Design of Work Teams." In J. W. Lorsch (ed.), *Handbook of Organizational Behavior.* Englewood Cliffs, N.J.: Prentice-Hall, forthcoming.

Hackman, J. R., and Oldham, G. R. *Work Redesign.* Reading, Mass.: Addison-Wesley, 1980.

Hersey, P., and Blanchard, K. *Management of Organizational Behavior.* (4th ed.) Englewood Cliffs, N.J.: Prentice-Hall, 1982.

Hollander, E. P. "Leadership and Power." In G. Lindzey and E. Aronson (eds.), *Handbook of Social Psychology.* (3rd ed.) New York: Random House, 1985.

Hollander, E. P., and Julian, J. W. "Studies in Leader Legitimacy, Influence, and Innovation." In L. Berkowitz (ed.), *Advances in Experimental Social Psychology.* Vol. 5. Orlando, Fla.: Academic Press, 1970.

House, R. J. "A 1976 Theory of Charismatic Leadership." In J. G. Hunt and L. L. Larson (eds.), *Leadership: The Cutting Edge*. Carbondale: Southern Illinois University Press, 1977.

House, R. J., and Mitchell, T. R. "Path-Goal Theory of Leadership." *Journal of Contemporary Business*, 1974, *3*, 81-97.

Katz, D., and Kahn, R. L. *The Social Psychology of Organizations*. (2nd ed.) New York: Wiley, 1978.

Kennedy, R. F. *Thirteen Days: A Memoir of the Cuban Missile Crisis*. New York: Norton, 1969.

Kerr, S., and Jermier, J. M. "Substitutes for Leadership: Their Meaning and Measurement." *Organizational Behavior and Human Performance*, 1978, *22*, 375-403.

McGrath, J. E. *Leadership Behavior: Some Requirements for Leadership Training*. Washington, D.C.: U.S. Civil Service Commission, 1962. (Mimeographed.)

Mintzberg, H. *The Nature of Managerial Work*. New York: Harper & Row, 1973.

Oldham, G. R. "The Motivational Strategies Used by Supervisors: Relationships to Effectiveness Indicators." *Organizational Behavior and Human Performance*, 1976, *15*, 66-86.

Peterson, D. R. "Functional Analysis of Interpersonal Behavior." In J. C. Anchin and D. J. Kiesler (eds.), *Handbook of Interpersonal Psychotherapy*. Elmsford, N.Y.: Pergamon Press, 1982.

Rauch, C. F., Jr., and Behling, O. "Functionalism: Basis for an Alternate Approach to the Study of Leadership." In J. Hunt, D. Hoskins, C. Schriesheim, and R. Stewart (eds.), *Leaders and Managers*. Elmsford, N.Y.: Pergamon Press, 1984.

Roby, T. B. "The Executive Function in Small Groups." In L. Petrullo and B. M. Bass (eds.), *Leadership and Interpersonal Behavior*. New York: Holt, Rinehart & Winston, 1961.

Schlesinger, A. M., Jr. *A Thousand Days: John F. Kennedy in the White House*. Boston: Houghton Mifflin, 1965.

Schutz, W. C. "The Ego, FIRO Theory, and the Leader as Completer." In L. Petrullo and B. M. Bass (eds.), *Leadership and Interpersonal Behavior*. New York: Holt, Rinehart & Winston, 1961.

Steiner, I. D. *Group Process and Productivity*. Orlando, Fla.: Academic Press, 1972.

Stogdill, R. M. *Handbook of Leadership*. New York: Free Press, 1974.

Vroom, V. H., and Yetton, P. *Leadership and Decision-Making*. Pittsburgh, Pa.: University of Pittsburgh Press, 1973.

Walton, R. E. "Establishing and Maintaining High Commitment Work Systems." In J. R. Kimberly, R. H. Miles, and Associates (eds.), *The Organizational Life Cycle: Issues in the Creation, Transformation, and Decline of Organizations*. San Francisco: Jossey-Bass, 1980.

Walton, R. E. "From Control to Commitment: Transforming Workforce Management in the United States." In R. H. Hayes and K. B. Clark (eds.), *The Uneasy Alliance: Managing the Productivity-Technology Dilemma*. Boston: Harvard Business School Press, 1985.

Walton, R. E., and Schlesinger, L. S. "Do Supervisors Thrive in Participative Work Systems?" *Organizational Dynamics*, Winter 1979, pp. 24–38.

4

═══◄◄◄◄◄◄◄◄◄◄►►►►►►►►═══

Impact of Task
and Technology
on Group Performance

Paul S. Goodman

The ultimate goal of this chapter is to provide an intellectual guide for the reader as he or she tackles the problem of understanding factors that contribute to effective groups in organizations. Specifically, we want to carefully delineate the meaning of the task and technology variables and their interrelationship, and we want to carefully think about how these variables work in a model of group performance.

The general rationale for focusing on groups appears in many places throughout this book. Groups are a pervasive phenomenon in our society. In organizations they are central building blocks for getting work done. While there has been a good deal of variation in researchers' interests in groups over the years, there has clearly been a resurgence of interest in groups in organizations over the last ten years. A major thrust comes from the action research effort tied onto the significant quality of work life effort (QWL) that currently is evidenced in autonomous work groups, quality circles, and labor-management participation teams. In addition, the emergence of new models of group performance, such as those by Hackman (1976), Glad-

Note: Support for this chapter was provided through Bureau of Mines Contracts J0100069, J0328022, and J0123040.

stein (1984), Kolodny and Kiggundu (1980), and others, attest to the current interest in understanding groups' effectiveness in an organizational setting.

The specific interest in task and technology is driven by a need for finer-grained models and the fact that these variables are critical in models of group performance in organizations. There are several current models of group effectiveness. They are often drawn in a fairly general way. The variables are listed and arrows are drawn but rarely are there any specific hypotheses or models that afford assessment of confirmability. The point is not that these models are faulty. They serve the important heuristic function of identifying the critical variables and their general relationship. The next step is to move to more finer-grained models, but it is difficult to draw finer-grained models of a large system of variables. So the immediate task should be to move to smaller-range theories and to delineate the relationship of a smaller set of variables while keeping in mind the broader models. This argument underlies one rationale for focusing on the task and technology variables. The reason for selecting these, as opposed to other sets of variables, is that they appear in most models of group performance. The meaning of the task and technology variables has not been well delineated, and they may play a more important role in explaining group effectiveness in organizations than is acknowledged by current models.

Boundaries

As we examine the relationships among task, technology, and group effectiveness, there is a need to limit inquiry. First, we are primarily interested in groups in organizations. The use of the organizational context will affect the meanings we ascribe to task and technology. We will obviously look to research on groups in other contexts, but our focus is within organizations.

Second, we are primarily interested in groups that produce something. The "something" could be a ton of coal, a manufactured part, a policy decision, or an approved bank loan. Groups serve functions in organizations other than producing or changing the value of objects (for example, receiving communication, politically legitimizing acts). Third, our primary interest is in groups that exhibit some degree of intradependence. In organizations we often see nominal designations of groups; that is, the organizational chart labels a set of workers as a group, but there is no interdependence among these individuals. In our analysis interdependence, the psychological awareness of group membership, and a common task goal are defining attributes of groups in organization.

Organization of the Chapter

This inquiry is organized in terms of sections. In the first section we explore how task and technology have been used in models of group effectiveness, by describing some representative approaches. Then, commonalities and problems are explored. In the second section an alternative view of task and technology will be presented. In section three some empirical information will be used to illustrate an approach to better understand how task and technology affect group performance. We will conclude with a set of guidelines for investigating the role of task and technology in performance.

Some Biases

Before this inquiry is finally launched, it is appropriate to acknowledge some assumptions or biases that underlie this discussion. The first bias concerns the ambiguous language used in the literature about tasks and technology and their relationship to group effectiveness. This lack of conceptual clarity, which characterizes many variables in the organizational theory, may be attributed to the following: First, a lot of our conceptualizations of tasks, for example, are influenced by laboratory work on group performance. The question is whether this extrapolation from the laboratory setting works in the organizational setting. The traditional laboratory setting is fundamentally different from work settings and the simplicity in terms of space and time precludes simulating the richness and complexity of variables such as technology. Second, much of the work on task and technology has been done by psychologists or sociologists with little link to engineering or production professionals. These social scientists may not have the alternative concepts and vocabulary to think about technology. In my review of studies of task, technology, and group effectiveness, dimensions of tasks or technology are described, but the reader is never told what actually happens or how goods are produced in that organizational setting. The language used to describe technology by many social scientists comes from other theories (for example, contingency theory) that may not be robust in characterizing technology. Third, many researchers do single-firm studies, examining the role of task and technology over multiple groups within a single organization. The problem with that strategy is that certain factors such as type of machinery, manning policy, and maintenance policy may appear to be held constant within the firm and are not a source of variation in group performance; thus they are ignored. However, in a larger context (that is, across organizations) they may be quite important. The point is that our intellectual background and experiences may have constrained how we think about these concepts. Perhaps, and this is our bias, we need to rethink the language we use.

Another bias concerns how generally we can think about models of group performance. In a sense the issue is whether one develops general models that cut across various groups and types of technologies or whether one adopts a more idiographic approach. Most of the current literature on groups in organizations (Cummings, 1981; Gladstein, 1984; and Hackman, 1976) articulates general models of group performance. Our bias is that technology plays a major, but not well-understood, role in models of group performance. To understand that role requires finer-grained analysis of a specific technology and the emergence of a model specific to that technology.

The final bias concerns the role of human factors as opposed to nonhuman factors (for example, capital, technology, environment) on group performance. A cursory view of the current models of group performance indicates an obvious bias toward human variables, such as effort, commitment, leadership, coordination, and norms. The assumption is that these variables are important and that changing these human variables in a particular way can enhance performance. An alternative view is that human variables play a relatively small role in influencing performance and other controllable variables (for example, type of equipment, manning policy, maintenance policy), and noncontrollable variables play a more important role in influencing performance. Our bias is that most models of group performance do not really acknowledge the importance of these structural policy variables and the uncontrollable variables.

Task

In identifying some representative characterizations of the task and technology constructs as they bear on models of group performance, our strategy is not to enumerate all classification systems. Rather, it is to note systems that have been influential and/or current and that bear on understanding groups in organizations and then to note some critical issues underlying these classification systems. We begin with the task variable.

If there is any stylized fact that emerges from the group literature, it is that the group task makes a difference in group performance. The relationships between performance and group size are moderated by the tasks. In disjunctive and additive tasks, size is positively related to performance. The effects of homogeneity or heterogeneity of group composition on performance depends on task requirements. Intragroup cooperation (versus competition) contributes to performance when the task requires interdependent activities (Nieva, Fleishman, and Rieck, 1978). All these "findings" portray task as a moderator variable. Other research shows tasks having a direct effect on performance (Hackman, 1976). In all cases, tasks make a difference.

Representative Schemes. Categorizing tasks is, of course, not a new activity. Carter, Haythorn, and Howell (1950) classified tasks into clerical discussion, intellectual construction, mechanical assembly, motor coordination, and reasoning. Shaw (1973) generated six dimensions along which group tasks varied: intellectual versus manipulative, task difficulty, intrinsic interest, population familiarity, solution multiplicity versus specificity, and cooperation requirements. In Steiner's *Group Process and Productivity* (1972), a category scheme was presented that has remained fairly influential. He distinguishes between divisible and unitary tasks. In divisible tasks members do different activities, the combination of which leads to the group product. In unitary tasks, individuals do the same activity, which gets combined into a single product. Unitary tasks can be disjunctive, where performance depends on the best individual, or conjunctive, where performance is a function of the weakest individual. Additive tasks (for example, a group shoveling snow) are all member activities added together to determine group performance.

McGrath's (1984) recent book provides the best overall summary of the current status of the group performance literature. In it he proposes a model of group task types. This model asserts that groups can do four things: generate ideas or plans, choose among alternatives, negotiate conflicts, and execute activities. A careful review by the reader of McGrath's typology will reveal it to be a nice way to organize the literature on groups.

The above schemes are primarily derived from research on the social psychology of groups. Organizational researchers also have generated possible task schemes. Sometimes it is difficult to know whether they are talking about group tasks or technologies, but we can leave that issue for later discussion.

Herold (1978) presents a scheme based on the complexity of technical and social demands on the group. Task complexity is based on three criteria: (1) the programmability of task activities (the lower the programmability, the more complex the task); (2) difficulty of task activities (the greater the effort, number of operations, and number of skills required—measures of difficulty—the greater the complexity of the task); (3) the diffusion of task information (the less knowledge is centralized, the greater the task complexity). Social demands refer to the quality of social interaction necessary for the group to perform effectively. The continuum ranges from tasks that require little or no interaction to tasks that require extensive and potentially problematic social interaction. Attributes that affect the complexity of social demands include: (1) the level of ego involvement, (2) agreement on means, and (3) agreement on ends. These two dimensions provide a simple classification of group tasks. This scheme then provides a basis for creating group effectiveness. For example, social process interventions are appropriate for groups low in technical demands and high in social demands as compared with groups low in social demands and high in technical complexity. The work by Katz and Tushman (1979) represents another approach to task descriptions. In their work on R&D project groups, tasks are described in terms of their predictability or routineness, the uncertainty in the task environment information requirements of the task, and the degree of task interdependence. These task dimensions, then, are related to communication structure and performance indexes.

As we review these category schemes (Table 4-1) there are some obvious commonalities and differences. Some of the

Table 4-1. Group Task Dimensions.

Researcher(s)	Task Categories
Carter, Haythorn, and Howell	Clerical, discussion, intellectual construction, mechanical assembly, motor coordination and reasoning
Shaw	Intellectual versus manipulative requirements, task difficulty, intrinsic interest, population familiarity, solution multiplicity versus specificity, cooperation requirements
Steiner	Unitary, divisible, conjunctive, disjunctive, additive
McGrath	Generate, choose, negotiate, execute
Herold	Task complexity, social complexity
Tushman	Routine, environmental uncertainty, interdependence

schemes use common or related labels. Programmability in Herold's (1978) schemes is similar to the routinization category in Tushman's (1979) studies. These concepts also are related to the solution multiplicity idea of Shaw. The task difficulty idea appears in Herold (1978) and Shaw (1973). Within McGrath's

(1984) "execute" category we could place some of the Carter, Haythorn, and Howell (1950) categories, such as clerical or mechanical assembly. There also are some obvious differences. Some of the schemes, such as McGrath's, classify task content or the nature of work that groups do. Other schemes seem to be about specific group task dimensions and these dimensions could fit into the general category schemes. For example, task difficulty or task programmability could cut across tasks that "execute" or "choose." The specific taxonomies seem more helpful in generating hypotheses. That is, if we know the level of task interdependence, we can predict the effect of cooperative or competitive reward systems on performance. The more general schemes (for example, McGrath, 1984) seem helpful in organizing knowledge about groups. There are other differences. The Tushman (1979) research includes a task attribute about task uncertainty concerning the environment. This focus on the task context or environment is different. Shaw (1973) includes a category—intrinsic interest—that focuses on the motivating potential of the task.

While it is interesting to review these different category schemes on group tasks, our primary objective is to understand work groups in organizations. Specifically, we are interested in the effect of group tasks on group performance. So, the general question is how valuable are these schemes in describing group tasks in organizations and explaining the performance of work groups in organizations. We begin this analysis acknowledging that these taxonomies have been derived from and applied primarily to laboratory research on groups.

Issues in Current Taxonomies for Group Tasks. Perhaps the best way to evaluate how well these taxonomies may help us describe group tasks in organizations and explain group performance would be to begin with a description of a work group in an organization. An underground mining crew is selected because it is a good example of a work group and we have been collecting data on mining crews. The primary group task is to transport coal from one place (the face) to another place (a conveyor belt), which in turn takes the coal outside for transportation to a consumer (for example, a utility). This task is done by eight to ten people per shift. There are three major pieces of equipment in the most common form of underground mining. The continuous miner removes the coal from the face, a shuttle car carries the coal from the continuous miner to a feeder that moves the coal to a belt for transportation outside, and a bolter puts bolts in the roof to prevent roof falls. Two workers work on each of these three machines. There also are a foreman and a mechanic with each crew. Most groups also contain some utility workers who perform indirect production work (for example, keeping the work area up to safety standards). The work flow begins with the continuous miner. The car operator takes the coal from the continuous miner. At the same time the bolter is preparing a new area for the continuous miner to enter. The utility workers are doing the indirect production work. The task environment is important to mining. Conditions are hazardous. The size of the work area, the lack of illumination, and noise prevent crew members from seeing or hearing each other. Mining typically is a multiple-shift operation, with the incoming crew picking up the work cycle completed by the outgoing crew.

Now let's go back to the various taxonomies and see how they fit in describing the task of a mining crew. Here are some of the critical issues.

1. *A working definition.* One of the problems with many of the discussions of the group task is the failure to define what we conceptually mean by the group's task. Typically researchers define the task by citing dimensions. It is clear that the level of interdependence is an important part of a group task, but it is an attribute, *not* a definition of the group's task. We would probably better understand the role of tasks in either laboratory or organizational settings if we better defined the conceptual space of tasks.

2. *Construct space.* While the schemes in Table 4-1 enumerate a number of possible dimensions, there are no intellectual guidelines about how to delineate the construct or dimensional space for a given group task. For example, the Herold (1978) scheme is based on multiple dimensions. We could use concepts such as programmability and difficulty to describe the

mining task, but do these dimensions represent a comprehensive list of dimensions relevant to group performance? The dimensions in Steiner's (1972) system do not really appear in Herold's (1978) system. Should they be included? The issues about dimensionality and definitions are really the same. If we really want to understand the role of the group task variables, it is important to define the construct space and then to present a dimensional structure of group tasks. Too often the selection of dimensions may be guided by convenience or fashionable paradigms. For example, the interest in task environmental uncertainty has been influenced to some degree by the interest in contingency theories. The point is, we should probably spend some time thinking about what the dimensional structure of group tasks might be, given a particular technology, rather than using dimensions of convenience or simply those used by other researchers.

Our position, which is discussed later in this chapter, is that the task dimensions are contingent on the type of technology, and the initial delineation of these dimensions should be generated on a specific set of technological arrangements in specific sets of homogeneous work groups. We reject the idea of group task and provide a way to think about the relationships among tasks, technology, and organizational structure.

3. *Single or multiple tasks.* Implicit in most of the analyses of the effect of group task on performance is the assumption that there is a single group task and this task can be dimensionalized in some way. That is, there is a task we can describe as a choose task as opposed to a negotiate task, or there is a task that is high in interdependence as opposed to low in interdependence. The problem with this assumption is that it is based on the existence of a single group task. If we go back to the mining example, we can see that there is a whole range of group tasks. First, there are two major types of mining activities—developmental and retreat. During developmental mining, the crew goes forward into new seams of coal. In retreat mining, the crew leaves an area and pulls out large coal pillars that had supported the roof. Eventually the roof collapses and the area is no longer useful. These two types of mining utilize the same crew but the

task requirements are substantially different and the expected productivity is different (greater under retreat mining). The dimensionalization of the developmental task is not the same as that of the retreat task. Second, within any of these two types of mining tasks there are sets of subtasks. For example, in developmental mining there are the direct and indirect production tasks. These two types of tasks differ on dimensions such as routineness, difficulty, complexity, and so on. The point is that most work groups have multiple tasks. It is presumptive to believe those tasks are homogeneous. If this is true, we need to be wary of aggregate descriptions of group tasks. In work situations there are bound to be multiple tasks. Also, it is difficult in some cases to know where the boundary of one task ends and the other begins. Aggregate descriptions are suspect.

4. *The language of task taxonomies.* Another issue concerns how well the language of the task taxonomies describes or helps us understand variations in group performance. Take the Steiner (1972) scheme—tasks can be unitary or divisible. But does this distinction apply to groups in organizations? Most, if not all, production groups in organizations exhibit some division of labor, so this distinction is not helpful. Performance work groups, in a definitional sense, are divisible. McGrath (1984) classifies groups into eight task types within the processes of generating, choosing, negotiating, and executing. His scheme is more robust in describing the group task than Steiner's (1972). However, his scheme would be used differently in an organizational setting. Instead of classifying groups into mutually exclusive task categories, the scheme would be used to classify activities within a work group. Mining crews do more than psychomotor tasks. They compete against other crews, they are involved in mixed-motive negotiation, they engage in decision-making activities, and they do planning and creating. Some of these tasks are done independently, others are done simultaneously with other tasks, and others are highly interdependent with other tasks. In addition, the boundaries among these tasks are often blurred at any point in time and clearly over time. The point is that this scheme may be used within a group task to describe different types of task activities (for

example, the percentage of time spent choosing as opposed to executing). However, given some of the blurred nature of task boundaries, this scheme may not provide a strong method for deciding on any factors that affect group performance.

5. *Functions of task taxonomies.* The last issue to be explored concerns the functions of task taxonomies in models of group performance. While a number of taxonomies have been generated, their functions seem rarely explored. The most obvious function of a taxonomy is to organize knowledge. When we were planning this book, it was natural to ask what we know about groups. This question implies that there is some way to organize this knowledge. McGrath's (1984) scheme provides a useful order to a diverse literature.

Another function of the task taxonomy is to serve as a moderator variable. In other words, groups differ in terms of their tasks. As we change input characteristics of groups, such as size, we should expect differences in performance as a function of task characteristics. Task variation moderates the effect of size on performance. The use of task as a moderator characterizes its primary use in literature on groups. A third possible function of groups' tasks is to directly impact on performance. Work by Hackman (1976) shows that task directly affects group process. In none of the current studies we reviewed were task characteristics portrayed as direct predictors of performance. We will examine this point further in our discussion.

Technology

Technology is another component in a model of group effectiveness. This concept has played a major role in understanding all levels of analysis in organizations. While our focus will primarily be on groups, it is informative to begin with more general conceptualizations.

Representative Schemes. Thompson and Bates (1957, p. 325) described technology as "those sets of man-machine activities which together produce a desired good or service." Underlying this definition is the idea of transforming an object from one state to another. Thompson (1967) also presented a typology of technology based on three types—long-linked, mediating, and intensive. Long-linked technology is defined by serial interdependence among activities and is represented by assembly lines. In mediating technology the main characteristic is linking one group (for example, depositors in a bank) with another (borrowers). In an intensive technology (for example, general hospital) a variety of different activities are directed to an object, but the combinations can change with different objects. Thompson focused not only on broad technical differences but also on the effects of environmental uncertainty on the core technologies. He argued that organizations need to buffer their core technologies from environmental influences and suggested a set of mechanisms such as stockpiling inventory, smoothing input and output transactions, and forecasting.

Perrow (1967, p. 195) viewed technology as "the actions that an individual performs upon an object, with or without the aid of tools or mechanical devices in order to make some change in that object." Again, the idea of transformation underlies the definition of technology. He also proposed two dimensions of technology: The first is the number of exceptional cases encountered in the work. The second is the nature of the search process that is undertaken when exceptions occur. These dimensions lead to a two-by-two classification of technologies. Some have few exceptions and analyzable problems (for example, producing screws and bolts) while others experience many exceptions and unanalyzable problems (for example, aerospace). It is important for the reader to note that these two dimensions were generated to better understand the interface between technology and organizational structure.

A major thrust in the 1960s and 1970s was an examination of the effect of technology on organizational structure, the so-called technological imperative. The focus is on how technology affects structure rather than how it contributes to performance. However, it is still instructive to look at this literature briefly because some of it occurs at the group or unit level and definitions and dimensions of technology are displayed.

Hickson, Pugh, and Pheysey (1969) propose three types of technologies. Operations technology concerns the equipping and sequencing of activities in the work flow, materials technology concerns the characteristics of the material in the work flow, and knowledge technology concerns the characteristics of knowledge in the work. Their research focuses on operations technology, which is dimensionalized in terms of (1) the level of automation of equipment, (2) the rigidity of the work flow, (3) the specificity of the evaluation of operations, and (4) the continuity of throughput. No strong findings are presented to support the effect of technology on structure.

Mohr (1971) examined the impact of technology on the structure and effectiveness of 144 work groups from fifteen health departments. Technology was conceptualized in terms of the manageability of tasks and materials. Manageability was composed of uniformity (of materials), analyzability, and complexity. Task interdependence was also used. Mohr (1971) reports weak support for the relationship of technology to structure and for the hypothesis that effectiveness is a function of the consonance between technology and its organizational structure. Comstock and Scott (1977) argue about the importance of separating technology at different levels of analysis: individual, group, and organization. They basically find that technology affects structure when you separate individual or task technology effects from work group technology effects. Their two major dimensions are task predictability (individual level) and work flow predictability.

Current work on technology and group effectiveness comes from a variety of traditions. There are tests of contingency theory at the group level or work unit level. Basically this theory suggests that the fit between structure and technology predicts effectiveness. For example, under conditions of technological uncertainty, destandardization of rules and decentralization should increase effectiveness. Schoonhoven (1981) did one of the more refined studies using this theory, with operating rooms in a hospital as the sample and morbidity as the criterion. She basically found that traditional theories of contingency theory underrepresent the complexities of the relationship between technological uncertainty structure and effectiveness. Symmetrical and nonmonotonic interactions between technology and structure are reported. Argote (1982), in a study of emergency rooms in hospitals, found that programmed means of coordination made a greater contribution to effectiveness under conditions of low input uncertainty, while nonprogrammed means made a greater contribution under conditions of high uncertainty.

Fry and Slocum (1984) found little support for the contingency hypothesis about group effectiveness. Technology in their study was conceptualized in terms of the number of exceptions in work, the analyzability or unanalyzability of exceptions, and interdependence. The sample was sixty-one work groups in a police department.

Other current models of work group effectiveness include dimensions of technology. Cummings (1981) argues that technology should be considered as a controllable variable, not just a contingent variable. He lists the following technological characteristics: work flow predictability, boundary-transaction predictability, spatial temporal relations, and mechanization. Kolodny and Kiggundu (1980) present an interesting sociotechnical analysis of wood-harvesting crews. While their analysis is rich with insights about technology, there is no formal definition of technology or presentation of technological dimensions. In their model they do introduce the concept of task conditions, referring primarily to the uncertainty and variability of the task environment. Sources of this variability came from variations in groups and weather conditions, tree size, species mix, and condition of equipment.

Table 4-2 summarizes the basic dimensions of technology that we have discussed. One is struck by the dominance of the uncertainty concept in all of the categories. Some researchers use different names, such as manageability (Mohr, 1971), but the underlying concept is the same. The dominance of the uncertainty term in one sense is surprising, in another sense not. On one hand, technology is a complex concept and it is unlikely to be primarily described by one dimension. On the other hand, forms of contingency theory have been a major intellectual force in organizational studies. The driving mechanism of that "theory" is the concept of uncertainty. That is, given certain levels of uncertainty, some organizational structures are more

Table 4-2. Technology Dimensions.

Researcher(s)	Technology Categories
Thompson	Long-linked, mediating, intensive
Perrow	Number of exceptions, nature search process
Hickson	Level automation, rigidity of work flow, specificity of evaluation, continuity of throughput
Mohr	Manageability, uniformity, analyzability, complexity
Comstock and Scott	Task predictability
Schoonhoven	Technological uncertainty
Argote	Input uncertainty
Fry and Slocum	Number of exceptions, analyzability, interdependence
Cummings	Work flow interdependence, work flow predictability, boundary transaction predictability, spatial and temporal relationships, mechanization

appropriate than others. Given the correctness of the fit between uncertainty and structure, we should find different levels of effectiveness. The pervasiveness of that theory even in the light of varied criticisms (Schoonhoven, 1981) explains in part the pervasiveness of uncertainty dimensions. The reader should note that while contingency theory is often considered an organizational-level theory, it has been used at the group level as indicated by the research cited above.

It is difficult to find substantial differences among the technological dimensions cited in Table 4-2. Some researchers have distinguished between types of predictability (Cummings, 1981). The dimension of work flow interdependence appears in a few discussions (Hickson, Pugh, and Pheysey, 1969; Cummings, 1981). However, it is the similarities that dominate the descriptions of technology.

Issues in Current Conceptualization of Technology. This description of technology in the context of group performance models raises a number of issues about the viability of current approaches to understanding technology and organizational effectiveness.

1. *Definitions versus dimensions.* Except for a few cases

(for example, Thompson, 1967, and Perrow, 1967), technology is defined by selected attributes or dimensions, not by what it is. Technology is not task predictability. Predictability is a descriptor of certain attributes of technology.

2. *Construct space.* This same issue appeared in the discussions of tasks, but it is more pronounced in the technology literature. Task or work flow uncertainty dominates the way we think about technology. However, technology is much too complicated to expect that a single attribute will be adequate. While there is always motivation in science to move toward parsimony, the power of these variables should be demonstrated. A review of the studies we cited does not provide clear support for the effect of technology on structure, or technology and structure on group effectiveness. There is no research we reviewed that shows uncertainty dominates other dimensional characteristics of technology. The point is that technology is more likely a multidimensional construct and the heritage of contingency theory will not be functional in designing models of group effectiveness. We need not only to define technology but to describe the dimensional space for a given type of technology.

3. *Dimensions versus description.* After reading all the empirical papers on task and technology (with the exception of Kolodny and Kiggundu, 1980), it is difficult to know what technology is. If technology refers to the activities applied to an object to change that object, the reader has little knowledge of what is going on.

In Mohr's (1971) study of 144 groups in fifteen local health departments, technology was described in terms of manageability. Mohr clearly tells the reader what manageability means, but we do not know how the technology operates in the 144 groups. In Fry and Slocum's (1984) study of 61 work groups in a police department, the work groups are described in terms of technological attributes (for example, interdependence), but we do not know what the groups do. How can we understand group effectiveness if we cannot describe what groups do—that is, how the technology process operates? In the Kolodny and Kiggundu (1980) study there is an excellent description of machinery, employees, organizational arrangements, and task conditions and how they interrelate. For example, there is a detailed discussion of the main type of machinery in the harvesting operation and how this machinery affects production. Downtime was a major problem that directly affected production. The authors identified some specific skills of the operator to assess and diagnose downtime and some specific types of exchanges between the operator and mechanic that had a significant impact on downtime and group performance. That description that is unique to that technology was very informative. It identified the critical points (or levers) for understanding and changing group performance. The point is that this is one of the *few* papers that tell us how the technology functions.

4. *Level of analysis.* Some of the early typologies (for example, long-linked, mediating technology, intensive) of technology were at the organizational level (compare Thompson, 1967; Woodward, 1965). These typologies can serve a useful purpose in comparative organizational analysis. Other research on the effect of technology also generated organizational measures of technology. An assumption underlying this research is that there is homogeneity of technology within the organization. A number of studies have questioned this assumption (Comstock and Scott, 1977) and indicated we should differentiate the meaning of technology at different units of analysis—specifically, individual, group, and organization. Indeed, a cursory review of this discussion of task and technology should indicate a reasonable amount of overlap. To some extent this overlap occurs because of blurring the distinction between technology at the individual and group levels. Indeed, one of the findings from Comstock and Scott (1977) was that the effect of technology on structure is more clearly revealed when one separates technology at the individual and group levels.

5. *Subjective versus objective reports.* A number of the technology–work group effectiveness studies use subjective reports to measure such technological dimensions as interdependence and uncertainty. Consider the recent study by Fry and Slocum (1984). A sample item for interdependence is "Mine is a one-person job; there is little need to work with others." Interdependence is really a group-level rather than individual-

level phenomenon, but the item rests at the individual level. Does aggregating individual-level responses adequately represent this group-level variable? Why not use more objective information or alternative measures to access convergent validity? In the mining crew example, interdependence can be simply demonstrated by the fact that when one of the three major pieces of equipment stops, all other equipment stops. The information is available observationally or from records. Again, in the Fry and Slocum (1984) study one of their dimensions of technology is the number of exceptions. This is measured by "the amount of variety in my work." Is variety a measure of exceptions, and if it is, does this measure individual or work group phenomena? This point is raised to question the use of subjective measures alone and the assumption of aggregate individual responses to group-level measures. The reader should note that some objective measure of dimensions such as work flow uncertainty have been generated by researchers such as Schoonhoven (1981) and Argote (1982).

6. *Technology and stability.* An assumption implicit in many of the discussions on technology is that it is a given or a stable variable. This assumption may arise from the belief that technology is always exogenous to a particular entity such as a work group. However, this assumption may not be true. We would expect continual change in aspects of technology by the group or other forces (for example, market).

7. *Technology as a predictor.* In the studies we reviewed, technology is used as an independent variable that causes changes in organizational structure or in a contingency framework. Since we are interested in effectiveness, the latter use appears more relevant. The basic hypothesis is that given certain levels of technological uncertainty, certain organizational arrangements are more likely than others to lead to effectiveness. It is clearly not in the scope of this chapter to review the merits of this theory other than to note the empirical findings supporting this contingency framework are not too robust and the theoretical framework has been severely criticized (Schoonhoven, 1981). The point is that the only way researchers have presented technology is as a contingency or moderator variable. None of

the studies treat technology as a main effect variable. Let's assume that equipment is a component of technology. If one mining crew has a machine with higher capacity than another, we would expect performance differences. If one machine is more reliable than another, we would expect direct performance differences. While these examples seem simple and even trivial, they illustrate important predictors of crew performance differences. They are presented to illustrate that technology may have a main effect on group performance—a point of view well understood by students of engineering but not of organizational behavior.

Alternative Approach

In this section an alternative approach to categorizing task and technology in models of group performance is presented. This approach builds from our prior discussion and indicates some different ways of dealing with task and technology.

Definitions. Let us begin with some key definitions.

1. *Technology.* Technology is a system of components directly involved in acting on and/or changing an object from one state to another. Following Perrow (1967), the object can be a living being, human or otherwise, a symbol, or an inanimate object. To change an object means to transform it. The word *directly* means that the system of components is proximate in space and time to the object being acted on and/or changed. The system concept is introduced to indicate that technology is made up of multiple components and all those components are interrelated.

There are four classes of components in the technological system—equipment, materials, physical environment, and programs. These four should appear with varying weights in all technological systems of groups producing goods or services. Equipment could refer to simple tools or complex programmable equipment (including both the hardware and the software). Materials could represent the object being worked or animate or inanimate objects necessary to transform the object in question. The physical environment refers to the physical context in which the transformation takes place. Programs are rules, procedures, or design heuristics used in the transformation process. In this analysis three types of programs are considered. *Task core programs* represent standard procedures for doing activities that directly bear on the transformation process. In the coal mining example discussed earlier, the miner operator and helper, the two bolters, and the two car operators directly change the coal from one state to another. These task core programs are typically organized by jobs. *Support task programs* represent procedures for doing activities that support the task core activities. Maintenance, material handling, or indirect production all represent jobs that would be covered by support task programs. Lastly, there is a set of *linking programs* that deal with the interdependencies between the task core programs and the support task programs. The programs to coordinate the work of the miner operator and the car operator or of the mechanic and the car operator are linking programs.

We can summarize the discussion of technology by noting the following: (1) Alternative combinations of these components can produce the same products or service. (2) The particular combinations of technological components will be determined by extraorganizational considerations (for example, the market) and organizational considerations (for example, past history, expertise). (3) All four components—equipment, material, physical environment, and programs are interrelated. (4) All will appear in any technological system with varying effects on performance. (5) Technology can appear at any unit or level of analysis. Our focus is on how the technological components operate at the group level of analysis.

2. *Task.* Task is a subcomponent of technology. It is a program or a set of operating rules, heuristics, and criteria for the transformation process. Tasks describe activities in a particular job or activities that must be accomplished between jobs. Multiple tasks can be assigned for a given job. Tasks for a particular job could be core tasks that directly (in space and time) act on the object in question or support tasks that permit the core task to function. In the coal mining example, the miner operator task is a core activity; maintenance, a support activity.

It is important to clarify the concepts of technology and task. The earlier review indicates these concepts often are not defined and are used by different researchers interchangeably. Our conceptualization treats task as a component of technology. The task is one of the four components in a technological system. The issue is not level of analysis, which appears as a source of confusion in other research on this topic. In that case, technology is an organizational variable and task is the group variable. Our use of these concepts is at the group level. Technology is the system of components at the group level that transforms objects from one state to another. Task represents the specific programs to accomplish the transformation process.

3. *Labor.* A technological system in our definition is composed entirely of nonhuman objects (for example, machinery and programs). Technological systems require a human component to operate them in the transformation process. The labor component refers to the skills, abilities, knowledge, motivation, and attitudes that characterize work group members.

4. *The production function.* This is the simplest representation of any production system. The basic model is that production is a function of labor and capital. In our framework capital is represented by the technological systems, so production of any group is a function of the labor and the technological system. The components of the production system are directly involved in the transformation process.

5. *Organizational system.* The technological systems exist in a larger organizational system. Organizations not only must transform objects (the role of the technological systems) but must acquire materials from the environment, dispose of transformed objects, and deal with maintenance functions. (See Katz and Kahn, 1976, for a more elaborate discussion.) We distinguish the technological system from the organizational system in that the former is focused only on the transformation of objects.

The discussion of the differences between organizational and technological systems has been and could be very elaborate. That, however, is not the focus of this chapter. Our interests focus on the technological system at the group level that is involved in transforming objects. Groups exist in a larger organizational system. Within this larger system a variety of important functions, such as adaptation and obtaining legitimation, are carried out. These functions are important to the survival of the organization and groups within the organization. At any time, however, these organizational functions are not directly involved in the transformation process.

Assumptions. Our conceptual strategy for understanding the role of technology and tasks is based on a set of assumptions.

1. *Type of variable.* Technology is a main effect variable. In most of the studies we reviewed, technology was considered a contingency or moderator variable. In models that portrayed technology as an independent variable (Cummings, 1981), its effect was always mediated through other variables. That is, technology would change effort that would change performance. We view technology as having an independent *and* direct effect on group performance. The effect of the technological system may be based on the relationship among the components (for example, machinery and programs) or on any of the components. Earlier we mentioned there are multiple configurations of technological system components for any product or service. Within these different configurations are different capacities for performance. We would expect that capacity differences would be associated with performance differences. The direct effect of technology may be more clearly understood as one considers the components individually. Equipment differs in terms of reliabilities or downtime. Downtime directly affects performance variations. Variation in the quality of materials will directly affect performance. The physical environment in the Kolodny and Kiggundu (1980) analysis of harvesting teams also directly affected performance. Some maintenance programs will lead to less downtime and performance than other programs will. The point is that the technological system directly affects group performance and these effects are independent of human interventions.

2. *Nonhuman and human factors.* The basic assumption in most of the research on groups is that the human component makes a difference. The focus on leadership, cohesive groups,

and autonomous work groups speaks to the belief that changing these human factors in groups makes a difference. In group effectiveness our argument is that human factors are important in some group situations and not in others. The unmodified assumption that human factors make a difference is misleading. The issue is the relative importance of these classes of variables. This assumption is highlighted because we want researchers to be more sensitive to the role of human *and* nonhuman factors in understanding group performance.

Perhaps an example will highlight this issue. The Rushton experiment (Goodman, 1979) was one of the early quality of work experiments designed to find new ways to restructure work and organizational forms. Rushton was a medium-sized coal mine in Pennsylvania and the object of change was the work group or the mining crew. The basic focus of the change team was on the human aspects of the group, and the basic intellectual focus was to redesign the human or social system to better fit the technological system. While the total intervention was fairly complex, a major thrust was to develop autonomous groups or self-managing teams. The initial results of the change effort were successful in the sense that highly cohesive self-managing teams were created. The question is whether these changes affected performance. The answer is that there were small positive effects. The lesson, however, is that while some change was successfully initiated, the magnitude of the changes was highly constrained by the technological system. These nonhuman factors (for example, physical conditions, equipment, reliability, market factors) varied independently of the intervention, and they explained a large portion of the variance in performance. In this case, the nonhuman factors were dominant. They created the constraints by which other systems (for example, the human or team component) could function. They created a "ceiling effect" on the impact of the team intervention.

The point of this example is not to criticize the QWL effort or the use of autonomous work groups. Rather it is to point out the need to acknowledge the role of human and nonhuman factors on group effectiveness. In some cases, the dominance of the technological system and other external factors will preclude any major impacts from interventions in the human systems. In other cases, where the technological system is not dominant, interventions in the human and team factors will create higher yields in effectiveness criteria. The point is to reject the unmodified assumption that manipulating human or team factors will make a significant difference.

There are some guides that may uncover the relative importance of the human and nonhuman factors. The implementation of these guides can be done relatively parsimoniously and efficiently. Human factors will be more important in understanding group performance to the extent that (1) there is considerable discretion in the transformation process, (2) the technology makes performance sensitive to variations in human effort, skill, and so on, (3) the redesign of the technological system is controlled by the group, and (4) there are not major exogenous variables that affect group performance.

3. *Multiple or single technology.* A problem with much research on work groups is that it is based on the assumption that a group uses a single technology. Indeed the attempts to measure concepts such as difficulty or predictability are based on the belief that there is some common or homogeneous technology for the work group. In our research we find that is not true. For example, coal-mining crews do developmental and retreat mining. These two "technologies" require different configurations of machinery and programs. That is, these work groups have multiple sets of technologies. Each particular technological system must be understood separately, and using general descriptors across different technologies confounds marked differences in these systems and how they operate. Our initial operating assumption is that groups have multiple technological systems and that these systems should remain in a disaggregated form.

4. *Idiographic or nomothetic.* In defining technology we noted it was composed of different components. Also, it was argued that different configurations of these components can produce the same product. When the labor component is combined with the technological system, there are other possible configurations to achieve the sample production end. For example, in our research we have twenty-six different mines that in a

sense use the same technology (for example, continuous mining), but the final production system varies greatly across these organizations. Given the large number of variables in each system and the large number of alternative configurations, our strategy is to treat each system separately and examine its unique property rather than to assume that the production systems are the same. We would not consider the production systems across organizations to be homogeneous. Indeed, in a within-firm study of "homogeneous" groups we would begin with the assumption that the production system of each group is different. We have tested this assumption and found it to be true—that is, apparently homogeneous groups defined in terms of the same technology were actually different.

5. *Specific or general criteria.* Many models of performance groups focus on a general effectiveness criterion. That is, by changing designated variables in these models, effectiveness should be increased. It should be clear from the more detailed literature on organizational effectiveness that such an approach is unlikely to be fruitful. Rather, we need to be explicit about what specific criterion we want to investigate. Then we have to develop some fine-grained models for that criterion (Goodman, Atkin, and Schoorman, 1983). This position is based on the assumption that properties of the criterion variables are different and different models are needed for different criteria. In group research we mean different models would be developed for quantity, quality, downtime, satisfaction, group stability over time, and so on. Following our discussion in point 4, different models also would be developed for different technological systems. The argument for moving to more fine-grained models rather than general models appears in other areas of organization theory (Goodman and Atkin, 1984).

6. *Language.* One major problem in the literature on technology and group performance is that we do not know what groups actually do. Fry and Slocum (1984) study groups in a police force, but we do not know what these groups do. Comstock and Scott (1977) study groups in a hospital, but we are never told what the technological system is for these groups. Another problem is that when group technology is described,

the researchers use broad abstract categories such as difficulty
and predictability. Since the technological system in a group is
a complex entity made up of multiple tasks, it is unlikely that
these abstract aggregate categories adequately sum the many
different nuances that exist in a technological system. Also,
these categories are often operationalized through subjective
indicators. To the extent that there is variation in the interpretation of words such as *difficulty* or *predictability*, the structural meaning of these technological dimensions is less clear.

Any language system for describing technology must reflect the issues described above. Most groups have multiple
technologies, so we must describe each technological system
rather than aggregate across systems. Also, we have argued
that each system may be configured in many ways, so we expect that the description of each system will have unique properties. There are unlikely to be general descriptors that cut
across different technological systems.

Since we believe that language systems will be specific to
a particular technological system, it is not possible to propose a
general set of descriptors. We can, however, identify some of
the constraints that need to be described. These came specifically from our definition of a technological system. There are
four components in that system—machinery, materials, environment, and programs. We rarely find descriptions of machinery
in most research on groups. The issue of whether the machinery
is automated, a typical descriptor used in the literature, seems
somewhat trivial. What we need to know are the properties of
each piece of machinery. What is the capacity of the equipment
for a given product? What is the machine cycle? What is the reliability of this machinery? Simply describing *what these characteristics are* will tell us some of the constraints of the technological system. Similar descriptions of the materials used in
the production and the physical environment are needed. Consider the physical environment variable. In mining the key areas
are the roof and the runways. The simplest descriptors of these
areas are whether the roof is solid and whether the runways are
wet or graded. These simple descriptions are concrete, easy to

verify or validate, and important to group performance. Different physical environments obviously require different descriptions.

The fourth component of the technological system, the task programs, contain the rules, procedures, and decision heuristics about the transformation process. We would represent the task programs by drawing process charts of work. To begin this description we need to look at a particular technological system and product. Then we would identify the task core programs and describe the processes involved in each task. The process description identifies the steps in the work cycle for that particular task. For example, we are doing a study on groups performing milling and grinding operations. The process description for milling machine A would include lifts up bar stock, places on machine, secures to jig, starts machine, and so on. After the process charts for the core task programs and the support task programs have been completed, we would move to a more macroprocess description of the work cycle at the group level for a given product.

This initial description provides a good account and hopefully an understanding of the major components in the technological system and how they interact. More description is needed to thoroughly learn the system. First, we need to separate how the intended system is suppose to operate and how the actual system operates. Departures from the intended system may be functional or dysfunctional for group performance. Second, we need to learn the major sources of variation in the technological system. What is the relative importance of the four components (for example, machinery as opposed to materials) in explaining whether the technological system diverges from its equilibrium? What are the critical or major sources of variation in group performance? In our mining example, the reliability of the continuous mining machine is a critical factor in variation of crew performance. When this machine goes down, production quickly stops. The source of the reliability or the frequency of downtime is typically exogenous (for example, the age or type of machine). The amount of downtime is related to inherent

characteristics of the machinery as well as the skills and motivation of the crew. The key point is that this is a major source
of variance in crew production.

7. *Group performance levers.* As previously stated, the
technological system is composed of four components: machinery, materials, physical environment, and task programs. The
technological system plus the labor system equals the group's
productive system. The word *system* means all these components are interrelated and necessary and absence of any component would affect performance. In a sense, all the components
are important. Our assumption is that all the components are
not equally important. Some are more important than others.
We start with the premise that all the components are present
(not absent) and operate in some equilibrium state. We are interested in what factors make a difference—that is, which factors substantially change variation in performance—and the
sources of variation in these critical factors.

In the mining example, we noted that downtime of the
continuous miner is a major factor affecting group performance.
A variety of sources, some uncontrollable (for example, physical conditions), some controllable but exogenous to the group
(age of machinery), and some controllable by the group (care of
machinery), affect variations in downtime. The controllable
sources are what we call group performance levers. They represent controllable points of intervention exogenous or endogenous to the group that affect group performance.

The idea of group performance levers is compatible in
some sense to other approaches to understanding group effectiveness, particularly those approaches that concern intervening
in groups. Herold's (1978) concept of work group effectiveness
is built around matching the intervention to group task characteristics. That is, the interventions or levers to improve effectiveness are tied to the social and task demands of the group.
For example, social skill training is appropriate for tasks low in
task complexity and high in social demands. Hackman's (1983)
discussion of work teams deals with the effect of organizational
contextual variables and design variables on a set of intermediate criteria that, in turn, affect work group effectiveness. Note

that the types of levers suggested by Herold (1978) and Hackman (1983) are general in nature (for example, social skill training) and seem to be drawn from human organizational behavior literature.

The difference between our use of the word *levers* and these other intervention approaches is that we focus on (1) both technological and human components, (2) factors that are exogenous and endogenous to the groups, and (3) factors that are controllable sources of variation.

Unfortunately, there is no simple path to find the levers of performance. One has to know the technology thoroughly and be totally immersed in the group's operation. Given our early position on the idiographic nature of group research, the immersion initially will be in a single group. Still, there are some general guidelines for this search. We would initially begin with the technological system, since that provides the basic constraints around the group's performance. Within the technological system we would first consider the configuration of machinery. Across different configurations of equipment there are inherently different strategies or levers that affect performance. In a continuous-process technology, machine balancing is key to performance, while in a batch operation, lot size and scheduling are key to performance differences. In both cases, but particularly in the continuous process, downtime is critical. The material component of the technological system is another possible group performance lever. In products requiring small quality tolerances, variations in material may be an important source of performance differences. The task programs are another set of performance levers. It is obvious that there are many possible task configurations for any product or service. One could look at the core tasks or the support-task or linking-task programs for group performance levers. The identification of these task performance levers will come from careful job analysis. In mining, the cutting strategy of the continuous miner has a major impact on performance. Maintenance, quality control, and inventory policies and programs are other sources of levers that in most cases are not scrutinized by group researchers.

The intersection between the labor component and the

technology system is another place to search for levers. The issue here is not whether a group is adequately manned in terms of numbers and skill but whether there are some critical paths or points in the intersection between the technology and labor components that substantially affect variance in production. Kolodny and Kiggundu (1980) provide a fairly rich description of work groups in their study of work groups harvesting lumber. One of the key paths in that production system is the relationship between the harvester machine, the operator, and the mechanic. Harvester downtime is a major predictor of low production. The frequency of downtime was probably explained by the age of the equipment, time since overhaul, amount of time run, and other factors. The length of downtime was explained by the type of failure, the operator's ability to diagnose, anticipate, and communicate the source of downtime to the mechanic, the proximity between the machine and mechanic (they operated in different areas), and the skills of the mechanic. The frequency of downtime was primarily exogenous to the group and uncontrollable. The length of downtime was controlled by the quality of operator and mechanic interactions. This was a critical path in explaining variations among the harvester crews.

The organization/management system is another source of levers for group performance and one that is ignored by most researchers. Here we are interested in policies that are established outside the group but bear on group performance. For example, in the twenty-six mines in our study there are major differences in the use of indirect labor—that is, people who work outside the regular mining crews. We could look at two mines whose crews have exactly the same equipment, job configuration, and labor, but who differ greatly on the number of people who work in the mines but not in the crews. We have seen 50 percent to 60 percent variation in the amount of indirect labor for mines with the same number of crews. There are two points to this illustration: (1) If we looked only at the productive system for the group, we would be unaware of other organization policies that may influence group performance, such as this difference in manning policy. Efficient indirect labor may facilitate the work of the crews. (2) These policies that apply to all groups may be more important levers than a within-group intervention. That is, a change in the indirect labor policy may have more impact on some group productivity indicators than any change at the group level.

Empirical Illustration

An empirical example will illustrate some of the ideas presented in this chapter. Although the illustration is not meant to be comprehensive or to represent formal model testing, it does demonstrate some themes in our discussion. It also articulates a strategy for estimating group performance that differs from other empirical investigations (Gladstein, 1984) of group performance.

The example focuses on predictors of group performance. The coal-mining crews are the subject of this investigation. The empirical question concerns predictors of crew performance, and performance is defined by the tons of coal produced per day per crew.

Technology. Coal mining can be generally described as a set of transportation activities. In underground mining, coal must be removed from the seam and transported out of the mine and then to a customer (for example, a power plant). The continuous miner, a large piece of machinery with a rotating drum with carbide bits, scrapes the coal from the seam and then passes it (by its own conveyor) to a shuttle car. The car, which is an open container on wheels, transports the coal to a feeder. The coal is dropped on the feeder, which places the coal on a conveyor belt that eventually takes the coal to the surface. On the surface the coal may be "cleaned," and then it is transported by rail or truck to the customer. Since our interest is in work group performance, we will focus our attention inside the mine on mining crews that work in an area called a section. In addition to the continuous miner, car, feeder, and belt, there are other pieces of machinery. The bolter inserts and secures bolts into the roof to prevent roof falls. Other pieces of machinery, such as scoops, are used to carry supplies and clean work areas.

Some of the major characteristics of this array of machinery and technological arrangement are the following:

1. Work is highly interdependent. Failure of any of the major pieces of equipment will stop the production process.
2. There is a high degree of interdependence between crews in the same section. Mining includes both direct production processes (for example, removing coal) and indirect production processes (for example, rock dusting, meeting safety requirements, cleaning belts). The total work cycle involving direct and indirect work activities extends beyond the normal eight-hour work cycle. Therefore, it is very important that each crew balance its direct and indirect activities. Conflict between crews can lower a crew's productivity.
3. Mining is both labor- and capital-intensive. On the average, eight to ten people in a crew are needed to mine coal. If the crew is undermanned, production suffers. Not only are numbers of workers important, but the appropriate skill levels are also important. Operators of the critical pieces of machinery such as the continuous miner and bolters require extensive training and experience. A mismatch between skill levels and these machines will mean lower productivity.

    As we noted earlier, there is a set of expensive machines assigned to each production section. Downtime of these machines will directly affect the performance of the crew. Some machines (for example, a continuous miner) have greater effects on output than others (for example, cars).
4. Mining activities are affected by the quality of physical conditions, particularly the roof and runways (the bottom). If the roof conditions are bad, production will be lower and chances for an accident increase. If the bottoms are wet, the transportation activities are slowed.

In the mine used for this illustration there were two kinds of basic technologies—continuous developmental and continuous pillaring. In continuous-developmental mining the goal is to mine ahead. The mining equipment and technological arrangements follow those outlined above. In continuous-pillaring mining, the mining crew retreats from the areas already mined. The goal in this type of mining is to remove large pillars (usually forty feet by forty feet) that have been used to support the roof. The differences between pillaring and developmental technologies include the following: Pillaring uses less bolting activities, pillaring generally uses less inside general workers, pillaring is somewhat more dangerous (the roof eventually falls), and pillaring is more productive since there are not a lot of indirect production activities. Following our earlier argument, we expect that the model of crew performance for developmental mining differs from that for pillaring mining.

Data. The data for this analysis come from a medium-sized mine located in the Eastern coal fields. The mine employs 180 workers and is unionized. Data will be reported on twelve crews over a one-year period. A crew is composed of six prime crew members who run the basic equipment in a mining crew (two miner operators, two car operators, and two bolters). In addition, other day laborers may be drawn from a general labor crew to help in special activities in a given crew. These people are called general inside laborers. There is also a mechanic and a first-line supervisor. The actual number of people in a crew at any time will depend on absenteeism, company replacement policy, and special mining conditions.

The data used in this example come from daily company production records. Each record, completed by the foreman, is fairly detailed, identifying crew, number of workers, who works on what job, coal produced, downtime, and so on.

Analysis. The analysis plan reflects some of the major themes in the chapter. The first analysis examines the effect of some of the technological variables on group performance. Then we examine the technological system and labor component on group performance. Implicit in the first two analyses is an assumption about homogeneity of technology. Throughout this chapter we have argued that this assumption is inaccurate and one should treat different types of technology differently. So we reestimated the labor and technology components for different types of mining. Other analyses briefly present crew effects and indirect effects.

Technological effects. Table 4-3 presents the regression

Table 4-3. Technology Variables and Production.

Technology Variables	Coefficients	t Value
Delay		
1. Continuous miner	−0.42	(41.27)
2. Miner move	−0.35	(10.54)
3. Car	−0.09	(11.89)
4. Bolter direct	−0.44	(16.15)
5. Bolter indirect	−0.02	(2.30)
6. Managerial	−0.49	(11.51)
7. Inside equipment	−0.38	(24.27)
8. Outside equipment	−0.35	(13.90)
9. Other activity delays	−0.40	(19.68)
Number of cars	17.95	(10.80)
Physical condition	−17.11	(2.87)
Sections		
2	−15.57	(6.40)
3	0.69	(0.31)
4	4.49	(1.98)
5	−16.99	(7.15)
6	−20.56	(4.91)
11	−26.34	(5.33)
Shift 2	3.49	(2.04)
Shift 3	5.05	(2.96)
Constant	211.40	(37.98)
R^2	0.586	

coefficients and t values for machinery variables and physical conditions variables. The machinery variables are measured by minutes of delay time per shift and the number of cars available per shift. The physical conditions are measured by a four-point scale that ranges from 4 = bad conditions to 1 = good conditions, and a section dummy. A section is a physical area in which multiple crews work. It is a surrogate for different physical conditions within a mine and for differences in machinery. All crews had the same type of equipment but some pieces were newer. A shift variable was introduced as a control variable since the mine operated on a twenty-four-hour basis, and there is reason to believe that the day shift (shift 2) and afternoon shift (shift 3) may be different from the eight-hour shift starting at midnight.

Basically the table shows that the technology variables are important in explaining crew production. The delay variables have the appropriate negative signs and are in general significant. The miner delay of −.42 means that every minute the continuous miner is down, .42 tons of coal is lost. The magnitude of effects of different delays also makes sense. For example, the continuous miner delay (−.42) should have a greater impact on production than car delay (−.09) because there is usually a second car that will continue to move coal. Direct bolter delay (−.44) that stops the continuous miner is greater than indirect bolter delay (−.02) that does not stop the continuous miner and thus production. In defining the technological system, we included the physical environment in which work is conducted. The direct measure of physical conditions (for example, bad conditions lead to lower production) and the section dummies are significantly related to production variation.

Reviewing the whole table we observe the following: (1) The signs are in the right direction, (2) the magnitudes in the coefficients fit the nature of the technology, (3) the coefficients for the major variables are significant, and (4) this model accounts for a reasonable portion of variance, at least compared with R^2 reported in similar studies.

Production system. The technological system and the labor system constitute what we have labeled the production system in the group. Table 4-4 shows the results for the production system. Prime crew is the number of miners in the six core jobs, and inside general represents the number of utility people who appear in a crew for a specific day. We have other labor measures such as the familiarity of group members with their job, crew, and section, but the derivation of this and other measures is complicated and outside the scope of this particular illustration. This table is similar to Table 4-3. The prime crew and inside general variables are significant. We have also examined these labor variables on production independent of the technology variables. The fact that they are not major explanatory variables is not surprising. There is not a great deal of variation in these variables. Crews cannot function unless there is a minimum number of workers.

Table 4-4. Technology Variables, Labor, and Production.

Technology Variables	Coefficients	t Values
Delay		
1. Continuous miner	−0.42	(41.27)
2. Miner move	−0.35	(10.54)
3. Car	−0.09	(12.06)
4. Bolter direct	−0.44	(16.25)
5. Bolter indirect	−0.03	(2.48)
6. Managerial	−0.49	(41.27)
7. Inside equipment	−0.38	(24.25)
8. Outside equipment	−0.35	(13.88)
9. Other activity delays	−0.39	(19.57)
Number of cars	16.13	(9.30)
Physical condition	−17.10	(2.88)
Labor		
Prime crew	4.42	(2.68)
Inside general	4.45	(4.07)
Sections		
2	−15.52	(6.38)
3	−0.57	(0.25)
4	3.66	(1.61)
5	−15.63	(6.58)
6	−20.09	(4.83)
11	−26.48	(5.39)
Shift 2	3.40	(2.00)
Shift 3	4.75	(2.80)
Constant	185.31	17.80
R^2	0.592	

Heterogeneity in production systems. Earlier we argued that technology in any given setting is likely to be heterogeneous, and we need to break down the technological system into homogeneous components. There are basically two types of mining—developmental and pillaring. Although the physical conditions remain the same and much of the machinery is the same, the task programs are very different for these two types of mining. Therefore, one would expect different descriptions of the production system for different types of mining. One analytic procedure is to test whether a single run that combines both developmental and pillaring (that is, the same coefficients for both types of mining) is different from combining two separate runs (that is, one from developmental and one from pillaring). Analysis of these data indicates that the model for development mining is statistically different from the model of pillaring (F = 12.2 < .001).

Other analyses indicated that the prime crew coefficient in pillaring is substantially greater than the inside general coefficient, and this coefficient appears greater than the prime crew coefficient in developmental mining. This is consistent with the fact that inside general workers play a less important part in the production process in pillaring and pillaring in general is a more productive form of mining than developmental. The magnitude of the delay coefficients has the correct signs and the magnitude among these coefficients appears in the correct magnitude, as we discussed earlier. The slightly higher delay coefficients in pillaring indicate that downtime costs more in terms of lost production, compared to developmental. The coefficient for physical conditions indicates that bad conditions lead to lower tonnage and the magnitude of this coefficient is greater in pillaring than developmental.

Crew effects. The data for Tables 4-3 and 4-4 are presented at the crew level; that is, the analysis generates one model from data across twelve crews. The assumption in this type of analysis is that the estimated coefficients for the different crews are the same. Our hypothesis, of course, is that crews are different. At this time in our research we have examined crew effect by using dummy variables. Other effects that might be related to crews (for example, machinery, conditions) have already been included in the model. While this is a crude or black box approach, our assumption is that crew effects represent the coordination or team aspects of the mining crew. (We are currently looking at alternative procedures to clarify the crew concept.) Given our hypothesis about crew effects, we did several analyses that led to the following findings:

- Crew effects by themselves generate an R^2 of about .09— using tons of coal as the dependent variable.
- Crew effects are significant with the physical conditions and

labor variables added. That is, the crew effect dummies are not merely picking up variation in physical conditions or the number of laborers.

- Crew effects are significant in the full model that contains the technology variables, labor variables, and the control variable.

Indirect effects. Figure 4-1 summarizes some of the results we have discussed thus far. The technological variables, machin-

Figure 4-1. A Production Model.

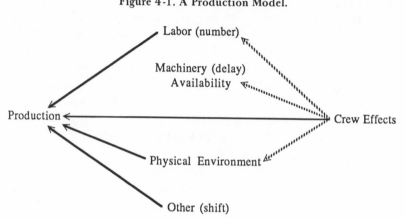

ery, and physical conditions contribute directly to performance. The labor and crew variables incrementally improve the explanatory power of our model. The relationships among the variables in the figure are, of course, more complicated than the simple direct effects we have portrayed. For example, crew effects may directly and indirectly impact on production through the machine availability or delay variable. Examining indirect effects provides a more comprehensive way to understand group performance. We have explored some of these indirect effects; others are still under investigation. The physical environment variables could increase machine delay time, which in turn would effect production. No relationship was observed. The labor variable could affect delays but no relationship was observed. The crew effects variable does seem to affect the length of delays;

some crews have shorter delays than others. There is some indication in the literature that there may be an interaction effect between the crew variable and environmental variables on production. That is, well-coordinated or cohesive crews perform better in bad physical conditions, but no differences appear in average or good conditions (Goodman, 1979). This relationship, as well as other possible indirect effects, is currently being examined.

Summary Discussion

In order to help the reader understand more about models of work group effectiveness, we have focused on the task and technology concepts because they are important in work group performance and these two concepts have not been well delineated.

The major problem with the role of task and technology in group performance has been the lack of definitional and conceptual clarification. Another problem has been that these two concepts have been used interchangeably. In this chapter technology was defined as a system of structural components involved in the transformation process. The task variable is one of the components of technology and consists of a set of core, support, or linking programs.

Throughout this discussion there has been a contrast between human and nonhuman factors. The reason for this theme was to reorient our thinking about groups. Variables such as leadership and cohesiveness are important but they are only part of the story about group effectiveness. The machinery, inventory policies, scheduling policies, and maintenance policies affect what goes on in the group. Our argument, or perhaps plea, is to take a more interdisciplinary view in studying work group effectiveness. The Rushton quality of work experiment (Goodman, 1979) was cited to show the important constraints created by the nonhuman factors. In that experiment some very powerful teams were created over a reasonable time period. However, the effect of these teams was marginal, given the dominance of certain nonhuman factors. That is, the technological system in many ways created little room for the team effect to be realized.

This issue about human and nonhuman systems is not just a recasting of the sociotechnical approach. Indeed, in that approach the social system is typically fit to the technology rather than any real joint optimization. Our position is that (1) both sets of factors should be represented in any study of effectiveness, (2) more attention should be given to the specific technical and economic factors that are involved in designing the technological system, and (3) more attention should be given to the interactions between these two sets of variables.

A related point is the need to estimate the direct effects of the technological system variables on performance. The moderator- and/or contingency-variable approach underestimates the role of technology on performance. It focuses on the question of how other variables affect performance, given variations of technology. A more appropriate analysis strategy would be first to determine the extent to which the technological system provides constraints on the human system. How much room, as in the Rushton case, is there for changes in group performance due to interventions in the human system? The second type of analysis would be to look for interactions between the technology system and crew or labor variables. For example, crew variables probably affect the length of downtime but not the frequency of downtime.

Another theme in this discussion concerns the homogeneity assumption, which appears often in both the task and the technology literature. This assumption leads to using global attributes such as uncertainty or difficulty. We have argued and illustrated that the heterogeneity assumption is probably more accurate and a better place to start. One implication of the heterogeneity assumption is that you estimate different models for different types of technology. So in our empirical example we separated the developmental and pillaring models. The equivalence or nonequivalence of empirical models then becomes a test for determining homogeneity of technology.

Another implication concerns analyzing groups across different organizations. An original assumption in our research program was to sample groups across a homogeneous population of organizations—that is, to get a large number of groups doing the same thing (continuous mining) in different organizations. This would permit looking at policy differences holding technology constant. What we found is that there is great variation in how the components of the "same" technological system are configured. Therefore, it becomes difficult to separate out the variations in the technological components and related policies. Our evolved strategy is to understand well one set of groups in a particular organization. The focus is more idiographic.

This idiographic approach to groups can lead to productive or unproductive scientific explorations. Since this is an important theme in the chapter, we should identify the potential problems with this approach. The basic argument is that we need different models of group performance for groups with different technologies. Given a common technology, we expect to have different models across different firms. And even within firms, different crews may have different models of performance. The basic problem with this idiographic approach concerns how we use information generated from this type of investigation. If we end up with only a model of description of crew A on shift 1 in mine X, our knowledge and scholarship will be quite limited. However, our definition of technology and the production systems identified a system of components. It was argued that alternative combinations of these components can produce the same product or level of effectiveness. If our investigation identifies the unique combination of components in work group A and in work group B, then we can begin to understand what some of the boundaries are for effective group performance. Our fine-grained analysis of crews A and B is conducted to better inform our general understanding of group performance. An idiographic approach does not mean you can only construct a model of crew A. On the other hand, this movement from the specific group to a more general understanding does not mean you will have a more detailed general model that will not let you predict crew A's performance. The basic argument is that there are large numbers of combinations of components in the technology and production system that lead to effective performance. We are not able to know or control all these combinations. However, knowledge of a particular combination, understood in the light of certain constraints, can improve our understanding of the group process.

A dilemma in the current literature is the language used by researchers in describing technology. In most cases, the transformation process is never described. In some of the other cases, the attribute approach (for example, predictability) is used. We have discussed the limitations of this approach. There is not now a good language to describe groups. A good language should inform us what goes on (both intended and actual) in the transformation process. It should be descriptive and easy to replicate or cross-validate. It should inform us where the critical levers are that can change group performance. Some of the concepts we have discussed (for example, technological system) provide some hints about what we should describe. The process and work flow charts used in engineering may be one method to represent the work of a group.

The idea of group performance levers was introduced because we want to know what makes a difference. We believe that in any group's productive system there is a small number of intervention points that will significantly impact performance. What would be nice to see in a report on group effectiveness is the researcher's identification and rationale at the critical levers of group performance. Some hints appear in Kolodny and Kiggundu (1980), but nothing is explicit. Unfortunately, there are no general levers for all groups, but some strategic points for search have been enumerated above.

The empirical example was introduced to illustrate *some* of the ideas in the text. There was some evidence that (1) the technology variables were important, (2) the technology was heterogeneous, and (3) both direct and indirect effects on performance need to be identified.

There were obvious limitations to this example. The focus was on one general type of technology—mining. Data from only one mine were presented, although other mines show similar relationships. The measures from record data were clearly loaded on the technological side rather than the human side.

On this last point, there is an interesting problem. Data on the technological and labor variables in many settings are available cheaply for frequent (for example, daily) time periods. Data we collected from interviews were expensive to gather and limited to one time period. For this reason, it is hard to usefully match these data. That is, we have the technological and labor variables daily but only a one-shot measure of some of the human-attitudinal variables. It may be preferable to collect the record data and some rich case studies based on selected groups over time. The record data would fit the more traditional modeling strategy. The case studies would provide ideas, contextual material, and confirmation for the modeling analysis. For example, it would be nice to have case studies for the crews to which we attached dummy variables. The case studies would be more valuable for identifying group performance levers.

A particular bias in our analysis has been the focus on production criteria as opposed to other group criteria. The bias was intentional. We do not believe there are general models of performance that cut across different criteria. From other work done in the organizational effectiveness area, it is relatively clear that attacking global measures of effectiveness has not been productive (Goodman, Atkin, and Schoorman, 1983). So we have focused on one criterion and built our discussion around performance. Our strategy in organizational effectiveness or group effectiveness studies is to select an appropriate criterion and work backward in developing a model specific to that criterion.

Other criteria, such as the satisfaction of group members, should be explored. That exploration would obviously end up with a different model than appears in Figure 4-1. But that is not the point of the chapter. All the themes we have reviewed in this section still hold. The definitions of the technological system, the issues of homogeneity, the need for a language, the direct effect of technology, and so on would still be the same.

Another bias in our approach has been the focus on production groups—that is, groups that produce or transform some goods. While there are important types of production groups in organizations, it is clear there are groups in organizations devoted to other functions, such as decision making (for example, approving a bank loan), communicating, or coordinating activities. Does the approach to groups advocated in this chapter fit these types of groups? The answer to that question is no; our focus has been primarily on groups that produce products. An underlying criticism in this chapter of other approaches to understanding groups is that they are too general. That is, general models are constructed to explain group effectiveness across different types of groups, technologies, and different organizations. The position advocated in this chapter is that we need to move away from this general approach to a more fine-grained approach. Therefore, the position taken in this chapter does not fit all types of groups. It seems more appropriate now to develop a good framework for understanding production groups and then do the same thing for decision-making groups. Then one can look for commonalities. The idiographic theme advocated in this chapter will not be of value to the person interested in decision making in organizations. However, concepts such as the group performance levers, the homogeneity assumption, and specific as opposed to general criteria should all be relevant to those interested in group decision making.

We conclude this discussion by noting some implications of this chapter for practice. This chapter was not written only for the researcher concerned with models of group performance. The intended constituency was anyone—researcher, manager, consultant—interested in improving group performance. There were a number of basic themes that directly bear on practice. First, if one wants to change a group, one needs more than a general model of performance that currently appears in the literature. Our idiographic argument means that the change agent has to learn in depth about the unique configurations of each group that is the object of change. Often consultants treat work groups as homogeneous entities. We view them as heterogeneous entities. Second, technology plays a powerful role in group performance. Despite the espoused acknowledgement of the importance of social and technical variables, most of the approaches to group performance ignore to a large extent the role of technology—that is, the focus is still on changing the social system. We have argued that in many cases the technological systems create a "ceiling effect" and there is little opportunity for any social intervention to have major effects (for example, the Rushton case). Similarly, we have argued that a careful analysis of the technological system will indicate areas (for example, inventory or maintenance policies) that are typically ignored by social change agents but are very important. Third, the determination of the interface between the human and nonhuman elements needs to be identified by both the researcher and the practitioner. In the mining example, one key interface occurs during the downtime situation. To some extent the frequency of downtime is affected by variables exogenous to and uncontrollable by the members of the group. However, the members' response to the downtime incident is key to increased productivity. If this observation is true, then the major intervention in the human system will be around this interface, not on how to change groups in general. Fourth, the concept of group levers is important for both theory and practice. These represent the key intervention points that substantially impact on group performance. Although there is no set of general levers for all groups or even for groups in the same technology, we did identify a strategy for identifying levers in performance groups.

References

Argote, L. "Input Uncertainty and Organizational Coordination in Hospital Emergency Units." *Administrative Science Quarterly*, 1982, *27* (3), 420-434.

Carter, L. F., Haythorn, W. W., and Howell, M. "A Further Investigation of Three Criteria of Leadership." *Journal of Abnormal and Social Psychology*, 1950, *45*, 350-358.

Comstock, D. E., and Scott, W. R. "Technology and the Structure of Subunits." *Administrative Science Quarterly*, 1977, *22*, 177-202.

Cummings, T. "Designing Effective Work Groups." In P. C. Nystrom and W. H. Starbuck (eds.), *Handbook of Organizational Design: Remodeling Organizations and Their Environments*. Vol. 2. New York: Oxford University Press, 1981.

Fry, L. W., and Slocum, J. W., Jr. "Technology, Structure and

Workgroup Effectiveness: A Test of a Contingency Model." *Academy of Management Journal,* 1984, *27* (2), 221-246.

Gladstein, D. "Groups in Context: A Model of Task Group Effectiveness." *Administrative Science Quarterly,* 1984, *29* (4), 499-517.

Goodman, P. S. *Assessing Organizational Change: The Rushton Quality of Work Experiment.* New York: Wiley-Interscience, 1979.

Goodman, P. S., and Atkin, R. A. "Effects of Absenteeism on Individuals and Organizations." In P. S. Goodman, R. S. Atkin, and Associates (eds.), *Absenteeism: New Approaches to Understanding, Measuring, and Managing Employee Absence.* San Francisco: Jossey-Bass, 1984.

Goodman, P. S., Atkin, R. A., and Schoorman, D. "On the Demise of Organizational Effectiveness Studies." In K. Cameron and D. Whetton (eds.), *Organizational Effectiveness: A Comparison of Multiple Models.* Orlando, Fla.: Academic Press, 1983.

Hackman, J. R. "Group Influences on Individuals." In M. D. Dunnett (ed.), *Handbook of Industrial and Organizational Psychology.* Skokie, Ill.: Rand McNally, 1976.

Hackman, J. R. "A Normative Model of Work Team Effectiveness." Technical Report No. 2, Research Program on Group Effectiveness, Yale School of Organization and Management, 1983.

Herold, D. M. "Improving the Performance Effectiveness of Groups Through a Task-Contingency Selection of Intervention Strategies." *Academy of Management Review,* 1978, *3* (2), 315-325.

Hickson, D. J., Pugh, D. S., and Pheysey, D. C. "Operations Technology and Organization Structure: An Empirical Reappraisal." *Administrative Science Quarterly,* 1969, *14,* 378-397.

Katz, D., and Kahn, R. L. *The Social Psychology of Organizations.* (2nd ed.) New York: Wiley, 1976.

Katz, D., and Tushman, M. "Communication Patterns, Project Performance, and Task Characteristics: An Empirical Evaluation and Integration in an R&D Setting." *Organizational Behavior and Human Performance,* 1979, *23* (2), 139-162.

Kolodny, H. F., and Kiggundu, M. N. "Towards the Development of a Sociotechnical Systems Model in Woodlands Mechanical Harvesting." *Human Relations*, 1980, *33* (9), 623-645.

McGrath, J. E. *Groups: Interaction and Performance.* Englewood Cliffs, N.J.: Prentice-Hall, 1984.

Mohr, L. "Organizational Technology and Organization Structure." *Administrative Science Quarterly*, 1971, *16*, 444-459.

Nieva, V. F., Fleishman, E. A., and Rieck, A. "Team Dimensions: Their Identity, Their Measurement, and Their Relationships." Final Technical Report for Contract No. DAHC19-78-C-0001. Washington, D.C.: Advanced Research Resources Organizations, 1978.

Perrow, C. "A Framework for the Comparative Analysis of Organizations." *American Sociological Review*, 1967, *32*, 194-208.

Schoonhoven, C. B. "Problems with Contingency Theory: Testing Assumptions Hidden Within the Language of Contingency." *Administrative Science Quarterly*, 1981, *26*, 349-377.

Shaw, M. E. "Scaling Group Tasks: A Method for Dimensional Analysis." *JSAS Catalog of Selected Documents in Psychology*, 1973, *3*, 8.

Steiner, I. D. *Group Process and Productivity.* Orlando, Fla.: Academic Press, 1972.

Thompson, J. D. *Organizations in Action.* New York: McGraw-Hill, 1967.

Thompson, J. D., and Bates, F. L. "Technology, Organization, and Administration." *Administrative Science Quarterly*, 1957, *2*, 325-343.

Tushman, M. L. "Work Characteristics and Subunit Communication Structure: A Contingency Analysis." *Administrative Science Quarterly*, 1979, *24*, 82-97.

Woodward, J. *Industrial Organization: Theory and Practice.* Oxford, England: Oxford University Press, 1965.

5

Groups Under Contrasting Management Strategies

Richard E. Walton
J. Richard Hackman

Groups pervade organizations and have long been recognized as significant in affecting both the quality of life of organization members and organizational productivity. We know of no scholar or manager who would argue that groups can safely be ignored in studying or leading an organization that has work to accomplish. Yet we perceive some changes in how groups are being used in contemporary organizations, changes that appear to be associated with some fundamental changes in how organizations are designed and managed.

There is a trend in many organizations away from management strategies dominated by top-down controls, narrowly defined jobs, and close supervision. Replacing a control-oriented strategy in these organizations is an approach that seeks to foster high member commitment and the greatest feasible self-

Note: Prepared for a conference on groups in organizations held at Carnegie-Mellon University, September 16–18, 1984. Support for the first author's work was provided by Lex Service PLC and the Division of Research, Harvard Graduate School of Business Administration. Support for the second author's work was provided in part by the Organizational Effectiveness Research Program, Office of Naval Research, through Contract N00014-80-C-0555 to Yale University. Helpful comments on an earlier draft were provided by participants at the Carnegie-Mellon Conference and by Shoshana Zuboff.

management (Walton, 1985; Hackman, 1985). We refer to organizations dominated by the first strategy as "control strategy organizations" and those dominated by the second strategy as "commitment strategy organizations." Also of interest are "mixed strategy organizations," particularly those in the midst of a transition from a control strategy to a commitment strategy.

By examining the kinds of groups found in the two types of organizations, we should be able to better understand both the management strategies themselves and the dynamics of organizational groups more generally. Questions of interest include the following: What kinds of groups are typically found in control as opposed to commitment organizations, and what functions do they serve for members and for the organization as a whole? How are groups used and managed in the two types of organizations? What roles do groups play in the transition from one management strategy to the other?

To explore these questions, we must first clarify what we mean by groups in organizations. Our use of the concept, adapted from the definition proposed by Alderfer (1977), is as follows:

- The group is perceived as such both by members (who should be able to distinguish reliable people who are members from those who are not) and nonmembers (who should be able to identify and characterize the group in relatively specific terms).
- Members have significantly interdependent relations with one another. While this does not necessarily mean that they have regular face-to-face interaction, it does require that they be dependent on one another to achieve some shared purpose.
- Members have differentiated roles within the group. There is agreement among them that different individuals are expected to behave in different ways as the group goes about its business.
- The group operates in an organizational context, managing relationships with other groups or their representatives.

Only if these attributes are all present does a group fall within our domain of interest; if they are not, we would refer to the entity as an aggregation rather than a group.

We further distinguish between two general types of groups within our domain: organizationally created work teams and self-enacted informal groups. *Work teams* are created by managers to accomplish specified organizational tasks. Although members of work teams always share responsibility for performance outcomes, the design of such teams can vary widely (for example, in size, in the significance of the work to be done, in the amount of authority members have to do the work, and in the way the team is managed). *Self-enacted groups* are created by members themselves and are an expression of the needs and aspirations of the people who comprise them—including needs to collectively make sense of and respond to organizational requirements and managers' behaviors. Although many such groups are formed in the absence of formal task responsibilities shared by members, they also may evolve as an elaboration of roles that already exist in structured work teams.

As will be seen, work teams and self-enacted groups play different roles and have different dynamics in control and commitment organizations.

Contrasting Strategies of Work Force Management

The traditional strategy for managing the work force was institutionalized over the first half of this century. Its component policies have a theme of imposing control to achieve efficiency. Although commitment is welcomed by management in a control-oriented organization, the organization is designed to function adequately even if member commitment is relatively low. As a consequence, control organizations tend to elicit little commitment from their members and offer few means other than effort by which any increase in commitment can be translated into improved organizational effectiveness.

An alternative management strategy was initiated by the founders of high-technology engineering companies such as Hewlett-Packard and Digital Equipment Corporation. In the last decade, the commitment approach, articulated as a generalizable management strategy, has been employed in the design of numerous new plants and companies and is now guiding system-wide change in many large companies. Its policies are designed to elicit commitment in order to achieve effectiveness and efficiency. A high-commitment work system, then, is designed to *generate* high commitment, to fully *utilize* commitment for business and human gains, and to *depend* on high commitment for organizational effectiveness (Walton, 1980).

Two Dimensions of Difference. Differences between control and commitment strategy organizations are found in virtually all policy areas that bear on human resource management, ranging from recruitment and selection practices to labor relations policy (see Walton, 1985). For present purposes, we highlight two dimensions of difference that have special relevance to groups in organizations. One has to do with how work is set up and managed, the other with how authority is distributed and exercised.

Work design and performance management. In control strategy organizations, work is divided into small, well-defined tasks that typically minimize the skill and judgment required. Performance is managed by reference to explicit standards (preferably based on systematic measurement of the work) that define minimum acceptable performance. Pay is based on individual performance or job classification, sometimes with the addition of incentive compensation for above-standard performance. In all, work is structured and managed using the lowest common denominator concept: The idea is to run the organization so that even the least skilled or motivated employees will perform at satisfactory levels.

In a commitment strategy organization, job responsibilities tend to be broad, combining planning and implementation activities. Employees are expected to manage themselves to a considerable extent, making adjustments in what they do or how they do it when circumstances change. Self-managing teams, rather than individuals, often are the accountable unit for performance. Rather than minimum standards of acceptable performance, commitment organizations typically set "stretch objectives" intended to motivate employees to seek the highest level of performance of which they are capable. These objectives emphasize continuous improvement and often change in response to changing requirements in the organization's marketplace. Compensation policies reward the acquisition of new skills, typically provide for significant gain or profit sharing, and often provide special reinforcement for group achievement.

Authority dynamics and compliance mechanisms. Management prerogatives and positional authority are emphasized in control organizations, consistent with the general strategy of top-down control and coordination. There typically are many hierarchical levels in these organizations, and status symbols are allocated in ways that legitimize and reinforce hierarchical differences. Bottom-up influence is minimized: Employees are expected to follow orders, not make suggestions. There typically are many rules in place to make sure people know what they are supposed to do and formal sanctions available to make sure they comply.

In contrast, authority in commitment-oriented organizations derives more from competence and experience than position. Commitment organizations tend to be flat with relatively few management perks and status symbols. Employee ideas are actively sought, and governance devices are installed to provide means for upward influence by rank-and-file organization members. Instead of rules, coordination and control are handled through shared philosophy, goals held in common, and group meetings of various kinds. Probably the most pervasive and powerful influence on compliance is influence from one's coworkers.

Trends and Complications. Historically, control and commitment strategy organizations evolved in two separate kinds of organizations, characterized by different types of work and different populations of employees. Yet today we see some signs of a countertrend in both kinds of organizations.

Control strategies, for example, originated and prospered in large blue-collar and clerical organizations, where there were large quantities of relatively routine work to be done. In the past fifteen years, however, the commitment model has been tested and has taken root in numerous firms of this type—including automobile, steel, rubber, electrical equipment, metalworking, communications, transportation, banking, food products, and wood products companies. Competitive challenges in these industries, particularly those arising from international trade and deregulation, appear to have spawned a variety of management strategies intended to increase employees' motivation and the utilization of their skills. Managers also have had to confront rising employee expectations regarding voice and fairness and have sought policies and practices that might meet these expectations and simultaneously improve organizational effectiveness.

Commitment strategies, in contrast, originated with (and traditionally have been reserved for) work done by high-level managers and skilled professionals, such as research scientists. In many professional organizations, the current interest is in improving the design and implementation of commitment policies, rather than replacing them. Yet a countertrend toward more control-oriented strategies has become evident in professional organizations in recent years, most obviously in some schools, religious organizations, and health care institutions.

The evolution of the two strategies in the future seems certain to be powerfully influenced (and complicated) by microprocessing technology. Some applications of this technology generate or reinforce a control strategy—for example, by routinizing, pacing, monitoring, and depersonalizing work. Other applications foster a commitment strategy—for example, by augmenting employees' skills, relieving them of tedious and repetitive work, and providing for decentralized decision making. Technological influences on work force strategy are likely to be particularly powerful in white-collar industries, where there are large numbers of people engaged in clerical work or in professional activities such as drafting, engineering, or purchasing. Managements in such industries, so far, have not taken initiatives to shape the applications of computer technology in ways that deliberately reinforce their preferred work force strategies.

The characterizations of control and commitment organizations we have offered in the preceding pages are, to some extent, idealized; few organizations of either type have all the features we have discussed. Yet many actual organizations approximate the ideals rather closely. Even more numerous are organizations that employ a mixture of policies, some of which impose top-down control and some of which foster commitment and self-management. Many of these mixed organizations are in transition from a control-oriented strategy to a commitment strategy, reflecting a broad trend in contemporary U.S. society from the former to the latter work force strategy.

Does this trend suggest that commitment strategies are inherently more effective than control strategies? Not at all. Indeed, a well-managed control-oriented organization (and there are many of them) will easily outperform a poorly managed commitment-oriented organization (and there are many of them, too). In the remainder of this chapter, we explore in some detail the role groups play in control, commitment, and mixed strategy organizations. For each type of organization, we will see multiple ways that groups can contribute—and detract from —overall organizational effectiveness.

Groups in Control Strategy Organizations

What kinds of groups are found in control strategy organizations? How is their development shaped by the policies of those organizations? What kind of power do these groups have, with respect to both their members and the larger organization, and how do managers respond to the exercise of that power?

Types of Groups. Control organizations turn out to be fertile breeding grounds for self-enacted groups. The research literature (particularly that generated at the Harvard Business School during the 1950s) shows the pervasiveness of self-enacted groups in control organizations, the variety of forms they can assume, and their complexity as a social form (Homans, 1950; Sayles, 1958; Lawrence and Seiler, 1965).

Self-enacted groups can range in size from three to a dozen or more workers. Although they usually are composed of people who report to the same supervisor, they may also form because of task similarity, work flow interdependency, or even simple proximity. Similarity in demographic characteristics (such as age, ethnicity, and social class) also promotes the formation of self-enacted groups. Some such groups are relatively isolated from neighboring groups, while others may be imbedded in a network of informal groups; indeed, individuals sometimes are members of multiple self-enacted groups. Despite their variability in composition and structure, self-enacted groups often wield considerable power in control organizations, as will be seen below.

What about work teams in control organizations—groups composed by the organization to accomplish organizational tasks? Here, too, the data are clear, even though the conclusion is different: Work teams are rarely seen in control organizations. As we explore below organizational dynamics that foster and shape emergent groups in control organizations, we also will see why work teams are so rarely used in these organizations.

Control Policies and Group Development. Even though informal, self-enacted groups can be as relevant as task groups to the well-being of both the enterprise and its employees, the most immediate and obvious functions of self-enacted groups are social. Such groups typically emerge as members develop regular patterns of friendly interaction—conversation, shared activities during breaks, off-hour social exchanges, and so on. In this way, a self-enacted group helps humanize the workplace for the direct benefit of its members. The effect of the group on the organization, however, varies, depending on whether the friendly interaction is at the expense of work activities.

Self-enacted groups also serve numerous purposes beyond this limited (and inwardly oriented) social function. It is, for example, common to find groups in control organizations assuming responsibility for "bargaining" about output standards on behalf of their members, defining and enforcing limits to supervisory control, and influencing various organizational practices and procedures. To understand these functions better, we will show how the policies of control organizations strengthen the power of the organization over individual members and how self-enacted groups can provide a counterbalance to the exercise of that power.

Work design and performance management. Narrow, specialized jobs in control strategy organizations keep the training investment in the individual low and thereby minimize the organization's dependence on the individual. Individual accountability for performance puts maximum pressure on the individual worker to meet standard expectations and helps supervision stimulate output competition among workers. Individualized incentives induce workers to act in their own individual short-term interest in ways that serve management's interest in the longer-term (yielding higher output immediately, thereby providing the basis for raising standards later and decreasing the labor required).

The emergent group frequently blunts these control measures. After the social function, perhaps the most commonly observed function of self-enacted groups is to regulate the output of group members. Self-enacted groups often develop a widely shared rationale for norms that restrict output—for example, "Our work is not appreciated, anyway"; "Management will always want more and more"; "They are not fair to us"; and "They will take advantage of us."

In the bank wiring observation room in the Hawthorne studies, for example, members respected a group norm that individuals would wire two pieces of equipment per day; they even underreported or overreported their actual output if necessary in order to maintain that output record (Roethlisberger and Dickson, 1939). Subsequent researchers repeatedly have documented this tendency of informal groups to decrease or eliminate the differences among workers' output (or at least to obscure actual differences) and thereby frustrate management's effort to stimulate competition among workers. The group is often successful in restricting output despite individual incentives administered by management. Groups also deflect the control tactic of individual accountability in other ways such as by informal helping out among members and job trading.

Authority dynamics and compliance mechanisms. As noted earlier, managers in control strategy organizations seek to maintain unilateral authority and to enforce compliance with management-specified rules about behavior in the workplace. Although managers may have to negotiate work rules institutionally with a labor union, they have little interest in renegotiating them in the workplace. Nonetheless, in both nonunion and union settings, groups are highly influential in determining what is and what is not acceptable behavior at work. Indeed, group norms may prevail over the organization's rules or the labor contract in innumerable areas—such as assigning overtime, taking breaks, punching out, horsing around, smoking or eating at the workplace, and accounting for resources used in the production process. Thus, the self-enacted group can defeat, at least in part, the policy of top-down control.

The expressed rationale for activities that violate rules, including those that increase group members' pay (such as punching in other employees and manipulating downtime to increase incentive earnings) include "We are giving full measure"; "We are underpaid"; "Everyone does it"; and "Management knows about it." Often unstated is a perhaps more important rationale—namely, that such activities give members a voice, a feeling of influence and control, that they are otherwise denied in control organizations.

Control strategy organizations typically reinforce the hierarchy by the allocation of status symbols. Status symbols are designed to denote subordination, to create social distance, and to reward proorganizational behavior. Thus, it is important that the differentiating symbols be prized by the general population of the organization. Self-enacted groups can, however, create alternative social realities, and hence, competing status criteria. They can develop a consensus that ridicules the organizational badges of status and that prizes other group-supplied status symbols. Thus, management's dress, office, and titles can lose their effectiveness in subordinating and controlling the work force. The symbols used to recognize superior performance (for example, awards and publicity) can come to be a source of embarrassment, not pride, to those who receive them.

Power of Groups. The above analysis depicting the group as neutralizing the control measures of the formal organization suggests that the more elaborate the system of control measures (for example, standards, incentives, detailed rules), the more developed will be the emergent group's devices for protecting its members.[1] But what are the *processes* by which self-enacted groups gain, consolidate, and exercise their power in control organizations?

First, how do these groups exercise power in relation to their *members*? They do, of course, have powerful incentives (such as approval and social satisfaction) to use in enlisting member support and conformity. Beyond this, they sometimes use a variety of punishment tactics to keep members in line—ranging from criticism, sarcasm, and ostracism, to sabotaging a target employee's work (hiding tools, maladjusting his or her equipment), destroying property (smashing a lunch box or ripping off an auto antenna), and physical intimidation.

Not all employees are equally susceptible to group influence. A study of salesmen found that the effectiveness of peer controls depended upon the individual identifying (in a reference group sense) with the sales group (French, 1960). Moreover, the more hostility and rejection directed at an individual salesman, the less likely he was to acquire identification. Thus, some pressure tactics groups employ to achieve compliance can be self-defeating. Even so, it is not uncommon for individuals who withstand the pressure of the group eventually to decide that the job situation is intolerable and quit, or request transfer.

How do self-enacted groups exercise power in relation to

1. It is, therefore, not surprising that the phenomenon of groups restricting output and otherwise limiting organizational demands has been most completely documented in blue-collar work settings. These organizations, historically, have had the most well-developed control systems. Yet the phenomenon also is observed in white-collar organizations. In the Federal Aviation Administration, for example, informal groups of controllers developed norms that supported noncompliant behavior. In academic settings, groups of students often develop norms about preparation and class participation. Even groups of faculty develop norms to limit responsibilities in relation to both administrators and students. Similar phenomena have been observed among salespersons, professional staffs of consulting firms, police officers, and Internal Revenue Service agents. The protective functions of self-enacted groups are *not* observed only in blue-collar industries.

supervision? Often the process can be characterized as "mutual boundary setting." Since neither the group nor the supervisor can dictate to the other, there is implicit bargaining over limits. What worker behaviors not countenanced by the formal organization will the supervisor actually tolerate? What supervisory behaviors will the group actually accept? The group and the supervisor tacitly agree that it is in their mutual interest to accommodate each other within certain boundaries rather than for either to escalate the influence tactics available.

Thus, self-enacted groups regulate behavior in ways that can be far more significant than the simple restriction of output. By actively redefining norms regarding such behaviors as attendance, effort, cooperation, production, and compliance with rules, a broad range of behavior can be controlled over an extended period of time. While the norms that emerge may not be exactly what management (the other party to the bargains that are struck) would have preferred, they provide a unique means for members to express their own views about what is fair and appropriate, and to have those views "count" in an otherwise management-dominated organization.

Observers differ in their interpretations of how consciously self-enacted groups exercise influence. Homans concluded that many of the group processes observed by Roethlisberger and Dickson in the Hawthorne studies were not conscious: "The protective functioning of the informal organization was not a product of deliberate planning. It was more the nature of an automatic response" (Homans, 1941, p. 86). In other studies, and in our own observations, the leaders of these informal groups are often quite aware of the instrumental nature of the group and are conscious of the way they mobilize and utilize power. These leaders may or may not be able to formulate explicitly the tacit bargain that has been struck with supervisors, but they certainly know when it is not being observed.

Management Responses to Groups. We can identify four responses managers in control-oriented organizations have to self-enacted groups. Each represents one way for management to deal with the potential power of those groups to blunt organizational control policies.

The first approach is to attempt to kill the group or to prevent it from forming in the first place. In one classic case study (Richards and Dobyns, 1957), a department manager tried to defeat a self-enacted group by controlling members' breaks, forbidding conversations, and removing a physical barrier to make its internal behavior more observable. The manager succeeded in changing the *manifest* pattern of the group's activities to his liking, but the net effect of the behavior change compromised the organization's interests. Self-enacted groups appear to be a robust social forum, even when subjected to concerted management opposition.

In some cases, managements have been able to limit, if not prevent, group formation completely. Physical layouts and production processes that make talk difficult, high levels of turnover, and heterogeneous membership all retard the development of informal groups. In one case (Goode and Fowler, 1949), management prevented group formation by employing a dozen or so employees, each of whom for one reason or another (such as physical handicap) needed a job "desperately" and therefore had a strong disincentive to resign. This cadre of individuals was controlled by management to set a fast work pace for others. The others were high-turnover personnel—either part-time workers, experienced workers on layoff elsewhere, or young newcomers to the labor market. The work force remained individualized and controlled.

A second management approach to groups in control organizations is to attempt to confine the group's activities and influence to the social domain. As noted earlier, the social functions of groups are important to individual members. These functions are particularly salient in control organizations, where individuals often must deal with the numbing effects of subordination, monotony, and work that is experienced as having little meaning. By neutralizing the negative side effects of control, social groups can make the organization more tolerable for their members. Some managements capitalize on the social function of groups by sponsoring various group-oriented activities, such as bowling or softball leagues, hobby groups, and other off-hours activities. The hope, apparently, is that the social benefits of groups, which accrue both to the organization and to individual employees, will be obtained—but in a way that obviates any inclination members have to engage in work-focused group activities, which would represent a threat to managers in a control-oriented organization.

A third response can be called containment. In this strategy, management has acknowledged the reality of self-enacted groups with agendas to protect their members and give them voice. Managers conclude that the consequences of applying control measures to break up groups or deny them influence only serves to strengthen the allegiance of their members and to drain or divert organizational energy. Upper-level managers are generally aware that supervision must strike bargains with the self-enacted groups, and they appreciate that the bargains involve compromise of the organization's official rules and efficiency standards. They do not know the nature or extent of these deals, however, and they are comfortable not knowing so long as production remains satisfactory. The containment strategy is undoubtedly the most common management response to groups in control organizations.

The fourth response in control organizations is "benign neglect." Like the containment approach, this involves a tacit exchange "agreement," but with an important difference. Here the "bargain" involves performance that meets or exceeds the organization's standards. The self-enacted group's norms call for superior performance in quality, volume, and/or methods improvement, but they also assume an absence of close external supervision. As the leader of one such group remarked, "They leave us alone and expect us to produce—and we do" (Lawrence and Seiler, 1965, p. 84). In this case, members punched the time clock for each other contrary to organizational rules, but the supervisor recognized that, overall, the group's activity was beneficial to the organization. Sometimes a supervisor is fortunate enough to be "offered" such a bargain (tacitly, of course) by a subordinate group. More often, the group has been nurtured by a supervisor whose particular style is deviant from the control strategy of the organization. Appreciating the constructive outcomes of the bargain, senior managers look the other way.

These benign neglect groups do not always live happily ever after, however. Such groups often have gone sour, because inadvertent actions by higher management or new supervision disrupt the membership or weaken group autonomy. When the "agreement" with management is broken, members feel betrayed and withhold standard performance. Because it already is a strong social unit, a "betrayed" group typically can respond vigorously and with discipline when members feel management has violated the implicit agreement.[2]

Groups in Commitment Strategy Organizations

We turn now to organizations that seek to foster employee commitment and self-management. The same questions discussed for groups in control strategy organizations will be examined, but with a difference. Whereas there is a substantial research literature upon which to draw for control organizations, research on commitment organizations is in its relative infancy, and there are very few studies that specifically address groups in them. Therefore, our treatment will be more speculative in tone, and we will summarize sections by providing hypotheses for further investigation rather than conclusions that summarize what is already known.

Types of Groups. Work teams pervade commitment organizations. In discussing such organizations writers often treat work designed for individuals and for teams as alternative options, but in practice teams are the dominant organizational forum used to accomplish work. We know of no commitment organization that does *not* rely substantially on teams of one sort or another for getting the organization's work done. The reasons for this state of affairs will become clear as we examine the social imperatives and incentives of commitment policies below.

2. Two aspects of this last management response should be noted, because the benign neglect groups contrast with the formal task teams in commitment-oriented organizations discussed next. First, benign neglect groups develop despite a control-oriented culture and therefore represent a deviant subculture. Second, they represent a specific "agreement," do not identify with the organization, and do not have a proorganization ideology.

What of self-enacted groups? They are scarcely mentioned in research and writing about commitment organizations. Are they as absent from these organizations as work teams are from control organizations? To the contrary: It appears that self-enacted groups are pervasive in such organizations and important to what happens there, although they play a very different role than they do in control organizations.

Indeed, some planners of commitment organizations actually count on task teams to elaborate their own internal structure and extend the scope of group roles beyond the work itself. The formal designs of task teams provide for certain group leadership functions and member roles, posit decision mechanisms that require negotiation among team members, and provide a means for teams to exercise influence upward in the organization. But not everything can be planned and structured formally, and the *emergence* of additional leadership within teams, further differentiation of roles, additional forms of peer pressure, and so on appears to be critical in creating a high-commitment culture. In the healthy commitment organization, then, the boundaries between organizationally created and self-enacted group phenomena are blurred and difficult to sort out. This may present research dilemmas, but it is also a phenomenon of potentially great significance.

Commitment Policies and Group Development. We will examine the functions served by task teams and informal groups in commitment organizations by analyzing them in relation to the main features and policies of those organizations, as we did in discussing groups in control organizations. Each of us has been directly involved in a number of cases where plants have been started up in greenfield sites or new companies have been founded. We draw on these cases and on the accounts of other newly founded organizations (for example, Hackman, 1984; Walton, 1980). To a lesser extent, we draw on our observations of high-commitment organizations that are well established. We present our thoughts as hypotheses rather than findings, since the amount of trustworthy research evidence on groups in commitment organizations is, so far, quite limited.

Work design and performance management. Overall, commitment organizations are structured and managed in ways that emphasize the mutuality of interests between employees and employers, the managed and the managers. Profits and gains from improved productivity are shared; all members, not just managers, have means to influence work-related decisions; there is relatively open information and two-way communication about organizational policies and practices; and hierarchical differences are minimized in ways that encourage all to feel that they are full members working together toward shared objectives.

Taken together, the impact of such policies is to bring the interests of employees and those of the organization into closer alignment than typically is observed in control organizations. This sense of common mission influences the kinds of norms that develop: Task teams and other groups in commitment organizations tend to develop norms that (a) support high productivity and (b) foster rather than undermine the well-being of the enterprise as a whole.

Regarding the work itself, the commitment strategy favors the creation of whole (that is, beginning to end) pieces of work that challenge the skills of those who perform them. And performance management involves the greatest feasible level of *self*-management by those who carry out the work. When teams are used to perform work, larger tasks (requiring diverse knowledge and skill) can be created, self-management can be accomplished through peer influence, and the fact that people are working *together* toward common ends is constantly reinforced. It is not surprising, therefore, that task teams often are used as the basic building block in commitment-oriented organizations.

Typically, teams of from five to fifteen members are assigned a set of interrelated tasks that comprise a meaningful segment of the overall work to be done. The team is asked to manage itself, within limits that depend upon the team's developed and demonstrated competence as a performing unit. The organization invests to build team competence in self-management skills through training, consulting, and coaching or modelling provided by a supervisor (who is often called a team adviser). The interdependence among various organizational tasks and units is highlighted by management whenever possible, as is the importance of cooperation in pursuing common goals.

The prominence of work teams in commitment organizations, and the considerable attention and nurturance they receive, suggests a number of hypotheses about *self-enacted* groups in these organizations:

Self-enacted groups in commitment organizations tend to have boundaries that coincide with (rather than cross) those of formal work units, include all (or nearly all) members of a given work unit, and form relatively quickly and remain relatively stable over time, with little interference from management.

Authority dynamics and compliance mechanisms. The commitment philosophy includes the ideal of direct participation: Everyone should have a "say" about matters that affect him or her. Groups are a major vehicle for enacting this part of the philosophy. Task teams regularly are invited to consider problems and suggest solutions to higher levels of the organization, and when broader questions arise, cross-team task forces often are created to wrestle with them. Often self-enacted or task teams convene at their own initiative to consider some matter of concern to members, forwarding their ideas to a member of management. The manager is likely to be receptive to what the group has to say, since the effectiveness of a commitment organization depends heavily on both (a) the commitment, talent, and energy of its employees and (b) maintenance of members' confidence in the competence and responsiveness of higher management. Thus, although individuals in commitment organizations are not wholly dependent on self-enacted groups or task teams to exercise influence upward, these groups provide powerful and legitimate vehicles for giving voice to employees.

Because formal status differentials are de-emphasized (with authority based more on information and expertise than on position), we would expect that groups in commitment organizations would have different internal structures than groups in control organizations. Indeed, in a study of two engineering groups, Barnes (1960) found that the informal pecking order among members was based less on demographic factors (and more on performance-related attributes of members) in the more "open" unit (which had some commitment-type policies) compared to the more "closed" unit (which had mostly control-type policies). Given this finding, and the fact that teams in commitment organizations typically are formed to accomplish work that is challenging to individuals as well as important to the organization, we hypothesize the following: Status and influence within task teams in commitment organizations are based more on task skills and expressed commitment than on personal qualities and demographic attributes, the reverse being true in self-enacted groups in control organizations.

Group dynamics in commitment organizations also are affected by the fact that compliance is governed more by shared philosophy and values than by a fixed set of rules. Such values typically are stated at a fairly high level of abstraction (for example, "Do what is right for the business and what is fair to people"), which means that a way must be found to interpret the philosophical statement so it can be applied to concrete situations. At times there may be no simple, integrative course of action that is fully in accord with the shared values—and a decision must be made about what to give priority in particular instances. In commitment organizations these decisions often are made more or less autonomously by self-managing teams. For the above statement, the expectation would be that the team has internalized the organization's goals and that it has a sense of what is fair to its members in the current circumstance. Its task, then, is to be as integrative as possible, and when no integrative solutions can be invented, to balance conflicting interests. Thus, task teams in commitment organizations often play a major role in interpreting, integrating, and balancing the interests of the organization and the needs of its own members.

Managers may regard peer pressure as an unhappy fact of life in control organizations, but they need it and count on it in commitment organizations. Planners assume that organizational policies will succeed in eliciting the commitment of a large majority of employees, and thus they are confident that peer pressure will be aligned with organizational interests. Because the planners eschew formal rules and controls, they must rely upon individuals to internalize the values and peers to influence one another. Both task teams and (usually overlapping) self-enacted groups play a role in mobilizing peer pressure. Task teams may formally influence the individual member's compensation and mobility opportunities, while the self-enacted aspects of the same group can strongly affect the individual's quality of work life on a daily basis. When peers have this much fate control, their pressure is hard to resist. Thus, groups in commitment organizations exercise greater peer pressure than do groups in control organizations, and they influence their members more powerfully.

Group Power and Management Responses. Whereas management reactions to groups in control organizations range from "kill" to "benign neglect," managers in commitment organizations are out in the organization actively promoting and empowering groups. As the discussion above should have made clear, groups are close to the heart of what managers are trying to create in high-commitment organizations.

Yet there is an important caveat here, a qualification that can reveal the limits of management's commitment to high commitment. When a group starts to function with a full head of steam, members feel both productive and powerful. They often develop an appetite for even more responsibility and especially for more "say" in the affairs of the organization. At some point, senior managers have to come to terms with the amount of voice and ownership they are prepared to share with others in the organization. At that time, it should be relatively easy to distinguish those managers who are fully committed to the high-commitment philosophy from those who view high-commitment policies mainly as a means to increase organizational performance or profitability. The former managers, we suspect, will be engaged with employees in discussions of ownership and organizational democracy; the latter managers will probably be engaged in discussions with each other about how to contain the rising tide of employee expectations without losing the organizational benefits gained thus far.

Groups Under Mixed and Changing Strategies

As seen above, control policies presume that employee and employer interests are fundamentally divergent, whereas commitment policies assume that the interests of the two parties can be aligned with one another—or, if not, that they can be balanced in a mutually satisfactory way. One can envision a continuum ranging from extreme control strategies on one end to extreme commitment strategies on the other. In some industries, management policies and practices have clustered toward the control end of the continuum—and, because controls typically beget more controls, the majority of these organizations are still there. A limited number of organizations (often in start-up situations or in response to new competitive challenges) have staked out strategies that cluster toward the commitment end. And a small but increasing number of organizations have begun to move away from the control end of the continuum and now have a "mixed" strategy.

Mixed management strategies tend to produce mixed reactions on the part of individuals and, hence, on the part of the groups they spawn. Mixed strategies increase the uncertainty about whether any emergent group phenomenon will be neutral, aligned with, or opposed to organizational interests. When management forms work teams, some of them probably will attend more to organizational work while others will focus more on members' personal agendas. In an ambiguous organizational context, this choice of alignment will be influenced by the prior dispositions (derived from prior employment history or personality) of individual team members and their attitudes toward supervision. Because the alignment of groups is relatively unstable, they are susceptible to shifts in orientation based on how employees interpret new developments. Consider, for example, a mixed-strategy organization where many work teams had begun to develop strong proproduction norms. Management reacted to a few instances in which individuals had abused a new privilege by reinstating some earlier restrictions. Because workers widely perceived this as a retreat from a tentative commitment strategy, the reaction of many groups was to withdraw from the spontaneous problem-solving activity that had begun to produce dramatic cost savings.

In view of the instability of the alignment of groups in mixed-strategy organizations, some managements have introduced work teams only in areas where conditions are relatively favorable for group alignment with organizational interests.

Other managements have reduced uncertainty in more fundamental ways, by signaling that work teams will be part of a
more comprehensive change toward commitment policies
and by continuing to move in that direction.

When there is an overall change from control to commitment, what role do groups play in the change process? How
does management involve groups, and how do groups respond
to management's initiatives? The following thoughts are based
partly on field observations and partly on inferences from
other findings reported earlier. We offer them in a speculative
spirit.

It is instructive to review briefly what those who have
studied transitional process have regarded as important. They
note that the change from a control to a commitment strategy
is a profound cultural change, involving alterations in values,
attitudes, skills, and behavior patterns from the top of the organization to the bottom. Therefore, we can appreciate that
it takes concerted action, sustained commitment, and time to
transform an organization and that the initiatives for change
must include both substantive policy changes and symbolic
acts. Supervisors, middle managers, traditional industrial relations specialists, and union officials frequently feel threatened
that a change will make their knowledge and skills obsolete.
Therefore, we can appreciate that the change strategy should
consider the potential opposition of these stakeholders and
plan ways for them to "let go" of old functions and policies in
order to acquire new ones. This perspective on the change process has within it the potential for groups either to impede or
accelerate the transition from a control to a commitment strategy.

Groups as Liability for Change. Existing informal groups
(from the control-oriented period) can be viewed as stakeholders who may be just as threatened as supervisors and union officials by the impending transformation of the organization—and
therefore just as capable as they are of undermining the change
process.

It is reasonable to assume that a network of informal
groups exists in a control-oriented organization, that they pro-

vide both social satisfaction and protection for their members, and that management has attempted to contain the extent of their influence. Now management announces that it intends to involve employees more in managing the work of the organization and increasingly to rely on commitment policies. How is an employee to know whether he or she should believe what upper management is saying? How is an employee to predict whether or not middle management and union officials actually can change to behave in accord with the newly espoused policies?

Given our earlier analysis that groups play a central role in affecting individuals' interpretations of organizational events and managerial actions generally, it is safe to predict that they will play such a role during the change process. Individuals' attitudes (such as about how trustworthy management is) are likely to change only after possible new perceptions and feelings are tested within the group. And new behaviors are likely to appear and persist only when the group is prepared to provide normative support for them. Thus, groups are likely to play a key mediating role in any significant cultural change in an organization.

When one combines the two hypotheses sketched above —namely, that groups may have a vested interest in the status quo and that groups mediate change in individual perceptions and behavior—then it is reasonable to conclude that informal groups often will be a significantly conservative force in the change process.

Groups as Asset for Change. When might groups accelerate rather than impede the change from control to commitment strategies? Consider a case when the majority of group members are prepared to give management the benefit of the doubt—perhaps because of a history of fair, above-board dealings with individual managers or because the vision of a commitment-style organization articulated by top managers has struck a hopeful chord in most members. In this case, individuals would find among their peers support for their own favorable inclinations, and the group would help leverage the majority view into a consensus. With the norms of the group now supporting the change, fence sitters and skeptics in the group would find their own positions increasingly untenable, and the group could become a positive force for change.

Many managers are aware of the positive potential of groups in the change process and often make tactical use of them in attempting to move the change along. One common device is the temporary problem-solving team, which draws volunteers from differing units (and therefore from different self-enacting groups). Members of such teams, partly because they are away from their home base, are relatively free to explore new ideas and to entertain different hypotheses about the intent of management and the prospects for constructive change. Moreover, because members of the team are volunteers, they may be more optimistic about change in the first place. Such temporary teams often generate norms and processes that support the change effort and, at the same time, provide a second home base for members, making it easier for them to return to their original groups to discuss and explain the new ideas they have been considering.

In sum, groups can either impede or facilitate change in mixed-strategy organizations, depending in part on the prior history of existing groups and the inclinations of their members and in part on the strategies change-oriented managers and consultants use in dealing with them. The creation of new, temporary teams and task forces as part of the change process appears to have considerable promise as a device for helping an organization move from control policies (under which groups are an anathema) to commitment policies (under which groups are a critical ingredient for effectiveness).

Summary of Functions and Effects of Groups in Organizations

In our examination of groups in control, commitment, and mixed organizations we have identified five generic functions of groups in organizations:

1. Social function. Humanizing the workplace for its members.

2. Interpretive function. Creating social reality for its members.
3. Regulative function. Generating and enforcing norms that govern member behavior.
4. Agency function. Voicing member concerns and influencing other organizational entities.
5. Task management function. Coordinating resources to perform organizational assigned tasks.

It is the ability of groups to perform these functions that gives them power with respect to both individual members and the organization. All five group functions can be observed in both control and commitment organizations, but their significance hinges on the organizational strategy pursued by management.

In the control organization, the only function planned for—and then only some of the time—is the social function. The next three functions emerge to serve the individual but not the organization. Only occasionally does the fifth occur—by benign neglect. In the commitment organization, on the other hand, planners typically key in on the fifth function—task management —but all four other functions are regarded as organizationally legitimate and are often taken explicitly into account in planning and management training.

We can review and deepen our understanding of the contrasting effects of control as opposed to commitment strategies by examining how they relate to each of the five group functions.

Social Relations. Groups provide a setting in which individual needs for social relationships can be satisfied. These social needs are universal and not readily set aside (Alderfer, 1969). In both control and commitment organizations, positive social relations can make the workplace relatively more satisfying for the individual.

In the control organization, social support helps individuals cope with policies that tend to produce a sense of futility, powerlessness, and anomie. In the commitment organization, social support within groups helps individuals deal with the stress, responsibility, and challenge that pervade such enterprises and provides them with a secure base from which to experiment with new learnings. Both are important. First, in fast-growing, high-commitment organizations, there often is significant personal stress among members. Second, commitment organizations as such (particularly, but not exclusively, at start-up) require large amounts of high-quality learning by staff throughout the organization.

The above contributions of groups to supportive relationships can benefit the individual and, in turn, the organization under both strategies. Group interaction patterns that chronically reject or withhold support from members cause problems for both the individuals and their employing organizations. While this is true under both strategies, destructive patterns of group interaction are more likely to be detected and addressed under the commitment strategy.

Interpretation of Reality. Groups create social reality (by their interpretations of "objective" reality and by constructing a new social reality), transmit it (making sure all members comprehend "how things are here"), and provide a setting in which groups can firm up their self-perceptions by comparing their attitudes and behavior with those of others. These activities are critical, both for individuals and organizations, because "objective" reality is usually difficult to determine in constantly changing social systems.

Consider, for example, an action taken by management that affects how things are done in the workplace. Once the action is noted, all parties who might be affected by it seek to understand what it *means.* The manager who took the action may state what he or she intended by it. A union official may advance a different interpretation. Various individuals may have immediate interpretations, based on their own previous experience (with that manager or with similar actions taken by others) or on their presumptive beliefs about what management is likely to be up to.

All these sources of data about the meaning of the event are relevant, and all are incomplete. Inevitably, individuals turn to others in their work teams or informal groups for help in making sense of what is going on. And once a group interpretation has been established, members are quick to convey this meaning to others—thereby further strengthening the credence of the interpretation and making sure that others will not disrupt the social order by basing their behavior on some alternative interpretation of the events.

Although groups are involved in interpreting a great diversity of actions and events in the workplace, it appears that special attention is given to organizational expectations about what is (and is not) appropriate behavior at work, to determinations about what is fair and just, and to assessments of the intentions and competencies of management. It turns out that these matters are close to the core of the difference between control-oriented and commitment-oriented organizations.

In control organizations, for example, major organizational policies (such as how work is designed, how authority is distributed, who has legitimate say about policy and decisions, and how status is conferred and symbolized) assume a conflict of interest between managers and rank-and-file organization members. It is not surprising, therefore, that the social reality created by groups in these organizations often includes a negative assessment of the motives and capabilities of organizational managers. Such interpretations serve a defensive function for groups and their members, but usually at the expense of organizational objectives.

In commitment organizations, policies send strong signals suggesting an alignment of interests between the organization and the individual. Often a published statement asserts the organization's commitment to participation, personal development, and human dignity, as well as to excellent performance and competitiveness in the marketplace. Such a philosophy offers a system of meanings that employees, by and large, *want* to believe and therefore will embrace if management's commitment appears genuine and is sustained. In commitment organizations, then, groups provide a means to transmit and support core organizational values, to the benefit of both individuals and the organization.

Internal Regulation. Groups develop and enforce norms for members' behavior—and, indeed, can be exceedingly powerful in affecting what people do (in contrast to the previous function that deals with how people comprehend the world). By regulating the workplace behavior of their members, groups provide social control that is both efficient and powerful (Hackman, 1976). It is efficient because the regulators and those being regulated are in frequent and close contact with one another and because groups have the capability of dealing responsively and in real time with special circumstances that may be affecting a member's behavior. It is powerful because the potential for approval and disapproval (or even rejection from the group) by one's peers is, for most people, an exceedingly strong incentive for compliance.

The main device used by groups to control member behavior is the group *norm,* a structural feature of groups that specifies what behaviors are approved and what behaviors are disapproved in the group. Norms typically form to regulate behaviors members deem important but for which no generally accepted formal rules or laws apply. They also provide a means for a group to enforce adherence to group standards that are at variance with formal rules and expectations (for example, expected levels of output, or check-in times, or even dress codes).

As we have seen, the content of group norms varies considerably between control and commitment organizations. In control organizations, the norms of self-enacted groups often run counter to management-specified rules and policies that members may view as unfair or oppressive. While the group requires its members to violate certain expectations of organizational authorities, it also makes it relatively safe for them to do so. In commitment organizations, on the other hand, norms provide readily available, low-overhead, high-potency ways to direct the work behavior of individuals toward the achievement of common objectives. Self-regulation within teams means that fewer coordination links are needed and, moreover, a well-designed and well-managed team can influence individual behavior more effectively than most supervisors can.

Agency and Voice. Groups provide a megaphone for amplifying individual voice. It is, for obvious reasons, difficult for individuals (at least those who do not occupy positions of prominence) to have their voices heard in large organizations. When most members of a group hold the same view of some matter, their collective voice can have greater impact than any individual can. When an expression of opinion is accompanied by group power—based, for example, on withholding cooperation—the group becomes an especially effective agency for representing the interests of its members.

In the control organization, this function is celebrated by individuals who gain voice and opposed by managers whose organizational authority is qualified. In contrast, providing people with a means to have "voice" is a crucial feature in high-commitment organizations. The idea of groups as agents is carried even further in some commitment organizations. The group not only represents members' views to management but also represents the needs and priorities of the organization as a whole. Because individual and organizational interests are relatively well aligned and because group members understand local circumstances, the group can be an efficient vehicle for seeking integrative solutions to organizational problems and for striking compromises between individual and collective needs, if that becomes necessary. By exercising this dual agency function, the group becomes something of an "honest broker," attempting to determine "what's right for the business" and "what's fair to the people."

Task Management. Groups provide a means for concerted, coordinated action to accomplish the work of the organization. Groups can accomplish certain kinds of tasks more efficiently and effectively than individuals can, even when managers have carefully choreographed and supervised individual behavior.

In the control organization, managers do *not* utilize work teams for many reasons. Two are fundamental. First, given the design features and policies that produce adversarial relations, management usually does not trust groups to work without direct, external monitoring and supervision. Second, management seeks to avoid encouraging strong groups that could undermine organizational policies or managerial authority. Individual supervisors do, however, occasionally strike a bargain with a particular self-enacted group to grant it some latitude in the way tasks are organized and performed in return for reliable performance at satisfactory levels.

As noted earlier, commitment organizations tend to rely heavily upon teams to accomplish the work of the enterprise and to do so with the maximum feasible group self-management. Yet difficult trade-offs remain between the exercise of managerial authority and group autonomy, both of which are ingredients of effective team performance (Hackman, forthcoming). While teams can develop over time from manager-led to self-managing to self-designing in commitment organizations, this progression has significant implications both for the distribution of authority in the organization and the evolution of *managerial* roles over time (Walton and Schlesinger, 1975). Despite the prevalence of self-managing teams in commitment organizations, a great deal remains to be learned about how to design and manage them well.

Conclusion

The broadest hypothesis proposed in this chapter is that group phenomena in organizations differ radically as a function of management strategy—specifically whether management policies attempt to impose control or to elicit commitment. Our major conclusions about the kinds of group phenomena produced by these two strategies are displayed in Table 5-1.

Managers who pursue a control strategy do not use task groups, while those who use a commitment strategy make frequent and purposeful use of both semipermanent teams and temporary task forces. Individuals enact groups under both strategies, but with very different intent and effect. In control organizations, self-enacted groups attempt to protect the individual by defeating management control policies. They often hinder task performance and undermine core organizational values. In commitment organizations, where policies have already attempted to align individual and organizational interests, self-enacted groups tend to be extensions of the formal task teams—in spirit, form, and function. These groups tend to promote effective task performance and transmit core organiza-

Table 5-1. Observed Patterns of Groups Under Different
Organizational Strategies.

	Control Strategy	Commitment Strategy
Organizationally Created Groups	Management does not use task teams.	Management makes frequent use of both temporary and permanent task teams. Management delegates progressive amounts of authority and responsibility to teams, requests teams to exercise upward influence, and may allow teams latitude in deciding how to trade off individual needs and organizational requirements.
Self-Enacted Groups	Management tries to prevent or contain the formation of groups.	Management expects and encourages the group to elaborate its roles, norms, and functions.
	Groups serve individual members' needs.	The task team and the enacted groups have merged interests and integrated norms and structures.
	Groups often hinder task performance and create deviant subcultures, constituting, in effect, a powerful foe of the organization.	The resulting group tends to become a powerful ally of the organization, promoting effective task performance and transmitting core organizational values.

tional values. In brief, the self-enacted group is an organizational foe under the control strategy and an ally under the commitment strategy. Not surprisingly, management tries to prevent or contain the self-enacted group in the first case and to encourage it in the second.

In mixed-strategy organizations, the alignments of formal and informal groups are difficult to predict and tend to be unstable. In the transitional phase from control to commitment, management often makes tactical use of task groups—such as participative problem-solving groups and temporary discussion groups. These new groups permit their members to consider new organizational possibilities in a context other than the groups they belong to (groups that members formed originally in response to control policies). Such established self-enacted groups are hypothesized to have conservative tendencies (similar to the conservative inclinations of other stakeholders whose role or status may be threatened by the transition from control to commitment).

There is a general trend in the United States toward commitment-oriented organizational strategies. One implication of this chapter is that the organizations involved in this trend will increasingly employ task teams either as a basic building block of the organization or as a major mechanism for accomplishing nonroutine work. Another implication is that if commitment strategies are effective in these organizations, the preexisting set of self-enacted groups will also dissolve and be replaced by other groups aligned structurally and normatively with the formal work organization.

There is a minority countertrend toward control in the management orientation in some professional service organizations and in some industrial organizations precipitated by basic changes in either the terms of employment or in the nature of the organization's task. We forecast that these organizations will rely progressively less on groups to accomplish work and that group phenomena will become increasingly problematic for management.

Students of groups should be able to find interesting questions to investigate in these organizational trends. And managers who appreciate the patterns hypothesized in this chapter should be better able to utilize groups in ways that serve both individual members' needs and organizational objectives.

References

Alderfer, C. P. "An Empirical Test of a New Theory of Human Needs." *Organizational Behavior and Human Performance,* 1969, *4,* 142-175.
Alderfer, C. P. "Group and Intergroup Relations." In J. R. Hack-

man and J. L. Suttle (eds.), *Improving Life at Work.* Santa Monica, Calif.: Goodyear, 1977.

Barnes, L. B. "Organizational Systems and Engineering Groups: A Comparative Study of Two Technical Groups in Industry." Boston: Division of Research, Harvard Business School, 1960.

French, C. J. "Correlates of Success in Retail Selling." *American Journal of Sociology,* 1960, *66* (2), 128-134.

Goode, W. J., and Fowler, I. "Incentive Factors in a Low Morale Plant." *American Sociological Review,* 1949, *14* (5), 618-624.

Hackman, J. R. "Group Influences on Individuals in Organizations." In M. D. Dunnette (Ed.), *Handbook of Industrial and Organizational Psychology.* Skokie, Ill.: Rand McNally, 1976.

Hackman, J. R. "The Transition That Hasn't Happened." In J. R. Kimberly and R. E. Quinn (eds.), *New Futures: The Challenge of Managing Corporate Cultures.* Homewood, Ill.: Dow Jones-Irwin, 1984.

Hackman, J. R. "The Commitment Model: From 'Whether' to 'How.' " In R. Hayes and K. Clark (eds.), *The Uneasy Alliance: Managing the Productivity-Technology Dilemma.* Boston: Harvard Business School Press, 1985.

Hackman, J. R. "The Design of Work Teams." In J. Lorsch (ed.), *Handbook of Organizational Behavior.* Englewood Cliffs, N.J.: Prentice-Hall, forthcoming.

Homans, G. C. "Committee on Work in Industry." In *Fatigue of Workers: Its Relation to Industrial Production.* New York: Van Nostrand Reinhold, 1941.

Homans, G. C. *The Human Group.* San Diego, Calif.: Harcourt Brace Jovanovich, 1950.

Lawrence, P. R., and Seiler, J. *Organizational Behavior and Administration.* Homewood, Ill.: Richard D. Irwin/Dorsey Press, 1965.

Richards, C. B., and Dobyns, H. F. "Topography and Culture: The Case of the Changing Cage." *Human Organization,* 1957, *16* (1), 16-20.

Roethlisberger, F. J., and Dickson, W. J. *Management and the Worker.* Cambridge, Mass.: Harvard University Press, 1939.

Sayles, L. *Behavior of Industrial Work Groups.* New York: Wiley, 1958.

Walton, R. E. "Establishing and Maintaining High Commitment Work Systems." In J. R. Kimberly, R. H. Miles, and Associates (eds.), *The Organizational Life Cycle: Issues in the Creation, Transformation, and Decline of Organizations.* San Francisco: Jossey-Bass, 1980.

Walton, R. E. "From Control to Commitment: Transformation of Work Force Management Strategies in the United States." In R. Hayes and K. Clark (eds.), *The Uneasy Alliance: Managing the Productivity-Technology Dilemma.* Boston: Harvard Business School Press, 1985.

Walton, R. E., and Schlesinger, L. S. "Do Supervisors Thrive in Participative Work Systems?" *Organizational Dynamics,* Winter 1975, pp. 24–38.

6

Intergroup Relations
in Organizations

Jeanne M. Brett
Jorn Kjell Rognes

In investigating intergroup relations in organizations, we assume that groups are the basic structural building blocks of organizations and that relations between groups in organizations must be managed. We want to know why some intergroup relations are more difficult to manage than others, how to distinguish well-managed intergroup interfaces from those that are poorly managed, and what factors lead to effectiveness.

We have drawn on a diverse literature in investigating these questions, including microtheory that focuses on the enactment of organizational roles, macrotheory that focuses on the internal structures of organizations, and organization-environmental theory that focuses on transactions between organizations. The conceptual framework for research on organizations developed in this chapter recognizes the interplay between these three types of theory.

Our framework assumes that the study of intergroup relations within organizations is important and that the appropriate conceptual approach is an integrative one. These are not idle assumptions. The importance of lateral relations within and between organizations has increased in recent years (Kochan and Bazerman, 1986). Organizations are becoming larger and associated with that growth is increased specialization of groups within organizations (Mintzberg, 1979). Another factor contributing to the specialization of organizational groups is increased complexity in the environment and in technology. A result of this increased specialization is that tasks requiring intensive coordination cannot be grouped into a single functional unit (McCann and Galbraith, 1981).

Lateral relations between organizations are also increasing in importance. There has been substantial growth in the long-term contractual relations between different organizations, for example, in partly integrated distribution channels (Stern and El-Ansary, 1977), in contractual relations in the construction industry (Stinchcombe, 1983), and in the international expansion of the service sector (Kochan and Bazerman, 1986). The recent surge of mergers and acquisitions has, in many cases, transformed lateral relations between organizations into lateral relations within organizations.

The increasing importance of lateral relations within organizations has spawned a plethora of structural forms—matrices, task forces, teams, and so on—that fall between the ideal types that have preoccupied management scholars (that is, bureaucracy) and economists (competitive markets). In hierarchical, bureaucratic systems, conflict is resolved by the dictates of the superior. In the competitive market, conflict can be resolved (dissolved) by changing transaction partners. But when groups, whether inside the same organization or in different organizations, have to engage in long-term, lateral relations, conflict management becomes problematic. Authority, responsibility, and appropriate behavior are unclear (Brown, 1983). Unlike hierarchical relations, there are often no norms about group interaction when conflict breaks out. Furthermore, managers leading such groups and representing them in dealings with each other are seldom selected for their negotiation skills and may not have had an opportunity to learn such skills. Probably the most important factor, however, is that they are not rewarded for the development and maintenance of cooperative lateral relations. Many managers holding key lateral positions talk about lateral relations in terms of problems, not conflict, and fail to recognize that what they are doing to manage those relations is negotiating.

While this chapter focuses on lateral relations within, not

between, organizations, there is much to be gained conceptually from recognizing the interplay between levels of theory. The issue of the effective management of transactions between units is central to both intra- and interorganizational relations. The problems of enactment are the same.

This chapter is organized as follows: First intergroup relations are defined and the characteristics of intergroup relations are identified. Second, criteria for effective intergroup relations are presented. Third, propositions about the effectiveness of various techniques of managing intergroup relations are developed.

Intergroup Relations in Organizations

In order to understand what an intergroup relationship within an organization is, we have to be able to know one when we see one. This entails being able to identify a group and a relationship and to determine whether the relationship is between groups in the same organization or between groups in different organizations. The first and last issues having to do with the definition of a group and an organization are relatively easy compared to the issue of defining a relationship.

An *organizational group* is a set of individuals who perceive themselves and whom nonmembers perceive as constituting an identifiable social aggregate within the organization. The group may be a small, primary work group, a task force whose members are formally assigned to a variety of different functional areas, or a huge functional department like marketing, production or accounting. The only definitional requirement is that members and nonmembers recognize the group as a distinguishable social aggregate that exists within the boundaries of the organization.

In most cases, organizational groups can be further distinguished in terms of specific work tasks and the technologies, goals and values associated with them. If each group were producing its own product or service, there might be little need for significant intergroup coordination. In most cases, however, identifiable groups in organizations are producing only a specialized segment of the organization's product or service. Coordination between such groups is a necessity. Even organizations whose groups have traditionally provided distinct services—for example, banks with their separate areas controlling loans, transfer of funds, and investment—are requiring significant intergroup coordination in order to provide full service to customers in an increasingly competitive environment.

An *intergroup relationship* within an organization is a coordinated link or bridge between two distinct organizational groups. The link or bridge is necessary because each group needs resources from the other group in order to complete its own task (Aiken and Hage, 1968). On an automobile production line, the trim department (group) needs to receive painted chassis from the paint department. If something goes wrong in paint, trim waits; it cannot put chrome on unpainted chassis even if they did come down the line. Likewise, if something goes wrong in trim, paint waits, for it has no other outlet for its product.

Power-Dependency Relationships. Theoretically, an intergroup relationship is a power-dependency relationship (Emerson, 1962). Each group is dependent on the other for resources. The degree of dependency is a function of the availability from other groups of the resources being exchanged and the value of the resources to each group. In our example, paint and trim are highly interdependent and the dependency is symmetric. Paint has no other place but trim to send chassis, and moving chassis through the paint shop is a major element of the paint group's performance evaluation. Trim has no other source of painted chassis and, like the paint group, is evaluated on how many cars are trimmed per shift.

Some intergroup relations are based on asymmetric dependencies. For example, marketing and manufacturing departments depend on each other to produce the market for the product and to produce the product for the market. But a marketing department that has top management approval to contract out production when a particular campaign generates demand in excess of manufacturing's capacity is less dependent on manufacturing than manufacturing is on marketing. Such asymmetrics in dependence imply differences in power between the two departments.

Power, according to Emerson's theory (1962), is a function of dependency. A group is powerful when the resource it provides is needed and scarce. A group is weak when the resource it provides is abundant and/or not very important to the other party. In an asymmetric power relationship, the more powerful party is able to get more from the exchange because the weaker party is willing to give more to maintain the relationship. In our example about marketing and manufacturing, manufacturing should be more willing to acquiesce to marketing's requests than vice versa because its alternatives are not as good as marketing's alternatives.

The example points out several other characteristics of power. First, strategic resources—that is, resources from which a party can derive power—are not limited to materials. Marketing's power in regard to manufacturing is embedded in its expertise and information. Marketing, through its prediction capacity, can smooth market demand for manufacturing that cannot respond quickly to changes in the market. Other resources that may be a source of power include financial and human resources, expertise and technology. For example, in the classic matrix design integrating functional departments and projects, the power of the functional department heads rests on their control of human and technological resources. The power of the project team directors rests in their financial resources.

A second important characteristic of power is that although it is situationally based, it is a psychological construct. The utility of marketing's power depends on manufacturing's perception of its dependence on marketing. Manufacturing is going to act on the basis of its own perceptions. Furthermore, manufacturing's own perceptions of its dependence may be at variance with marketing's perceptions of manufacturing's dependence. We propose that in a dyadic relationship perceived power has four elements:

- Party A's perception of own power
- Party A's perception of B's power

- Party B's perception of own power
- Party B's perception of A's power

The empirical research on situational power (Rubin and Brown, 1975; Bacharach and Lawler, 1981; Greenhalgh, Neslin, and Gilkey, 1985) conceptualizes power as a psychological construct but, with the exception of the Greenhalgh, Neslin, and Gilkey study, treats power as a situational variable for analytic purposes. Results show that in the laboratory, parties with high situational power use it and get higher outcomes (Rubin and Brown, 1975). Greenhalgh, Neslin, and Gilkey (1985) take this research one step further by showing that own perceived power is indirectly related to outcome. We propose that perceptions of others' power may also have a significant impact on a negotiated outcome. So, going back to our marketing and manufacturing example, manufacturing's perception of its own power may affect the negotiation, but so may marketing's perception of manufacturing's power.

We offer a third characteristic of power as a proposition. We propose that power relationships between groups in organizations are stable at least in the short term. There are two reasons why. First, in an organization each group usually has a monopoly on its task. Structural change to break that monopoly either from within the organization or through contracting out is likely to require top management approval. Such change will not occur swiftly. Second, while we concede that in a dyadic relationship within an organization control over resources and the values attached to them varies between parties across issues, we note that power is a perception and thus it carries all the biased baggage of any other perception. In particular, we suspect a large halo effect across issues such that power distinctions between issues tend to blur. We propose that perceptions of power based on accumulated experience across a range of interface issues define stable social influence relationships between groups.

Over time, of course, changes will occur in power-dependency relationships between groups. These changes will be functions of changes in each group's environment that make its resources less valued or less scarce to the other group. For example, the power of groups within organizations that offer centralized computing facilities to other organizational groups has diminished significantly with the widespread availability of powerful personal computers.

Intergroup Transactions. An intergroup transaction occurs "whenever individuals belonging to one group interact collectively or individually with another group or its members in terms of their group identification" (Sherif, 1966, p. 9). Most intergroup transactions occur between representatives of groups acting in the interests of their groups, not of themselves. Thus, an intergroup transaction is not the same as an interpersonal transaction. What the representatives "get personally from the encounter is not strictly germane to the question of what they have secured for those persons whom they represent" (Stephenson, 1981, p. 177).

In theory, any member of a group is an equally viable representative of the group's interests. In practice, group members frequently do not have homogeneous values and interests and are therefore not fully interchangeable in the role of group representative. Two factors serve to reduce variability in representative behavior. First, the role of group representative carries with it strong expectations about appropriate role enactment. These expectations are shared by the role incumbent, group members, and members and representatives of the other group. So even when group representatives are representing their own interests and not the group's, the other group's representatives believe they are representing the group. The reward contingencies are such that they are better off representing their group, not themselves, for they are ultimately accountable to their group. Groups that elect or select their own leaders remove leaders whom group members perceive to have negotiated an intergroup relationship that violates the group's interests (Bok and Dunlop, 1970). In organizations, intergroup representatives often also hold roles of hierarchical authority within their own groups (for example, unit manager). They are not typically accountable to their groups for their jobs, but they are highly dependent on group members to implement the intergroup relationship. Group representatives with hierarchical authority are ultimately evaluated based on the effectiveness of their groups. A group that fails to implement an intergroup transaction negotiated by its representatives makes the representatives look bad to higher management.

The justification for theory at the intergroup level rather than the interpersonal level is the fact that group representatives act on behalf of the "group," not themselves. The reason for the representatives' interaction is an interface issue that exists at the group, not the individual, level.

Interface Issues. There are three types of interface issues: conflict, constraints, and interdependent action (Dale, 1981). In this chapter we are primarily interested in intergroup conflict and its management. Constraints and interdependent action are outcomes of the management of intergroup conflict. Constraints refer to limits placed on a group. For example, marketing could agree to suspend advertising for a product with which manufacturing was having quality control problems. Interdependent action refers to coordinated action between two groups. In our assembly line example, the speed of the line is a coordinated action; if paint moves chassis at the rate of sixty per hour but trim can move them only at the rate of fifty per hour, coordinated action will break down and conflict erupt. One solution, a constraint on intragroup action, might be for paint to slow down.

Intergroup conflict occurs when two groups linked in a power-dependency relationship disagree about one or more aspects of the terms of that relationship. Conflict is endemic to groups in organizations. The products or services of all but the smallest organizations are the result of coordinated action of functionally differentiated groups. Since each group performs only a monopolistic set of tasks, transfer of resources among groups is a critical part of organizational functioning. Coordination between groups is exacerbated by the fact that differentiated groups vary not just with respect to task but also in terms of technology, goal and time orientation, reward systems, and member characteristics (Lawrence and Lorsch, 1967; March and Simon, 1958). The very elements that support differentiation between groups inhibit integration because they cause interdependent groups to take positions on interface issues that maximize their own parochial interests.

While the fundamental causes of intergroup conflict are interdependence and differentiation, the intensity of conflict between groups is partly a function of scarce resources. If one group has excess resources (slack), it can develop excess capacity and thereby buffer its relationships with other groups and reduce intergroup conflict. When slack is not an option, lateral relationships between interdependent groups are likely to be conflictive. U.S. firms, reducing slack under pressures of deregulation and foreign competition, are learning that they have to improve coordination between groups within organizations as well as with suppliers. Interestingly, firms are beginning to recognize that one way to improve intergroup relations is to improve managers' negotiating skills.

While the causes of conflict are structural, the actual management of conflict takes place between individuals representing the groups. The process by which group representatives determine new terms and conditions of their exchange relationship is negotiation or bargaining (these terms are used interchangeably). Negotiation is an intergroup (or interpersonal) decision-making process under conditions of dependence and conflicting interests. Dependence needs no further definition at this point; conflicting interests do. An interest is the reason why a group (party) wants an exchange structured in a particular fashion. For example, manufacturing has two major related interests: labor costs and long production runs. Marketing, in contrast, is interested in a quick response to changes in the market environment. Both groups want to sell the product. So while marketing and manufacturing share an important interest, manufacturing's interest in long production runs and marketing's interest in quick responses are in conflict. This conflict will surface from time to time (depending on the dynamism of the market environment). The process by which the conflict is managed is negotiation. Note that the conflict is not resolved by the negotiation. Conflicting interests are structurally based and do not disappear when an issue has been successfully negotiated. Conflicting interests are simply subordinated to the joint gain of coordinated action (or intragroup constraints), at least until the environment changes and the coordinated action (or intragroup constraints) no longer is more valuable than the parochial interests of at least one of the parties.

Summary. This section provides the conceptual definitions and theoretical basis for the propositions about the effectiveness of various techniques of managing intergroup relations in organizations. The main points are as follows:

- A group is an identifiable social aggregate within an organization.
- An intergroup relationship is a coordinated action between two groups that exchange resources.
- Power is a function of dependency.
- Power is a psychological construct.
- Power relationships are stable, at least in the short term.
- An intergroup theory is necessary because while groups interact through individual representatives, the representatives present their group's interests, not their own, on interface issues that exist at the group level, not the individual level.
- Intergroup conflict occurs because interdependent groups have differentiated parochial interests that are stable only so long as each group's environment is stable.
- Scarce resources exacerbate intergroup conflict.
- Negotiation (or bargaining) is the process by which groups determine the terms and conditions of their exchange relationships.

Effectiveness of Intergroup Relations

In order to develop propositions about the effectiveness of various techniques of managing intergroup relations in organizations, we must develop criteria of effectiveness that are meaningful at the intergroup level of conceptualization. The intergroup effectiveness criteria must be conceptually the product of an intergroup exchange; they must be capable of characterizing the intergroup relationship over time, and they must provide an index of the quality of the exchange.

We found the literature evaluating alternative modes of dispute resolution to be a better source for ideas about intergroup effectiveness criteria than either the group or organizational effectiveness literature. This is because dispute resolution studies focus on the results of a dyadic exchange, whereas the group and organizational effectiveness studies focus on a single entity acting in its environment. A good example of the latter type of evaluation study, which would have benefited from knowledge of the former type of study, is Gladstein (1984). Gladstein was studying group effectiveness. Her dependent variable, however, was the result of an intergroup transaction rather than an intragroup process. It is not surprising, then, that intragroup variables did not predict sales, but market factors did.

In the alternative dispute resolution evaluation studies—for example, Brett and Goldberg's (1983) study of grievance mediation and Pearson's (1982) study of the mediation of child custody disputes—researchers have focused on the cost of the process, the endurance of the settlements, and participants' evaluations of the process (procedural justice) and the outcomes (distributive justice). We have focused on the first two of these criteria. We believe that in organizations, agreements that are perceived by the implementors to be unjust on either procedural or distributive grounds will not endure. This is a testable proposition. If it is true, then justice issues need not be formally included in our conceptualization of intergroup effectiveness. By not including justice in our definitions, we do not mean to denigrate their importance in research on intergroup relations and negotiations. Indeed, we draw heavily on the procedural justice research in developing propositions about the effectiveness of various techniques for managing intergroup relations.

We propose that the effectiveness of an intergroup relation can be evaluated in terms of efficiency and quality. Efficiency refers to the management costs associated with transforming an intergroup conflict into actions agreed upon by the groups. Those actions include constraints on intragroup activities and/or coordinated intergroup activities. Manpower costs associated with developing the transaction terms are part of the efficiency criterion. Management costs associated with implementing an exchange either in terms of constraints or coordinated action are not part of the efficiency criterion. Quality refers to the degree to which the intergroup negotiation results in a well-defined exchange agreement that endures until changes in relevant environmental factors make the exchange agreement obsolete.

Our concept of effectiveness is related to, but not synonymous with, Williamson's concept of transaction costs. Transaction costs are incurred, according to Williamson (1975), when at least one of the parties in an interdependent exchange relationship pursues its own interests rather than maximizing the two parties' joint benefits. Transaction costs can take two forms: Costs are incurred when parties engage in needless haggling over the terms of the transaction and/or when the terms of the transaction are advantageous to one party but suboptimal for the relationship as a whole (Williamson, 1979).

We propose that at the intergroup level of conceptualization, transaction costs have two elements: efficiency and quality. Our efficiency criterion refers to costs associated with the establishment of transaction terms; that is, the manpower and resources expended during the intergroup negotiations. A major challenge associated with operationalizing our efficiency criterion is to be able to distinguish between the costs of negotiating the transaction terms and the costs of implementing them in terms of coordinated action or intragroup constraints. Our quality criterion refers to the nature of the negotiated transaction terms. We propose that transaction costs are incurred when transaction terms are renegotiated even though no relevant environmental factor has changed.

Why do negotiators reopen agreements? We doubt they do so because they have been to a negotiations training workshop and now believe they can better the other party. We doubt they do so because they think they have more power. (Recall we proposed that the power distribution between two parties or groups is stable in the short term.) We expect negotiators reopen negotiations after a settlement because the settlement was poor, either because it was incomplete or ill defined. A complete, well-defined settlement is one that covers all aspects of the interface issue. Procedures, responsibilities, tolerances, and timing are all specified so that new issues, which require new negotiation, do not arise during implementation. Despite the arguments by some theorists of the utility of ambiguity in getting agreement among groups with conflicting interests (Weick, 1969, 1979), we believe that exchanges defined in ambiguous terms will quickly break down because of unmet expectations. The result is increased transaction costs as the details of the intragroup constraints or the coordinated action are worked out.

We do not expect parties to achieve complete, well-defined settlements in all situations. Bounded rationality will often inhibit completeness and it may not be possible to establish terms for all possible contingencies. There may also be occasions when parties wish to come to agreement in principle and work out the details of the exchange as the relationship develops. If a complete, well-defined settlement is not worked out, effectiveness is a question of the parties' abilities to readjust settlements, when needed, without incurring excessive management costs.

We recognize that there will be occasions when negotiations need to be reopened or extended. We are primarily concerned, however, with negotiations that result in ill-conceived settlements due to the parties' failure to make an explicit agreement on one or more of the known intergroup issues.

Efficiency and quality are separate constructs. Intragroup constraints or coordinated actions that endure justify significant costs in the negotiation phase, though enduring settlements are not necessarily the result of significant negotiation expenses. High-quality solutions justify high development costs; low-quality solutions do not. Thus, we propose that, controlling for the rate of environmental change, intergroup relations that incur low negotiation costs relative to their endurance are effective intergroup relations.

The rate of environmental change is an important factor in this criterion. Groups in organizations that face dynamic environments will have to negotiate more frequently and their solutions will be less enduring than those of groups in organizations that face stable environments. Thus, it is essential that the rate of environmental change be considered when evaluating the effectiveness of an intergroup relationship. Groups that nego- tiate more frequently than the rate of change in their environ- ment are ineffective by our conceptualization and incur transac- tion costs, according to Williamson (1979).

The rate of environmental change, however, may be much more rapid for one of the groups in the relationship than the other. When there is substantial disparity between groups in the rate of environmental change, we expect the normal rate of negotiation to fall somewhere between the rate expected if both groups were in dynamic environments and the rate expected if both groups were in stable environments.

We recognize that Williamson's transaction costs concept has been difficult to operationalize for interorganizational rela- tions. We know that operationalization of our conceptualization of transaction costs at the intergroup level will be difficult, if only because there are sometimes no price mechanisms for intraorganizational exchanges. But, as Jennergren (1979) points out, transfer prices can be estimated for exchanges between or- ganizational subunits. Furthermore, it is not uncommon that profit centers are charged for use of centralized staff functions (for example, computer services). In principle, prices can be put on the exchange of resources within organizations.

Assuming that intergroup transaction costs can be esti- mated, we can then compare transaction costs across different interfaces. Then, controlling for interdependence and rate of environmental change, we can begin to test causal models of intergroup effectiveness.

Our conceptualization of transaction costs provides sig- nificantly more precision than Williamson's ecologically ori- ented framework. From the ecological perspective, intergroup relations that persist over time must be effective. Otherwise, the groups would decouple or be integrated into one unit. While the ecological perspective may be quite useful in showing how groups couple and decouple in response to environmental changes over the long term, it provides no insight into the causes of variation in effectiveness across intergroup dyads in the relatively short term. Since many intergroup relations are stable for relatively long periods of time, it becomes important to study the utility of different ways to manage the interfaces. Our operationalization of the transaction costs concept makes such research possible.

To summarize, we have defined in this section the effectiveness of intergroup relations in terms of transaction costs. We proposed the following:

- A transaction is of high quality when the negotiated exchange agreement endures until changes in relevant environmental factors make it obsolete.
- Groups in dynamic environments will have to negotiate more frequently than groups in stable environments, and their exchanges will be less enduring.
- Assuming that such transaction costs can be measured, then, controlling for environmental change and dependency, it is possible to test causal models of intergroup effectiveness.

Techniques for Managing Intergroup Relations

The major technique for managing conflict between groups in organizations is to dissolve the relationship either by changing the organizational structure, hence redefining intergroup relations (McCann and Galbraith, 1981), or by transferring key people (Brett, 1984). Kolb (1986) presents a particularly rich description of how a division manager, familiarly known as "Reorganize it Rogers," manages a classic conflict between planning and operational units. Rogers attributes conflict to personalities and individual styles of the managers involved. He says to Kolb: "Did you ever meet such a cast of characters? I can't get them to do anything I want. I've tried." Kolb continues:

> The fact that meetings are acrimonious, that individuals complain to him, that the "chemistry" seems poor, that he has to order people to attend meetings and do tasks suggests to him that this is an interpersonal conflict. These are the facts that

he attends to and tries to remedy. He deals with
conflicts episodically as they surface. When complaints about what somebody is doing or not doing
reach his ears (and they do frequently), he reshuf-
fles. He moves people and responsibilities around
so that they will have less occasion to interact and,
hence, disagree with each other [footnote omitted].
Indeed, behind his back they call him "Reorganize
it Rogers." Every few weeks or so, somebody's
position on the organization chart has changed.
The irony of this label is, of course, that his actions
actually preserve the structure—the matrix relationship of planning and operations—only people are
moved around [Kolb, 1986, p. 25].

Rogers's responses reflect the two different approaches to
conflict management in organizational theory and organizational psychology. The former views the inability to manage
conflict as a structural problem; the latter, as a personality
problem. If, according to Rogers, people were less rigid and
more flexible, problems between managers would not occur.
Note that Rogers fails to recognize that his managers' "problems" are conflict associated with their matrix roles.

The view of intergroup relations developed in this chapter
is consistent with the organizational theory view that conflict
has structural causes. However, we do not believe that structural change is a sufficient condition for managing intergroup
conflict. Organizational structures merely determine group
interdependencies. The interaction occurs between people. We
propose that people's skills in managing intergroup relations,
though not their personalities (Greenhalgh, Neslin, and Gilkey,
1985), make a significant contribution to the effectiveness of
any particular structural configuration. Furthermore, we propose that negotiation skills can, to some extent, compensate for
structure. In this section we discuss various structural techniques for managing intergroup conflict and propose the type
of skills necessary to manage intergroup relations effectively in
each.

Hierarchy and Negotiations. In organizational theory, intergroup relationships have traditionally been controlled by hierarchy and legitimate authority (McCann and Galbraith, 1981). Conflict between groups is managed by appealing to a common superior. Hierarchy, however, has important shortcomings as a conflict management device. Hierarchy becomes overloaded in dynamic environments when spans of control are too broad or when decision making is centralized with top management (McCann and Galbraith, 1981). The effect of an overloaded hierarchy is slow response to situations that require quick decisions. The other problem with hierarchy is poorquality decisions about the terms of an intergroup exchange setting up intragroup constraints or coordinated action. There are several reasons why hierarchical decisions may be poor. First, hierarchical leaders may be cognizant of the organization's superordinate goals but lack detailed knowledge and understanding of each group's interests on a particular interface issue. Second, hierarchical managers, either because they are already overloaded or because they perceive that their role in conflict management is to make decisions, fail to investigate conflict issues thoroughly. Sheppard (1983) found that managers making decisions to control conflict act like inquisitors. They investigate the issue by asking questions of their own formulation and then impose their own power-based solution. Kolb writes about Rogers in similar terms: "Rogers' role definition is shaped by his position as manager of the division. Indeed, he reaffirms his authority when he decisively solves the problems. His subordinates contribute to this definition. They complain to him about their colleagues. They ask him to order people to perform particular tasks. They ask him to clarify roles, responsibilities, and objectives. As one manager said, 'If he would tell us which objective—the product or the methodology—was more important, there wouldn't be any problems.' They look to him to resolve the situation, which he does. However, in doing so, he seems to create a dependence on him that limits the ability of his managers to deal with conflict and ambiguity in the future" (Kolb, 1986, p. 26).

Rogers, when he is not reorganizing, makes unilateral decisions that resolve the question of which objective is more important on an issue-by-issue basis. The tension between product orientation and method orientation continues to generate "problems" that get sent up the hierarchy to Rogers.

We propose that three other conflict resolution models associated with a hierarchical structure will be superior to this style found by Sheppard (1983) and Kolb (1986). The first alternative is for the hierarchical manager to act as a judge and require that each group make a presentation outlining positions, interests, and potential settlements. In this way the hierarchical manager should be able to make a better-informed decision, for it behooves each group to explain why the other group's position is untenable.

The second alternative is mediation. The manager acting as a mediator will try to facilitate an agreement between conflicting groups. Techniques may include getting the group representatives to recognize their own group's and the other group's interests with respect to the interface issue; getting the groups to generate proposals that package issues so that some of each group's interests are met; and suggesting that a particular proposal be tried on an experimental or nonprecedent-setting basis, putting pressure on powerful groups to look to the long term and "leave a little money on the table" and putting pressure on nonpowerful groups to withdraw. (See Carnevale, 1986, for a theoretical and Shapiro, Drieghe, and Brett, 1985, for an empirical discussion of what effective mediators do.)

Recent research (Brett and Goldberg, 1983; Pearson, 1982) shows that mediation is effective in high-conflict situations in which the disputing parties are also highly interdependent and thus have substantial common interests as well as interests in conflict. Brett and Goldberg (1983) report that 80 percent of grievances between labor and management were settled in one form or another after mediation. The "one form or another" settlements turn out to be an important aspect of mediation. Unlike hierarchical decisions that frequently split the difference between disputing parties, mediation can result in acquiescence by one or the other party, a purely integrative compromise, or a split-the-difference settlement. Pearson's research points out another important aspect of mediation. It appears to be more successful in developing enduring settlements than the judicial style of dispute resolution. Pearson found recidivism rates to be significantly lower when child custody agreements were reached through mediation than when such agreements were imposed by the court. Low recidivism translates into a high quality of solution according to our criteria of effectiveness. An additional potential benefit of mediation is that subordinates might learn some negotiation skills. Mediators use many of the same techniques used by negotiators intent on solving the problems. Advocates of mediation make the social learning theory argument that disputants can learn negotiation skills by modeling the mediator-manager. While there is plenty of research to support social learning theory, we know of no research that has studied the impact of mediation on disputants' negotiation skills.

The third alternative decision-making style that should be superior to hierarchy is direct lateral negotiation. The manager using this approach to conflict management pushes the conflict back down the hierarchy to the groups that are experiencing it. The hierarchical manager refuses to resolve conflict between subordinates but instead makes it clear that group representatives are the best ones to resolve the matter and must do so. The effectiveness of this approach will depend on the group representatives' negotiation skills. Not all group representatives will be skilled negotiators, and even those who are skilled may have difficulty seeing beyond their group's position to a creative solution or putting an interface issue into the context of the group's long-term relationship. Direct lateral negotiation may be particularly difficult when power is unequally distributed between groups. In this situation, the powerful group may adopt a tough, exploitative negotiation strategy and the low-power party may adopt a soft strategy (Pruitt, 1981). The result of such a negotiation is likely to be a distributive settlement that favors the powerful party to an extent greater than one should expect, given its power. The low-power party, however, is likely to be dissatisfied with the settlement and, thus, the settlement may not survive implementation.

Another problem with direct lateral negotiations is that

groups may negotiate exchanges that are optimal for them but distinctly suboptimal for the organization as a whole. Direct lateral negotiation is an extremely decentralized mode of conflict resolution (Hage, 1983). Without control systems such as an appraisal system that rewards integrative intergroup exchanges, direct lateral negotiations may be difficult to manage.

Which of these hierarchical conflict resolution models should a manager choose—inquisition, judicial, mediation, or direct lateral negotiation? The answer depends on a number of factors, including efficiency and quality of the solutions generated by each approach, the skills of the parties, the power distribution between groups, and the organization's culture.

The inquisition model is likely to incur the lowest negotiation costs, since it will take less time than the others. It is difficult to compare the judicial, mediation, and direct lateral negotiation alternatives in terms of negotiation costs. In the dispute resolution literature, judicial proceedings and mediation are used only after parties have reached an impasse. This need not be so in the management context. Rogers's behavior, for example, discouraged subordinates from engaging in direct lateral negotiations.

The important issue from our perspective is the relationship between negotiation costs or efficiency and the quality of the solution. Here the dispute resolution literature is more helpful. Disputants may prefer direct lateral negotiations to any third-party mode of dispute resolution. Among third-party modes of dispute resolution, disputants seem to prefer mediation to arbitration (Brett and Goldberg, 1983) and arbitration to inquisition (but see Sheppard, 1985). The reason for this preference ordering has been the subject of a scholarly dispute (Folger, 1986). However, Brett and Shapiro's (1985) recent data show clearly that the reason for the preference ordering appears to be satisfaction with and control over outcome. We note that both of these factors have been identified in the organizational change literature as factors contributing to commitment to organizational change and ease in the implementation of change. Thus, we propose that mediation and judicial models may be superior to the inquisition model of dispute resolution typically used by managers, because they generate higher-quality exchanges.

When parties are not skilled negotiators, third-party modes of dispute resolution may be more effective than direct lateral negotiations. Direct lateral negotiations may result in impasses that increase groups' adherence to positions. They may result in poor-quality exchanges when power is unevenly distributed. Alternatively, direct lateral negotiations may result in exchanges that are optimal for the two groups but distinctly suboptimal for the organization as a whole.

Finally, some of these modes of conflict management within a hierarchy may be more appropriate to the organization's culture than others. Richard Walton (personal communication, 1985) illustrated this point nicely in telling us about his experience doing third-party workshops to aid in managing border disputes in the Horn of Africa. He noted that the Somalis preferred direct dialogue between equals, because this dispute resolution mode was dominant in their tribal society. The Ethiopians preferred appeals to an authority or elder, since this was the dominant mode of dispute resolution in their society. Organizations whose cultures are tied to traditional hierarchical control mechanisms may only be able to move from an inquisition to a judicial model. But even that change in approach may have significant impact on the ease with which a coordinated action or an intragroup constraint is implemented. An organization that is trying to rely on cultural norms, rather than hierarchy, for control might be able to use the mediation or negotiation mode, if managers have these skills. For example, Walton and Hackman in Chapter Five discuss the role of groups in high-commitment, as opposed to high-control organizations. While they do not discuss intergroup relationships and conflict resolution, an inquisition or even a judicial mode of conflict management would be inconsistent with the way hierarchical management in high-commitment organizations deals with groups.

Lateral Relations and Negotiations. The structural response to an overloaded hierarchy is to institute formal lateral control structures, such as liaison roles, task forces, teams, integrating departments, and matrices (Galbraith, 1977). These structures add a set of lateral interface roles to the organization in addition to those already in the organization's hierarchical structure. The major issue concerning lateral structures in organizational theory is whether or not they can be controlled (McCann and Galbraith, 1981; Pfeffer, 1981). As in direct lateral negotiations, there are two aspects to this issue. First, there is the problem that agreements between groups negotiated at low levels in the organization may be optimal for the groups at the interface but suboptimal for the organization. Second, a structural provision for low-level lateral contact may result in impasses, not settlements. In both situations, subsequent hierarchical management costs must be added to the costs of the lateral structure.

We propose that lateral structures will operate more effectively in managing conflict if the structures are staffed with properly skilled people and if the organization's reward system contingently rewards effective (as previously defined) settlements.

The organizational theory literature treats all lateral structures similarly. We distinguish between temporary structures and permanent ones. The distinction is based on how the person's performance in the lateral structure is evaluated. In temporary structures like task forces, members of the task force are representatives of primary groups. Their performance is evaluated by their primary group manager based on how well the task force's settlement (solution) meets the primary group's interests. In permanent structures (for example, a matrix) the manager's performance is evaluated by two direct superiors and ideally also by the third-level boss. The matrix manager should be evaluated based on our quality criterion, his or her success in facilitating lasting settlements of interface issues.

It is a bit difficult to classify various lateral structures as temporary or permanent, because the classification depends on the performance evaluation relationship. In general, liaison roles and task forces are temporary structures. Teams,[1] integrating departments, ombudsmen, and matrices are permanent. Task

---

1. Many organizations call task forces teams. Teams are groups to which people are assigned for 100 percent of their time and for an indefinite period.

force leaders, if they are temporarily pulled from their primary group and assigned to a vice-president for the duration of the task force, should be considered as permanent structures though the members may have only temporary assignments.

Temporary lateral structures. Temporary lateral structures are used as communication vehicles to transform intergroup conflict into intragroup constraints or coordinated action. The roles of group representatives—for example, on a task force—are to represent the preferences and provide the skills of their primary group. Control over performance appraisal lies with the primary group manager, not the task force leader. Politically wise task force members know they will have to justify any settlement to their primary group. As a result, temporary lateral structures tend to stimulate a positional approach to negotiations. There are numerous terms used to identify different negotiation strategies. Positional negotiations, as described by Fisher and Ury (1981), are conceptually similar to distributive negotiations, as described by Walton and McKersie (1965). We prefer Fisher and Ury's term because we believe the term *distributive* connotes a single-issue negotiation. We contrast positional negotiating with a problem-solving approach. Problem solving is called principled negotiations by Fisher and Ury (1981), and integrative by Walton and McKersie (1965). We use the term *integrative* interchangeably with *problem solving.* We do not use the term *principled* because of its ethical connotation.

We note that unless one or the other group completely capitulates on an interface issue, settlements achieved through either positional or problem-solving negotiations that transform intergroup conflict into intragroup constraints or coordinated action are all compromise settlements. A manager assigned to a task force is likely to stake out a position on the conflict issues that is favorable to his or her group and only move from it when more powerful groups exert other power. The task force member may work to build coalitions with representatives of other groups but is unlikely to enter into problem-solving discussions, because such discussions are time-consuming and a creative, integrative solution would probably be more difficult to sell to the primary group than a solution, albeit a compromise solution, which is a variant of the group's original preferences.

Task forces provide structural opportunities for powerful groups to exploit less powerful groups in ways that may not be consistent with overall organizational strategy. We have three suggestions for controlling temporary lateral structures. First, in order to minimize exploitation, we think it is important for group representatives to task forces to recognize that intergroup negotiations have simply been transformed into intra–task force negotiations. Regardless of the language used in creating the task force, group representatives who do not approach task force deliberations as a negotiation are setting their group up to be exploited. Groups should select representatives to task forces who can expertly present and defend the group's interests. This task requires individuals who have both positional and problem-solving negotiation skills.

Secondly, in order to reduce the likelihood of impasses, task force members need to be motivated to complete the task force's mission. The most direct way of accomplishing this is to make the achievement of a high-quality settlement a central element of each task force member's performance appraisal. Ideally, the hierarchical manager, who would have to manage the conflict if the task force were unsuccessful, should be involved in each task force member's performance appraisal. Contingent rewards and visibility are two factors contributing to a problem-solving mode of task force deliberation. Another factor may be the task itself. Hackman's (1984) model of group decision making emphasizes the fact that decision making should be enhanced when the decision-making task itself has motivational properties. Task forces that provide opportunities for personal skill development or challenges unavailable in normal humdrum jobs are also likely to be motivating and cause group representatives to look beyond the parochial interests of their own groups to the broader interface issues.

If motivation factors are not sufficient to stimulate the task force to move from a positional to a problem-solving approach, it may be necessary for groups to actually instruct their representatives to take a problem-solving approach to task force deliberations. There is support for this proposition in the research on representative-constituency relationships (Benton and Druckman, 1974). In general, negotiators representing constituencies take a tougher positional approach to negotiations than negotiators who do not represent constituencies even when the constituency gives the representative no instructions. Instructions from constituencies to take a problem-solving approach do have an effect on negotiator behavior and settlements. The problem with extrapolating from this research to the organizational setting is that the research was done in the laboratory and the leaders were elected or appointed. Instructions to take a problem-solving approach may have no effect if the group representative also holds a position of hierarchical authority in the group.

Permanent lateral structures. Integrating roles, matrices, and ombudsmen (see Kolb, 1986, for a discussion of the latter) are permanent intergroup interface positions.[2] They are an expensive structural alternative, since they are full-time conflict management positions, but they may also be cost-effective in terms of long-term settlements. "Reorganize it Rogers," our example of a hierarchical manager, was managing a matrix. The degree of conflict in Rogers's matrix illustrates that permanent lateral structures, when they do not operate properly, can add significantly to transaction costs. Kolb does not tell us much about the lower-level matrix managers in her case, other than that they were engineers and that their method for managing intergroup conflict was to push it up the hierarchy. This conflict management style violates the whole concept of the matrix. Obviously, design is not enough. What else is necessary to make permanent lateral structures operate as intended? We be-

2. The best example of an integrating role is a brand or product manager who coordinates activities associated with the product across the functional departments. A matrix structure lays an integrating dimension across functional areas. Popular two-dimensional matrices integrate projects and functions or geographic regions and functions. The ombudsman role is widely used to structure nonunion grievance procedures but it also appears as a line position with a troubleshooter title.

lieve organizational systems that demand and reward high-quality intergroup settlements and role incumbents who have good negotiation skills are essential for making these lateral structures effective.

We have already discussed reward systems in some detail. Incumbents in permanent lateral structures should be evaluated on the quality of the settlements of interface issues that they negotiate. One factor that makes the tasks particularly difficult is that group representatives, with whom a matrix manager or ombudsman interacts, are evaluated on how well their groups' interests are maintained in an interface settlement, not on integrative criteria. Furthermore, incumbents in permanent lateral roles have interests of their own. High-quality interface solutions may be the means for achieving an outcome, but in many organizations the outcome is the most visible criterion and is what is rewarded. As a result, it may be difficult for incumbents in permanent lateral structures to distinguish effective and ineffective means.

We propose that problem solving is a more effective style of negotiation than a positional or distributive approach in permanent lateral structures. These structures seldom have the formal authority (power) that is necessary to successfully negotiate a position. For example, product managers in marketing departments (an integrating structure) frequently have no budgetary control. Their power comes from their ability to absorb uncertainty by predicting or managing markets and to manage conflict with quality interface solutions. Quality interface solutions either on their face or over the long run are most likely to be those arrived at through integrative negotiation.

Do managers have integrative bargaining skills? Some obviously do, but even those who do may lack a structure or framework for planning a negotiation. The current popularity of negotiation training courses in master of business administration (M.B.A.) and executive programs suggests that these are skills managers want to acquire.

The most accessible description of the problem-solving approach to negotiation is in Fisher and Ury (1981). They suggest: (1) focus on interests, not positions; (2) separate the people from the problem; (3) invent options for mutual gain; (4) invent objective criteria; and (5) know your *Best Alternative to a Negotiated Agreement* (BATNA). The Fisher-Ury principles provide a useful guide in preparing for negotiations. The negotiator intent on approaching the conflict from a problem-solving perspective first anticipates what the groups' positions are likely to be on the interface issues. The next step is to think through the reasons underlying those positions and consider possible hidden agendas. Underlying reasons or hidden agendas are called interests by Fisher and Ury (1981). Then analyze what will happen if no settlement is reached. Will the groups continue the status quo, interacting on the issue using old procedures? Will the conflict get escalated up the hierarchy? This analysis step is called BATNA. An assessment of groups' BATNAs is really an assessment of their power. The group with the better BATNA is the more powerful group. The reasoning goes like this: A's power is a function of B's dependency on A, and B's power is a function of A's dependency on B. If A is relatively less dependent on B—that is, has a better BATNA—than B is on A, then A has relatively more power than B.

These three steps—positions, interests, and BATNAs—provide the information necessary to analyze whether or not there is likely to be an area of agreement for the groups. The analysis of interests is particularly useful in searching for alternative settlements that maximize both groups' interests, regardless of their original positions. All of this analysis is done before the negotiation. This means that chance meetings in the hall, on an elevator, or by a coffeepot are not appropriate for negotiations, unless one is fully prepared. Such meetings might be appropriate for checking out anticipated interests or exploring BATNAs, but a problem-solving negotiation session needs to be a serious joint attempt to develop a mutually beneficial settlement. The chances of negotiating an agreement that a group representative can successfully sell to his or her primary group are better when that representative was fully involved in the deliberations.

Incumbents in permanent lateral roles may also frequently find themselves in a mediation role between conflicting groups. Recent research (Kolb, 1986; Shapiro, Drieghe, and Brett, 1985) has demonstrated that successful mediators are not artists who approach each conflict uniquely, but systematic practitioners of a style. Shapiro, Drieghe, and Brett (1985) found, further, that several different styles are effective in getting settlements.

Managers have much to learn from mediators. Mediators use the Fisher-Ury techniques, particularly the one about separating the people from the problem. Many mediators literally separate the opposing groups and shuttle back and forth between them. This works very well when there are emotional tensions between people that are interfering with the negotiation. It is not, however, necessary in all situations.

Other mediator techniques make settlements more palatable. Three of these are as follows: (1) add issues to the conflict so that every group can get something out of the settlements, (2) get the groups to agree that a particular settlement is a one-time agreement and cannot stand as a precedent, and (3) get the groups to try a settlement for an experimental period. Another technique used in mediating multi-issue conflicts is the one-text procedure (see Fisher and Ury, 1981; also Carter, 1982). In this procedure, the mediator provides a settlement proposal written in simple language that focuses on the primary issues. The mediator then shuttles back and forth between the parties, asking them to discuss the proposal. For example, "What might you be willing to do to change the undesirable clause?", and so on.

We are more confident of our prescriptions for mediation techniques for incumbents of permanent integrating roles than of the problem-solving negotiating style. We know successful mediators use these techniques (Shapiro, Drieghe, and Brett, 1985).[3] There is no research contrasting the problem-solving and positional styles of negotiation. A major problem with such research would be to get advocates of both styles to

---

3. We cannot be sure that unsuccessful mediators do not use these techniques, since all the mediators in the Shapiro study had about the same settlement rate.

agree on effectiveness criteria. Given the effectiveness criteria developed in this chapter, we propose that the problem-solving approach is more likely to be effective.

Summary and Research Issues. This section integrates the organizational theory and negotiations literature in a series of propositions about the effective management of intergroup conflict. The main points are as follows:

- In hierarchical structures, superiors need mediation skills, subordinates need negotiation skills.
- In temporary lateral structures (for example, liaisons, task forces, or teams), when performance is evaluated in the primary group and not in the task force or team, group representatives may use positional negotiation skills.
- In permanent lateral structures (for example, ombudsmen, task force, or team leaders, integrating departments or matrices), incumbents need problem-solving negotiation skills and mediation skills.
- The balance of power between the groups, the organization's culture, and the reward/incentive system must be considered when designing a management form for an intergroup relationship.

There are numerous research issues identified in this section. A major challenge is to test the effectiveness of various negotiation (positional as opposed to problem-solving) and third-party approaches (inquisition, judicial, mediation) in different intergroup structural arrangements and under different distributions of power and organizational cultures. In this chapter we propose that in general in organizations, (1) problem-solving is more effective than positional negotiation and (2) third-party procedures that place control over the interface exchange with the interfacing groups will be most effective. But we caution that under conditions of unbalanced power, or when the organization's culture is tied to hierarchical control, direct lateral negotiations and mediation may not be effective.

A second challenge is to determine whether problem-solving negotiation skills actually affect the quality of intergroup exchanges. Lawrence and Lorsch (1967) found that a "confrontation style" of decision making was crucial for interdepartmental effectiveness. Can such necessary confrontations be implemented more effectively in a problem-solving rather than a positional style? Lawrence and Lorsch's research does not tell us. The framework developed here suggests researchers should examine skill, structure, power, and the organization's culture and its incentive system in studying the causes of effective intergroup relations.

It is interesting to speculate about the substitutability of skill for structure. Since lateral structures are permanent management devices, they are costly. The structure should be chosen by evaluating the interdependence between the groups, environmental uncertainty, and the negotiation skills of managers. Lateral structures required by the environment, but staffed by unskilled managers, will only increase transaction costs. On the other hand, managers skilled in negotiations may be able to cope with less hierarchy and few permanent lateral structures, holding environmental dynamism and interdependence constant.

One research issue that has not been fully discussed is the long-term viability of an organization that manages conflict via the techniques discussed in this chapter. In periods of dramatic environmental change, organizations must survive revolutions to remain viable. The approaches to managing conflict discussed in this section are not appropriate for revolutionary change during which the organization questions its fundamental operating assumptions. We think the approaches to managing conflict discussed here are appropriate under conditions of moderate change. All the techniques discussed recognize a multiplicity of interests, all recognize that conflict is legitimate, and all are focused on lasting solutions. While it is possible that a solution will outlast its viability in the environment, this seems less likely to occur when the situation requires the concurrence of groups that will be differentially affected by environmental change.

Conclusion

The dominant approach to examining intergroup relations has been structural (for example, Galbraith, 1977). But as

Strauss (1978) points out, many structural theories have negotiation at the heart of their framework without examining
the process of negotiation itself. To understand the process of
intergroup relations in organizations, structural considerations
must be linked to the process of negotiation. Different structural arrangements allow for different negotiation models. The
weak link is that structural interfaces are enacted by group representatives with different degrees of negotiation skills. In this
chapter it is argued that research integrating the structural approaches from organization theory with negotiation theory is
the most fruitful avenue to pursue for intergroup research.

In presenting our ideas for this integration of theory, we
have drawn no causal models, stated no formal hypotheses, proposed no formal research, and presented no computerized literature review. We have only written a theoretical statement
about intergroup relations: why they are conflictive, how they
can be evaluated, and how they can be managed. We have focused on intergroup conflict, though we know many managers
talk about intergroup problems, not conflict. We have also emphasized the conflictive aspect of intergroup relations, though
we recognize that for an intergroup interface to be effective, the
majority of the interface time should be consumed in coordinated intergroup action or on constraints on intragroup behavior.

We have also focused on negotiation skills, though there
is no research showing that successful managers act as we prescribe. Certainly Kipnis, Schmidt, and Wilkinson's (1980) research that reports that managers use power when they have it
and Sheppard's (1983) research showing that managers deal
with conflict like inquisitors are discouraging. Yet why should
we expect managers to have negotiation skills honed as finely as
their financial and market analysis skills or even their skills in
managing people? Most people learn negotiating skills in the
course of everyday life. They take a problem-solving approach
with their families and a positional approach with their car deal-
ers. The problems come in the transfer of skills from the everyday to the organizational setting. It is not legitimate to treat
your counterpart in another group the way you do your spouse
or a car dealer. So what do you do? Few managers have models,

few have had formal training. Most managers are unprepared to manage intergroup conflict effectively. So while the research task of confirming or disconfirming our theory of managing conflict between groups is formidable, the training task, assuming a confirmed theory, is greater.

References

Aiken, M., and Hage, J. "Organizational Independence and Intraorganizational Structure." *American Sociological Review,* 1968, *33,* 912-930.

Bacharach, S. B., and Lawler, E. J. *Bargaining: Power, Tactics, and Outcomes.* San Francisco: Jossey-Bass, 1981.

Benton, A. A., and Druckman, D. "Constituents' Bargaining Orientation and Intergroup Negotiations." *Journal of Applied Psychology,* 1974, *4,* 141-150.

Bok, D. C., and Dunlop, J. T. *Labor and the American Community.* New York: Simon & Schuster, 1970.

Brett, J. M. "Managing Organizational Conflict." *Journal of Professional Psychology,* 1984, *15,* 664-678.

Brett, J. M., and Goldberg, S. B. "Wildcat Strikes in the Bituminous Coal Mining Industry." *Industrial and Labor Relations Review,* 1979, *32,* 467-483.

Brett, J. M., and Goldberg, S. B. "Grievance Mediation in the Coal Industry: A Field Experiment." *Industrial and Labor Relations Review,* 1983, *37,* 49-69.

Brett, J. M., and Shapiro, D. "Procedural Justice: A Test of Two Theories." Working paper, Kellogg Graduate School of Management, Northwestern University, 1985.

Brown, L. D. *Managing Conflict at Organizational Interfaces.* Reading, Mass.: Addison-Wesley, 1983.

Carnevale, P. "Strategic Choice by Third Parties: A Theory of Dispute Resolution." In R. J. Lewicki, B. H. Sheppard, and M. H. Bazerman (eds.), *Research on Negotiations in Organizations.* Greenwich, Conn.: JAI Press, 1986.

Carter, J. *Keeping the Faith: Memoirs of a President.* New York: Bantam Books, 1982.

Dale, A. "Interface Issues." In R. Payne and C. Cooper (eds.), *Groups at Work.* Chichester, England: Wiley, 1981.

Emerson, R. M. "Power Dependence Relations." *American Sociological Review,* 1962, *27,* 31-41.

Fisher, R., and Ury, W. *Getting to Yes.* Boston: Houghton Mifflin, 1981.

Folger, R. "Process and Outcome in Dispute Resolution." In R. J. Lewicki, B. H. Sheppard, and M. H. Bazerman (eds.), *Research on Negotiations in Organizations.* Greenwich, Conn.: JAI Press, 1986.

Galbraith, J. R. *Organization Design.* Reading, Mass.: Addison-Wesley, 1977.

Gladstein, D. "Groups in Context: A Model of Task Group Effectiveness." *Administrative Science Quarterly,* 1984, *29,* 499-517.

Greenhalgh, L., Neslin, S., and Gilkey, R. "The Effects of Negotiator Preferences, Situational Power and Negotiator Personality on Outcomes of Business Negotiations." *Academy of Management Journal,* 1985, *25,* 9-33.

Hackman, J. R. "A Normative Model of Work Group Effectiveness." Technical Report No. 2, Program on Group Effectiveness, Office of Naval Research, 1984.

Hage, J. "Communication and Coordination." In S. M. Shortell and A. K. Kalunzy (eds.), *Health Care Management.* New York: Wiley, 1983.

Jennergren, L. P. "Decentralization in Organizations." In P. C. Nystrom and W. H. Starbuck (eds.), *Handbook of Organizational Design.* New York: Oxford University Press, 1979.

Kipnis, D., Schmidt, S., and Wilkinson, I. "Intraorganizational Influence Tactics: Explorations in Getting One's Way." *Journal of Applied Psychology,* 1980, *65,* 440-452.

Kochan, T., and Bazerman, M. H. "Macro Determinants of the Future of the Study of Negotiations in Organizations." In R. J. Lewicki, B. H. Sheppard, and M. H. Bazerman (eds.), *Research on Negotiations in Organizations.* Greenwich, Conn.: JAI Press, 1986.

Kolb, D. "Who Are Organizational Third Parties and What Do They Do?" In R. J. Lewicki, B. H. Sheppard, and M. H. Bazerman (eds.), *Research on Negotiations in Organizations.* Greenwich, Conn.: JAI Press, 1986.

Lawrence, P. R., and Lorsch, J. W. *Organization and Environment.* Boston: Graduate School of Business Administration, Harvard University, 1967.

McCann, J., and Galbraith, J. R. "Interdepartmental Relations." In P. C. Nystrom and W. H. Starbuck (eds.), *Handbook of Organizational Design.* New York: Oxford University Press, 1981.

March, J. G., and Simon, H. A. *Organizations.* New York: Wiley, 1958.

Mintzberg, H. *The Structuring of Organizations.* Englewood Cliffs, N. J.: Prentice-Hall, 1979.

Pearson, J. "An Evaluation of Alternatives to Court Adjudication." *Justice System Journal,* 1982, 7, 420–444.

Pfeffer, J. *Power in Organizations.* Marshfield, Mass.: Pitman, 1981.

Pruitt, D. G. *Negotiation Behavior.* Orlando, Fla.: Academic Press, 1981.

Rubin, S. B., and Brown, B. R. *The Social Psychology of Bargaining and Negotiations.* New York: Academic Press, 1975.

Shapiro, D., Drieghe, R., and Brett, J. M. "Mediator Behavior and the Outcome of Mediation." *Journal of Social Issues,* 1985, *41* (2), 101–114.

Sheppard, B. H. "Managers as Inquisitors: Some Lessons from the Law." In M. H. Bazerman and R. J. Lewicki (eds.), *Negotiating in Organizations.* Beverly Hills, Calif.: Sage, 1983.

Sheppard, B. H. "Justice Is No Simple Matter: A Case for Elaborating Our Model of Procedural Fairness." *Journal of Personality and Social Psychology,* 1985, *49,* 1–10.

Sherif, M. *In Common Predicament: Social Psychology of Intergroup Conflict and Cooperation.* Boston: Houghton Mifflin, 1966.

Stephenson, G. M. "Intergroup Bargaining and Negotiation." In J. C. Turner and H. Giles (eds.), *Intergroup Behavior.* Oxford, England: Basil Blackwell, 1981.

Stern, L. W., and El-Ansary, A. I. *Marketing Channels.* Englewood Cliffs, N.J.: Prentice-Hall, 1977.

Stinchcombe, A. "Contracts as Hierarchical Documents." Working paper, Stanford University/Department of Sociology, Northwestern University, 1983.

Strauss, A. *Negotiations: Varieties, Context, Processes, and Social Order.* San Francisco: Jossey-Bass, 1978.

Walton, R., and McKersie, R. A. *A Behavioral Theory of Labor Negotiations.* New York: McGraw-Hill, 1965.

Weick, K. E. *The Social Psychology of Organizing.* Reading, Mass.: Addison-Wesley, 1969.

Weick, K. E. *The Social Psychology of Organizing.* (2nd ed.) Reading, Mass.: Addison-Wesley, 1979.

Williamson, O. E. *Markets and Hierarchies.* New York: Free Press, 1975.

Williamson, O. E. "Transaction Cost Economics: The Governance of Contractual Relations." *Journal of Law and Economics,* 1979, *22,* 233–261.

7

Research on Work Group Effectiveness: An Anthropological Critique

Helen B. Schwartzman

Anthropologists are fond of citing the proverb "It would hardly be fish who discovered the existence of water" when they are asked to describe the anthropological perspective. When Clyde Kluckhohn first introduced this proverb in *Mirror for Man* (1957), he used it to describe the anthropologist's ability to examine the taken-for-granted features of everyday life in American as well as exotic societies: "Studying primitives enables us to see ourselves better. Ordinarily, we are unaware of the special lens through which we look at life. It would hardly be fish who discovered the existence of water. Students who had not gone beyond the horizon of their own society could not be expected to perceive custom which was the stuff of their own thinking. The scientist of human affairs needs to know as much about the eye that sees as the object seen" (p. 16).

Anthropologists, however, have for the most part been associated with the study of "primitives" and their ability to study complex societies (and especially complex organizations) has been overlooked and is unrecognized by many researchers, including many anthropologists. This is unfortunate, because anthropologists have produced a variety of unique and insightful studies of American society. In particular, they played an important role in the establishment of the field of organizational research. In this chapter the value of an ethnographic approach is illustrated by presenting an anthropological critique of recent research on work group effectiveness. This critique suggests that research on this subject has been guided by several generally unrecognized cultural assumptions that have affected the research methods as well as theoretical constructs used by investigators in this field.

Anthropological Study of Organizational Behavior

For some time now, anthropologists have been outsiders to the array of theories, shifting emphases, and methodological controversies that characterize the field of organizational behavior research. Recently, however, ethnographers have begun to step back into this field. In fact, this is the discipline's second foray into the area, because anthropologists played an important, though now largely forgotten, role in the Hawthorne studies of the 1930s and the subsequent "human relations movement." Today, the tradition of industrial ethnology is rejuvenating itself as the anthropology of work (for example, Gamst, 1980; Nash, 1979; Wallman, 1979), at the same time that ethnographic studies of public bureaucracies as well as investigations of the culture of corporations are appearing (for example, Britan and Cohen, 1980; Gregory, 1983; Nader, 1980; Schwartzman, 1980). These studies have been encouraged by a growing recognition among anthropologists that all societies, no matter how remote, are affected by the actions taken by governmental as well as private organizations.

Anthropologists have made important theoretical and methodological contributions to this research field. For example, according to Burrell and Morgan (1979), one of the most important effects of the Hawthorne research (Roethlisberger and Dickson, 1939) was the introduction of systems equilibrium concepts and an organic metaphor into the organizational literature. The influence of researchers associated with the functional school of anthropology (especially Malinowski and Radcliffe-Brown) on the development and application of this metaphor is apparent throughout the Hawthorne investigation,[1] and the impact of their work on subsequent systems models of organizations has been specifically reviewed by Burrell and Morgan (1979).

The influence of anthropologists in the development of new research methods for the study of organizational behavior is also apparent beginning with the Hawthorne investigation. The research conducted in the bank wiring observation room was designed specifically as an observation/fieldwork investigation instead of a controlled experiment. The observation techniques used there, as well as the conception of the group as a type of small society, were suggested by the anthropologist W. Lloyd Warner, who had become involved with the project in 1930. Warner (a student of Radcliffe-Brown) had recently returned from conducting fieldwork among the Murgin in Australia, and he suggested that the bank wiring room could be treated as an analog to a primitive society such as the Murgin and was accessible to study using fieldwork techniques (especially participant observation).[2]

The use of systems equilibrium models as well as participant observation techniques continued with the work of human

1. For example, the influence of Radcliffe-Brown's ethnography *The Andaman Islanders* (1933) is specifically noted in Roethlisberger and Dickson's (1939) discussion of supervisors' complaints and social equilibrium (see pp. 358–387). The work of Malinowski (see especially 1927), Pitt-Rivers (1927), and again Radcliffe-Brown (1933) also influenced the development of the investigators' interview method (see Roethlisberger and Dickson, 1939, p. 272).

2. Roethlisberger and Dickson (1939) note a particular debt to Warner in their discussion of "Method and Procedure in Studying a Shop Department": "The general methodological concepts employed throughout this study [the bank wiring observation room] were chiefly derived from Mr. Warner; however, he should not in any sense be held responsible for their detailed application to this industrial situation. Mr. Warner frequently discussed the investigators' problems with them and called their attention to the similarity between the problems confronting them and those confronting the anthropological field-worker. He also directed their attention to the works of such people as Durkheim, Malinowski, Radcliffe-Brown, and Georg Simmel, from which a wealth of background material was obtained" (p. 389).

relations researchers. Many of these individuals were trained as anthropologists and sociologists, and they produced a variety of detailed and contextually rich descriptions of life in American industrial organizations in the 1940s and 1950s (for example, Chapple, 1941, 1953; Gardner and Moore, 1964; Walker and Guest, 1952; Walker, Guest, and Turner, 1956; Richardson and Walker, 1948; Roy, 1952; Sayles, 1964; Warner and Low, 1947; Whyte, 1948).

This research provides the foundation for the variety of studies of formal organizations in which anthropologists are currently engaged. This research includes studies of schools and schooling in traditional and modern societies (see Singleton, 1967; Khleif, 1971); investigations of mental hospitals and the mental health treatment system (Salisbury, 1962; Schwartzman, forthcoming); research on trade associations, the Better Business Bureau, and state departments of insurance (Nader, 1980); and analyses of New England apparel factory workers (Lamphere, 1979), Bolivian tin miners (Nash, 1979), Japanese bankers (Rohlen, 1978), and even the United States Congress (Weatherford, 1981).

Although these populations differ greatly, the researchers do share a common research approach that may be characterized as the anthropological perspective. The hallmark of this perspective is the tradition of ethnographic research, which may be defined as the observation, recording, and analysis of behavior in the multiple and nested contexts in which it occurs. The anthropologist is specifically concerned with presenting a systematic description of social systems that examines interrelationships among particular behaviors, customs, rituals, beliefs, and values in terms of broader patterns of cultural understanding, social structure, and environmental constraints. The anthropological perspective is holistic because it encompasses a wide range of social, cultural, economic, and psychological variables within a single conceptual frame (Foster, 1969). This approach requires several things of investigators, briefly enumerated as follows:

1. Researchers must go into the field (not bring the field to them).

2. Researchers must immerse themselves in the field (although this should be immersion, not conversion, as in "going native"). This is essential because there is no other way to become familiar with the world of one's informants than to participate in their activities on a day-to-day basis. This is what is meant by *participant* observation as anthropologists use the term.

3. Researchers must allow the research problem to develop, evolve, and even change dramatically during the study, and likewise methods appropriate to the problem must be allowed to develop, evolve, and change.

4. Researchers are concerned with the meaning and not the frequency of events (see Van Maanen, 1979). This does not mean that investigators do not count things but that counting is not the purpose of the research.

5. Researchers must be willing to allow themselves to function as the major instrument of the study. Investigators' reactions to differences between their culture and the informant's culture are legitimate and important data in this approach.

6. Researchers must be willing to collect and handle contextually rich data that have been collected from multiple sources and by multiple techniques.

7. Researchers must be willing to search for the informant's point of view while at the same time attempting to examine what is unproblematic to (and often not articulated by) the informant.

It is this approach, described here as the anthropological perspective, that allows researchers to understand seemingly inexplicable and presumably unrelated social and psychological events and problems in terms of the subtly patterned cultural beliefs, decisions, and forms that organize an individual's experience of everyday life. My "informants" for the anthropological analysis offered in this chapter are the recent research reports of investigators studying work group effectiveness.[3]

---

3. As an outsider to this research field, I found the prospect of reviewing the literature on work group effectiveness somewhat overwhelming. I decided to let the two selected bibliographies that we received as

Cultural Lenses and Research
on Work Group Effectiveness

It should come as no surprise to anyone that researchers are creatures of their own personal and sociocultural contexts. Even though it can be recognized that this is the case, however, most researchers (including anthropologists) act as if the development of research questions, the choice of methodological approach as well as specific methods used, the interpretation and presentation of research findings, and the development of strategies and interventions for change occur in a cultural vacuum. It is argued here that an examination of certain of the cultural lenses that affect the way that researchers look at the topic of work group effectiveness makes it possible for investigators to begin to perceive "the custom which is the stuff of their thinking" about this subject. Such an examination may also produce new research questions, as well as encourage the use of various methods, and lead to new conceptualizations of strategies for change.

Methodological Lenses. Anthropologists assume that all societies are characterized by a distinctive *world view,* that is, the basic premises that orient a people's view about the nature of the world and of humans' place in it. While it may seem relatively easy to characterize the world view of small and generally homogeneous societies, such as the Hopi, it seems almost impossible to describe a set of basic assumptions for Americans or Westerners. However, by using the cross-cultural comparative perspective of anthropology, as well as historical and philosophical analyses such as Grene (1969) and Matson (1966), we can see that certain basic premises affect the beliefs and actions of

---

participants in the Conference on Work Group Effectiveness held at Carnegie-Mellon University, September 16–18, 1984, define the recent literature. Therefore, the dates covered here are, in general, 1979–1984. I reviewed most but not all of the studies included in the annotated list and a selected number of investigations in the nonannotated bibliography. I also included a few studies and literature overviews outside these lists (for example, papers in the Goodman, Pennings, and Associates' 1977 book) that seemed relevant to the topic of work group effectiveness.

even large and diverse populations, such as Americans or Chinese. One of the bedrock propositions of what is referred to here as the American world view is the view that "the universe is a physical [mechanistic] system that operates in a determinate manner according to discoverable scientific laws" (Hoebel, 1966, p. 499). A corollary of this primary assumption is the view that people can and should seek to understand the universe in order to control it as well as to manipulate and change it. This view produces an active orientation toward the world, as it is believed that it is not necessary to accept things as they are because it is always possible to manipulate and redesign the world. Therefore, "the conditions of living are improvable, materially, biologically, and socially" (Hoebel, 1966, p. 499). To members of American (and Western) society, these beliefs seem obvious, natural, and true, and they are taken for granted and rarely discussed by most individuals.

It is also the case that these beliefs provide the foundation for the development of science and the scientific method in American and Western societies (see Matson, 1966, for a detailed historical analysis). This view places faith in the development of science and technology as *the* means by which humankind will be able to improve the world. It is science that makes it possible to stamp out disease, wipe out illiteracy, and conquer space (Hoebel, 1966). Science in this case is equated with the experimental method, and it is this model of research that has come to be the standard that laypeople as well as researchers use to judge the validity of specific studies. The goal of scientific research, therefore, is the discovery of determinate cause-and-effect relationships.[4] If the universe operates according to discoverable scientific laws, then it is the scientist's responsibility to discover these laws.

4. Of course, this goal has been questioned and debated by a variety of researchers, generally in the domain of philosophy of science or philosophy of social science discussions. One of the questions that repeatedly stirs debate in this area is whether or not the goals and methods of the natural sciences are appropriate for the social sciences. Of the many discussions related to this issue that appear in the literature, I have found the varied perspectives offered by Bateson (1972), Giddens (1974), and von Wright (1971) to be particularly informative.

The above cultural premises as briefly described here manifest themselves in the literature on work group effectiveness in a variety of ways. The most obvious is that virtually all of the researchers who have conducted research on this have adopted some form of the experimental model to guide their investigation. Although there are many differences in the use of specific methods among the investigations in this area, almost all the studies are, in one way or another, searching for *determinants* of group effectiveness. This search for determinants is coupled with the belief that once these determinants are discovered, it will be possible to manipulate them, to redesign group structures, processes, environments, and so on, to improve effectiveness and make things better. It is my suggestion here that this goal "feels right" to researchers (it is rarely questioned) because it is congruent with basic cultural premises about the nature of the universe and our place in it.

This search for determinants feels right to researchers, but it has led them to let the canons of experimental research dictate the following:

1. *The type of group studied and the place where it is studied.* Frequently a laboratory group is formed from the population of college students that is most convenient to the researcher (Drory and Gluskinos, 1980; Hawley and Heinen, 1979; Herbert and Yost, 1979; Lichtman and Lane, 1983; Lord and Rowzee, 1979; Miner, 1979; Rohrbaugh, 1979, 1981; Tjosvold and Field, 1983; Woodman and Sherwood, 1980; Yetton and Bottger, 1982). These are groups generally with no previous experience interacting with one another and have had no previous exposure to the decision task that they are presented. This approach is used because the researcher wishes to have as much control over the situation as possible. In this way the size of the group can be varied, as can the group's task; group membership is also controlled, as well as leadership structure, and so forth. The researcher assumes/hopes that the findings from such studies may be generalized to natural groups functioning outside the experimental situation.

2. *The type of question asked.* A recurring question given the experimental framework is "Does A cause B?" or "Does ABC cause D?" In general, as Weick has suggested, researchers appear to do a fine-grained analysis to isolate separate causes and a coarse-grained analysis to examine effects (1974).

3. *The specific type of methods used in the research.* Attitude questionnaires seem to be the most popular (Abbey and Dickson, 1983; Allen, Hitt, and Greer, 1982; Awal and Stumpf, 1981; Koch, 1979; Rotheram, LaCour, and Jacobs, 1982; Schriesheim, 1980; Tjosvold and Field, 1983). Individuals are asked about their perceptions, evaluations, ratings, and so on of a host of variables of concern to investigators (for example, perceptions of innovativeness, effectiveness, stress, work group structure; evaluations of organizational climate, performance, ratings of job satisfaction, assessments of leader influence, style, and so on). This approach assumes that questionnaire data can be taken at face value, except possibly for measurement error and bias, which can be statistically remedied or estimated, and it also assumes that "human conduct can be described and predicted from variables which characterize individual actors" (Knorr-Cetina, 1981, p. 9) (see discussion of individual-centered beliefs below).

4. *The type of data collected.* Data are almost always quantified and subjected to a range of statistical analyses. This need for quantifiable data has also created a subgrouping of articles that discuss and/or evaluate accepted quantifying procedures used in the field (for example, Hawley and Heinen, 1979; Lane, Mathews, and Buco, 1981).[5]

5. Recently, several researchers working in the symbolic interaction tradition (for example, Bogdan and Ksander, 1980) have begun to conduct studies of "enumerology," which should contribute greatly to our understanding of the quantification process in social research as well as everyday life. Enumerology is defined as "the study of the social processes by which numbers are generated and the effect of these processes on behavior and thought" (Bogdan and Ksander, 1980, p. 302). Adopting this approach, "number-generating strategies in all their various aspects become

5. *Presentation of suggestions for future research.* Data are
frequently said to be suggestive but not conclusive and always in need of more refined tests; future research needs
frequently focus on the importance of more methodological precision and rigor and sometimes more theoretical clarity.

6. *The type of interventions suggested.* Interventions that
have been tested by an experimental design are generally
favored. The interventions most frequently evaluated are
team development (DeMeuse and Liebowitz, 1981; Hughes,
Rosenbach, and Clover, 1983; Woodman and Sherwood,
1980), the nominal group technique (Herbert and Yost,
1979; Rohrbaugh, 1981; Scott and Deadrick, 1982; Stephenson, Michaelson, and Franklin, 1982; Willis, 1979) and
quality circles (Stimson and Mossburg, 1983; Wood, Hull,
and Azumi, 1983). It is interesting to note that the results
of this research, though frequently very difficult to interpret (for example, Was it really the nominal group tech-

---

the subject of study, rather than (as conventionally used) a tool of study"
(p. 307).

Culturally different approaches to the idea of counting are nicely
illustrated in a quotation from an old Eskimo woman in Coles (1977;
quoted in Bogdan and Ksander, 1980, p. 308).

> My grandson counts the days in a month. I don't
> know how old I am. He thinks I am kidding him when I
> shrug my shoulders and say I am many winters old. He ask
> me, to have fun, how many. I tell him more than he would
> care to count up. He is sure I have done the counting. But I
> haven't.
>
> Once he asked me how many summers I've lived. I
> told him a winter or two worth of summers. He was so in-
> terested in those numbers they teach the children at school,
> he repeated his question—as if what I'd said has nothing to
> do with what he asked. I didn't repeat myself—and he sur-
> prised me. He had heard me—and understood me. He told
> me that he wished he could just forget all the arithmetic he
> was learning, and play in the winters and go hunting and
> fishing in the summers. . . . He is twelve, he tells me. So
> what! All these numbers. What do they have to do with
> life? Does the sun have numbers for itself? The bears and
> caribou? The fish? The snow that greets us, stays with us."

nique or actually the membership composition that affected the performance rating?), are always used to support the need for more research on group interventions.
(This relates to number 5 above.)

7. *The standard used to judge proper and improper research
    studies.* Research is reviewed and critiqued according to
    whether or not it adheres faithfully (or as faithfully as pos-
    sible given "field" research conditions) to the experimental
    model. Questions are frequently raised about the research
    design, the use of control groups as well as sample selec-
    tion, and random assignments to groups (DeMeuse and
    Liebowitz, 1981; Hughes, Rosenbach, and Clover, 1983;
    Rohrbaugh, 1979, 1981; Sonnenfeld, 1983; Woodman and
    Sherwood, 1980).

Researchers working within this field (Campbell, 1977;
Hackman and Morris, 1975) have begun to criticize the literature on work group and organizational effectiveness by suggesting that the research produced so far is inconclusive, "helter-
skelter," noncumulative, and inconsistent. Factors found to be
important in one study are found to be "less important, not important at all, or even inversely important in another study"
(Abbey and Dickson, 1983, p. 362, discussing correlates of innovation in work groups). The response to this inconsistency,
however, is generally to call for greater methodological rigor
and precision. The suggestion almost always seems to be that researchers should do more of the same thing, only better. Only
rarely does this frustration with the literature (as in "Where is it
getting us?") seem to produce a call to question basic premises
about the basic goals of research and the types of methodological orientations employed, although Campbell (1977) hints at
this, and Weick's (1977) definition of organizational effectiveness seems to require it. This is true even though frustrations
with the research status quo and calls for rethinking goals and
standard methodological orientations are evident in the field of
organizational behavior in general (for example, Burrell and
Morgan, 1979; Fineman and Mangham, 1983; Morgan, 1983;
Van Maanen, 1979, 1983). It will be argued here that such a call

requires stepping outside one's culture and questioning basic premises about the world that have been learned early and reinforced repeatedly throughout one's life. Since this is not an easy thing to do, most researchers do not respond to such calls.

Theoretical Lenses. The formulation of research questions, the interpretation of data, and the development of interventions are also greatly affected by cultural context. Two types of theoretical lenses are considered here: individual-centeredness and a focus on the content as opposed to the form of group activities.

Where many societies locate responsibility for events in one's life on supernatural powers, kin, class, or other collectivities, the American world view locates responsibility *in* the individual. Even though Americans are widely given to group organization, their world view is individual-centered (Hoebel, 1966). Under the related ideal of self-reliance, it is believed that every individual is his or her own master, in control of his or her destiny, and able to advance or regress in society only according to individual efforts (Hsu, 1961). This latter belief places a strong value on individual self-improvement. Every individual should, it is believed, strive to improve himself or herself.

The conception of the person that this view supports is that of "a bonded, unique, more or less integrated motivation and cognitive universe, dynamic center of awareness, emotion, judgment, and action organized into a distinctive whole and set contrastingly both against other such wholes and against a social and natural background" (Geertz, 1973, p. 48). The individual-as-central view assumes that "actions, decisions, and behavior flow from internal, personal characteristics as opposed to contextual relationships" (Hall, 1983, p. 90). The American and Western "contextless" idea of the person has been contrasted with "contexted" concepts in other cultures by several anthropologists, including Geertz (1973) for the Balinese, Schweder and Bourne (1982) for Oriyas (Orissa, India), and Read (1955) for the Gahuku-Gama (New Guinea).

The impact of this individual-centeredness on research on group effectiveness is apparent in several ways. One of the most prominent research topics in this area is a direct reflection of this focus on the individual. The study of leaders, leadership behavior, leadership effectiveness, and so on, as it appears in the literature (for example, Curtis, Smith, and Smoll, 1979; Drory and Gluskinos, 1980; Fiedler, 1967; Konar-Goldband, Rice, and Monkarsh, 1979; Schriesheim, 1980), is premised on several assumptions congruent with the American world view as presented so far. One of the dominant concerns in this area is the relationship between leader traits, leader behavior, and leader and group performance. This approach assumes that there are, in fact, traits of effective leaders (as well as characteristics of specific situations) that can be isolated and discovered by scientific research, and once understood can be used by all individuals (that is, leaders) wishing to improve themselves and the effectiveness of the groups they lead. Campbell, Daft, and Hulin (1982) note that interest in leadership studies in the general field of organizational behavior continues "almost unabated" although the results of this research have been very disappointing. Researchers appear to be asking a recurring series of questions that have changed very little over the last twenty years: Do leader behaviors influence subordinate behaviors, or vice versa, or both? How much of the variance in leader performance can be explained by leader traits, or leader behavior, or the job/task, or organizational structure? (Campbell, Daft, and Hulin, 1982).

While it is true that a variety of discrete traits have been isolated, identified, and compared in these studies (Drory and Gluskinos, 1980; Christie and Geis, 1970), the relationships between these traits and group performance is not at all clear. This is one of the reasons why the literature on group effectiveness is said to be inconclusive. I suggest that this leadership research continues "unabated" because it validates an important cultural belief, that is, that individuals (especially certain individuals) and their actions determine what happens in group settings. Hall (1983, p. 91) makes a similar point in his recent critique of the concept of individualism and its impact on applied behavioral science:

> Despite the fact that many scholars have argued the principles of emergence or the reality of

the social and bemoaned tendencies toward reductionism, their audience has been less than per-
suaded. . . . One reason reductionism at individual
and unitary levels has become so popular and successful is that it falls within common sense and
does not contradict the basic view of reality. Psychology, for example, may be well-rewarded, not
only because of its scientism,[6] but because it looks
inside the individual for sources of physiology, cognition, motivation, learning, intelligence, attitudes,
and behavior. . . . Even the most common studies
by sociologists look at the attitudes and behaviors
of individuals as measured by surveys and questionnaires. It is an easily grasped and easily studied
entity—the individual. And each study or act of research done from that perspective maintains, reinforces, and recreates that common-sense construction.

The interventions that the leadership effectiveness studies
suggest also support this individual-centeredness value, as not
surprisingly they almost always involve some form of leader improvement (that is, individual self-improvement). Therefore, a
variety of leadership training seminars, skills workshops, discussion groups, and so on have been developed and tested because
it is believed that by improving leaders, and leaders' understandings of groups, group performance will be improved (for example, see Miner, 1979, regarding problem-centered leadership
skills). A basic and generally unchallenged assumption that supports this research and these interventions is that individuals
(leaders) and/or groups want to improve themselves, although it
is recognized that *improve* may mean different things to different individuals. However, insofar as I could tell, almost everyone assumes the "motivation" to improve and then differs on
what intervention best fosters improvement. (It is important to

6. Of course, this "scientism" is congruent with other core cultural
values as described in the methodology discussion in this chapter.

reiterate the point that the idea of researchers' developing and testing *interventions* to improve group or organizational functioning is itself a cultural belief specifically related to the values outlined in this chapter—for example, the belief that it is not necessary to accept things as they are because it is always possible to redesign and change the world, the view that research will lead the way toward change, and the value of self-improvement.)

If individuals determine what happens in group settings and some individuals are more powerful than others, then it follows that one focuses attention on the perspective of those individuals who are believed to be in control. Therefore, the cultural value placed on the individual supports the researchers' emphasis on the study of management, their views, perspectives, relationships (especially with subordinates), and so on as well as the researchers' adoption of management's perspective in framing research questions. Even though the adoption of this perspective has been questioned by some researchers (for example, Bittner, 1974), it continues to guide and direct a great deal of the research on work group effectiveness. For example, Schriesheim (1980) notes that nearly 75 percent of recent leadership research has focused on the leader-subordinate dyad rather than the work group despite well-established evidence of the importance of group factors in interpersonal behavior. I suggest that the dominance of this perspective is due not just to the fact that researchers must please managers to have their research accepted and supported but also to the fact that this approach supports the widespread cultural view not only of managers but also workers and researchers, that specific *individuals* do (or, at least, should) determine what happens in work group situations.

The individual-centeredness of the American world view also affects basic theoretical constructs in the literature on group effectiveness. For example, the issue of how effectiveness is defined appears to be greatly affected by these beliefs. In discussing organizational effectiveness, Campbell (1977) and others (for example, Ghorpade, 1971; Scott, 1977) have suggested that there are two general models of the effectiveness construct in use by investigators: goal-centered models and natural systems models. In discussions of these models, researchers almost always emphasize their differences, which has excluded recognition of some fundamental similarities between these two orientations.

The goal-centered view has very obvious roots in individual-centered beliefs. A primary assumption of this model is that a group or organization is composed of rational individuals who have agreed-upon goals that they wish to pursue, that these goals can be defined, and that criterion measures can be developed to assess whether the goals have been achieved (Campbell, 1977). In this case, the group or organization is treated *as if it were an individual,* subject to the same types of experimental measures of individual performance, competence, and so on already developed by psychological researchers (Campbell, 1977). In general, the research designs for studying work group effectiveness seem to enact this model—that is, the researcher assumes that the groups they create are composed of individuals who will respond rationally to the goals and structures set by the experimenter. Furthermore, it is assumed that measures can be developed to assess what the level of goal attainment is and this becomes the measure(s) of effectiveness.

Systems models of group effectiveness are also rooted in American individual-centeredness. This core belief is most obvious as it has been used by researchers and practitioners to develop interventions to change groups or organizations in order to improve their effectiveness. It is believed that a group's effectiveness will increase as more individuals in the group have an opportunity to "actualize" their goals as well as to maintain their integrity and uniqueness (Campbell, 1977; Beckhand, 1969). The concern here is to create more possibilities for more *individuals* to be responsible for and make decisions about their actions. Such interventions as T-groups and sensitivity training, team building, process consultation, and participatory democracy flow from this basic belief. When investigators attempt to test the effectiveness of the specific interventions, they tend to utilize the above goal-oriented approach for designing the research and in this way the differences between goal and systems models of effectiveness seem to me to be much less than advertised.

Cummings (1977) takes the individual focus evident in the above models one step further by suggesting that an organization can best be defined as "an instrument or an arena within which participants can engage in behavior they perceive as instrumental to their goals" (pp. 59-60). According to this view, "an effective organization is one in which the *greatest percentage of participants* perceive themselves as free to use the organization and its subsystems as instruments for their own ends" (pp. 59-60). As Cummings notes, this definition is entirely psychological, as it very clearly makes the individual the centerpiece of the construct. One of the interesting ideas that this approach suggests is that "profitability and productivity" are no longer viewed as the goals of organizational effectiveness, but instead as the means to the end—that is, they make it possible for the organization to become a place for individuals to fulfill their needs.

Researchers' views and definitions of what constitutes group ineffectiveness are also related to the individual-centeredness value. In general, the view seems to be that when group concerns (cohesiveness, maintenance, process) override the assumed ability and inclination of individuals to rationally deliberate, evaluate, and examine issues, problems, and so on, then the group is believed to be ineffective, and decisions produced by it are thought to be defective.[7] One of the best examples is the phenomenon known as groupthink. Groupthink is described as the tendency of decision-making groups to focus on group involvement rather than on a function or task that is believed to seriously jeopardize the effectiveness and adequacy of group decision-making processes (Janis, 1972; Moorhead, 1982). Janis defines this phenomenon as "a mode of thinking that people engage in when they are deeply involved in a cohesive in-group, when the members' strivings for unanimity override their moti-

7. I am aware that a variety of researchers in the field of organizational studies have questioned rational-human models of decision making. One of the most interesting critiques of this model, in my view, is offered by March and Olsen (1976). However, I did not observe that these critiques have had any significant impact on the majority of studies reviewed in this chapter.

vation to realistically appraise alternative courses of action" (p. 9). In Janis's terms, cohesiveness seems to be implicated as the central cause of consensus-seeking tendencies in groups (Swap, 1984). This high cohesiveness is related to a tendency of group members to become euphoric, to believe that the group is all-powerful and all-protective, and to the creation of an illusion of invulnerability. Along with this, members tend to develop stereotypic views of the opposition as weak, incompetent, or stupid; there is also an unquestioned belief in the group's moral-ity, as well as a shared illusion of unanimity, direct pressure on any member who deviates coupled with self-censorship of devi-ations, and the emergence of self-appointed mindguards and collective efforts to rationalize in order to discount warnings (Janis, 1972).

When group members adopt a groupthink mode of think-ing, then it is said that they are more likely to make highly risky decisions that are defective and sometimes dangerous because the group does not consider and evaluate alternatives as well as consequences of group decisions (see Janis, 1972; Swap, 1984). Janis believes that groups can avoid this groupthink phenome-non by opening the group up to the opinions of trusted asso-ciates while at the same time consciously bringing in experts to challenge members' opinions.

Janis focused his original analysis of groupthink on for-eign policy decisions including the Bay of Pigs invasion, the in-vasion of North Korea, and the lack of defense of Pearl Harbor. The value of this approach for understanding behavior in vari-ous everyday work contexts has recently been suggested by Manz and Sims (1982), who used it to analyze the potential for groupthink in autonomous work groups, using observational data collected in the study of a battery assembly plant in the southern United States. Moorhead (1982) also outlines the need for testing the groupthink hypothesis and relates this approach to previous group dynamics research, especially in the area of group cohesiveness.

The effect of group norms/consensus/cohesiveness on in-dividual behavior in groups is, in fact, a major subtheme of re-search on group (including work group) effectiveness. Reflecting

the ambivalence that researchers feel about group as opposed
to individual behavior, a variety of studies have focused on this
issue (see Yetton and Bottger, 1982, for a brief review, as well
as Swap, 1984). The general question is "To what extent is the
quality of group performance above or below that of its members?" (Yetton and Bottger, 1982). Researchers have claimed
that groups are superior to individuals in solving problems (at
least certain types of problems), but some researchers have begun to question this view. The work of Janis (1972) and others
(Swap, 1984) specifically examines what is viewed as the destructive effect of groups on individuals, and many researchers
have suggested that groups fail to reach their full potential because of "process losses" and "affective reactions of group
members" (Birrell and White, 1982; Guzzo and Waters, 1982;
Rohrbaugh, 1979, 1981; Steiner, 1972).

Attempts to improve group effectiveness also reflect this
ambivalence about the individual and the group. Consistent
with the view that groups outperform individuals but suffer
process losses and so on, a variety of interventions focus on improving group dynamics and structure. One approach that has
received a great deal of attention in the recent literature is the
nominal group technique (NGT). This approach very clearly attempts to structure and "individualize" the decision-making
process. Van de Ven (1974) suggests this in the following description:

> Imagine a meeting room in which seven to
> ten individuals are sitting around a table in full
> view of each other. However, they are not speak-
> ing. Instead, each individual is writing ideas on a
> pad of paper in front of him. At the end of ten to
> twenty minutes, a very structured sharing of ideas
> takes place. Each individual in round-robin fashion
> provides one idea from his private list. This is writ-
> ten by a recorder on a blackboard or flip-chart in
> full view of other members. There is still no discus-
> sion, only the recording of privately generated
> ideas. This round-robin listing continues until each

member indicates he has no further ideas to share. The output of this nominal process is the total set of ideas created by this structured process. Generally, spontaneous discussion then follows for a period (in the same fashion as an interacting group meeting) before nominal voting. Nominal voting simply means that the selection of priorities, rank-ordering, or rating (depending on the group's decision rule) is done by each individual privately, and the group decision is the pooled outcome of the individual votes [p. 2].

Recent attempts to evaluate the effectiveness of NGT include studies by Herbert and Yost (1979), Rohrbaugh (1981), Scott and Deadrick (1982), Stephenson, Michaelson, and Franklin (1982), and Willis (1979). Other approaches attempting to improve group dynamics and structure include the use of social judgment analysis (Rohrbaugh, 1979, 1981), team development (DeMeuse and Liebowitz, 1981; Hughes, Rosenbach, and Clover, 1983; Woodman and Sherwood, 1980), problem-centered leadership (Miner, 1979); and quality circles (Stimson and Mossburg, 1983; Wood, Hull, and Azumi, 1983).

Questions about group effectiveness in general have also led to the development of interventions that restrict or eliminate face-to-face interaction and discussion among group members. The Delphi approach (Linstone and Turoff, 1975), which in general relies on rounds of questionnaires and information feedback, is an example of such an approach (see also Rohrbaugh, 1979). Birrell and White (1982) also review recent electronic alternatives (such as video-teleconferencing) to groups meeting face-to-face and suggest that these interventions may be used to increase decision-making effectiveness (see also Johansen, Vallee, and Spangler, 1979).

All of the above judgments made by researchers about the nature of group effectiveness and ineffectiveness seem to reflect an American ambivalence about group activities. Ineffectiveness in most instances is associated with group process, affect, cohesion, and so on, and interventions are designed to correct this emphasis, whereas effectiveness is equated with individual responsibility. These definitions are also related to the second theoretical lens to be described here—the concern of most researchers with examining the content as opposed to the context or form of group activities.

The assumption that "reality" is reducible to the sum of the "least particulars" that compose it is another important, though generally taken for granted, feature of the Western and specifically American world view (Schwartzman, 1977; see Grene, 1969, and Whyte, 1965, for extensive discussion of this point). Adopting this perspective, often referred to as atomism or particularism, the world is perceived as a world of *things* (objects, forces, individuals, events) that must be labeled, categorized, and classified if understanding and eventual manipulation of them are to be achieved. Scientific typologies are elaborate expressions of this particular orientation, but it is evident as well in the central origin myth for this population.

In the beginning God created the heaven and the earth. And the earth was without form, and void; and darkness was upon the face of the deep. And the Spirit of God moved upon the face of the waters.

And God said, Let there be light: and there was light. And God saw the light, that it was good: and God divided the light from the darkness. And God called the light Day, and the darkness he called Night. And the evening and the morning were the first day.

And God said, Let there be a firmament in the midst of the waters, and let it divide the waters from the waters. And God made the firmament, and divided the waters which were under the firmament from the waters which were above the firmament: and it was so. And God called the firmament Heaven. And the evening and the morning were the second day.

And God said, Let the waters under the

> heavens be gathered together unto one place, and
> let the dry land appear: and it was so. And God
> called the dry land Earth, and the gathering to-
> gether of the waters called he Seas: and God saw
> that it was good [Genesis 1:1-10].

As pointed out by Bateson (1972) in his more extensive analysis of this myth, many of the fundamentals and problems of modern science are foreshadowed in this document. In particular, the passage deals at length with the problem of the origin of order, and order is seen as a matter of sorting, dividing, classifying, and naming the *things* in the universe. It is especially important to emphasize that these ordering acts are seen as unproblematic.

Since Western science is a logical extension of this concern with naming and ordering the "things" in the world, it has been very difficult for researchers to move away from a concern with things to a study of contexts. It has been particularly difficult for researchers to conceptualize relationships, patterns, and form as opposed to the more culturally congruent studies of content and substance. And when researchers do attempt to study context or process, they almost invariably transform it into entity (because "it" must be measured) (Schwartzman, 1977). Furthermore, this concern with things is tied directly to the search for causes (determinants) as discussed earlier in this chapter.[8] As these views appear in the philosophical tradition known as positivism, which appears to support the majority of work effectiveness studies reviewed here, it is assumed that "all basic processes of nature lend themselves readily to unambiguous description, permanent classification, and scientific analysis according to a 'linear' conception of causality" (Toulmin, 1981, p. 361).

---

8. I hope it is obvious that the different features of the American world view that I have described here are systematically related to one another and it is only for the purpose of emphasis that I have examined different features in the methodological and theoretical sections of this chapter.

This atomistic orientation expresses itself in the literature on work group effectiveness in several ways. For example, much of the work of researchers seems focused on categorization and classification efforts. Researchers have developed typologies for just about everything in their area of interest (for example, typologies of different types of groups, types of individuals, types of learning styles, types of compatibilities, types of organizations). In conjunction with this, researchers develop and rely on elaborate classification and coding systems for scoring survey questionnaires or for observing behavior in groups (Bales and Cohen, 1979). Researchers also use decision problems or group tasks that require their "subjects" in experiments to atomize and rank "things"; for example, the National Aeronautics and Space Administration (NASA) moon survival test seems to be very popular (Yetton and Bottger, 1982; Herbert and Yost, 1979).

Researchers have also been led by their own culture's concern with the content and/or substance of group activities to ignore analyses that focus on the form or context of group activities. Most small-group and decision-making studies treat the group's defined task (to make a decision about something) as the "thing" that needs to be explained. However, this focus on group task or function has placed the social form that organizes most of these group activities *in real-world settings* (that is, the ordinary, everyday meeting) in the background, as it has not been defined as a proper subject of study. When the context for group discussion is examined in studies, it is generally only by varying discussion formats to examine differences in task effectiveness (see the intervention studies discussed above). The focus of this research, in my view, remains on the task or content of the group, not on the context. In this way, meetings have been *used* as tools for research on the variety of topics that guide this field—leadership effectiveness, structural effects, evaluations of group effectiveness interventions, and so on. Therefore, while the literature seems crowded with the above types of studies, only a very few researchers have attempted to examine the culturally patterned and highly significant social forms, such as meetings, that organize the interaction of individuals in naturally occurring groups.[9]

Alternative Studies of Work Group Effectiveness

It has been suggested here that in order to reorient research on work group effectiveness, it may be important for researchers to step away from their own cultural context. This is not easy to do, because it means questioning basic assumptions about the nature of the world that are generally taken for granted. Nevertheless, it is my view as an anthropologist that new questions and approaches are most likely to be generated in the field of work group effectiveness studies by researchers consciously adopting culturally incongruent methodologies and theoretical constructs in their investigations. If the field continues to pursue the well-worn research and theory paths that are now being traveled, I believe that the research will continue to produce inconclusive results and always arguable causal statements about the *content* of group activities. This research will also, of course, continue to validate basic cultural premises about the nature of the world and the place of our species in it, which may be its most important function.

However, if researchers wish to generate new ideas and new approaches for the study of work group effectiveness, then I suggest that they may have to move into foreign (exotic) methodological and theoretical territory. Some of the directions that have been suggested in this chapter are as follows:

1. *A move away from reliance on experimental models and the search for deterministic relationships that has dominated most of the research in this field.* This change should also move researchers away from the use of attitude surveys and toward the use of participant observation and ethnography for studying naturally occurring groups. The importance of such a shift for the entire organizational behavior field has been pointed

9. A more extensive analysis of the meeting as a neglected social form in organizational studies is presented in Schwartzman (1981, 1984, forthcoming).

out by several researchers, including Sayles (1973), Mintzberg (1973, 1979), Weick (1979), and Van Maanen (1979, 1983). The importance of such a shift for the specific study of work group or organizational effectiveness has been less readily recognized and, based on my review of the literature, rarely implemented, although Campbell called for a move toward more observational studies in 1977: "There have been very few observational studies of what organizations actually *do*. Perhaps this is a mistaken impression, but behavioral scientists interested in organizations (with the exception of some sociologists, perhaps) seem to have lost their powers of observation. We are neck deep in questionnaires, but observations of actual behavior are rare" (p. 51).

What could these observational studies produce? First and most importantly, these should be ethnographic observations of actual work groups where the central aim of the method "is to understand another way of life from the native point of view" (Spradley, 1980, p. 3). A variety of models for the collection of this type of data have been suggested, but methods outlined in Spradley (1979, 1980) and Agar (1980) and used recently by Gregory (1983) in a study of organizational culture would seem to be most relevant for research on work groups. Adopting an ethnographic approach to work group studies would allow researchers to produce in-depth descriptions of the meanings that work activities have to participants. In conjunction with this, attention could be focused on the participants' (natives') criteria of work group effectiveness. Almost all researchers in this area seem to have imposed their own criteria of work group effectiveness onto the groups that they have studied (criteria such as task performance, task completion, goal attainment, productivity, and decision quality) without considering the fact that the members of a work group may have their own very different views of what constitutes "work" as well as "effectiveness."[10] This information would seem particularly

10. It would seem that the Hawthorne studies, especially research conducted in the bank wiring observation room, would have underlined the importance of understanding workers' perceptions of "work" and "ef-

important to collect for individuals wishing to improve or change work group activities. Ethnographic fieldwork methods are particularly well suited for collecting and analyzing this type of data.

Ethnographic observational studies would also be able to document the processes of problem setting and problem solving that actually occur in organizational settings. As revealed in this review of the literature, current studies continue to build into the design of experiments the idea that all groups approach "problems" and "problem solving" in a rational, linear, and systematic fashion (Starbuck, 1982). In contrast, ethnographic observations would be specifically designed to produce rich, contextually "thick" descriptions of the actual problem-solving processes adopted by particular work groups. I would also suggest that these studies be specifically designed *not* to prove, test, predict, or change anything. If organizations act in order to discover what they are doing, as Weick (1977) has suggested, then researchers must be allowed to conduct research in order to discover what they have been studying. Ethnographic methods come closest to facilitating this activity, and if it sounds strange to adopt this as a research approach, it is only because it violates basic cultural premises (already outlined in this chapter) about what the goal of scientific research should be.

2. *A move away from the individual-centeredness of most theoretical constructs utilized in this field.* Researchers must begin to develop and use constructs that do not locate the source of control and power in organizations in individuals, and that do not view the organization *as if* it is an individual subject to the same measures already developed for assessing individual motives, goals, and so on. Studies of group norms, work group climate and organizational culture (see Smircich (1983) for a recent review) attempt to move in this direction, but in my view

fectiveness," but unfortunately, detailed documentation of the activities of work groups is still the exception, not the rule, in the field of organizational research. W. F. Whyte has recently observed that *Management and the Worker* (Roethlisberger and Dickson, 1939) "remains unsurpassed for detailed, systematic observational records of the behavior of work groups" (1978, p. 418).

they have been specifically hampered by the tendency of researchers, as described above, to treat the organization or group as if it were an individual or a collection of individuals (for example, use of aggregated individual scores to describe subunit and organizational characteristics), as well as the atomistic orientation of most researchers that leads them to continually transform process concepts into entities for measurement purposes (see Schwartzman, 1977).

It is also important in this regard to begin to question the cultural assumption that individuals want to improve their effectiveness and more generally to attempt to understand why effectiveness is such a common problem "setting" (see Schön, 1979) for individuals involved with work T-groups in American society. In one sense it is a predictable problem, given the cultural lenses described here, as the problem can conveniently be located *in* individuals, or in work groups that are treated *as if* they are individuals. As these lenses focus attention on the problem of effectiveness, they also lead to solutions that focus on improving individual or group productivity efficiency, motivation, satisfaction, and so on. Alternative problem settings either do not seem possible, or they do not seem natural. For example, Weick's (1977) suggestion that effective organizations are garrulous, clumsy, superstitious, hypocritical, monstrous, wandering, and grouchy seems to directly contradict typical understandings of effectiveness. It has this effect, in my view, because Weick is presenting a culturally incongruent view of effectiveness, and this makes it a potentially useful way to reframe our research as well as practical problems regarding work groups.

This issue is also set very differently in organizations in other cultures where, for example, the harmony of work groups may become a major goal. This point has been made in a variety of publications on Japanese companies, but it is probably best understood and illustrated in Thomas Rohlen's ethnography of a Japanese bank (1978). This study is also particularly useful because it illustrates the value of using ethnographic observations (as discussed above) for generating alternative views of work group relationships and effectiveness.

3. *Alternative studies that would not attempt to under-stand and conceptualize group forms, processes, and relation-ships as if they were entities, thus avoiding the perpetuation of the focus on group tasks that dominates this field.* When content is given precedence over form, then this leaves us with many interesting theories and prescriptions about decision making, leadership, conflict resolution, and ways to solve problems, but it also leaves us without a theory of meetings as the most common social *organizing* form in organizations. Alternative studies suggested here include making meetings the *topic* of research interest as opposed to using meetings as a *tool* for research on other subjects. The functions and uses of meetings for individuals and especially for groups and organizations would be of specific concern here.

A major question guiding this research would be: What do we know about the impact of the meeting as a social form on naturally occurring work groups? For the most part, researchers have acted as if meetings were a sort of "blank slate" organizational structure that individuals can use to make decisions, discuss issues, solve problems, and so forth. The content (or task) of the meeting is assumed to be the reason for its existence. As a social form, however, it has typically been assumed that the meeting has no particular effect on a group or organization's activity; it is simply there to be used by individuals. The fact that individuals may use meetings for a variety of purposes (for example, the "hidden agenda" phenomenon) has, of course, been recognized (see Bradford, 1976). American individual-centered beliefs would seem to dictate this view as well as the interventions that have been designed to "deal" with it. However, the idea that meetings may be important forms for groups and organizations precisely because they provide individuals with opportunities to engage in a variety of expressive activities (while they appear to be engaged in instrumental behavior) has been less readily recognized (busy as most practitioners and researchers seem to be in correcting "process losses" and other expressive "problems" in groups).

Even more importantly, the fact that meetings *as a social form* use individuals to accomplish a variety of organizational or group ends is rarely considered. For example, if we assume that

organizations need meetings because they are important symbols of organizational activity, then new research questions
emerge. Our focus is no longer on examining the content of
meetings but rather on attempting to understand how organizations or groups generate meetings and what purposes these
meetings serve. In other words, interest is no longer centered on
studying how or whether meetings allow individuals to achieve
their specific ends but instead on understanding how a group or
organization uses individuals to achieve group ends. This view
relates in some ways to systems models of organizational effectiveness as discussed above, but it does not assume that the
meeting exists in order to make a decision. In fact, it suggests
the opposite—that is, that the decision exists because it makes a
meeting. In other words, I am suggesting that research investigations might profit by reversing the content-focused and culturally congruent view that suggests that meetings exist in order to
facilitate such activities as making decisions. This reversal suggests that individuals in groups or organizations need to make
decisions, or to develop or create problems or crises, *because
these are occasions for meetings,* and groups and organizations
(especially certain groups and organizations) need meetings because it is through the meeting that the group or organization
creates and maintains itself.[11]

The implications of this anthropological critique and the
alternative directions that have been suggested in this chapter
are several. The alternative methodologies suggested here would
provide participants as well as planners of work groups with a
way to discover and describe the meaning of work for actors in
specific work groups. This approach would counter the tendency described earlier for researchers to continually investigate
and impose their own categories and meaning systems on the
groups that they have studied.

One of the most important implications of this approach

11. Campbell, Daft, and Hulin (1982) include a number of interesting reversals, some of which are related to the approach suggested here,
in their analysis and review of research questions in the field of organizational behavior—for example, "Under what conditions do leader characteristics contribute to group performance?" becomes "Under what conditions
does group performance proceed independently of the leaders?" (p. 53).

is that it does not present recipes for "how to" improve work group effectiveness. Instead, it raises a number of questions that typically are not raised in the literature because of the cultural lenses outlined here. New questions may not seem very helpful to practitioners in this field who may be looking for specific answers to improvement questions. However, it has been suggested here that the field of work group effectiveness does not need more answers to the same questions that have continued to guide this area of study. Instead, it is my view that this field needs to develop some way to generate new questions as well as problem frames. The following are examples of the kinds of questions that this particular critique raises:

- How do specific work groups define *work, effectiveness,* and *improvement*?
- What evidence do we have that groups/individuals want to improve their effectiveness?
- Are individuals responsible for group activities?
- How do social forms such as meetings control and affect what happens in organizations?
- Do meetings exist because they facilitate making decisions or solving problems; or do decisions and problems exist because they generate meetings?
- Should interventions be directed to individuals?
- Should interventions be directed to the content or form of group activity?
- How might "ineffective" activities actually be valuable for individuals, groups, or the entire organizational system?
- Is effectiveness the way to set our research problem?

Conclusion

In reviewing the literature for this paper, I was struck by the fact that many researchers lament the lack of agreement among studies about basic definitions, measurements, perspectives, and so on. For example, on the related issue of organizational effectiveness, Scott (1977) begins as follows: "After reviewing a good deal of the literature on organizational effectiveness and its determinants, I have reached the conclusion that this topic is one about which we know less and less. There is disagreement about what properties or dimensions are encompassed by the concept of effectiveness. There is disagreement about who does or should set the criteria to be employed in assessing effectiveness. There is disagreement about what indicators are to be used in measuring effectiveness. And there is a disagreement about what features of organizations should be examined in accounting for observed differences in effectiveness" (pp. 63-64).

In contrast to this view, I was struck not by the differences across studies but by their similarities: the uniformity of methodological approach as well as specific methods used, the recurring questions asked as well as question frames, the similar approach taken to defining basic theoretical constructs. I believe this is what led me to examine what I have discussed here as the cultural lenses that affect how researchers are looking at their research topic, in this case work group effectiveness. I believe that it is these generally unrecognized cultural lenses that produce the uniformities that I see. Individuals working specifically within this field, as it currently constitutes itself, are not generally aware of these lenses, and so when they scan the literature, they tend to see diversity and worse—confusion, contradiction, a hodgepodge of theories, methods, and results. This anthropological analysis of the literature has been suggestive of an alternative view of this research field. Unless researchers are content to let their research continue to validate, but rarely challenge, core cultural premises, it is important to begin to examine some of these alternatives.

References

Abbey, A., and Dickson, J. W. "R&D Work Units and Innovation in Semi-Conductors." *Academy of Management Journal,* 1983, *26,* 362-368.

Agar, M. *The Professional Stranger.* Orlando, Fla.: Academic Press, 1980.

Allen, R. D., Hitt, M. A., and Greer, C. R. "Occupational Stress and Perceived Organizational Effectiveness in Formal Groups: An Examination of Stress Level and Stress Type." *Personnel Psychology,* 1982, *35,* 359-370.

Awal, D., and Stumpf, S. A. "Differentiating Between Perceived Organization and Work Group Climates." *Journal of Management,* 1981, *7,* 33-42.

Bales, R. F., and Cohen, S. P. *Symlog: A System for the Multiple Level Observation of Groups.* New York: Free Press, 1979.

Bateson, G. *Steps to an Ecology of Mind.* New York: Ballantine, 1972.

Beckhand, R. *Organizational Development: Strategies and Models.* Reading, Mass.: Addison-Wesley, 1969.

Birrell, J. A., and White, P. N. "Using Technical Interventions to Behavioral Advantage." *Behavior and Information Technology,* 1982, *1,* 305-320.

Bittner, E. "The Concept of Organization." In R. Turner (ed.), *Ethnomethodology.* Harmondsworth, England: Penguin, 1974.

Bogdan, R., and Ksander, M. "Policy Data as a Social Process: A Qualitative Approach to Quantitative Data." *Human Organization,* 1980, *39,* 302-309.

Bradford, L. P. *Making Meetings Work.* San Diego, Calif.: University Associates, 1976.

Britan, G., and Cohen, R. (eds.). *Hierarchy and Society: Anthropological Perspectives on Bureaucracy.* Philadelphia, Pa.: ISHI Press, 1980.

Burrell, G., and Morgan, G. *Sociological Paradigms and Organizational Analysis.* London: Heinemann Educational Books, 1979.

Campbell, J. P. "On the Nature of Organizational Effectiveness." In P. S. Goodman, J. M. Pennings, and Associates, *New Perspectives on Organizational Effectiveness.* San Francisco: Jossey-Bass, 1977.

Campbell, J. P., Daft, R. L., and Hulin, C. L. *What to Study: Generating and Developing Research Questions.* Beverly Hills, Calif.: Sage, 1982.

Chapple, E. D. "Organization Problems in Industry." *Applied Anthropology,* 1941, *1,* 2-9.

Chapple, E. D. "Applied Anthropology in Industry." In A. Kroeber (ed.), *Anthropology Today*. Chicago: University of Chicago Press, 1953.

Christie, R., and Geis, F. L. *Studies in Machiavellianism*. Orlando, Fla.: Academic Press, 1970.

Coles, R. "The Madness of Dark." *American Poetry Review*, Nov./Dec. 1977, p. 22.

Cummings, L. L. "Emergence of the Instrumental Organization." In P. S. Goodman, J. M. Pennings, and Associates, *New Perspectives on Organizational Effectiveness*. San Francisco: Jossey-Bass, 1977.

Curtis, B., Smith, R. E., and Smoll, F. L. "Scrutinizing the Skipper: A Study of Leadership Behaviors in the Dugout." *Journal of Applied Psychology*, 1979, *64*, 391-400.

DeMeuse, K. P., and Liebowitz, S. J. "An Empirical Analysis of Team Building Research." *Group and Organization Studies*, 1981, *6*, 357-378.

Drory, A., and Gluskinos, U. M. "Machiavellianism and Leadership." *Journal of Applied Psychology*, 1980, *65*, 81-86.

Fiedler, F. E. *A Theory of Leadership Effectiveness*. New York: McGraw-Hill, 1967.

Fineman, S., and Mangham, I. "Data, Meanings and Creativity: A Preface." *Journal of Management Studies*, 1983, *20*, 295-300.

Foster, G. *Applied Anthropology*. Boston: Little, Brown, 1969.

Gamst, F. C. *The Hoghead: An Industrial Ethnology of the Locomotive Engineer*. New York: Holt, Rinehart & Winston, 1980.

Gardner, B. B., and Moore, D. G. *Human Relations in Industry*. Chicago: R. D. Irwin, 1964. (Originally published 1945).

Geertz, C. *The Interpretation of Cultures*. New York: Basic Books, 1973.

Giddens, A. (ed.). *Positivism and Sociology*. London: Heinemann Educational Books, 1974.

Ghorpade, J. (ed.). *Assessment of Organizational Effectiveness*. Pacific Palisades, Calif.: Goodyear, 1971.

Goodman, P. S., Pennings, J. M., and Associates (eds.). *New Perspectives on Organizational Effectiveness*. San Francisco: Jossey-Bass, 1977.

Greenbaum, H. H., Ellsworth, J., Jr., and Spataro, L. "Organizational Structure and Communication Processes: Study of Change." *Group and Organization Studies,* 1983, *8,* 61-82.

Gregory, K. "Native-View Paradigms: Multiple Cultures and Culture Conflicts in Organizations." *Administrative Science Quarterly,* 1983, *28,* 359-376.

Grene, M. (ed.). *The Anatomy of Knowledge.* Amherst: University of Massachusetts Press, 1969.

Guzzo, R. A., and Waters, J. A. "The Expression of Affect and the Performance of Decision-Making Groups." *Journal of Applied Psychology,* 1982, *67,* 67-74.

Hackman, J. R., and Morris, C. G. "Group Tasks, Group Interaction Process and Group Performance Effectiveness: A Review and Proposed Integration." In L. Berkowitz (ed.), *Advances in Experimental Social Psychology.* Vol. 8. Orlando, Fla.: Academic Press, 1975.

Hall, P. M. "Individualism and Social Problems: A Critique and an Alternative." *Journal of Applied Behavioral Science,* 1983, *19,* 85-94.

Hawley, K. E., and Heinen, J. S. "Compatibility and Task Group Performance." *Human Relations,* 1979, *32,* 579-590.

Hendrick, H. W. "Differences in Group Problem-Solving Behavior and Effectiveness as a Function of Abstractness." *Journal of Applied Psychology,* 1979, *64,* 518-525.

Herbert, T. T., and Yost, E. B. "A Comparison of Decision Quality Under Nominal and Interacting Consensus Group Format: The Case of the Structured Problem." *Decision Sciences,* 1979, *10,* 358-370.

Hoebel, E. A. *Anthropology.* (3rd ed.) New York: McGraw-Hill, 1966.

Hsu, F. L. K. "American Core Values and National Character." In F. L. K. Hsu (ed.), *Psychological Anthropology.* Homewood, Ill.: Dorsey Press, 1961.

Hughes, R. L., Rosenbach, W. E., and Clover, W. H. "Team Development in an Intact, Ongoing Work Group: A Quasi-Field Experiment." *Group and Organization Studies,* 1983, *8,* 161-186.

Janis, I. L. *Victims of Groupthink.* Boston: Houghton Mifflin, 1972.

Johansen, R., Vallee, J., and Spangler, K. *Electronic Meetings.* Reading, Mass.: Addison-Wesley, 1979.

Khleif, B. B. "The School as a Small Society." In M. L. Wax, S. Diamond, and F. O. Gearing (eds.), *Anthropological Perspectives on Education.* New York: Basic Books, 1971.

Kluckhohn, C. *Mirror for Man.* Greenwich, Conn.: Fawcett, 1957.

Knorr-Cetina, K. D. "Introduction; The Sociological Challenge of Macro-Sociology: Towards a Reconstruction of Social Theory and Methodology." In K. Knorr-Cetina and A. V. Cicourel (eds.), *Advances in Social Theory and Methodology.* Boston: Routledge and Kegan Paul, 1981.

Koch, J. L. "Effects of Goal Specificity and Performance Feedback to Work Groups on Peer Leadership, Performance, and Attitudes." *Human Relations,* 1979, *10,* 819–840.

Konar-Goldband, E., Rice, R. W., and Monkarsh, W. "Time-Phased Interrelationships of Group Atmosphere, Group Performance, and Leader Style." *Journal of Applied Psychology,* 1979, *64,* 401–404.

Lamphere, L. "Fighting the Pieceputs System: New Dimensions of an Old Struggle in the Apparel Industry." In A. Zimblest (ed.), *Case Studies in the Labor Process.* New York: Monthly Review Press, 1979.

Lane, I. M., Mathews, R. C., and Buco, S. M. "Toward Developing an Unbiased Scoring Algorithm for 'NASA' and Similar Ranking Tasks." *Group and Organization Studies,* 1981, *6,* 235–243.

Lichtman, R. J., and Lane, I. M. "Effects of Group Norms and Goal-Setting on Productivity." *Group and Organization Studies,* 1983, *8,* 406–420.

Linstone, H. A., and Turoff, M. (eds.). *The Delphi Method.* London: Addison-Wesley, 1975.

Lord, R. G., and Rowzee, M. "Task Interdependence, Temporal Phase, and Cognitive Heterogeneity as Determinants of Leadership Behavior and Behavior-Performance Relations." *Organizational Behavior and Human Performance,* 1979, *23,* 182–200.

Malinowski, B. "The Problem of Meaning in Primitive Languages." In C. K. Ogden and I. A. Richards (eds.), *The Meaning of Meaning.* Supplement 1. New York: Harcourt Brace Jovanovich, 1927.

Manz, C. C., and Sims, H. P. "The Potential for 'Groupthink' in Autonomous Work Groups." *Human Relations,* 1982, *35,* 773-784.

March, J. G., and Olsen, J. P. *Ambiguity and Choice in Organizations.* Bergen, Norway: Universitetsforlaget, 1976.

Matson, F. W. *The Broken Image: Man, Science, and Society.* Garden City, N.Y.: Anchor Press, 1966.

Miner, F. C., Jr. "A Comparative Analysis of Three Diverse Group Decision-Making Approaches." *Academy of Management Journal,* 1979, *22,* 81-93.

Mintzberg, H. *The Nature of Managerial Work.* New York: Harper & Row, 1973.

Mintzberg, H. "An Emerging Strategy of 'Direct' Research." *Administrative Science Quarterly,* 1979, *24,* 582-589.

Moorhead, G. "Groupthink: Hypothesis in Need of Testing." *Group and Organization Studies,* 1982, *7,* 429-444.

Morgan, G. (ed.) *Beyond Method.* Beverly Hills, Calif.: Sage, 1983.

Nader, L. (ed.) *No Access to Law.* Orlando, Fla.: Academic Press, 1980.

Nash, J. *We Eat the Mines and the Mines Eat Us: Dependency and Exploitation in Bolivian Tin Mines.* New York: Columbia University Press, 1979.

Pitt-Rivers, G. H. L. F. *The Clash of Culture and the Contact of Races.* London: Routledge, 1927.

Radcliffe-Brown, A. R. *The Andaman Islanders.* Cambridge, England: Cambridge University Press, 1933.

Read, K. "Morality and the Concept of the Person Among the Gahuku-Gama." *Oceania,* 1955, *25,* 233-282.

Read, R. W., Bender, L. R., and Vitters, A. G. "Leader Sex, Follower Attitudes Towards Women and Leadership Effectiveness: A Laboratory Experiment." *Organizational Behavior and Human Performance,* 1980, *25,* 46-78.

Richardson, F. L. W., and Walker, C. R. *Human Relations in an*

Expanding Company: A Study of the Manufacturing Depart-
ments in the Endicott Plant of the International Business Ma-
chines Corporation. New Haven, Conn.: Yale Labor and Management Center, 1948.

Roethlisberger, F. L., and Dickson, W. J. *Management and the*
Worker. Cambridge, Mass.: Harvard University Press, 1939.

Rohlen, T. *Harmony and Strength: White-Collar Organization*
in Japan. Berkeley: University of California Press, 1978.

Rohrbaugh, J. "Improving the Quality of Group Judgment: Social Judgment Analysis and the Delphi Technique." *Organiza-*
tional Behavior and Human Performance, 1979, 24, 73-92.

Rohrbaugh, J. "Improving the Quality of Group Judgment: Social Judgment Analysis and the Nominal Group Technique."
Organizational Behavior and Human Performance, 1981, 28,
272-288.

Rotheram, M., LaCour, J., and Jacobs, A. "Variations in Group
Process Due to Valence, Response Mode, and Directness of
Feedback." *Group and Organization Studies, 1982, 7,* 67-75.

Roy, D. "Quota Restrictions and Goldbricking in a Machine
Shop." *American Journal of Sociology, 1952, 57,* 427-442.

Salisbury, R. *Structures of Custodial Care: An Anthropological*
Study of a State Mental Hospital. Berkeley: University of
California Press, 1962.

Sayles, L. *Managerial Behavior.* New York: McGraw-Hill, 1964.

Sayles, L. "Preface." In H. Mintzberg, *The Nature of Manage-*
rial Work. New York: Harper & Row, 1973.

Schön, D. A. "Generative Metaphor: A Perspective on Problem-
Setting in Social Policy." In A. Ortony (ed.), *Metaphor and*
Thought. London: Cambridge University Press, 1979.

Schriesheim, J. F. "The Social Context of Leader-Subordinate
Relations. An Investigation of the Effects of Group Cohesiveness." *Journal of Applied Psychology, 1980, 65,* 183-
184.

Schwartzman, H. B. "The Bureaucratic Context of a Community Mental Health Center: The View from 'Up'." In G. M.
Britan and R. Cohen (eds.), *Hierarchy and Society: Anthro-*
pological Perspectives on Bureaucracy. Philadelphia, Pa.:
ISHI Press, 1980.

Schwartzman, H. B. "Hidden Agendas and Formal Organizations or How to Dance at a Meeting." *Social Analysis,* 1981, *9,* 77-88.

Schwartzman, H. B. "The Meeting of Cultures in Organizational Settings." Paper presented at the annual meeting of the American Anthropological Association, Denver, Colo., 1984.

Schwartzman, H. B. "The Meeting as a Neglected Social Form in Organizational Studies." In B. M. Staw and L. L. Cummings (eds.), *Research in Organizational Behavior.* Vol. 8. Greenwich, Conn.: JAI Press, forthcoming.

Schwartzman, H. B., Kneifel, A. W., Barbera-Stein, L., and Gaviria, E. "Children, Families, and Mental Health Service Organizations: Cultures in Conflict." *Human Organization,* 1984, *43,* 297-306.

Schwartzman, J. "Art, Science and Change in Western Society." *Ethos,* 1977, *5,* 239-262.

Schweder, R. A., and Bourne, E. J. "Does the Concept of the Person Vary Cross-Culturally?" In A. J. Marsella and G. M. White (eds.), *Cultural Conceptions of Mental Health and Therapy.* London: D. Reidel, 1982.

Scott, D., and Deadrick, D. "The Nominal Group Technique: Applications for Training Needs Assessment." *Training and Development Journal,* 1982, *36,* 26-33.

Scott, W. R. "Effectiveness of Organizational Effectiveness Studies." In P. S. Goodman, J. M. Pennings, and Associates (eds.), *New Perspectives on Organizational Effectiveness.* San Francisco: Jossey-Bass, 1977.

Singleton, J. *Nichū: A Japanese School.* New York: Holt, Rinehart & Winston, 1967.

Smircich, L. "Concepts of Culture and Organizational Analysis." *Administrative Science Quarterly,* 1983, *28,* 339-358.

Sonnenfeld, J. "Commentary: Academic Learning, Worker Learning, and the Hawthorne Studies." *Social Forces,* 1983, *61,* 904-909.

Spradley, J. *The Ethnographic Interview.* New York: Holt, Rinehart & Winston, 1979.

Spradley, J. *Participant Observation.* New York: Holt, Rinehart & Winston, 1980.

Starbuck, W. H. "Congealing Oil: Inventing Ideologies to Justify Acting Ideologies Out." *Journal of Management Studies,* 1982, *19,* 3-27.

Steiner, I. D. *Group Processes and Productivity.* Orlando, Fla.: Academic Press, 1972.

Stephenson, B. Y., Michaelson, L. K., and Franklin, S. G. "An Empirical Test of the Nominal Group Technique in State Solar Energy Planning." *Group and Organization Studies,* 1982, *7,* 320-334.

Stimson, R. A., and Mossburg, P. A. "Quality Circles—The Latest Fad?" *National Contract Management Journal,* 1983, *17,* 41-45.

Swap, W. C. "Destructive Effects of Groups on Individuals." In *Group Decision-Making.* Beverly Hills, Calif.: Sage, 1984.

Tjosvold, D., and Field, R. H. G. "Effects of Social Context on Consensus and Majority Vote Decision Making." *Academy of Management Journal,* 1983, *26,* 500-506.

Toulmin, S. "The Charm of the Scout." In C. Wildermott and J. H. Weakland (eds.), *Rigor and Imagination.* New York: Praeger, 1981.

Van de Ven, A. H. *Group Decision-Making Effectiveness.* Kent: Ohio State University Center for Business and Economic Research Press, 1974.

Van Maanen, J. "Reclaiming Qualitative Methods for Organizational Research: A Preface," and "The Fact of Fiction in Organizational Ethnography." *Administrative Science Quarterly,* 1979, *24,* 520-526, 539-550.

Van Maanen, J. "Introduction." In J. Van Maanen, J. M. Dabbs, and R. R. Faulkner, *Varieties of Qualitative Research.* Beverly Hills, Calif.: Sage, 1983.

von Wright, G. H. *Explanation and Understanding.* Ithaca, N.Y.: Cornell University Press, 1971.

Walker, C. R., and Guest, R. A. *The Man on the Assembly Line.* Cambridge, Mass.: Harvard University Press, 1952.

Walker, C. R., Guest, R. A., and Turner, A. *The Foreman on the Assembly Line.* Cambridge, Mass.: Harvard University Press, 1956.

Wallman, S. (ed.). *Social Anthropology of Work.* Association of

Social Anthropologists Monograph 19. Orlando, Fla.: Academic Press, 1979.

Warner, W. L., and Low, J. *The Social System of the Modern Factory.* New Haven, Conn.: Yale University Press, 1947.

Weatherford, J. *Tribes on the Hill.* New York: Rawson Wade, 1981.

Weick, K. "Middle Range Theories of Social System." *Behavioral Science,* 1974, *19,* 357–367.

Weick, K. "Re-Punctuating the Problem." In P. S. Goodman, J. M. Pennings, and Associates, *New Perspectives on Organizational Effectiveness.* San Francisco: Jossey-Bass, 1977.

Weick, K. *The Social Psychology of Organizing.* (2nd ed.) Reading, Mass.: Addison-Wesley, 1979.

Whyte, L. L. "Atomism, Structure, and Form." In G. Kepes (ed.), *Structure in Art and in Science.* New York: Braziller, 1965.

Whyte, W. F. *Human Relations in the Restaurant Industry.* New York: McGraw-Hill, 1948.

Whyte, W. F. "Review of the Elusive Phenomena, F. J. Roethlisberger." *Human Organization,* 1978, *37,* 412–420.

Willis, R. E. "A Simulation of Multiple Selection Using Nominal Group Procedures." *Management Science,* 1979, *25,* 171–181.

Wood, R., Hull, F., and Azumi, K. "Evaluating Quality Circles: The American Application." *California Management Review,* 1983, *36,* 37–53.

Woodman, R. W., and Sherwood, J. J. "Effects of Team Developmental Intervention: A Field Experiment." *Journal of Applied Behavioral Science,* 1980, *16,* 211–227.

Yetton, P. W., and Bottger, P. C. "Individual Versus Group Problem Solving: An Empirical Test of a Best-Member Strategy." *Organizational Behavior and Human Performance,* 1982, *29,* 307–321.

8

Responsibility
and Effort
in Organizations

Bibb Latané

Organizations, like individual human beings, have distinct identities, and in the form of corporations, they have the same kinds of legal rights and responsibilities as individuals, including being able to do business, own property, enter into contracts, and make profits.

In economic competition with individuals, however, organizations almost always win, because they have many advantages. Organizations provide for the multiplication of human effort—by assigning many people to the same tasks, much more can be done than if only one person were doing it all. They also allow for an efficient division of labor—by assigning different people to different tasks, people can specialize in those things they do best, leading to greater concentration of skill. Like individuals, organizations have stability, and because they are not subject to the same biological and physical constraints that face any single person, they can act continuously and simultaneously at several locations over considerable periods of time, certainly beyond the life span of any one person.

Research reported in this chapter was supported by grants from the National Science Foundation and the Office of Naval Research. I thank John Levine and Richard Moreland for helpful suggestions on an earlier draft.

Organizations, because they can take advantage of the efforts of many individuals, have overwhelming competitive advantages as compared with single individuals, and they have proliferated. Today in the United States and to a lesser extent in other societies, it is almost impossible for an individual to function productively except as a member of a formal organization. But this should not be taken to imply that organizations as they function today are an efficient way to use the human and other resources available to them.

Tasks within organizations are done by individuals, but often they are defined, accomplished, and evaluated in a social context. Frequently this involves groups, which may range from temporary to permanent, informal to formal, with varying degrees of role differentiation and specification of rules, norms, and goals. In any case, this social context can have profound, and as yet poorly understood, effects on the quality of individual effort.

For the last ten years, a number of colleagues and I have been studying these consequences. We have discovered a pervasive tendency for individuals to exert less effort when working in groups than when alone, a process we have labeled *social loafing*.

In order for an organization to function successfully, it must effectively mobilize and direct the efforts of the individuals who comprise it. Explicit reward structures provide salaries, commissions, bonuses, expense accounts, and other perquisites —subordinates, access to facilities, and so on. The degree to which these rewards are or should be contingent on the fulfillment of explicit goals, the performance of specific levels of activity, or the achievement of specified levels of success has been a matter of debate in the organizational literature and by the management of organizations.

One school of thought seems to be that the greater the degree of actual or perceived contingency between individual effort and reward, the better—so people will know what is expected of them, believe they have control over their own outcomes, and see the system as fair. A second school, however, might claim that explicit links between performance and reward stifle initiative and undercut the development of responsibility. Commission systems based solely on individual sales can lead sales personnel to concentrate exclusively on customer relations and neglect the collective backstage tasks of stocking the shelves and maintaining inventory records. More generally, explicit reward structures may interfere with the development of a sense of individual responsibility to be aware of and to contribute to solving the needs of the organization.

If precise and complete job descriptions for every member of an organization can be specified in advance, if the appropriate reward for every likely individual input can be identified, and if these are likely to remain stable in the face of changing circumstances, as in the case of many repetitive tasks, it may make sense to develop and elaborate organizational manuals of goals and reward contingencies. More usually, however, organizations must function in an unstable environment with changing job requirements, and an alternative approach—enlisting to the maximum extent possible the alertness, ingenuity, creativity, good judgment, and responsibility of each of its members—may be far preferable.

The question for this chapter, then, is to consider how a sense of individual responsibility may be mobilized, encouraged, and allowed to flourish in organizations. The dilemma for organizations is that they are so often explicitly designed to limit the individual assumption of initiative and responsibility.

Scientific Background

For the past twenty years, I have been involved in research on responsibility—how it is aroused and what happens when it is shared with other people. My interest in the problem originated with the murder of Kitty Genovese. As you will no doubt remember, although this murder on the streets of the Kew Gardens section of Queens elicited little attention by itself (it was reported the next day in a single paragraph on page 57 of the *New York Times*), it received national prominence when it was discovered that thirty-eight people had watched and done nothing while she was stalked and killed. The apparent apathy and indifference of these thirty-eight witnesses scandalized the nation and the story, now front page news, became the journalistic sensation of 1964.

Social Inhibition of Bystander Intervention. The horror with which the case was met belied the usual explanation for it —that people really do not care about the fate of their fellows. It was left to John Darley and myself to suggest that the feature of the story that made it so newsworthy—that not just one or two, but thirty-eight people had watched and done nothing— contained within it a possible explanation for the facts. If each of the thirty-eight, isolated in his or her own apartment, was aware that others also were witnesses to the event, each may have felt a lessened sense of personal responsibility to shoulder the onus of action.

In a series of laboratory studies in which realistic, involving emergencies were created, bystanders were consistently more likely to respond if they were the sole person available to help than if others were also present. The social inhibition of bystander intervention in emergencies, discovered by Latané and Darley (1970), has proved to be an extraordinarily robust phenomenon (Latané and Nida, 1981).

Although several psychological processes may contribute to the widespread tendency for people witnessing an emergency individually to be more likely to intervene than those who see it together, diffusion of responsibility is certainly one. According to this idea, individuals are less likely to behave responsibly if the responsibility is shared. The process is not limited to emergencies. Similar effects have been repeatedly reported for such behaviors as answering the telephone or a knock on the door, tipping in restaurants, performing before audiences, attending town meetings, voting, and working.

Social Impact Theory. The diffusion of responsibility can be understood within the larger context of my theory of social impact (Latané, 1981), which deals with how an individual's physiological states, subjective feelings, motives, emotions, cognitions, beliefs, values, and behavior are affected by the presence or actions of other people in his or her environment. When others are the source of impact and the individual the target, impact should be a multiplicative function of the strength, immediacy, and number of other people, $I = S*I*N$. Thus, the more people who need help, the more responsibility you may feel to provide it. Further, impact is a power function of the number of people involved, with an exponent less than one, $I = sn^t$. This means that there is a marginally decreasing effect of adding more persons to a social setting. Finally, however, when others share with you the impact of outside events, as when many people are exposed to the plight of a victim in distress, their impact and the responsibility for dealing with them should be diffused or divided, and thereby reduced, $I = sN^{-t}$.

In many work settings, one or more individuals are subjected to pressures to work hard from management and from their supervisors. According to social impact theory, we should expect a decrease in individual effort in such circumstances as a function of the number of other persons who are also responsible for the work to be done. In other words, responsibility is diffused throughout the group and each individual exerts less effort than he or she would if alone.

Social Loafing. It is commonly believed that when people engage in collective activity, as when they perform together in work groups, task forces, and teams in organizations, team spirit can spur individual effort and enhance productivity. Some social psychological theorists and many of those who advocate reorganizing industrial production to focus on work groups assume that the presence of other people encourages greater output by each one. Not necessarily so. Decreasing individual effort with increasing group size—a phenomenon I call *social loafing*—has been a consistent finding of a program of research initiated with Steve Harkins and Kipling Williams (Latané, Williams, and Harkins, 1979). Since much productive activity is performed in collectives, social loafing has obvious implications for societies, both developing and developed, that are concerned about productivity and its impact on the quality of life of its citizens.

The earliest research evidence of social loafing is an unpublished study by a German student of industrial psychology named Ringelmann, reported by Moede in 1927. Ringelmann simply asked German workers to pull on a rope, alone, in pairs, in trios, and in groups of eight. Rope pulling is a simple, well-learned skill and can be considered a maximizing, unitary, and additive task, according to Steiner's (1972) classification. For a maximizing task, success depends on how much or how rapidly something is accomplished and presumably on how much effort is expended. A unitary task cannot be divided into separate sub-tasks—all members work together doing the same thing and no division of labor is possible. In an additive task, group success depends on the sum of the individual efforts rather than on the performance of any subset of members.

These characteristics of rope pulling lead one to expect the force exerted on a rope to be directly proportional to the number of people pulling on it. However, Ringelmann found that dyads pulled only 93 percent of their potential capacity while trios pulled 85 percent and groups of eight a mere 49 percent. When more individuals pull on a rope, the total force increases but the amount per person decreases. Some of this inefficiency can be attributed to the failure of people working together to coordinate their efforts optimally, so that the whole is not as great as the sum of the parts. Some, however, results from the fact that workers may reduce their efforts when working together, so that the parts themselves are smaller (Ingham, Levinger, Graves, and Peckman, 1974).

The existence of such gross inefficiency in such a simple form of collective effort led Williams, Harkins, and me to initiate a series of studies to see whether it can be reduced or reversed (Latané, Williams, and Harkins, 1979). For many of our studies, we have chosen noise production as our task instead of rope pulling. Making noise by shouting or by clapping is an effortful task that is maximizing, unitary, and additive. In addition, it does not involve any training and can be done without fatigue for a considerable period of time. Finally, the development of sophisticated battery-operated stereophonic tape recorders and sound level meters has made it possible to control experimental administration precisely and to record the actual amount (not just the psychological perception) of physical effort exerted without the necessity for cumbersome laboratory equipment. As we shall see, this has allowed us to study social loafing around the world.

CAPS Panelists: A

On a number of weekday afternoons in March and April 1984, forty-eight pairs of college students came to the Institute for Research in Social Science, located in the heart of the Chapel Hill campus of the University of North Carolina (UNC), for an hour of shouting and clapping. They shouted and clapped, not from enthusiasm or desire, but because it was one of a number of tasks associated with their part-time job—being a "professional" respondent in the UNC Computer-Administered Panel Survey (CAPS), an omnibus research facility administered by the institute and discussed more fully below.

Told that we were interested in the effect of sensory feedback on noise production and that they were to try to make as much noise as they could, individually and in pairs, they donned earphones and blindfolds (to control sensory feedback) and completed a series of thirty-two trials of shouting and clapping. For each trial, a tape-recorded voice announced over their individual earphones who was to perform ("A alone," "B alone," or "A and B" together) and whether they were to shout or clap. This was followed by a countdown and the prerecorded sound of six people shouting and clapping (justified as a means of holding sensory feedback constant). The prerecorded feedback was just loud enough to keep each participant from hearing the other perform, which had the desirable effects of preventing the development of group norms and of keeping each person from realizing that on the trials for which they believed they were performing with their partner, they were actually performing alone.

In order to separate losses due to faulty coordination and sound cancellation from those resulting from reduced individual effort, we devised a procedure for allowing participants to shout and clap either alone or in "pseudopairs" in which they thought another person was shouting with them, but they actually performed alone. With the aid of the stereophonic tape recorder, each person heard somewhat different instructions over their individual earphones. Under the pseudopair condition, one individual hears that both partners are to shout or clap together but the other hears that only the one is to perform. Therefore, the focal individual works believing that the other is also working too. These trials can be compared with others where each participant works and thinks he or she is working alone, and any differences must be due to changes in effort rather than coordination loss, since in all cases, only one person is actually making noise.

The actual amount of noise participants produced was measured on a sound level meter and the decibel units (scaled to reflect the perceived loudness of sound) were transformed to dynes/cm^2 (scaled to reflect the physical energy involved in producing it). Finally, as our measure of social loafing, we calculated the amount of noise produced when individuals believed their partner was working with them as a percentage of their loudness when they thought they were working alone.

It was no surprise to us—we had done similar versions of this study a number of times before with the same result—to discover that participants made more noise when they shouted and clapped alone than when they believed others were working with them. Females produced only 95 percent as much noise when shouting or clapping in pairs compared to when they performed alone, and the loafing ratio for males was only 89 percent. Both these percentages are significantly lower than 100 and reflect the degree of reduced motivation from having only one other person with whom the responsibility for working is shared.

What leads individuals to loaf? One possibility is that people have learned from their previous group involvement that other people are likely to shirk, and therefore they decrease their own effort in groups in order to maintain equity. However, asking individuals who have never participated in social loafing experiments how they think others will behave does not support this hypothesis. Overwhelmingly, individuals predict that others will try harder in groups.

An alternative possibility is that participants may have learned to conserve their energy for the times when they were asked to make noise alone. In an experiment designed to test this hypothesis, however, participants who always worked in groups produced less noise than those who always worked alone, suggesting that they were using a minimizing, rather than an allocational, strategy (Harkins, Latané, and Williams, 1980).

Another explanation for social loafing in groups and organizations is that individual outcomes are less contingent on their inputs. On a collective task, each individual receives only 1/Nth unit of extra reward for each unit of his or her extra effort, while receiving a free bonus of 1/Nth extra reward for the efforts of everyone else. By decreasing their input while exhorting others to increase theirs, individuals can increase their relative reward/cost ratio. Support for this line of thought comes from experiments in which participants were led to believe that their relative contributions could be individually identified, virtually eliminating social loafing (Williams, Harkins, and Latané, 1981).

I have now talked about social loafing on dozens of occasions to hundreds of people. Many of them, thinking about how little intrinsic value shouting and clapping have for most of us, wonder whether the phenomenon would hold up with more interesting tasks or in more involving social settings. A common reaction is to say, "Well, maybe, but if you had a task that was more interesting, or if success made more difference, you wouldn't get the effect." My first response usually is to point out that jobs in many organizations lack intrinsic interest, so that noisemaking may not be such a bad analog to the daily work life of their employees. My second response, however, has been to keep an ear open for opportunities to explore this question.

Cheering Cheerleaders

For one short week early every summer, hundreds of bubbly young beauties bounce into Chapel Hill for the start of cheerleaders' camp, one of a series of programs for high and junior high school athletes from across North Carolina and the South. Dressed each in her distinctive school uniform, they attend sessions on the tactics and techniques of cheerleading, roam the streets of the village in groups, and occasionally break out in spontaneous outbursts of enthusiastic noisemaking. For most of these girls, this week is the apex of a brief but intense stage of life during which the ability to make noise and generate enthusiasm is the key to helping their athletic teams win glory for their schools and to achieving their own social identity.

Although for most of the rest of us, the ability to make lots of noise by yelling or clapping our hands together is not highly valued and the activity not highly rewarding, for these young cheerleaders, temporarily at least, it is. If social loafing is a phenomenon that occurs only for tasks viewed as unimportant and meaningless, cheerleaders should not loaf. If people loaf only on tasks motivated simply by obedience to a supervisor, cheerleaders should not loaf when they are competing for recognition. Finally, if loafing occurs only when responsibility is shared with strangers, cheerleaders should especially not loaf when their friends are dependent on them to win.

With the cooperation of the camp directors, Charles and Rebecca Hardy and I set out to test these implications. Building on earlier work with cheerleaders by Hardy and Perry Prestholdt, we used the noisemaking task described above to find out exactly how cheering cheerleaders can be.

Three questions guided this experiment. Do people loaf on tasks that are important and involving to them or just on ones they find trivial, meaningless, or menial? Would the presence of competitive motives, either individual or group, help arouse collective orientations and thus reduce or reverse the tendency to loaf when working with others? Do people loaf only when responsibility is shared with strangers, or does being jointly responsible with friends reduce the effect?

The most attractive and perky member of our research team approached cheerleaders in their dormitory and asked them to "give us a hand for about twenty minutes so that we might measure how loud you cheer." Almost all who were asked agreed, and they were ushered, two at a time, into a small room furnished with a screen and two chairs. They were asked to shout and clap, alone and in pseudopairs, using the same instructions and procedures as in the CAPS study described above, for three practice and thirty-two regular trials.

During a rest period following this first series of trials and before starting the second, cheerleaders heard one of three announcements designed to induce either individual or group competitiveness. A randomly assigned third of the teams were told, "I should mention that we are keeping track of who is the best individual performer and at the end of camp, we are going to announce the six winners. I know you would like to be among the six best, so let's go one more series and really try" (individual competition). A second third were told that we were keeping track of "the best team" and that we would be announcing "the three best teams" (team competition). The final third heard simply that "we are keeping track of your performances. I know you want to do the best you can, so please shout and clap as loud as you can" (no competition).

Cheerleaders were recruited so that half the twenty-four pairs were wearing uniforms and came from the same high school cheerleading squad and half were from different schools. Conversations and postexperimental questionnaires confirmed that girls wearing the same uniforms knew each other well, unlike girls from different squads.

Girls seemed to enjoy the task, although they found it tiring, and they produced prodigious quantities of sound, especially when shouting. The average shout, from a distance of four feet, was ___ decibels (21.4 dynes), far louder than the sound of a New York subway train as heard from the platform. Noise production increased continuously throughout the series of sixty-four trials, presumably with practice and the reduction of any initial inhibitions about making undue amounts of noise.

Although girls seemed very excited about the chance to earn recognition for their cheering and although they made significantly more noise in the second block of trials after the induction of competition, they did so equally in the different experimental conditions, suggesting that competition did not itself affect their performance. The introduction of the opportunity for either individual or group competition also had no effect on social loafing.

As with CAPS participants and consistent with all our previous research, there was a strong and significant effect of the social context of performance—cheerleaders who thought they were cheering together produced only 92 percent as much noise as cheerleaders cheering alone. Thus there is social loafing, even when people perform a task that is meaningful and important to them.

Finally, although there was a hint of a difference in the degree of social loafing between girls who were paired with another person from their own team and those who were paired with a stranger, this difference was in the opposite direction to that we had anticipated. Cheerleaders loafed more with their own squad mates, making noise at only 90 percent of their alone rate, compared with a 94 percent rate when working with a girl from a different school.

I am not entirely certain how to interpret this finding, because I do not know just how cheerleaders from different squads regarded each other. A cynical view would hold that girls were more willing to take advantage of their friends than they were of strangers because it was somehow "safer" and less likely to lead to negative repercussions in the future. A more charitable interpretation is that girls regarded their partners, with their similar backgrounds, interests, and aspirations, as "friends-to-be" and, hoping to be ingratiating, were less likely to slough off the responsibility of working hard on them.

The conclusion reached in this study is that social loafing is not restricted to tasks that are seen as unimportant or meaningless or that lack intrinsic interest, and even if it were, it would still have negative effects on the productivity of organizations that have to impose some ration of such tasks on their employees. Although the introduction of competitive motives or of the opportunity to work with people with whom one has an ongoing relationship may in future studies prove to moderate social loafing, the present results provide no reason to believe they will be a panacea, or at least an easy panacea to administer. Nonetheless, I believe that social loafing can be overcome with changes in how group tasks are structured, a belief that receives some support from research on social loafing in India.

Indian Friends

Social loafing has been studied most extensively in Western societies, in which people are highly achievement oriented and work in an economic system that almost exclusively rewards individual as opposed to group effort. In addition, they live in a culture that places a high value on rugged individualism, self-reliance, and individual responsibility. The Protestant work ethic, so prevalent in the United States, emphasizes hard work and individual accomplishment; even in team sports, individual achievement is singled out for praise. It is possible that social loafing is a result of, and therefore limited to, particular cultural influences that reinforce effort in individual rather than group settings.

On the other hand, social loafing may be a consequence of more general biological forces. If exertion of effort is physically tiring, unpleasant, or painful, individuals may have a tendency to economize on effort when possible. Economizing is likely to result when one's effort cannot be distinguished from that of others in the group and when all group members share equally in the outcomes of group performance regardless of individual effort.

If loafing is socially determined, we should expect differences in its exhibition from culture to culture. If, on the other hand, it is a more general human response, the phenomenon should be observable in individuals raised in differing cultures. My own hunch is that both propositions are true—namely, that the potential for loafing is universal and observable in all cultures but that the factors leading to loafing may be moderated by cultural background, level of economic development, urbanization, religious orientation, philosophy, or political ideology.

Some cultures stress the good of the whole, while others stress individual costs and benefits. Individual as opposed to group orientation or socialistic as opposed to free enterprise economic systems may affect the degree of social loafing. Investigation needs to be made as to what extent social loafing occurs in different nations and in different social contexts, and what cultural characteristics moderate or modify individual motivation in collective work settings. If cultural differences lead to differences in social loafing, we can infer that the latter condition is not immutable in the human organization, and the specific nature of the differences may help us discover techniques for curing this social disease.

Two questions guided this phase of the research. Is the

phenomenon limited to U.S. society, with its emphasis on rugged individualism and its ideological anticollectivism? Can the phenomenon be reversed when collective orientations are highly mobilized?

Two experiments conducted with Indian school children help answer these questions. Indian society emphasizes the "extended ego" rather than the rugged individualist and the concept of "aram" rather than the Protestant work ethic. The extended ego develops from the tradition of the joint or extended family that makes the group rather than the individual the more important social unit (Long and Seo, 1977). Members of joint families live together communally in groups of up to seventy individuals. Resources are shared communally, but deference is paid to the authoritarian family head who is responsible for the care of all family members. Aram represents a focus on rest and relaxation and emphasizes a low value on hard work, which may be seen as an instrument to achieve desired rewards but is not valued for its own sake. The ideal job, according to aram, has high pay and prestige in return for little or no effort.

Each experiment followed the same basic model as described above, but a special version of the tapes was prepared with the instructions spoken in Hindi.

Participants in experiment 1, conducted by Janak Pandey from the University of Allahabad, Nan Weiner from the University of Toronto, and me, were thirty-two twelve-year-old male and female students at Saint Mary's and Saint Joseph's schools in Allahabad. Although these day schools, like many others throughout India, are run by members of a Catholic order, students are Hindu and represent a predominantly middle- to upper-middle-class range of parental occupations. Dressed in their normal school uniforms, they came in same-sex pairs from their regular classrooms to the music room of the school, where the experimenters explained the study to them, recorded their efforts, and gave them throat lozenges and a Polaroid picture of themselves at the end. These proved to be highly popular with the students and their parents, and much curiosity and favorable comment about the study pervaded the school for some time.

Janak Pandey and Saroj Kakkar conducted a second study among boarders at the Allahabad Boy's School, a government school that serves not only the city of Allahabad but the neighboring villages as well. Village boys from lower-middle- to middle-class backgrounds come to this school, for which their parents pay modest tuition. The research team recruited fifty-six of the nearly one hundred junior and senior boy boarders to participate in the study. Sociometric questionnaires were used to identify pairs of boys who were close to each other and regarded each other as friends and other pairs who did not feel friendly toward each other.

Indian children, like children in the United States and in other nations, made less noise in pseudopairs than when they thought they were alone (95 percent while shouting, 94 percent while clapping). This decrease, while small in absolute amount, is highly reliable—twenty-eight of the thirty-two children made less noise in pseudopairs than when alone, while one showed no difference ($p = .0001$ by sign test). Thus, the evidence is very clear that social loafing occurs within a society very different from that of the United States. However, the level of social loafing found among Indian children is much less than the 88 percent found among twelve-year-old children in Des Moines, Iowa (Williams and Williams, 1981).

Thus, the social loafing phenomenon is not limited to the United States but does indeed occur in a nonindividualistic society. However, the evidence also indicates that culture does make a difference. Unlike studies with U.S. schoolchildren, the gender of the participant was significant, with girls showing much greater social loafing, working in pairs at 91 percent of their alone rate, than boys, who worked together at 98 percent of their alone rate. It appears that traditional Indian society reinforces a lower emphasis on personal responsibility for women than for men. Women are always taken care of by a male head of household. Married daughters traditionally leave their own families and live with their husband's family. It is possible that girls in India take less personal responsibility for group output for two reasons—they depend on others to care for them, and they are less likely to feel commitment to any group.

A second interesting difference between the U.S. and

Indian studies is the participants' knowledge, or at least admission, that they socially loaf. The Indian children in a postexperimental questionnaire clearly saw themselves as working less hard on group trials, while in the United States, college students and twelve-year-olds alike consistently indicate that they work as hard or harder in the group situation, indicating that, consistent with the value of aram, social loafing may be more acceptable in India than in the United States.

The results of experiment 2 suggest that when collective orientations are very high, as among boarding school boys who identify each other as friends, the social loafing effect can be reversed. Unfriendly Indian boys did not show much social loafing, exhibiting the same 98 percent of their individual effort when shouting and clapping together as in experiment 1. Indian friends however, not only failed to loaf, they worked much *harder* when working together than alone, producing an astonishing 119 percent as much noise in pairs as alone.

These results certainly illustrate the pervasiveness of social loafing as, literally, a worldwide phenomenon. In addition to India and the United States, social loafing has now been found in Japan, Malaysia, Taiwan, and Thailand, so it is clearly not limited to Western culture. Instead, I believe, it does indeed have a biological and economic base in the desire to reduce costly effort when possible.

However, the results show equally clearly that social loafing can be moderated and even reversed under special circumstances, at present not well understood but involving cultural and social structural variations. To date, the only exception to our general rule has been for males from India who are exceptionally close friends. We do not know what it is about male Indians and their friends that makes them special—in fact, we do not know whether the same would hold for Indian girls or for close friends in other parts of the world, because the necessary research has yet to be done.

The results are hopeful, implying that if we can discover the critical elements allowing responsibility to be focused rather than diffused, we may be able to bring the process under control.

CAPS Panelists: B

The research findings I have presented so far clearly indicate, to me at least, that social loafing is a pervasive, if reversible, phenomenon. Is there any reason to believe that it operates in business organizations or that it has any negative effects on economic productivity? The next line of research I shall describe attempted to find out whether the phenomenon holds for the kinds of tasks and in the kinds of social settings that characterize business establishments.

Four questions guided this phase of the research program: (1) Do people loaf on tasks requiring mental as well as physical effort? (2) If it does affect mental effort, does social loafing affect the quality or only the quantity of thought? (3) Does social loafing require the immediate physical face-to-face presence of co-workers or can it occur when different people share responsibilities for actions occurring at different times, as in organizations in which interpersonal contact is largely mediated through interoffice memos, telephone calls, or, more recently, teleconferencing? (4) Does social loafing occur in standing or real groups as well as in ad hoc aggregations of people?

In order to answer these questions, with the help of a grant from the Office of Naval Research, John Barefoot, Beverly Wiggins, and I attempted to create a research organization in which to study the possible existence of and factors affecting social loafing. In doing so, we attempted to solve simultaneously a number of methodological problems that have long plagued research on groups and organizations, and although we certainly did not achieve complete success, our initial gropings have been quite encouraging.

There are a number of desirable features that should be included in any self-respecting program of research on groups and/or organizations. At a minimum, one would want to be able to study, over time, intact groups with a past and a future that are working on meaningful tasks under laboratory control with the opportunity for introducing experimental manipulations. It would, of course, be desirable to have extensive information about each of the individual members of the group as well as about how the group interacts and performs. Finally, given the shortage of personnel and funds for research, it is important to develop cost-efficient procedures for data collection and analysis.

Unfortunately, no method yet developed simultaneously satisfies all these criteria. However, a new facility initiated in the fall of 1983 at the University of North Carolina is designed to take maximum advantage of new technology in providing a continuing omnibus data collection facility that responds to these needs (Beza and Latané, 1983).

The version of the UNC Computer-Administered Panel Survey conducted during the 1983–84 academic year (CAPS/84) consisted of a sex-stratified but otherwise random sample of 300 UNC undergraduates who were sent an invitation to participate, reduced by self-selection to a group of 129 who showed up at the initial meeting, from which the final panel of 96 (48 male, 48 female) participants was selected on the basis of scheduling convenience. They were employed part-time as professional respondents for the academic year, during which time they reported to the Institute for Research in Social Science for twenty weekly sixty- to ninety-minute sessions in front of the computer terminal and answered questions or completed tasks assigned by it. Their job was to provide information about themselves, their family background, their aptitudes and achievements, their beliefs and attitudes, their life-styles and their habits, and they seemed to enjoy it.

Respondents were each assigned to a standing three-person group with whom they communicated and worked together on some tasks. At the end of and often during every session, respondents were allowed to send messages to the other members of their group via the computer. We were pleased to learn that computer-mediated interaction can still be human. CAPS participants sent lengthy, responsive messages to each other. They asked personal questions and disclosed personal information. They made extensive use of humor and even went to the trouble of writing out their "Argh's" and "Haha!'s." They apologized if they had missed a chance to communicate and, in general, seemed to treat their partners as real people (as, of course, they were) rather than as figments of the computer.

When respondents appeared for their weekly sessions, they would find an unoccupied computer terminal, enter their individual identification code, read any broadcast messages as well as specific messages to them from their supervisor and their co-workers, and check their earnings balance. In the meanwhile, the computer's executive system would check their task list and select the next uncompleted task module, randomly assign an experimental condition, and present the appropriate program module. As respondents worked, the executive would keep track of the amount of time remaining in the session, using this information in conjunction with the task list to select new modules. Finally, as the end of the session approached, the system would administer a closing questionnaire, give each participant a final chance to send messages to the supervisor and co-workers, record all data, update the task list, and calculate new account balances.

Respondents performed a wide variety of tasks, such as completing questionnaires and personality inventories and participating in experimental procedures. During the course of the year, each participant completed over a hundred research modules contributed by a dozen social scientists from eight departments on campus. Research projects covered a variety of topics and approaches, ranging from time diaries and self-reports of eating habits, drinking behavior, social life, and physical activities, to questionnaires measuring national and sex-role stereotypes, to weekly assessments of their political attitudes as the presidential primaries approached.

Perhaps the most important and encouraging thing we learned from our first experience with CAPS is that it is feasible. Participants apparently liked the program, despite (or perhaps because of) its intense interest in and scrutiny of their personal lives. They were very diligent in their work and got so they could answer questions at a rate faster than the computer could supply them (a newer model computer and improvements in the operating system have solved this problem), producing far more information per minute than if they had been restricted to the more traditional paper-and-pencil format. The data they produced were exceptionally "clean," in part because the computer had been programmed to wait for a formally appropriate answer before continuing to the next question and in part because they learned with practice how to operate the keyboard effectively.

Participants showed great interest in the project and worked diligently to provide large quantities of very clean data. They were also conscientious about their participation, enabling us to continue the study over an entire academic year, with an attrition of only seven respondents (who were replaced).

We used several cognitive tasks to measure the effect of social loafing in addition to the physically effortful tasks of shouting and clapping reported above. Three tasks were chosen to tap cognitive effort—a symbol manipulation task, an idea generation task, and a task involving judgment. In the first, participants were asked to solve anagrams, in the second to brainstorm uses for objects, and in the third to judge the creativity of the uses suggested by others.

On four occasions throughout the year, participants were asked to work on anagrams—forming new words at least four letters long by rearranging stimulus words such as *MASTER, RAMBLE*, or *DETAIL*. The computer would present each word and evaluate the responses, accepting correct answers and rejecting incorrect or repetitive ones. Participants could work as long as they wished on each stimulus word.

Participants worked on two stimulus words in each session. For one, they were responsible for completing the task alone, the results of which would be entered into the computer files under their individual names. For another, they worked as part of a three-person group, the members of which were jointly responsible for the score that would be entered into the files under the group's name. For half the team efforts, participants believed they were working with their regular standing group, the people they knew and "talked" with every week. On the other half, they were told that they were working with two other anonymous individuals whose identities they would never know. Of course, the association of stimulus word with condition, the order of words, and the order of conditions were all counterbalanced across respondents.

In the first two sessions, respondents were aware that everyone was given the same stimulus words, allowing them to feel that their efforts were redundant with those of their fellow participants when working in groups. In the last two administrations, respondents working together were given different words to work on, although they were actually composed of the same letters presented in different orders. For example, one group member might be assigned CANTER, while the other two would work on NECTAR and TRANCE.

Thus, our research included two general manipulations common to social loafing studies: (1) comparison of performance of the individual to that of the group and (2) comparison of the social loafing effect when working with a standing group as opposed to working with an anonymous collection of individuals.

As one might expect, practice at doing anagrams led to an improvement in performance, in this case averaging about 16 percent in the number of words per minute from the first to the second session within each word set. Some of this improvement in skill was used to produce more anagrams, but much was used to justify quitting sooner—respondents reduced the amount of time they spent on each word from 10.3 minutes in the first session to 9.6 in the second and 7.7 in the third and fourth. This suggests that whatever intrinsic interest the task may have had tended to dissipate and that participants were not motivated to work beyond the limits of their perceived responsibility.

Respondents produced more new words when working as individuals than they did in groups. Overall, they found an average of 14.5 different correct words when working as individuals but only 13.4 words, 92 percent of their alone rate, when working as part of a group ($p < .001$). Participants reduced their output when working in their regular standing groups as well as when working in anonymous ad hoc groups, although males did show statistically higher levels of social loafing in anonymous groups than in their regular groups.

What accounts for this difference? Did participants concentrate on the task more when working for themselves? Did they work more rapidly? Were they more persistent? The evidence points to the time spent on the task as the primary mediator of the effect. When working in groups, respondents spent an average of 8.3 minutes on each word, only 89 percent of the 9.4 minutes they spent trying to find anagrams by themselves $(p < .02)$.

If the difference in performance were due to differences in concentration, pace, or other aspects of thought quality, it should lead to more efficient performance and the production of increased numbers of correct anagrams per unit of time, but there was no significant difference between performance in the individual and group settings on this measure.

Finally, there was also a significant tendency for the size of the loafing effect to decrease over repeated administration of the task $(p < .03)$. There are a number of possible reasons for this trend (for example, decreasing salience of the manipulation, ceiling effects), but there is no way to decide among them without further research.

In summary, we found social loafing, even on a cognitive task and even in the absence of direct contact among group members, and we found it to about the same extent (92 percent) as in research on noisemaking. Interestingly, the amount of loafing decreased over time and/or experience with the task and the group, but it is impossible to determine the cause of this effect from the data. Finally, these effects were entirely due to the amount of time devoted to the task—participants produced the same number of solutions per minute in all conditions but differed only in how many minutes they persisted in looking for solutions, suggesting that sharing responsibility with others affects only the quantity, not the quality, of cognitive effort.

We used a variant of the popular brainstorming task to see whether there would be social loafing on a cognitive task requiring the generation of ideas. Respondents were asked to suggest uses for everyday objects, such as a knife, a shoe box, a detached doorknob, or a burned-out light bulb. As in the anagrams study, there were four administrations of the task with respondents performing in both group and individual conditions within each session, again with both their standing and with an anonymous group. In sessions 1 and 2 (weeks 4 and 7) the goal of the task was the production of a large number of uses. In sessions 3 and 4 (weeks 11 and 13), respondents were asked to be as creative as possible in their uses.

Results of the brainstorming studies support the conclusions of the anagrams studies. Respondents produced fewer possible uses for the objects when working in groups—7.37, only 95 percent of the 7.74 suggestions generated when working as individuals ($p < .01$). This appears to be due to reduced persistence, since the 4.5 minutes they worked on the task was only 96 percent of the time they spent when working as individuals ($p < .05$). There is no evidence that social loafing affects efficiency (suggestions per minute) or the quality of the product as measured by judgments of the creativity of the suggestions (see below). As in the anagrams task, respondents spent less time on task when working with others, leading to reductions in the amount but not the quality of the product. Thus, these two sets of studies agree. There is social loafing on cognitive tasks. It appears to operate by influencing the amount of time spent working on the task, rather than by affecting the amount of concentration or efficiency of thought.

We asked all CAPS/84 participants to serve as judges in evaluating the creativity of each other's suggestions in the idea generation task. Judges were given sets of actual suggestions and asked to rate them. Each saw four suggestion sets generated by other (unidentified) respondents plus two common suggestion sets. For some ratings, respondents were told that they were the only judge of a particular suggestion set; for others, they were told that they were one of five judges who would be determining the creativity of that set.

Whether responsibility was focused or shared had no effect on the average rating of creativity, but it did affect the degree to which judges differentiated their judgments. Participants were far more discriminating in the individual condition. When working with a list of three sets of uses to be rated, respondents made larger differentiations when they believed themselves to be the sole judge and relatively few discriminations when they believed themselves one of five judges. The variance of judgments of creativity was significantly higher when the judges believed they were the only ones responsible for rating a suggestion set than when they believed others were also evaluating the same materials ($p < .03$).

Of the research to date on social loafing, this is the only hint we have so far that actual decision-making strategy—that is, the quality of thought—is subject to social loafing. While it is possible that the reduced discrimination was simply the result of spending less time on the task, it seems unlikely.

Conclusions and Implications for Organizations

Social loafing does occur on cognitive as well as physical tasks, for standing as well as ad hoc groups, even when interaction is computer mediated. Therefore, there is every reason to believe that the potential for social loafing exists in modern business organizations. Every time people walk away from a problem because they think someone else will solve it, every time a group of committee members sit around a table waiting for one another to come to grips with a problem rather than knuckling down to concentrated thought, every time managers fail to run through all the permutations and possibilities just because they have not been specifically assigned to do so, social loafing may be to blame.

Much, however, has yet to be learned about social loafing in organizations. The present line of research, like the theory of social impact that generated it, does not deal directly with organizations or even, for that matter, with groups. Rather, the emphasis is on how individuals define their own priorities and goals as a function of the social context in which they work. Diffusion of responsibility may lead individuals to exert less effort on shared tasks. Is it possible that comparable processes operate at the level of the group itself?

An organization can be seen as consisting of an interrelated set of groups, usually with incompletely defined charges and responsibilities. Is there diffusion of responsibility among the subgroups in an organization? Are some kinds of groups (newly formed groups, groups with internal conflict, groups with a history of past failure) more likely to loaf than others? How can an organization best develop procedures for the assignment of responsibility and the communication of expectations about performance to its subunits and for holding them accountable for meeting them? Does social loafing occur only in the absence of well-defined norms, or can it be overcome through negotiation, contracting, and the focusing of responsibility?

Advantages of Collective Action. Collective action clearly has much to recommend it, and it proliferates, even in our ideologically antagonistic society. Several persons working together should always be able to accomplish at least as much as one person working alone, simply by letting each additional person watch. In most circumstances, of course, a group should be able to accomplish much more. If you can get someone to work with (or for) you, you can accomplish more with the same amount of effort than if you work alone. This advantage is appropriate for maximizing tasks in which more is better, as when you are producing goods for an unlimited market. Or, if you can get someone to work with (or for) you, the same task can be completed with less of your own effort. This advantage is most relevant for optimizing tasks in which excess production is redundant or useless. (Perhaps part of the process leading to social loafing is that people expect the second benefit in situations where the first is more appropriate.)

Finally, in many situations, people working together can be expected to do much better than the same number working alone. Success in many tasks involves overcoming some threshold or attaining some minimal standard of performance. Some tasks, impossible for any individual to complete alone, may be no problem for a group because of its greater resources—for example, lifting a heavy weight.

Advantages of Responsibility. People want responsibility when it carries power or conveys the rights of ownership. Having "responsibility" for something is often taken to mean having the right to decide how some resource is to be used, and that right, of course, carries the benefit of being able to enjoy the resource oneself. Individuals seem less enthusiastic about assuming responsibility when the payoff for its faithful discharge is collective rather than personal.

Advantages of Social Loafing. Social loafing can be seen as the legitimate enjoyment of one of the benefits of collective action—the opportunity to accomplish unpleasant tasks with much less effort. Few people believe in work for its own sake, and it may be that loafing contributes to job satisfaction and the quality of work life. Although loafing would seem to have primarily negative effects on short-term productivity, it is possible that its individual or long-range effects are more positive. Although the lack of individual recognition and control may lead people to dislike collective tasks, if people prefer work settings that allow for the sharing of responsibility, this potential may attract them to group tasks. It is therefore important to discover whether social loafing can be eliminated only at the expense of individual satisfaction and enjoyment of the task.

Although some people still think science should be value free, I must confess that I think social loafing can be regarded as a kind of social disease. It is a "disease" in that it has negative consequences for individuals, groups, organizations, and societies. Social loafing results in a reduction in human efficiency that leads to lowered outcomes and benefits for all. It is "social" in that it results from the presence or actions of other people. As in the tragedy of the commons, where the short-run advantage for each in taking destroys the long-run advantage for all in having, the danger of social loafing is that the short-run benefit of not giving results in lost opportunities in the long run for all.

The cure, however, is not to do away with groups, because despite their inefficiency, groups make possible the achievement of many goals that individuals alone could not possibly accomplish. Groups and organizations do perform better than individuals, and most of us spend most of our lives in them. Collective action is a vital aspect of our lives.

I think the "cure" will come from finding ways of channeling social forces so that the group will serve as a means of intensifying individual responsibility rather than diffusing it. Group cohesion and an increased sense of individual control, identifiability, and accountability may neutralize or reverse the effects of social loafing. I hope that through further study of cheering and other group tasks we will be able to discover techniques for getting people to pull together without pulling less hard. This would allow the old saying "Many hands make light the work" to be true in a less negative sense than documented in this chapter. If we can learn to structure collective jobs so that the help of many hands reduces the onus but not the joy of work, working together could make our work lives brighter.

References

Beza, A., and Latané, B. "Multipurpose Data Collection Facility at the Institute for Research in Social Science." *Social Science News Letter*, 1983, *68*, 27–31.

Gabrenya, W., Latané, B., and Wang, Y. "Social Loafing in Cross-Cultural Perspective: Chinese on Taiwan." *Journal of Cross-Cultural Psychology*, 1983, *14*, 368–384.

Harkins, S., Latané, B., and Williams, K. "Social Loafing: Allocating Effort or Taking It Easy?" *Journal of Experimental Social Psychology*, 1980, *16*, 457–465.

Ingham, A. G., Levinger, G., Graves, J., and Peckman, V. "The Ringelman Effect: Studies of Group Size and Group Performance." *Journal of Experimental Social Psychology*, 1974, *10*, 371–384.

Latané, B. "The Psychology of Social Impact." *American Psychologist*, 1981, *36*, 343–356.

Latané, B., and Darley, J. M. *The Unresponsive Bystander: Why Doesn't He Help?* East Norwalk, Conn.: Appleton-Century-Crofts, 1970.

Latané, B., and Nida, S. "Ten Years of Research on Group Size and Helping." *Psychological Bulletin*, 1981, *89*, 307–324.

Latané, B., Williams, K., and Harkins, S. "Many Hands Make Light the Work: The Causes and Consequences of Social Loafing." *Journal of Personality and Social Psychology*, 1979, *37*, 822–832.

Long, W. A., and Seo, K. K. *Management in Japan and India*

with Reference to the United States. New York: Praeger, 1977.

Moede, W. "Die Richtlinien der Leistungs-Psychologie." *Industrielle Psychotechnik,* 1927, *4,* 193-207.

Steiner, I. D. *Group Process and Productivity.* Orlando, Fla.: Academic Press, 1972.

Williams, K., Harkins, S., and Latané, B. "Identifiability and Social Loafing: Two Cheering Experiments." *Journal of Personality and Social Psychology,* 1981, *40,* 303-311.

Williams, K., and Williams, K. "The Development of Social Loafing in the United States." Paper presented at the Second Asian Conference of the International Association for Cross-Cultural Psychology, Taipei, 1981.

Williams, K., Williams, K., Kawana, Y., and Latané, B. "Social Loafing in Japan: A Developmental Cross-Cultural Study." Paper presented at meeting of the Midwestern Psychological Association, Chicago, 1984.

9

Thought Experiments
and the Problem
of Sparse Data
in Small-Group
Performance Research

James H. Davis
Norbert L. Kerr

The steady increase in social research during this century is astonishing. For the past three decades the effort has been especially rapid and has led to a very large literature of empirical studies. However, beginning about a decade and a half ago, a strong movement developed to demonstrate the relevance of social research to society's needs. Applied social psychology was not new, but the *intensity* of interest was different; indeed the particular focus of application continues to change. Along with the "new concern" there arose considerable disappointment about the degree of apparent usefulness of much empirical social research. There seem to have been at least two general kinds of disappointment: (1) Findings were judged to be "unstable." Often results from research conducted at one place or

Note: This research was supported in part by the National Science Foundation, grant SES 83-10797, to the University of Illinois, James H. Davis, principal investigator.

305

time was not consistent with data gathered earlier from elsewhere. (2) Despite the large number of empirical findings there rarely appeared to be a good one-to-one match between available empirical results and an applied question. Such poor matches often resulted in a plea to "do one more study" and sometimes in outright condemnation of the social psychology enterprise as irrelevant.

These two sources of discontent seem to have figured significantly in the rise of the "crisis in social psychology" so important to critics of the day (for example, Gergen, 1973). One general response to the "crisis," or disappointment with social research, was to advocate collecting more data, especially in the "field" or the "real world." The real world or the field were generally thought to be places such as organizations and institutions where people typically behaved "naturally." Among the more important activities of an especially interpersonal character were those associated with deciding criminal guilt, constructing corporate policy, establishing cabinet positions, or selecting new personnel.

This chapter will address the collection of problems we have outlined above, not by suggesting a reduction in our commitment to empirical research but by suggesting that thought experiments *supplement* such efforts. The *thought experiment* is an aid to extrapolating from known empirical results and interpolating between existing sets of findings. At the most fundamental level, the thought experiment is simply another name for simulation/modeling. We have chosen the label *thought experiment* partly as a disguise in order to achieve greater acceptability than heretofore among social researchers and partly to stress the implications of results rather than the mechanics of calculation.

Mathematical models in social psychology have typically been used, as in other fields, for explanation and prediction of empirical phenomena. There has been almost no use of modeling in the fashion we shall suggest here—a sharp contrast to other sciences, ranging from aeronautical engineering to economics. There are probably several reasons for this reluctance to use models in the design of institutions, the evaluation of social change, or the description of organizational systems that are too complex for direct study in a simple way. We suspect at least one of these may be due to a history in which schools of psychology, grand systems for understanding "man," and armchair psychology for so long played a significant role with minimal guidance from systematically gathered data. From another perspective, the political and religious ideologies of social thought have sometimes been so coherent, comprehensive, and intuitively compelling that data seem superfluous—a problem that has plagued social and behavioral science from earliest times to the present day. Indeed, statements of "show me your data" or "let the data do the talking" have proved valuable tools for refuting ideologically derived assertions about social behavior.

In any event, it now seems useful to consider some kinds of formal theory (whether mathematical or computer models, or something else) for assessing the practical impact of social and institutional changes, and especially proposals for such. In the future we may find that many rich and interesting theories of social behavior, now largely posed in verbal form, may benefit from the quantitative treatment we see routinely in, say, economics. In this connection, it is worthwhile to note that Harris (1976) has advanced the notion that many logical consequences of current theories in social psychology are not intuitively obvious. Moreover, unsuspected contradictions and inconsistencies are sometimes evident upon more formal treatment that allows extended examination.

We will explore below several examples of thought experiments taken from the general area of group performance. Again, our major objective will not be to supplant data by theory but to supplement existing empirical data with plausible theoretical models. Thought experiments, too, require data, if for no other reason than the replacement of assumptions about parameters with good estimates.

Group Decision Making: Jury Verdicts

We first consider extrapolations from a substantial set of data to a fairly specific social institution: the jury. This shift entails restrictions on potential thought experiments as a result of custom and law. A full description of the current role of the jury in contemporary civil and criminal proceedings in the United States is beyond the scope of this discussion. (See Gleisser, 1968, and Van Dyke, 1977, for comprehensive accounts.) However, we might note that the jury is a popular institution. Legislative or judicial actions affecting it stimulate considerable interest among experts and laymen alike. For our purposes, jury research illustrates well the difficulties often associated with obtaining social system information.

There are strict legal restrictions on directly gathering data from juries during actual deliberation. Moreover, trial records are frequently ambiguous, and, in any event, represent a single jury hearing a unique case. Finally, there is no single entity that can be clearly labeled *the* jury. In addition to the federal court system, the various state court systems may differ and judicial practices vary in subtle but important ways from jurisdiction to jurisdiction. With not one but several "targets," thought experiments are an especially important supplement to empirical research in jury behavior.

In a criminal trial, the jury is assigned the task of determining guilt, whereas in a civil trial it must assign culpability. The former setting occasionally finds the jury subsequently recommending or even setting sentence in a few instances, and the latter usually must award damages or the like. Most of the empirical research effort to date has focused upon criminal trials and the behavior of individual jurors. The obvious difficulty in obtaining sufficient samples of juries has proved to be a serious handicap. Finally, it is important to recognize that most data (for the reasons mentioned earlier) come from mock trial experiments in which subjects are recruited to play the role of jurors (Bray and Kerr, 1982). (See Davis, Bray, and Holt, 1977, and Kerr and Bray, 1982, for comprehensive reviews of empirical and theoretical research on jurors and juries alike.) This discussion will be concerned only with criminal juries and with just three features of juries: jury size, jury composition, and assigned decision rule.

Social Decision Scheme Theory. Historically, criminal juries in the United States have deliberated to a unanimous verdict; whatever the initial array of opinion might have been, the

verdict was returned when all members of the jury agreed upon
a verdict. Supreme Court decisions in recent years have held
that state or federal law permitting juries less than unanimous
verdicts are not prohibited by the Constitution (*Apodaca and
others* v. *Oregon,* 1972; *Johnson* v. *Louisiana,* 1972). Indeed,
the controversial nature of these decisions led to much of the
current interest in group social decision rules. Currently, some
social decision rules less than unanimity are permitted, most frequently a two-thirds majority being sufficient to establish a verdict. From the standpoint of the social researcher, we are concerned with any effects from the array of various majorities
running from simple to some higher order; an exhaustive evaluation of jury performance would inspect this entire array.
Moreover, the social decision rule *assigned* to a jury may influence but may not completely determine the social combination
process that actually provides the best prediction of the final
verdict. Consequently, we may think of the social combination
rule actually best describing the social deliberation process,
whatever the voting mechanics, as a *social decision scheme.* A
social decision scheme is a summary principle describing the
interpersonal interaction that acts upon the initial individual
member input and yields the final group output—in this case,
the verdict. More precisely, for every possible array of opinion
at the outset of group deliberation, there is some probability
of this interaction yielding a *guilty, not guilty,* or *hung* outcome (for the jury that cannot satisfy the decision rule). Some
alternative decision schemes for six-, nine-, and twelve-person
juries are given in Table 9-1 by way of illustration.

Observe that the distribution of initial preferences of individual jurors (along the rows) is between a guilty and a not
guilty verdict, since the undecided juror is obligated to favor
not guilty under legal norms. Jury deliberation, however, has
three possible outcomes: guilty, not guilty, or hung. Entries in
the matrices show outcomes under four different social decision schemes. The first matrix of the top row shows that a
two-thirds majority (also a simple majority for the six-person
jury) determines a verdict when it exists after the start of deliberation, but for an initial three-three split the predicted out-

Table 9-1. Matrices of Social Decision Rule Possibilities for Criminal Juries.

Initial (G, NG) Distribution	Outcome														
	G	NG	H	G	NG	H	G	NG	H	G	NG	H	G	NG	H
Six-Person Juries															
(6,0)	1	0	0	1	0	0	1	0	0	1	0	0	1	0	0
(5,1)	1	0	0	1	0	0	1	0	0	1	0	0	0	0	1
(4,2)	1	0	0	1	0	0	0	0	1	0	0	1	0	0	1
(3,3)	0	0	1	0	0	1	0	0	1	0	0	1	0	0	1
(2,4)	0	1	0	0	1	0	0	0	1	0	0	1	0	0	1
(1,5)	0	1	0	0	1	0	0	1	0	0	0	1	0	0	1
(0,6)	0	1	0	0	1	0	0	1	0	0	1	0	0	1	0
Nine-Person Juries															
(9,0)	1	0	0	1	0	0	1	0	0	1	0	0	1	0	0
(8,1)	1	0	0	1	0	0	1	0	0	1	0	0	0	0	1
(7,2)	1	0	0	1	0	0	1	0	0	0	0	1	0	0	1
(6,3)	1	0	0	1	0	0	0	0	1	0	0	1	0	0	1
(5,4)	1	0	0	0	0	1	0	0	1	0	0	1	0	0	1
(4,5)	0	1	0	0	0	1	0	0	1	0	0	1	0	0	1
(3,6)	0	1	0	0	1	0	0	0	1	0	0	1	0	0	1
(2,7)	0	1	0	0	1	0	0	1	0	0	0	1	0	0	1
(1,8)	0	1	0	0	1	0	0	1	0	0	1	0	0	0	1
(0,9)	0	1	0	0	1	0	0	1	0	0	1	0	0	1	0

Twelve-Person Juries

(12,0)	1	0	0	1	0	0	1	0	0	1	0	0
(11,1)	1	0	0	0	1	0	1	0	0	0	1	0
(10,2)	1	0	0	0	1	0	0	1	0	0	1	0
(9,3)	1	0	0	0	1	0	0	1	0	0	1	0
(8,4)	1	0	0	0	1	0	0	1	0	0	1	0
(7,5)	1	0	0	0	1	0	0	1	0	0	1	0
(6,6)	0	1	0	0	1	0	0	1	0	0	1	0
(5,7)	0	1	0	0	1	0	0	1	0	0	1	0
(4,8)	0	1	0	0	1	0	0	1	0	0	1	0
(3,9)	0	1	0	0	1	0	0	1	0	0	1	0
(2,10)	0	1	0	0	1	0	0	0	1	0	1	0
(1,11)	0	1	0	0	1	0	0	0	1	0	1	0
(0,12)	0	1	0	0	0	1	0	0	1	0	0	1

Note: G = guilty, NG = not guilty, H = hung jury.

come is hung. The second matrix in the top row shows a majority of five-sixths determining a verdict; otherwise the outcome is hung. All matrices in the table are read in a similar fashion. Observe that the *size* of the jury determines what social decision schemes are even possible. Size is especially important in determining the opportunity for ties or preference arrays that do not meet a majority rule. For example, there is no possible tie between jurors inclined to guilty and not guilty in nine-person juries, but the possibility exists for six- or twelve-person juries. Such nuances of size and rule interaction can play an important, though often quite subtle, procedural role in determining outcomes.

Next, we entertain the notion that, given a particular distribution of opinion at the outset, there may be only some *probability* that a guilty, not guilty, or hung verdict will follow. The confluence of numerous personal and social interaction variables moderates a certain determination of outcome by relative numbers of advocates. Thus, conditional probabilities, $[d_{ij}]$, replace the binary entries in the social decision scheme matrices. Examples for juries of six, nine, and twelve are given in Table 9-2.

The $m \times n$ social decision scheme matrices, D, of Table 9-2 summarize the many complexities of social interaction, whereby the ith of the m possible initial distributions of member opinion will ultimately lead to the jth of $n = 3$ outcomes (for the case at hand) with probability d_{ij}. Thus, the matrix D may constitute a social theoretical summary of the deliberation process. (For a detailed discussion of social decision scheme theory, see Davis, 1973, 1980; Stasser, Kerr, and Davis, 1980; and Stasser, Kerr, and Bray, 1982.)

In general, social decision scheme theory is a means of connecting the probability distribution, $p = (p_G, p_{NG})$, of individual jurors' verdict preferences with the outcome distribution, $P = (P_G, P_{NG}, P_H)$, of juries by means of summary assumptions about the social process implicit in D, which are only imperfectly observable in most circumstances. Empirical estimates, $\hat{p}$ and $\hat{P}$, are sometimes available but usually for only a few mock jury studies!

Before evaluating the effects of size and social decision scheme in light of various changes in juror guilt preferences, it might be useful to note that the present approach deals only with procedural, not distributive, justice. Moreover, correctness of verdict is not at issue. The true verdict, guilty or not guilty, is unknown. There is no probability attached to that event, and we have no means of discovering it in any case.

Thought Experiments: Jury Size and Assigned Decision Rule. In order to make projections about the effects of different jury sizes, it is necessary to assume something about the social decision scheme. Consequently, consider Table 9-2 again. The middle two matrices in each row of the table represent idealizations of a two-thirds majority rule, differing only in the way nonmajorities are treated. In one case, if a two-thirds majority does not exist, then the jury is as likely to choose guilty as not guilty; in the other, observe that the lack of a two-thirds majority results in a hung jury with a probability near 1.00. (Since entries are probabilities, values of 1.00 and 0.00 should be regarded as very near 0 or 1.) Some jury sizes, of course, require some further rounding (for example, note that two-thirds majorities are imperfectly realizable in a jury of ten persons).

Next, matrices in the first and last columns of Table 9-2 represent less familiar social decision schemes. Arrays in the first column reflect a proportionality principle, and those in the last a majority of sorts, but one with a dependent protection bias—a tendency actually observed in six-person mock juries (Davis, Stasser, Spitzer, and Holt, 1976; Davis and others, 1977). The first and last matrices for nine- and twelve-person juries are idealizations or extrapolations from the six-person cases. Thus, they represent plausible conjectures to aid us in illustrating verdict outcomes with juries not operating on the tidier (and more nearly symmetrical) social decision schemes implied by such phrases from conventional wisdom as *majority rules.*

Calculations have been carried through using the social decision schemes of Table 9-2. Figure 9-1 shows P_G, P_{NG}, P_H as a function of p_G for juries of six, nine, and twelve. The role of size is perhaps even more evident in Figure 9-2, left-

Table 9-2. Possible Social Decision Scheme Matrices for Criminal Juries.

(G, NG) Distribution	Outcome											
	G	NG	H	G	NG	H	G	NG	H	G	NG	H

Six-Person Juries

(G, NG) Distribution	G	NG	H	G	NG	H	G	NG	H	G	NG	H
(6,0)	1.00	.00	.00	1.00	.00	.00	1.00	.00	.00	1.00	.00	.00
(5,1)	.83	.17	.00	1.00	.00	.00	1.00	.00	.00	.93	.07	.00
(4,2)	.67	.33	.00	1.00	.00	.00	1.00	.00	1.00	.84	.16	.00
(3,3)	.50	.50	.00	.50	.50	.00	.00	1.00	.00	.16	.68	.16
(2,4)	.33	.67	.00	.00	1.00	.00	.00	1.00	.00	.06	.94	.00
(1,5)	.17	.83	.00	.00	1.00	.00	.00	1.00	.00	.00	1.00	.00
(0,6)	.00	1.00	.00	.00	1.00	.00	.00	1.00	.00	.00	1.00	.00

Nine-Person Juries

(G, NG) Distribution	G	NG	H	G	NG	H	G	NG	H	G	NG	H
(9,0)	1.00	.00	.00	1.00	.00	.00	1.00	.00	.00	1.00	.00	.00
(8,1)	.89	.11	.00	1.00	.00	.00	1.00	.00	.00	.97	.03	.00
(7,2)	.78	.22	.00	1.00	.00	.00	1.00	.00	.00	.90	.10	.00
(6,3)	.67	.33	.00	1.00	.00	.00	1.00	.00	.00	.80	.15	.05
(5,4)	.56	.44	.00	.50	.50	.00	.00	1.00	1.00	.70	.20	.10
(4,5)	.44	.56	.00	.50	.50	.00	.00	1.00	1.00	.05	.85	.10
(3,6)	.33	.67	.00	.00	1.00	.00	.00	1.00	.00	.05	.90	.05
(2,7)	.22	.78	.00	.00	1.00	.00	.00	1.00	.00	.00	.95	.05
(1,8)	.11	.89	.00	.00	1.00	.00	.00	1.00	.00	.00	1.00	.00
(0,9)	.00	1.00	.00	.00	1.00	.00	.00	1.00	.00	.00	1.00	.00

Twelve-Person Juries

	G	NG	H	G	NG	H	G	NG	H	G	NG	H
(12,0)	1.00	.00	.00	1.00	.00	.00	1.00	.00	.00	1.00	.00	.00
(11,1)	.92	.08	.00	1.00	.00	.00	1.00	.00	.00	1.00	.00	.00
(10,2)	.83	.17	.00	1.00	.00	.00	1.00	.00	.00	.97	.03	.00
(9,3)	.75	.25	.00	1.00	.00	.00	1.00	.00	.00	.95	.05	.00
(8,4)	.67	.33	.00	1.00	.00	.00	1.00	.00	.00	.85	.10	.05
(7,5)	.58	.42	.00	.50	.50	.00	.00	.00	1.00	.80	.15	.05
(6,6)	.50	.50	.00	.50	.50	.00	.00	.00	1.00	.10	.75	.15
(5,7)	.42	.58	.00	.50	.50	.00	.00	.00	1.00	.00	.90	.10
(4,8)	.33	.67	.00	.00	1.00	.00	.00	1.00	.00	.00	.90	.10
(3,9)	.25	.75	.00	.00	1.00	.00	.00	1.00	.00	.00	.95	.05
(2,10)	.17	.83	.00	.00	1.00	.00	.00	1.00	.00	.00	1.00	.00
(1,11)	.08	.92	.00	.00	1.00	.00	.00	1.00	.00	.00	1.00	.00
(0,12)	.00	1.00	.00	.00	1.00	.00	.00	1.00	.00	.00	1.00	.00

Note: G = guilty, NG = not guilty, H = hung jury.

Figure 9-1. Thought experiments showing the probability of conviction,
P_G (first row), acquittal, P_{NG} (second row), and hung, P_G (third row),
as function of individual jurors voting for a guilty verdict. The curves on
each panel reflect juries of different size (six, nine, and twelve).
The four panels in each row correspond exactly to the four social decision
schemes defined by the four columns of matrices of Table 9-2—informally
labeled Proportionality; Two-thirds Majority, Otherwise Hung; and
Defendant Protection (suggested by empirical data).

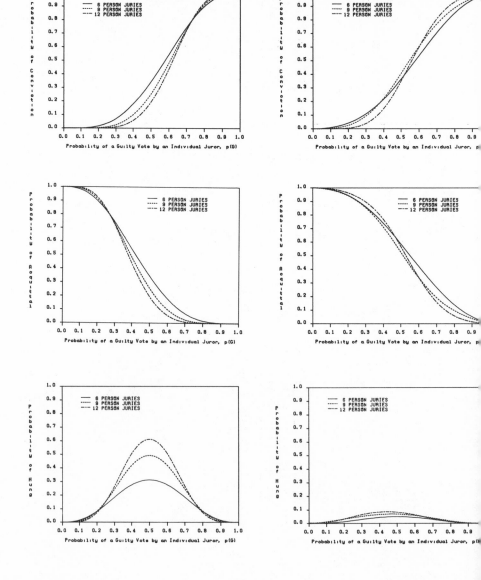

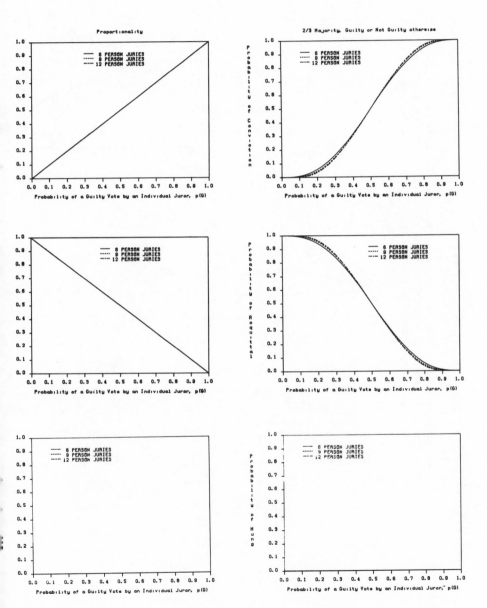

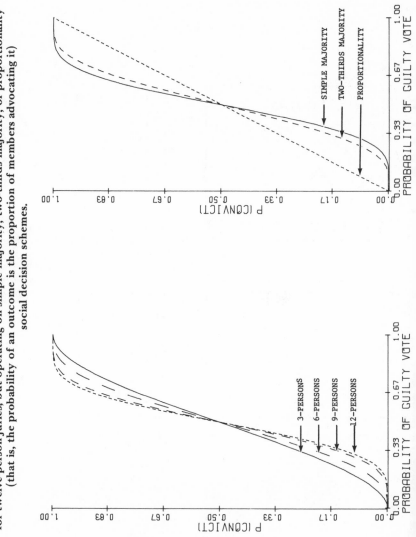

Figure 9-2. The left-hand panel shows the probability of conviction as a function of juror guilt preferences for various jury sizes, under the assumption of a simple majority; otherwise guilty or not guilty verdicts are returned with equal probability. The right-hand panel shows the same for twelve-person juries, but operating on simple majority, two-thirds majority, or proportionality (that is, the probability of an outcome is the proportion of members advocating it) social decision schemes.

hand panel, which assumes for purposes of our comparisons here a simple majority social decision scheme and only two outcomes (guilty, not guilty), chosen with equal probability if no majority exists. The right-hand panel of Figure 9-2 also reflects a simpler task (guilty or not guilty verdicts) but demonstrates for twelve-person groups the effect of three different social de-- cision schemes on the probability of a conviction as a function of the probability a juror will vote guilty.

Perhaps the most obvious conclusion evident from Figures 9-1 and 9-2 is that no single answer satisfies the question "What is the best size for a criminal jury?" When the probability of a guilty vote by an individual juror is small, the smaller jury is more likely to convict than the larger. Under most prevailing philosophical dispositions, this would suggest that the larger jury is a better choice than the smaller one; convicting the innocent is a more serious error than acquitting the guilty. When the probability of an individual voting guilty is high, the twelve-person jury is more likely to convict than, say, a six-person jury. Again, given the usual philosophical dispositions for protecting the defendant, the smaller jury might be regarded as superior to the larger, although some might favor the converse in "society's interests." Notice in Figure 9-1 that the larger jury is more likely to hang than a smaller one, particularly for very close cases (that is, $p_G \cong .50$).

Figures 9-1 and 9-2 also imply an important lesson for the conduct of empirical research intended to address the question of optimum size. A study (for example, a mock trial) with a case disposing jurors to respond such that p_G is small will yield one result, whereas a separate study using a case causing p_G to be large will yield a quite different result. This illustrates another important point. Thought experiments not only require data upon which to base model parameters (for example, the D matrix of the social decision scheme model), they can also help guide the collection of new data. The application of the two-thirds majority–hung otherwise decision scheme in Figure 9-1 suggests that the major impact of reducing jury size could be to reduce the rate of hung juries when cases are very close. Further, all the thought experiments to date suggest that jury size effects are rather small by typical social research standards. These conclusions suggest that previous studies of jury size may have generally failed to find any effect on jury verdicts (Hastie, Penrod, and Pennington, 1983) because their sample sizes were too small to detect such effects, their cases were not close enough, and/or they didn't examine the appropriate outcome measure (namely, hung jury rate). With these suggestions in mind, Kerr and MacCoun (1985) empirically reexamined the effects of mock jury size. But in contrast to previous work, they restricted their attention to rather close cases, focused mainly on hung jury rates, and made every effort to maximize the power of their tests. And, as suggested by the thought experiments reviewed above, Kerr and MacCoun found that for very close cases, mock jury size was directly and significantly related to hung jury rates, while there was no significant relation between jury size and conviction/acquittal rates. Thus, while research that was largely unguided by theory suggested that jury size did not affect deliberation outcome, research guided by thought experimentation (based on available theory *and* research) suggested quite a different conclusion. (See also Nagao and Davis, 1980, for further discussion of small effects and sample sizes in social research.)

The concern with jury size, like that of assigned decision rule, arose largely after Supreme Court decisions (*Colgrove* v. *Battin*, 1973; *Williams* v. *Florida*, 1970; *Ballew* v. *Georgia*, 1978). Overall, there seems to be little to support the notion of reducing jury size. Besides the antidefendant bias inherent in a reduction in overall hung jury rates (compare Kerr and others, 1976), it can also be shown (for example, Lempert, 1975) that reducing jury size also has pronounced and adverse effects on jury representativeness. Others (for example, Hastie, Penrod, and Pennington, 1983; Tanford and Penrod, 1983) have explored the effect of varying the jury's assigned decision rule through thought experimentation. Their primary finding—that nonunanimous juries are less likely to hang, especially for very close cases—has also been empirically confirmed (for example, Kerr and others, 1976). Many commentators have viewed with considerable distress, even alarm, the tendency of the criminal jury in the United States to decrease in size and the relaxation of the assigned decision rule (for example, Zeisel, 1971; Lempert, 1975). Thought experimentation has clearly guided empirical work to identify the small but nevertheless important effects of these changes in the jury system.

Summary. The relative unpopularity of group size research has been noted repeatedly. Research on the effect of assigned or institutionally imposed decision rules has, if anything, been even less popular. Thought experiments, such as the examples discussed above, provide an important supplement to the verbal theories that have heretofore been the only aid to conventional wisdom. Increases in group size tend generally to accentuate, in the group decision distributions, whatever perturbations exist in the individual decision preference distributions and to increase the probability of a hung jury. Reducing the level of consensus required for a verdict not only decreases the likelihood of a hung jury, it also has a similar effect of accentuating individual preferences. The outcome to be expected from changes in both simultaneously is not simple and not intuitively obvious.

We should also note that, in principle, there is no reason why size and assigned rule effects like those discussed here should be restricted to juries. Other task-oriented groups whose decision-making process can be accurately summarized by D matrices in similar fashion should exhibit similar effects. In particular, the jury-inspired social decision scheme matrices seem likely to provide at least a fair summary for groups in which each member has roughly equal formal power, in which initial majorities usually win, and which are more likely to deadlock as the initial split between subgroups or factions becomes more nearly equal in size. Intuition and theory (for example, Laughlin and Adamopoulos, 1982) suggest that this includes a very wide range of common decision-making groups located in a wide range of organizations and institutions.

Jury Selection

Between the abstract concept of a jury—a group of laypersons, untrained in the law, acting as referees of fact—and the realization of that concept lie a series of juror selection procedures. Juror selection is a multistaged, complex process that varies considerably across jurisdictions (Hans and Vidmar, 1982; Van Dyke, 1977). There are certain common features, however. First there must be legislation defining eligibility rules (for example, citizenship, fluency in English), rules governing waiver of service (for example, to certain professions like police officers and physicians), and terms of duty (varying from one day/ one trial to several weeks). A local official must maintain a list of potential jurors (most commonly based on voters' registration lists). Then a panel of potential jurors must be assembled at the court for final selection procedures. In all common-law countries those who have a demonstrable bias (for example, a relationship with a litigant or a personal interest in the outcome of the case) must be excluded; this is termed a *challenge for cause*. And in U.S. courts, opposing counsel are also given several additional "peremptory" challenges that may be exercised without explanation or justification.

A relatively new feature in jury selection is the use of social science methods to assist attorneys. A number of procedures, collectively referred to as *scientific jury selection* (SJS), have been used systematically by some (namely, Kairys, Schulman, and Harring, 1975; Schulman and others, 1973) in an attempt to secure advantage for, in these instances, the defense. For example, entire jury panels have been challenged using statistical data that establish that they are unrepresentative of the population of potential jurors (for example, *Castaneda v. Partida*, 1977; Michaelson, 1980). Another technique has been to provide evidence in support of a change in the location or venue of a trial. For example, social scientists have collected public opinion data using survey methods to support the argument that there is a general bias against a defendant in a particular locale (for example, due to extensive pretrial publicity—McConahay, Mullin, and Frederick, 1977; Vidmar and Judson, 1981). And an elaborate and controversial (for example, Berk, Hennessy, and Swan, 1977; Berman and Sales, 1977; Etzioni, 1974; Spector, 1974) technology has been developed to assist attorneys in the exercise of their challenges (for example, Schulman and others, 1973). These techniques include (1) investigating individual potential jurors through their neighbors, acquaintances, or other members of the local community; (2) surveying public opinion on key trial issues to develop demographic and attitudinal profiles of jurors favorable and unfavorable to one's case; and (3) using expert consultants in court to evaluate potential jurors' verbal and nonverbal behavior. Because of the expense involved, such techniques have been employed mostly in major cases that have attracted considerable public attention and support (for example, the Wounded Knee trial, the Joan Little trial).

In addition to the controversy concerning the ethics of SJS in practice, there is also disagreement about the effectiveness of such techniques (Berman and Sales, 1977; Saks and Hastie, 1978). Of course, the ethical and practical problems associated with a thorough empirical evaluation of SJS's effectiveness are enormous, and it is not surprising that none has been undertaken. Again, thought experiments offer a useful supplement to empirical research.

Thought Experiments: Scientific Jury Selection. Tindale and Nagao (1984) have carried out several thought experiments to explore the likely effects of SJS under various scenarios. First, they note that proponents of SJS (for example, Schulman, 1973) feel that SJS may be most valuable in helping to win changes of venue. So, the first issue Tindale and Nagao addressed was, how much impact on jury verdicts might be reasonably attributed to a change of venue? Of course, such effects would depend in part upon how different the jurors were in the venues in question. Tindale and Nagao contrasted three hypothetical venues: one in which only a large majority of jurors favored conviction (80 percent voting for guilty, 20 percent voting for not guilty); one containing a substantial minority favoring acquittal (60 percent guilty; 40 percent not guilty); and one for which there was equal support among individual jurors for conviction and acquittal (50 percent guilty; 50 percent not guilty). They assumed that twelve-person juries were randomly composed from each venue's juror population and that their deliberation process was summarized by a "two-thirds majority—defendant protection otherwise" social decision scheme, which is presented in Table 9-3. Such a matrix combines elements of the two-thirds majority–hung otherwise and majority with defendant protection schemes presented earlier in the third and fourth columns of Table 9-2. Asymmetric social decision schemes favoring the defendant have frequently been observed in mock trial studies (for example, Davis and others, 1975, 1977; Kerr and others, 1976).

Table 9-3. Social Decision Scheme for Twelve-Person Juries.

Initial (r_G, r_{NG}) Opinion Distribution	Jury Outcomes		
	G	NG	H
(12,0)	1.00	.00	.00
(11,1)	1.00	.00	.00
(10,2)	1.00	.00	.00
(9,3)	1.00	.00	.00
(8,4)	1.00	.00	.00
(7,5)	.00	.75	.25
(6,6)	.00	.75	.25
(5,7)	.00	.75	.25
(4,8)	.00	1.00	.00
(3,9)	.00	1.00	.00
(2,10)	.00	1.00	.00
(1,11)	.00	1.00	.00
(0,12)	.00	1.00	.00

Note: G = guilty, NG = not guilty, H = hung jury. Principle: Two-thirds majority establishes guilty, not guilty verdict with probability near 1.0, otherwise $P(NG) = .75$, $P(H) = .25$
Source: Adapted from Tindale and Nagao (1984), with permission.

Figure 9-3 shows the results of Tindale and Nagao's thought experiment. Focusing on the acquittal rates, we see that under their assumptions, jury acquittal rates would range from 5 percent (in the venue where 20 percent of the jurors acquit), to 44 percent (in the 40 percent juror acquittal venue), to 64 percent (when half of the jurors acquit). Thus, a venue-based difference of only 30 percent in *individual* acquittal rates would, under reasonable assumptions, translate into a striking 59 percent difference in *jury* acquittal rates due to change of venue. Clearly, even small between-venue differences can have dramatic effects on trial outcomes.

Figure 9.3. Predicted jury verdict consequences as a result
of a change in venue.

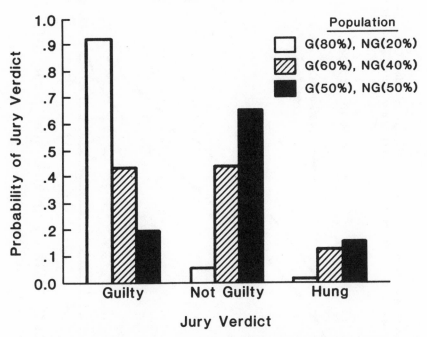

Note: Reprinted with permission from Tindale and Nagao, 1984.

Tindale and Nagao next considered the impact that SJS
might have during the juror selection phase of the trial. Assuming for the moment that SJS techniques have at least some
validity, they asked how much "better" could a hypothetical
defense counsel expect to do in a trial having used SJS than not
using these procedures? In particular, Tindale and Nagao made
the modest assumption that the net consequences of *all* SJS
procedures affected by the defense attorneys would be to ensure that the jury would have *one more advocate* for acquittal
than it would have had without using SJS techniques. Again
they assumed that twelve-person juries were randomly composed and deliberated under the same decision scheme as before. The results of their thought experiment appear in Figure
9-4 as a function of the probability, p_G, that an individual juror

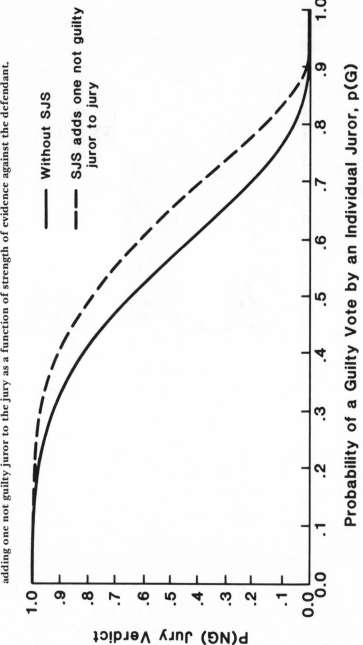

Figure 9-4. Predicted not guilty verdict consequences of scientific jury selection adding one not guilty juror to the jury as a function of strength of evidence against the defendant.

Note: Reprinted with permission with Tindale and Nagao, 1984.

votes for conviction. Clearly, when the case is lopsided (that is, p_G is near 0.0 or 1.0), SJS would not have much impact, but for more uncertain cases (that is, $p_G \cong .50$) it could have a fairly substantial effect (reaching a maximum effect of 19 percent for cases that are moderately strong against the defendant). One can easily imagine the difficulty of establishing this result through empirical study alone, unguided by theory. However, thought experiments (such as those of Tindale and Nagao) could help focus research effort and more efficiently use resources (for example, subjects) by suggesting research targets that would be most likely to yield an effect, as well as its likely magnitude.

Thought Experiments: "Nonscientific" Jury Selection. The actual practice of juror selection stands in sharp contrast to the prescriptions of SJS. Observational research (for example, Broeder, 1965) has shown that in the average trial, examination of potential jurors is cursory and few if any of the available peremptory challenges are used. Further, the average attorney does not generally have the wealth of data on jurors generated by SJS. Rather, counsel must usually rely on superficial background characteristics that can be obtained through casual observation or questioning (for example, juror sex, occupation, ancestry). Although there exists an extensive folklore among lawyers attesting to the utility of such factors (for example, Bailey and Rothblatt, 1971), direct empirical research (for example, Penrod, 1979; Saks, 1976) suggests that such factors show, at best, a very weak relationship with verdict.[1]

Under typical constraints, just how much impact on jury verdicts can an attorney expect to have by recognizing a potential source of bias in a juror and exercising a challenge to eliminate that juror? In a recent series of thought experiments, Kerr and Huang (1984) explored this issue. Suppose some individual

---

1. One should also note, though, that there are exceptions to this rule. For example, a number of studies indicate that female mock jurors are more likely to vote for conviction in a rape case than males (Nagao and Davis, 1980). Other special-case exceptions can also be identified (for example, Catholic as opposed to nonCatholic jurors in a euthanasia case; Becker, Hildrun, and Bateman, 1965).

juror characteristic, X, is related to individual verdicts, as indexed by a product moment correlation coefficient r_J. Kerr and Huang asked the following question: How well would knowledge of one juror's status on X predict the verdict of his or her jury?

In their initial thought experiment, Kerr and Huang assumed that juries deliberated under a social decision scheme suggested by Zeisel and Diamond's (1978) observations of actual juries. That scheme is presented in Table 9-4. One can see

Table 9-4. Zeisel and Diamond's Decision Scheme.

Predeliberation Distribution		Final Group Decision		
%G	#G/#NG	G	NG	H
100	12/0	1.0	.0	.0
92	11/1	.97	.02	.01
83	10/2	.95	.03	.02
75	9/3	.91	.07	.02
67	8/4	.83	.13	.04
58	7/5	.70	.23	.07
50	6/6	.42	.46	.12
42	5/7	.21	.72	.07
33	4/8	.12	.85	.03
25	3/9	.06	.92	.02
17	2/10	.01	.97	.01
8	1/11	.0	.99	.01
0	0/12	.0	1.0	.0

Note: G = guilty, NG = not guilty, H = hung jury.

that it is similar to some of the previously discussed schemes: Large initial majorities usually prevail, hung juries are more likely when the jury is initially evenly split, and there is some indication of a prodefendant bias (although it is less pronounced than for some of the social decision scheme matrices that have been observed in mock jury studies, for which deliberation times are often limited). Kerr and Huang compared the amount of variance accounted for in jury verdicts (that is, r^2_{Jury}, where r_{Jury} = the correlation between a juror's status on X and the jury's verdict) with the amount of variance X accounts for in individual jurors' verdicts (namely, $r_I{}^2$). (See Kerr and Huang, 1984, for computational details.)

In Figure 9-5 we see the ratios of these two squared correlations as a function of the overall conviction rate for individual jurors, p_G, and the strength of X as a predictor (that is, r_I). As in Tindale and Nagao, the ratio is highest when the case is close; when the case is lopsided, knowledge of even a valid predictor of a juror's verdict is of less utility in predicting the jury's verdict. Also, unsurprisingly, the larger the value of r_I, the larger is the ratio, except for very lopsided cases. But the most important finding is that one can account for so little of the variance in jury verdicts from knowledge of a juror's status on X; under the present assumptions, the ratio was always less than .04. However, this result is consistent with the perennial finding that member personality traits are very poor predictors of group performance (Mann, 1959; Heslin, 1964), an empirical result usually attributable to poor assessment techniques, dependent as they are on questionnaire answering. However, the above results suggest that there may be a limit on the predictability of group outcomes from trait knowledge (at least using indices of linear relationships) that has a more complex origin than suspected heretofore. (See also the discussion by McGrath and Altman, 1966.)

Earlier we explored the effect of jury size on deliberation outcome. Similarly, Kerr and Huang examined the relevance of jury size for the current question by means of a thought experiment. They generalized from the decision scheme implied by Zeisel and Diamond's (1978) observations, discussed earlier, for one group size (namely, twelve-person juries) to other jury sizes (namely, six-, four-, and two-person groups). For this thought experiment, they also assumed that X was a moderately strong predictor of individual juror verdict preferences (specifically, that $r_I = .40$). Results are given in Figure 9-6. As intuition would suggest, a juror's characteristic became more predictive of the group's verdict as jury size decreased; but somewhat counter to intuition, it was never possible to predict more than about a quarter as much variance for the jury as for the juror, even in dyads.

Figure 9-5. Ratio of variance accounted for in a jury of twelve persons to variance accounted for in individual juror verdict preferences as a function of strength of evidence against the defendant and strength of the predictor of individual juror verdicts.

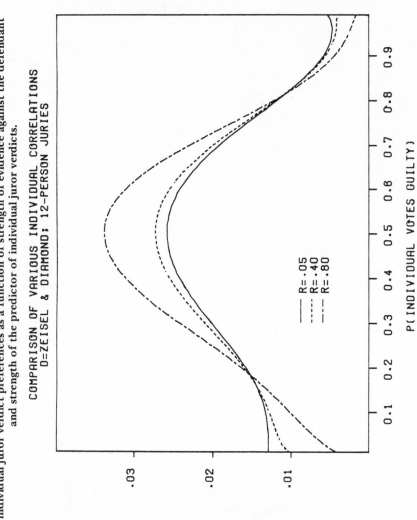

COMPARISON OF VARIOUS INDIVIDUAL CORRELATIONS
D=ZEISEL & DIAMOND: 12-PERSON JURIES

R=.05
R=.40
R=.80

P(INDIVIDUAL VOTES GUILTY)

Note: Reprinted with permission from Kerr and Huang, 1984.

Figure 9.6 Ratio of variance accounted for in the jury (of two, four, six, and twelve persons) to variance accounted for in juror verdict preferences as a function of strength of evidence against the defendant and jury size ($r_I = .40$, and the matrix D taken from Zeisel and Diamond, 1978).

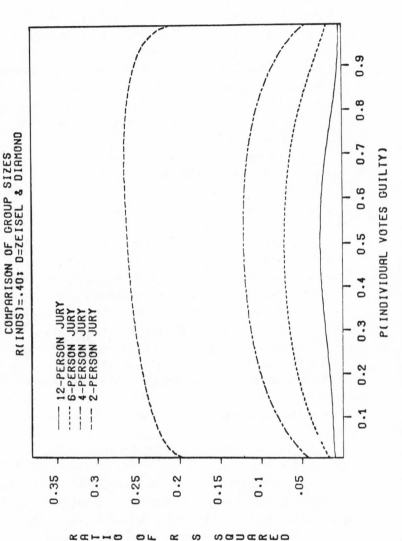

Note: Reprinted with permission from Kerr and Huang, 1984.

Summary and Implications. The preceding thought experiments demonstrate that different ways of approaching jury selection have rather different implications, some of which are counterintuitive. Even small differences between juror populations are exaggerated when one contrasts juries composed exclusively of members of one population with juries composed exclusively of those from another. On the other hand, even strong predictors of an *individual* juror's verdict preference will be far less useful in predicting the verdict of the jury of which that person is a member.

As noted earlier, it is important to recognize that the thought experiments discussed here have broader relevance than for jury behavior alone. Indeed, the results reported above have implications for various decision-making groups or committees whose deliberation processes can be reasonably summarized by the social decision schemes applied here and the conditions assumed in these conceptual studies. For example, a personnel manager can expect an *exaggeration* among decision-making committees of even relatively small differences in opinion found between alternative pools of committee members. Thus, one cannot reasonably expect to change the decisions of a committee very much by changing one committee member, A, for another, B—even if it is known that A and B hold opinions that differ a great deal. (Of course, such a conclusion would perhaps have to be modified under different conditions—changes in agenda structure, leader-follower relations, and so on.)

Organizational Structure and Decision Making

A fundamental problem in organizations is how to structure the system to best satisfy the organization's goals. For many organizations, these goals include reaching decisions that accurately and honestly reflect the preferences of the organization's members. Potentially relevant factors to be engineered include the number, size, and composition of constituent units in the organization and the formal (or informal) consensus criteria that apply at various levels of the organization (for example, the applicable decision or voting rules). The importance of such factors continues to be a matter of some controversy, not unlike the continuing debate about runoff elections in state primaries.

One approach to such questions, particularly popular in some areas of economics, has been to develop highly formal, axiomatic models of social choice (for example, Arrow, 1963). Social choice models (for example, Fishburn, 1973) resemble social decision scheme models in that they aim to translate individual decision preferences into group decisions. The two approaches differ in that social choice models typically work with a preference order (a set of ranked decision alternatives) and generally are not as concerned with the psychological plausibility of their assumptions; the latter concern with normative models usually leads to simulations that discover which group decisions (preference orders) are possible, desirable, optimal, and so on under various interesting conditions. Both approaches have much to offer in connection with thought experiments, depending upon one's purposes. (Indeed, descriptive and normative research efforts have independent and supplementary contributions to make to our understanding of group performance in general.) However, we are interested here in extending the social decision scheme model (especially those special cases that have been well supported in past, somewhat similar applications) to the organizational levels question implied above; that is, we will explore the behavior of the "flow of decisions" in hierarchically structured organizations composed of small, decision-making groups by means of thought experiments. Obviously, we must work with an idealized organization for this purpose but recognize that actual organizations are likely to be much less orderly in both structure and process.

Thought Experiments: Minority Size, Minority Integration, and Decision Process. Davis's (1973) exploration of the effect of several alternative social decision processes for final organizational decision offers a useful initial illustration. That investigation showed that if the original distribution of individual preferences was nonuniform, if the organization had a simple hierarchical structure (such that the decision made at one level would be carried on by that group's representative and ad-

vocated in the group at the next highest level), and if the decision-making process of groups at every level of the organization
could be summarized by a common decision scheme (namely, a
plurality determines the group choice), then the net effect of
the process of moving from individual members' preferences to
the final organizational decision would be to exaggerate at the
top (the final distribution of group decisions) the strength of
preference at the bottom of the organization. That is, the initially more popular alternatives become even more popular and
the less preferred alternatives become less preferred still as the
information (decision distribution) ascends the levels. If the organization has enough levels, minority preferences can be almost entirely suppressed. The thought experiment also demonstrated that different group decision processes (summarized by
different social decision schemes) would produce rather different effects. Various sorts of plurality schemes summarize decision processes for which there is strength in numbers, but depending on task demands and social context, among other
things, quite different social decision processes are likely to
emerge. (See Davis, 1982, for a discussion of social decision
schemes as a function of task types.) One process that seems to
characterize intellective tasks with no immediately obvious answer (for example, Davis, Hornik, and Hornseth, 1970) is the
equiprobability scheme, which holds that all alternatives with at
least one advocate are equally likely to be the group's choice. It
turns out that such a decision scheme tends to level the distribution of preferences, an effect that is compounded in a multileveled hierarchically structured organization—the leveling pro-
gressing as the hierarchy is ascended. Finally, we may note that
it is also possible to preserve the original distribution of individual preferences as the decisional information flows upward in
the organizational hierarchy as described above. Such preserva-
tion is maintained by a proportionality social decision scheme,
for which the probability of the group adopting an alternative is
equal to the relative frequency of advocates for a position.

The levels effect of the social decision processes just described is illustrated in Figure 9-7. In addition, the consequences
of an averaging social decision scheme (the group choice is the

arithmetic mean of the positions advocated) are shown for purposes of comparison. Clearly, the way interaction effectively aggregates member choices, as well as the number of levels to be traversed within the organization, exerts a powerful influence on the form of the information finally available at the top of the hierarchy. Observe, once more, that the degree of distortion (in the sense of inaccurately reflecting the grass-roots opinion) that may characterize the final distribution can be the consequence of a straightforward, sincere, democratic process, and in practice may go unrecognized by organization members.

The thought experiments just described assumed a single underlying population of individuals in the organization—a fairly unlikely lack of individual differences. Indeed, it is a more plausible assumption that an organization has several distinct subpopulations, possibly with different preference functions for each. Organizations also may differ in the organizational level at which their various subpopulations are integrated. In some cases, only units at the bottom of the organizational hierarchy may be homogeneous with respect to subpopulation membership—just as there may be less interpersonal variability within than between precincts in elections. In other cases, there may be more thorough integration of subpopulations throughout the organizational hierarchy.

Using a thought experiment, Ono and Hulin (1984) recently extended earlier (Davis, 1973) analyses to examine the impact of minority group integration in an organizational structure. In the interests of simplicity, they assumed that there were just three ordered decision alternatives, A_1, A_2, and A_3, and two subpopulations—a majority subpopulation that most strongly preferred alternative A_1, where the distribution of individual preferences was given by the probability vector p_M = (.433, .333, .233), and a minority subpopulation in which A_3 was the most preferred alternative, given by p_m = (.050, .100, .850). They further assumed five-person groups meeting at each level of a five-level organizational hierarchy. Again, the distribution of group decisions at one level was taken as the distribution of individual preference at the next higher level. Finally, Ono and Hulin contrasted three decision schemes: strict equiproba-

Figure 9-7. The initial individual and group distributions of decisions at each level of an organization for each of several common social decision schemes.

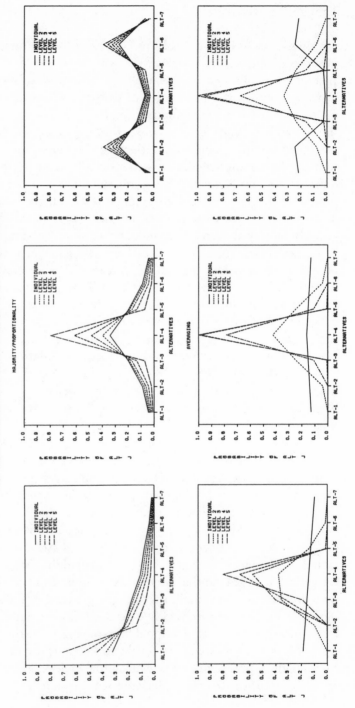

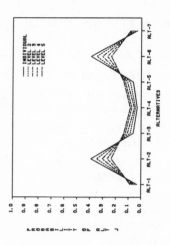

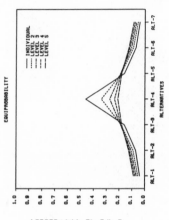

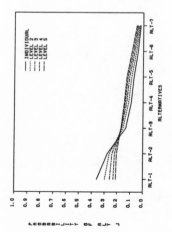

bility (STEQ); plurality if one exists, equiprobability otherwise (PLEQ); and plurality if one exists, proportionality otherwise (PLPR). Due to the inherent constraints of a five-person group choosing from among three alternatives, all pluralities were also majorities; therefore, PLEQ = MAEQ (majority wins if one exists, equiprobability otherwise). Similarly, PLPR = MAPR.

Five alternative models of minority integration were examined. They are depicted in Figure 9-8. Model A has com-

Figure 9-8. Alternative models for integration of minority and majority subpopulations in a hierarchical organization.

DECISION HIERARCHY

	Level-1	Level-2	Level-3	Level-4	Level-5
Model A	M & m ---->	M & m ---->	M & m ---->	M & m ---->	M & m
Model B	M / m ⟩-->	M & m ---->	M & m ---->	M & m ---->	M & m
Model C	M --------> / m -------->	M / m ⟩-->	M & m ---->	M & m ---->	M & m
Model D	M -------> / m ------->	M ---------> / m --------->	M / m ⟩-->	M & m ---->	M & m
Model E	M -------> / m ------->	M ---------> / m --------->	M --------> / m -------->	M / m ⟩-->	M & m

M = Majority

m = minority

Note: Reprinted with permission from Ono and Hulin, 1984.

plete subpopulation integration throughout the organization. Succeeding models retain subpopulation segregation at ever higher levels of the organization, such that by model E, representatives of the two subpopulations do not join the same group until the fifth and highest level. A final parametric variation in Ono and Hulin's thought experiment was the size of the majority; the majority subpopulation was assumed to represent 60 percent, 70 percent, 80 percent, or 90 percent of all the individuals in the organization and identical percentages of groups at the segregated levels of models B through E.

The thought experiment's results are plotted in Figure 9-9 in terms of the level of support by the final level of the organization for alternative A_3, the minority's most preferred alternative. Several patterns are evident. First, integration model and majority size are irrelevant under a STEQ decision rule; as noted above, this type of group decision process tends to produce a uniform preference distribution, and repeating its effect five times as in the present thought experiment completely flattens the preference function (that is, under STEQ, alternative A_3 is favored 33 percent of the time at the top of the organization). Second, and unsurprisingly, under more plausible decision processes (namely, majority or plurality wins), as the minority gets smaller, its preference becomes less likely to survive the organizational decision-making process. Third, and most importantly, as long as the minority is not too small, the more fully integrated the organization is, the more likely minority preference is to be reflected at the top of the organization.

Summary and Implications. Many, if not most, organizations are hierarchically organized. And it is not uncommon for there to exist some degree of segregation of distinctive subpopulations within organizations. Conventional wisdom holds that minorities will have more impact on the organization's decision by electing their own representative (that is, by maintaining segregation of group composition at lower organizational levels). But Ono and Hulin's analysis suggests that under familiar group decision processes, quite the opposite is true—minority opinion is more likely to emerge by fuller integration of the minority with the majority.[2] Of course, as in all thought experiments,

2. Of course, it may be important for a minority to have its own representatives for other reasons: pride, ensuring that its position is force-

the usefulness of results depends upon the plausibility of the generating assumptions. Further simulations under alternative assumptions will in time add to our store of information.

The Thought Experiment as a Method of Research

Utility of Thought Experiments. We have tried to show in the preceding sections that thought experiments can serve a number of useful functions. First, they can reveal unanticipated regularities or complexities in behavior. Ono and Hulin's findings on minority integration nicely illustrated this point. Second, they can identify the most informative or important range of parameters for direct empirical study. For example, Kerr and MacCoun's (1985) recent study of jury size used the findings of previous thought experiments to identify the types of cases and measures that should (and did) yield a jury size effect. Third, they can provide methodological aids. Kerr and Huang's thought experiments point out the apparent futility of drawing strong inferences about the strength of predictors of individual decision-making behavior when one can only obtain group decisions. Such thought experiments could also be used to develop normative baselines as methodological tools. For example, suppose one is interested in determining whether a single group member from a population of interest (for example, a juror who has encountered some prejudicial pretrial publicity) has disproportionate influence on the group outcome. The techniques used by Kerr and Huang would enable one to predict groups' decisions under the assumption that group members are indistinguishable except for their preferences. Deviations from this prediction in the direction of the distinctive member (for example, higher than predicted conviction rates for the pretrial publicity example) would disconfirm the equal-influence assumption. Finally, thought experiments can aid in theory development. Alternative social decision schemes can plausibly be viewed as alternative special-case theoretical models of the

---

fully articulated, and so on. Different results are also possible under different assumptions, for example, fewer organizational levels, alternative decision schemes.

Figure 9-9. Final probability of preference for alternative 3 under alternative decision schemes, majority sizes, and integration models.

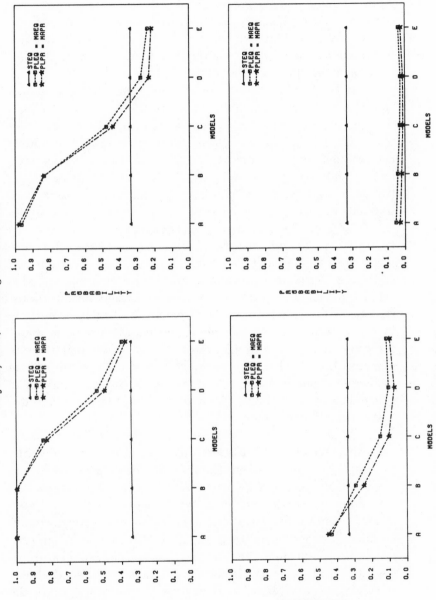

Note: Reprinted with permission from Ono and Hulin, 1984.

group decision-making process, with implicit assumptions about social influence processes. Further, they have the virtue of providing point predictions, which permits more nearly decisive falsification, and perhaps subsequent model revision and improvement (Kerr, Stasser, and Davis, 1979).

It is also important to reemphasize that we are *not* advocating thought experiments as a substitute for data. Ideally, a thought experiment, like any conceptual tool, must be consistent with the relevant data, when they exist. Rather, we advocate thought experiments as an adjunct and guide to data collection and theory development, which can be particularly useful at the early stages of inquiry, especially for questions with unusual ethical or practical barriers to thorough empirical study.

General Prescriptions for Thought Experiments. The greatest impediment to further exploitation of thought experimentation is the scarcity of suitable theory. This approach generally requires explicit, formal mathematical or computer models. Unfortunately, the norm in the social and organizational sciences is the conceptual model that is cast largely or entirely in verbal terms, which may be interesting and provocative but typically yields only predictions, at best. Indeed, it is quite common for verbal models of social behavior to permit several formal mathematical versions, at least some of which may make contradictory predictions. (See Harris, 1976, for a thorough discussion and illustrations.)

Again, the results of a thought experiment are no more valid than its assumptions. For this reason, whenever possible, thought experiment assumptions should be empirically tested. Even though there may be instances where one can perform useful thought experiments even when assumptions cannot be checked empirically, our confidence in the results will generally be directly proportional to the quality of the empirical support for key assumptions. Thus, we have a considerable measure of confidence in the jury thought experiments described above, since empirical research has strongly supported the form of the social decision schemes they employ. But since we have very little good data on the nature of the decision-making process within large multileveled organizations, we must be more guarded about the general applicability of Ono and Hulin's simulation at this time. On the other hand, we have noted above that it is precisely at this early stage that thought experiments can be especially useful.

Finally, mindful of the inherent weakness of thought experimentation, one should make every effort to capitalize on its strengths. At relatively little cost, one can vary parameters through quite wide ranges and include many different special cases or versions. Such parameter variation not only permits one to explore the robustness and generality of results but also helps increase the chances for making interesting new discoveries, perhaps unexpected. For example, had Hulin and Ono been content to restrict their attention to very small minorities, we would not have their interesting results on minority integration.

Closing Thoughts

There are frequent disappointments in the application of social research results to various problems, whether from an engineering or evaluation perspective. We have been stressing here a better marriage between theory and data, a match that heretofore has perhaps favored data gathering. We argued earlier that it is often unlikely that sufficient data will be available or forthcoming in view of the phenomena with which social psychology must deal. Actually, the problem is rather general, as has been noted by Boulding (1980): "Empirical regularities sometimes lead to the discovery of theoretical necessities, as happened in celestial mechanics, but science can never be satisfied with empirical regularities unless it can discover the theoretical necessities behind them. The idea that science consists merely in the discovery of empirical regularities is a total misunderstanding of its methods and its power. Without logical necessity, empirical regularity is little better than superstition" (p. 834). It is our thesis that the same disposition to search for empirical regularities without a parallel appreciation of theory lies behind many current difficulties in application, especially those involving task-oriented groups within organizations and institutions.

In a sense *thought experiment* is another name for simulation or the logical exploration of models—but perhaps a label that better captures the idea of extrapolating from data or social practice. Abelson's (1968) summary of simulation and its virtues conveys much the same spirit. For example, "Simulation is the exercise of a flexible imitation of processes and outcomes for the purpose of clarifying or explaining the underlying mechanisms involved. The feat of imitation per se is not the important feature of simulations, but rather that successful imitation may publicly reveal the essence of the object being simulated" (p. 275).

We conclude by noting that program evaluation has been highly successful during the past decade. Policymakers now routinely expect assessment data to be part of the tools available for decision making. Part of the success of program evaluation may be attributed to research methods that make possible the efficient handling of large data sets and large-scale analyses. The notion of organizational and institutional accountability provided an additional stimulus for public agencies, policies, and programs to be evaluated. The result has been a strong commitment to gathering empirical data to replace intuitive conclusions about the effects of social policy and programs—intuitions often influenced by political ideology and conventional wisdom.

Just as the program evaluation revolution provided the means of improving decisions about current institutions, policies, and so on, so might one hope that simulations, which we have camouflaged here as thought experiments, might provide a social engineering revolution, of sorts, about proposed organizational changes. Formal models have moved scientists and policymakers alike from data to orderly projections in areas varying from economics to meteorology—in just the fashion suggested (and illustrated) herein—but rarely in social and organizational psychology. (Gelfand and Solomon, 1973, and Penrod and Hastie, 1979, are among the striking exceptions.) However, there may be little alternative in the years ahead to the use of thought experiments to improve on hunches and ideologically derived policies and programs, especially those involving potentially "expensive" changes to sensitive institutions such as the jury.

References

Abelson, R. P. "Simulation of Social Behavior." In G. Lindzey and E. Aronson (eds.), *Handbook of Social Psychology.* Vol. 2. Reading, Mass.: Addison-Wesley, 1968.

Apodaca and others v. *Oregon. United States Supreme Court Reports,* 1972, *406,* 404–415.

Arrow, K. J. *Social Choice and Individual Values.* New York: Wiley, 1963.

Bailey, F. L., and Rothblatt, H. B. *Successful Techniques for Criminal Trials.* New York: Lawyers Cooperative, 1971.

Ballew v. *Georgia. United States Law Week,* 1978, *46,* 4217–4224.

Becker, T. L., Hildrun, D. C., and Bateman, K. "The Influence of Jurors' Values on Their Verdicts: A Courts and Politics Experiment." *Southwestern Social Science Quarterly,* 1965, *45,* 130–140.

Berk, R. A., Hennessy, M., and Swan, J. "The Vagaries and Vulgarities of 'Scientific' Jury Selection." *Evaluation Quarterly,* 1977, *1,* 143–158.

Berman, J., and Sales, B. "A Critical Evaluation of the Systematic Approach to Jury Selection." *Criminal Justice and Behavior,* 1977, *4,* 219–240.

Boulding, K. E. "Science: Our Common Heritage." *Science,* 1980, *207* (4433), 831–836.

Bray, R. M., and Kerr, N. L. "Methodological Considerations in the Study of the Psychology in the Courtroom." In N. Kerr and R. Bray (eds.), *The Psychology of the Courtroom.* Orlando, Fla.: Academic Press, 1982.

Broeder, D. "The Negro in Court." *Duke Law Journal,* 1965, 19–31.

Castaneda v. *Partida. United States Supreme Court Reports,* 1977, *430,* 482.

Colgrove v. *Battin. United States Supreme Court Reports,* 1973, *149,* 413.

Davis, J. H. "Group Decision and Social Interaction: A Theory of Social Decision Schemes." *Psychological Review,* 1973, *80,* 97–125.

Davis, J. H. "Group Decision and Procedural Justice." In M. Fishbein (ed.), *Progress in Social Psychology*. Vol. 1. Hillsdale, N.J.: Erlbaum, 1980.

Davis, J. H. "Social Interaction as a Combinatorial Process in Group Decision." In H. Brandstatter, J. H. Davis, and G. Stocker-Kreichgauer (eds.), *Group Decision Making*. London: Academic Press, 1982.

Davis, J. H., Bray, R. M., and Holt, R. W. "The Empirical Study of Decision Processes in Juries: A Critical Review." In J. L. Tapp and F. J. Levine (eds.), *Law, Justice, and the Individual in Society: Psychological and Legal Issues*. New York: Holt, Rinehart & Winston, 1977.

Davis, J. H., Hornik, J. A., and Hornseth, J. P. "Group Decision Schemes and Strategy Preference in a Sequential Response Task." *Journal of Personality and Social Psychology*, 1970, *15*, 397-408.

Davis, J. H., Stasser, G., Spitzer, C. E., and Holt, R. W. "Changes in Group Members' Decision Preferences During Discussion: An Illustration with Mock Juries." *Journal of Personality and Social Psychology*, 1976, *34*, 1177-1187.

Davis, J. H., and others. "The Decision Processes of 6- and 12-Person Juries Assigned Unanimous and 2/3 Majority Rules." *Journal of Personality and Social Psychology*, 1975, *32*, 1-14.

Davis, J. H., and others. "Victim Consequences, Sentence Severity, and Decision Processes in Mock Juries." *Organizational Behavior and Human Performance*, 1977, *18*, 346-365.

Etzioni, A. "Creating and Imbalance." *Trial*, 1974, *10*, 28-30.

Fishburn, P. C. *The Theory of Social Choice*. Princeton, N.J.: Princeton University Press, 1973.

Gelfand, A. E., and Solomon, H. "A Study of Poisson's Models for Jury Verdicts in Criminal and Civil Trials." *Journal of the American Statistical Association*, 1973, *68*, 271-278.

Gergen, K. J. "Social Psychology as History." *Journal of Personality and Social Psychology*, 1973, *26*, 309-320.

Gleisser, M. *Juries and Justice*. New York: Barnes & Noble, 1968.

Hans, V. P., and Vidmar, N. "Jury Selection." In N. Kerr and R. Bray (eds.), *The Psychology of the Courtroom*. Orlando, Fla.: Academic Press, 1982.

Harris, R. J. "Handling Negative Inputs: On the Plausible Equity Formulae." *Journal of Experimental Social Psychology,* 1976, *12,* 194-209.

Hastie, R., Penrod, S., and Pennington, N. *Inside the Jury.* Cambridge, Mass.: Harvard University Press, 1983.

Heslin, R. "Predicting Group Task Effectiveness from Member Characteristics." *Psychological Bulletin,* 1964, *62,* 248-256.

Johnson v. *Louisiana. United States Supreme Court Reports,* 1972, *406,* 356-403.

Kairys, D., Schulman, J., and Harring, S. (eds.). *The Jury System: New Methods for Reducing Prejudice.* Philadelphia, Pa.: Philadelphia Resistance Print Shop, 1975.

Kerr, N. L., and Bray, R. M. "The Psychology of the Courtroom: An Introduction." In N. Kerr and R. Bray (eds.), *The Psychology of the Courtroom.* Orlando, Fla.: Academic Press, 1982.

Kerr, N. L., and Huang, J. Y. "How Much Difference Does One Person Make in Group Decisions?: A Thought Experiment." Paper presented at annual convention of American Psychological Association, Toronto, 1984.

Kerr, N. L., and MacCoun, R. J. "The Effects of Jury Size on Deliberation Process and Product." *Journal of Personality and Social Psychology,* 1985, *48,* 349-363.

Kerr, N. L., Stasser, G., and Davis, J. H. "Model Testing, Model Fitting, and Social Decision Schemes." *Organizational Behavior and Human Performance,* 1979, *23,* 399-410.

Kerr, N. L., and others. "Guilt Beyond a Reasonable Doubt: Effects of Concept Definition and Assigned Rule on Judgments of Mock Jurors." *Journal of Personality and Social Psychology,* 1976, *34,* 282-294.

Laughlin, P. R., and Adamopoulos, J. "Social Decision Schemes on Intellective Tasks." In H. Brandstatter, J. H. Davis, and G. Stocker-Kreichgauer (eds.), *Group Decision Making.* London: Academic Press, 1982.

Lempert, R. O. "Uncovering 'Nondiscernible' Differences: Empirical Research and the Jury-Size Cases." *Michigan Law Review,* 1975, *73,* 643-708.

McConahay, J., Mullin, C., and Frederick, J. "The Uses of Social Science in Trials with Political and Racial Overtones: The Trial of Joan Little." *Law and Contemporary Problems,* 1977, *41,* 205–229.

McGrath, J. E., and Altman, I. *Small Group Research: A Synthesis and Critique of the Field.* New York: Holt, Rinehart & Winston, 1966.

Mann, R. D. "A Review of the Relationships between Personality and Performance in Small Groups." *Psychological Bulletin,* 1959, *56,* 241–270.

Michaelson, S. "History and State of the Art of Applied Social Research in the Courts." In M. Saks and R. Baron (eds.), *The Use/Nonuse/Misuse of Applied Social Research in the Courts.* Cambridge, Mass.: Abt Books, 1980.

Nagao, D. H., and Davis, J. H. "Some Implications of Temporal Drift in Social Parameters." *Journal of Experimental Social Psychology,* 1980, *16,* 479–496.

Ono, K., and Hulin, C. L. "Simulation Study of Group Decision Making and Linking Pin Theory of Organization." Paper presented at annual convention of American Psychological Association, Toronto, 1984.

Penrod, S. "Study of Attorney and 'Scientific' Jury Selection Models." Unpublished doctoral dissertation, Department of Psychology, Harvard University, 1979.

Penrod, S., and Hastie, R. "Models of Jury Decision-Making: A Critical Review." *Psychological Bulletin,* 1979, *86,* 462–492.

Saks, M. "The Limits of Scientific Jury Selection: Ethical and Empirical." *Jurimetrics Journal,* 1976, *17,* 3–22.

Saks, M., and Hastie, R. *Social Psychology in Court.* New York: Van Nostrand Reinhold, 1978.

Schulman, J. "A Systematic Approach to Successful Jury Selection." *Guild Notes,* Nov. 1973.

Schulman, J., and others. "Recipe for a Jury." *Psychology Today,* May 1973, pp. 34–44, 77, 79–84.

Spector, P. "Scientific Jury Selection Warps Justice." *Harvard Law Record,* 1974, *58,* 15.

Stasser, G., Kerr, N. L., and Bray, R. M. "The Social Psychology of Jury Deliberation: Structure, Process, and Product." In

N. L. Kerr and R. M. Bray (eds.), *The Psychology of the Courtroom*. Orlando, Fla.: Academic Press, 1982.

Stasser, G., Kerr, N. L., and Davis, J. H. "Influence Processes in Decision Making: A Modeling Approach." In P. Paulus (ed.), *Psychology of Group Influence*. Hillsdale, N.J.: Erlbaum, 1980.

Tanford, S., and Penrod, S. "Computer Modeling of Influence in the Jury: The Role of the Consistent Juror." *Social Psychology Quarterly*, 1983, *46*, 200–212.

Tindale, S., and Nagao, D. "Some 'Thought' Experiments" Concerning the Utility of 'Scientific Jury Selection.' " Paper presented at annual convention of American Psychological Association, Toronto, 1984.

Van Dyke, J. M. *Jury Selection Procedures*. Cambridge, Mass.: Ballinger, 1977.

Vidmar, N., and Judson, J. "The Use of Social Science in a Change of Venue Application." *Canadian Bar Review*, 1981, *59*, 76–102.

Williams v. *Florida. Supreme Court Reporter*, 1970, *90*, 1893–1914.

Zeisel, H. ". . . And Then There Were None: The Diminution of the Federal Jury." *University of Chicago Law Review*, 1971, *38*, 713–715.

Zeisel, H., and Diamond, S. "The Effect of Peremptory Challenges on Jury and Verdict: An Experiment in a Federal District Court." *Stanford Law Review*, 1978, *30*, 491–531.

10

Reexamining
Our Thoughts
Concerning Groups
in Organizations

L. L. Cummings

In reviewing the chapters in this book, I think I see two sets of themes. One I would label content themes and the other style themes.

Content Themes

I think there was considerable struggling—sometimes creatively, sometimes doggedly—with domain issues, and that struggle was reflected through almost the entirety of the first two-thirds of the chapters. And while I agree with Jim Davis that that is aggravating, I think it is necessary. The issues of construct definition and validation, I think, were central on our minds from the beginning. As I listened to Guzzo's presentation and reflected on the ensuing discussion, my first assumption was that there had been some ground rules established; that is, that we were going to have a discussion about what groups are, what our boundaries and domains are for the conference. It became obvious to me that there were no ground rules established, probably advisably so. Several interpretations can now be placed on that. One is that, in general, the presentations that we

350

were to hear and study were ordered systematically by our coordinator to lead us in the direction of specificity, ranging from Professor Guzzo's wide-ranging invitation to wrestle with broad constructs and domain issues to the last presentation dealing with extremely specific issues, so specific as to raise questions concerning the relevance to social settings and groups. The second possibility is that transition and development somehow reflect the natural evolution of a group, our group at Carnegie-Mellon in this case—that is, that we generally move from broad to specific topics on almost any generic topic. The third possibility is that the ambiguity about domain provided us an opportunity to get to know one another a bit. We could share how our biases and perspectives have changed for those of us who knew one another before. For those of us who did not know one another before, one can express some things about groups that signal and symbolize our own representation of groups and their roles in organizational contexts. I concluded the evening thinking that there is no intellectually honest way the area should avoid the construct problem as a continuing one and as a topic that should repeatedly come up. It clearly has done so in the intervening day and a half subsequent to our initial session.

Secondly, in terms of content, I think the focus by and large has been on relational issues between a group and other actors or other agendas to the neglect of group processes—that is, of things that happen within groups. Professor Guzzo talked about groups and organizational effectiveness. Professors Hackman and Walton talked about groups with leaders being outside of groups. No one challenged them on this. Groups without leaders and leaders without groups are interesting concepts in themselves. And the Walton/Hackman chapter, arguing that organizational cultures are a way to get a handle on groups, represents yet another variation on this theme. In other words, we are encouraged to step outside of groups again in order to understand groups. Certainly Professor Schwartzman's comments about the importance of mind sets and world views that come from a very different perspective to get a handle on groups represents this same consistent theme. Professor Brett's introduction to the idea of interrelationships between groups as a means to understanding group performance is also interpretable within this theme.

So it seems to me that a second theme is the tendency, even a strain at times, to *look outside of groups* for insights and creativity concerning group functioning *rather than searching within the groups* themselves for the infrastructures and the processes. Perhaps some would argue enough of that has been done. Many contributors to this conference have spent a lot of time and energy doing that and perhaps it is old hat, boring, and stale. On the other hand, one way to read it is that somehow we found ourselves in a position (trap) of looking at, if you like, the organizational context of groups as opposed to processes within groups to gain understanding of what enhances task performances of groups.

The third theme is one of hope and optimism, mixed with a bit of arrogance and a bit of contentiousness, in dealing with some slightly alien concepts, whether they happen to come from our anthropologist colleague (Professor Schwartzman) or from other sources. But the theme of hope and optimism is coupled with the helpful myth that we are among the selected, self-selected at that, who possess the combination of call and ability to bring vitality back to the study of groups in organizations. Obviously represented at the conference are scholars who have been at it a long time—some from the earliest days of their careers, others who are returning to the study of groups after explorations of other topics. I view that as very hopeful. Perhaps this is due to stubbornness, perhaps it is pure energy and perseverance, perhaps it is a shared belief that there is something worth pursuing in terms of trying to understand performance variances between organizations and within organizations. I am not sure of the reason, but I do think there are themes of hope and optimism.

Fourthly, there is clearly the theme of action. There is a theme of achieving groups, and while that was comfortable to most of us, Professor Schwartzman pointed out that we should be cautious about that comfort. The two extremes might be the position that groups are interesting in and of themselves, on the one hand, and Professor Guzzo's position that the only reason to study groups is to enhance the task performance of the group. Of course, that is an overly drawn contrast, but the differences in the views are striking.

What are the consequences of emphasizing this action theme? It clearly facilitates links of group processes and structures to important issues of performance and productivity in achievement settings. Secondly, it facilitates links to other topical areas—not just in social psychology and organizational behavior but also in economics, technology, and engineering. It suggests ways to link up with these disparate disciplines. That appears explicitly in Professor Goodman's presentation. Clearly, several members of the workshop felt that this explicit, tight linking may be pushing too hard and too far in the direction of relevance and application. The theme also appears in Professor Davis's associations of simulation and social engineering, particularly with reference to evaluation research in policy studies.

The conference discussions did not reflect much concern about what is lost when focusing our study of groups on task performance outcomes, either directly or indirectly via simulation. I am suggesting that we seem to have slipped into the action and application framework without due consideration of this orientation for the scientific and intellectual study of groups. Do we lose rigor in the pursuit of real applications? Can we adequately model the realities of group processes in natural settings with meaningful tasks?

The fifth content theme centers on the strain, both in the chapters themselves and in the discussions between general models, on the one hand, and what Professor Goodman labeled "fine-grained analysis," on the other hand. The strain is most fully developed between Professor Goodman's chapter presenting a discrete, fine-grained analysis and in Professor Brett's chapter presenting an extremely broad view of analysis of intergroup relations. My colleague, Professor McGrath, in his companion discussion piece, argues that the Goodman approach will not produce generalizable science. Yet, the fine-grained understanding is the essence of description, an important, even necessary to some minds, first step of science.

Style Themes

We finally broke the data barrier. I came in about 9:30 on the opening evening (Sunday) and thought, "Well, now, that is a rather unrealistic expectation to start off with data." I checked at 11:00 Monday morning and still found no data around. One of our colleagues had asked, I think at that point, if there were any data. That first query was clearly perceived with humor by most present. Nevertheless, by noon on Monday, I was getting hungry for data. One of our colleagues had asked twice by now and by 2:10 Monday, we still had no data. We were getting into arguments about how to collect data and what constitutes data, but still no data. By 4:00 Monday afternoon we still had no data. Nobody had talked about or presented any data. We finally broke the barrier Tuesday about 8:30. Paul Goodman's chapter clearly broke the barrier. In the last two chapters, we have lots of data. In one case, I question whether those data are real and meaningful. But we have been data rich on Tuesday. Again, we might attribute that to our conference organizer, who established the order of the presentations, but I cannot see how we can attribute it to the immaturity of this group, given the rich years of empiricism represented in it.

A second style theme focuses on our apparent lack of acceptance of the advocacy of active listening. One of the member skills that are frequently advocated in effectively performing teams is active listening. We here at the conference have illustrated considerable opportunity for each of us to improve these skills. Each of us has said or implied, "I have not made myself clear." That represents the more polite among us. More aggressively, "I have been misunderstood," and, finally, I do not think we have had anyone say, "Damn it, you are just not listening." We are, naturally enough, formulating our own response while others are contributing. That has been a style that I think is worth reflecting on, and it has led to a certain sense of discontinuity. That discontinuity is real in the sense that the chapters were not integrated in any logical order or systematically coordinated by the contributors. However, our own styles have led to a greater sense of discontinuity than, in fact, may have been the case in the substance of the chapters themselves.

Finally, in terms of style, I asked myself, "Did we become a group?" I used three criteria that are, in fact, articulated in some of the chapters. First, did we have a common goal? Perhaps we had an image of an emerging book coupled with the intention of experiencing an intellectually and socially enjoyable time. But was that an articulated common goal? Not really; rather, it appeared to me as an emerging goal. We certainly took ourselves seriously. As a matter of fact, I think Professor Schwartzman used the term *playful* when describing a disturbing absence in our discourse. In fact, I think that occurred as a specific response to Professor Goodman, who was saying, "Helen, you should *worry* about that or you should work on that." I think that Professor Schwartzman's response was something like "I will *play* with it or deal with it *playfully*." The essence seems to be that we have been too rigid, too traditional, too bound to our received paradigmatic ways. Perhaps playfulness would contribute to our creativity. Perhaps taking ourselves seriously to a fault, intellectually at least, is a commentary on our early assumptions and definitions of what the conference process ought to be in order to *generate* some kind of common goal. Perhaps we worked too hard at that. And, more importantly, perhaps task groups in work organizations frequently commit similar errors of process, yielding similar losses of creativity.

Secondly, are we interdependent through our work flows or social systems? Clearly not, except as perhaps pooled through the coordinator of the session and the editors of the book.

Thirdly, is there some sense of a common image of what we are generally about, short of an explicitly articulated and shared goal? There does seem to be a desire to struggle toward some common sense of membership. Movement toward that end will partially depend upon what happens after the conference itself, both with regard to the book and the exchange of chapters. But there is an implicit belief that if we attain interdependence through reflections across chapters, then that will produce outcomes that are likely to make an intellectual contribution and will also enhance the maintenance of our good feelings about three days well spent. It is clear that we are concluding our time together with that hope. Whether we achieve those ends depends partly upon technology but mostly on our efforts over the next six to twelve months.

Disturbing Contributions

I wish to address what I consider to be the most disturbing contributions made at the conference. It is difficult to find a socially acceptable label for this task. The term *disturbing* generally means bothersome, troublesome, even undesirable. In this context, I am referring to the *variance-creating potential* of an idea. These ideas disturbed my status quo, my intellectual slumber. They woke me up. They bothered me. Some I indexed as intellectually disturbing, others as emotionally disturbing. The underlying criterion is that the idea yields suggestions for elaboration and amplification.

Let us begin with Professor Guzzo's chapter. Here I was struck by the exclusive focus on groups with tasks. Certainly task-performing groups are the center of our attention and study at this conference. However, there are definitely insights to be gained about task groups from studying groups *searching* for tasks, groups *letting go* of tasks, and groups that have *tasks different* than most observers of the group think they have. The narrow focus suggested by Professor Guzzo's chapter would seem to lead us to an unfortunately static (as opposed to developmental) understanding of how groups find, perform, evaluate, and change their tasks.

Professors Hackman and Walton's chapter offers the disturbing idea that leaders of groups do not necessarily need to be group members. This strikes me as a novel notion because it implies mechanisms of influence by the leader on the group that are not neatly embedded in the existing literature and theory on influence. Of course, in a very simplistic sense, it is possible that a group has a formally appointed leader who has no social relations with any group member. That is straightforward but so simplistic as to be unrealistic. Of course, I believe that Hackman and Walton have something beyond this in mind, and not being able to discern the underlying influence mechanisms operating between such leaders and group members is disturbing. The authors do not clarify what these mechanisms might be.

The Walton and Hackman chapter argues that transitions between management philosophies or cultures provide opportunities for enlightening and understanding group functions. I think their conception of what transitions are useful to examine should be broadened to include transitions from commitment to control (as well as control to commitment). In addition, control can lead to revolt rather than commitment. Articulating the conditions for each transition would be a major contribution. It is a very Americanized and certainly a Western version of transitions presented here, even myopic in its focus.

In the case of Professor Schwartzman's chapter, my disturbance was that she implied that somehow the existing social psychological work on groups can be allowed off the hook merely by clearly articulating that these psychological and anthropological differences are differences of taste, differences of focus, differences of preference. I believe these differences should be treated as fundamentally different world views, different research paradigms, different research strategies. As the conference progressed, Professor Schwartzman opened fire just a bit on Professor Goodman for only meekly pursuing the research subject's world view in his work. That is, although Goodman's fine-grained analysis represented a proper step, it failed to recognize the fundamental differences in world views and paradigms necessary to actually understand the participants' views. But the scenario wasn't over yet because Professor Hackman opened fire on our colleague from anthropology by recognizing that while the group had been listening to her for quite a while, Professor Schwartzman had not yet actually described exactly what *she* would do if studying task groups. And, of course, Professor Schwartzman was ready. I suspected she was ready two days earlier to respond to that and when she finally did respond to it, she gave us an actual example of an agenda of how she or someone of her background, training, and orientation would go about studying that phenomenon. So perhaps the hook finally sunk it.

In Professor Brett's chapter, the thing that caused my

mind to twirl was her position that intergroup exchanges are best conceptualized in a complex paradigm focusing on negotiation and bargaining. It is not clear that the leverage is greater using that approach to understanding intergroup relations than looking at intergroup relationships as opportunities for cooperation, for cooptation, or for creative disengagement. We need to examine the conditions and rules for abandoning the premise of interrelating. This outcome and the processes antecedent to it seem neglected in her framework. In addition, there needs to be a connection made between within-group processes and intergroup relations. Brett's negotiation orientation neglects the impact of within-group negotiations. Within-group bargaining itself is likely to be a valuable arena for the acquisition of the kinds of skills that Brett is calling for in lateral negotiations. There are likely to be reciprocal influences as well—that is, the nature of intergroup relationships will affect the structure and the allocation of resources within groups.

In Professor Goodman's chapter, the disturbing element is the creeping turtle of fine-grained analysis. It creeps up on us through the general distrust of general models for group task performance. Some of us seem to want to move to generalizations about groups without data and to very broad generalizations at a hare's pace. Goodman's chapter challenges that strategy. Of course, Goodman's prescriptions and applications were challenged, not only by Schwartzman but by Professor Walton as well. But I was disturbed that the turtle and the hare never met; that is, they were passing each other with little recognition because of the different languages. The creative potential in the combination of the two strategies was missed. Are the differences just around the issue of pace and the slowness of the pace implied by this creeping turtle of fine-grained analysis? I doubt that. It may center on a deeper kind of notion about the benefits of starting with broad generalizations and working toward detailed, fine-grained understanding as opposed to the richness contained in understanding the discrete details in the beginning and then building carefully bounded, limited domain models.

Goodman also tends to view the work group as a manager would do. His is the most managerially oriented chapter. He warns of early generalizations. He advocates getting into the *field* with early descriptive approaches to understanding the work group. I think that disturbed some of us. Why does it disturb us? Well, first of all, what he has done is not really a Harvard Business School case. We could understand our anxiety about that! We could classify that and know what to do with it. Yet, it really is not an ethnographic study either, as Professor Schwartzman clearly pointed out. The world that he is viewing is still the world of the researcher, *not* the world that he claims to be studying. Perhaps some of us are disturbed because his approach is not the most elegant route to conceptual and empirical generalization.

Professor Davis's chapter introduces the aging-scholar syndrome. He used it metaphorically by asserting, "This is the mirror I'll hold up to myself, and if I see myself having the symptoms of the aging scholar, I will become very tense about it." The syndrome's most telling symptom is advocating types of research that one does not conduct oneself. Professor Davis advocates and conducts what he labels as "thought experiments" (simulations of the more mundane). He defines a thought experiment as an aid to extrapolate from known empirical results in interpolating between existing sets of findings. That is disturbing because he is limited to studying the known and those problems about which we already have a body of empirical evidence from which to build models. So we have the disturbing possibility that, on the one hand, we most need simulation to study phenomenon about which we know little because of feasibility constraints—economic, ethical, political— and, on the other hand, we need some kind of empirical data on phenomena prior to generating and creating simulations. We need a basis for building the simulation and it probably must be something other than the experiments of Professor Davis's mind (and others). He has presented us a very interesting and disturbing dilemma. How much data do you need before you start? How do you start to build a model? At one place Davis even uses the terminology "going from mind experiments to *simulations.*" Somehow this progression leads Davis to allowing himself to use the term *model.* That is, indeed, a hare's leap of considerable proportions. Equally disturbing is Davis's assertion that conclusions drawn from simulations would have any influence on opinions of important individuals making important decisions. Of course, these are decisions on relatively unaccessible social judgments where going to simulations may be necessary; that is, accessing "real" data is not feasible. Three central issues should be raised concerning this advocacy. First, what types of persons, particularly in terms of their cognitive processing, would likely be susceptible to influence by simulation data? Second, are there such persons presently in significant decision roles? Third, under what political and organizational conditions are they most likely to be susceptible to such influence?

Professor Latané's chapter was very disturbing because what he is really saying is that groups are not necessarily the most appropriate avenue for enhancing organizational performance—and that was supposed to be the central position and theme of the whole conference. That position seems counterculture at the extreme! But beyond this, and the most disturbing element of Latané's chapter, is his creative, if misleading, labeling. Social loafing could just as easily be viewed as *individual leisure generation.* The positional biases need to be recognized. Individuals may well seek refuge within groups in order to express leisure (nonperformance) behaviors. The reduced group performance is a by-product, not an intent, as loafing implies.

Conclusion

My guess is that if we had had in attendance a person or persons playing the role of *broker,* they would have easily taken much of the caution and uncertainty out of our conclusions. In almost every chapter there are translatable conclusions, arguments, and findings (in a few cases) of direct relevance to organizational functioning. The greatest barrier to our having an impact is our extreme caution that we may not (or do not) know enough to make prescriptions. I challenge that, and I believe that an assigned broker for our ideas would find our caution unnecessary and a blockage to our creativity. We establish a culture for ourselves not to be useful. Beyond that, it is unlikely that we would not make it easy for someone to perform these translations to real world applications. But I think that there is an intelligent, sophisticated audience who wouldn't even question us. They would be convinced that our theoretical and evidential basis is more than ample to expect accountability for use of our ideas and evidence in addressing important organizational and social problems centering on groups.

11

Studying Groups at Work: Ten Critical Needs for Theory and Practice

Joseph E. McGrath

This book deals with the task performance of work groups in organizations. One central premise of this book seems to be that *task performance of work groups in organizations* ought to be a major field of inquiry. Many of the chapters imply such an idea and further imply that such a topic would be a feasible and valuable focus for systematic research. Only in a few spots have questions been raised about the proper scope or definition of the topic: Should things other than task performance be included? How should the contributions of members of those work groups be dealt with? Should any group phenomena that take place outside work organizations be given consideration? But nowhere does the book question the value or feasibility of building a field of study that concentrates on task performance of work groups in organizations.

I wish to thank Janice R. Kelly for her helpful comments on an earlier draft of this chapter. Correspondence about the chapter should be addressed to Joseph E. McGrath, 235 Psychology Building, University of Illinois, 603 E. Daniels Street, Champaign, Ill. 61820.

Such questions would seem worth asking, I think, because of the history of research in related areas. There is a long history of study of task performance in groups, as well as productivity and task proficiency in work organizations. There is ample reason to question whether research in either of those two areas has been as successful as we would wish. Why, then, should we expect that a concentrated effort in what appears to be the intersection of those two areas of study will somehow be more successful?

That question can be asked in another, more optimistic form, namely, what could we do differently, in our study of work groups in organizations, to increase the chances that such work will be more successful than past work in related areas? This chapter addresses the latter, optimistic form of the question—what are the requirements for successful study in this area?

If we are to build a full-fledged field devoted to the study of task performance of work groups in organizations, we will need to handle certain methodological, conceptual, and substantive issues better than they have been handled in past work in related fields. Specifically, we need:

1. To use better methodological *tools,* primarily data collection tools
2. To use broadband *strategies* that are multivariate, multimethod, and multioccasion
3. To put more emphasis on *theory*
4. To study groups as *intact social systems* and to do so at a *group level* of analysis
5. To build a conception of *how groups vary in type*
6. To build a conception of *how group tasks vary in type*
7. To use a broader conception of the range of *content* to be included in our study
8. To study *groups in context*
9. To take seriously the idea of *temporal patterns* in groups
10. To take seriously the idea of *group process*

Some of these critical needs are surely old hat. I call them

the "of course" requirements of our field. In much of our literature, they are recognized as needs, and simultaneously dismissed, by prefacing statements about them with "of course.
. . ." To wit: "Of course, we need new and better data collection tools and a broadband methodology." "Of course, we need
to give more attention to theory." "Of course, we need to
worry about the context within which these behaviors take
place." But those "of course" needs are far more often honored
in the breach than in the observance.

Others of these critical needs are less often talked about,
and perhaps they are therefore more important to dwell upon.
These include, especially, the need to study groups as intact social systems, in a context that involves time as well as place and
situation, and to focus on process. Therefore, this chapter gives
more emphasis to these less familiar needs than to the more
familiar "of course" requirements.

I will argue that these ten critical needs are important
considerations in any systematic attempt to build a field of
study that deals with groups at work. I will argue further that,
if we give only lip service to them in our study of task performance of work groups in organizations (as we have done for
many of them in other related areas of study), we may once
again find that we have spent a lot of time and effort to build a
"pile of data" that we then cannot translate into a "body of
knowledge"—knowledge about task performance of work
groups in organizations.

The remainder of this chapter will present brief discussions of these ten critical needs and reflect on parts of the conference in relation to those requirements. The critical needs will
be dealt with in three clusters. The first three are methodological, the middle four are conceptual, and the last three are substantive. They are, I think, in order of increasing importance.

Some Methodological Requirements:
To Use Better Tools, Broader Strategies and More Theory

The main methodological requirements for successful systematic study of work groups in organizations, I believe, are for
a more balanced array of data collection tools, a broader array

of strategic approaches, and, especially, a stronger emphasis on theory.

Data Collection Tools. We need improved methodological tools, especially better data-generating tools. We have a powerful array of sophisticated tools for data processing and analysis. They are, if anything, too strong for the data we usually feed them. We need better data to put into them.

We particularly need a better balance of data collection methods that do not rely entirely on self-reports of workers or of managers. It may seem unnecessary to bring up this matter in the present context. Everyone knows it! I would agree that this is surely one of the major "of courses" in our field. Everyone agrees that we need to use measures of different kinds that compensate for each other's strengths and weaknesses. But it is still the case that a very large majority of all empirical evidence in research on work organizations is based on such self-reports.

This is not to downgrade the value of such self-report data. I would join Webb and colleagues (Webb and others, 1981), and many others, in praising the substantial strengths of questionnaires and other self-reports, while at the same time warning of their serious limitations if used exclusively. Research on work organizations, as well as behavioral science research in general, has too often relied totally on such self-reports. Direct observations, with or without mechanical aids, also have serious weaknesses and limitations, but they constitute a powerful *complement* to self-report measures. Similarly, trace measures, so eloquently urged by Webb and colleagues, have serious limitations. But their very strengths (nonreactivity) are the major weaknesses of self-reports; hence, they are valuable *in combination with* self-reports and methods of other types. Many behavioral scientists seem to shun the use of archival information, or at least to be uncomfortable with it. But such evidence often could serve valuable purposes, especially in research on continuing work groups within organizations.

This is not an argument for any one method; rather it is an argument for *no one method.* The need for a better balance of data collection methods is certainly one of those "of course" requirements that we too often accept in principle and ignore in practice.

Diverse Research Strategies. Not only do we need to employ a variety of measurement methods, we also need to bring a broader band of methodological strategies (for example, field studies, experiments, computer simulations, sample surveys, and so on) to our study of work groups in organizations. Furthermore, within each of the strategies that we might employ, we need a broadband approach to data collection. We need sets of data that are multivariate and that involve multiple types of measures from multiple sources for each of those variables. Such bodies of data also need to reflect evidence from multiple occasions and a dynamic view of the systems under study.

At least two chapters in this book give special emphasis to this critical need for a wider array of research strategies than are generally employed in research on work groups in organizations. Davis and Kerr (Chapter Nine) argue eloquently for the value of using a class of research strategies that they term thought experiments and that I call formal theories. These thought experiments are a means to extend and multiply our intellectual muscle, so to speak. Indeed, thought experiments offer us a means to pose, systematically, some questions that we cannot ask at all in a direct empirical fashion. Davis and Kerr do not propose thought experiments as a substitute for experimentation and careful observation. On the contrary, they argue for the use of formal models that are built on the best evidence we have from empirical and theoretical work of the past and that can be used to assess the complex consequences of the most promising hypotheses currently considered of interest in a given topical area.

Schwartzman (Chapter Seven), in contrast, calls for broadening the array of empirical strategies that are used in research on task performance of groups in organizations to take the perspective of the individual into account. She argues that virtually all work in these areas is done from the point of view of the "system," of the work organization, rather than from the perspective of its members. She suggests that we could learn a lot by asking about the system and its operation from the perspectives of the "natives" who inhabit it and whose behavior is the putative topic of interest. Schwartzman's prescription is quite in keeping with the critical need to use a wider array of research strategies, whose strengths and limitations can complement and offset one another.

More Focus on Theory. We must stop acting as if *theory* were either a naughty word to be shunned or a public relations consideration to be tacked onto our work later, when it needs to be packaged and sold. We must stop acting as if it were possible (let alone desirable) to have *evidence without interpretation.*

Since I consider formal theory to be one class of research strategy (Runkel and McGrath, 1972; McGrath, Martin, and Kulka, 1982; Brinberg and McGrath, 1985), the need for more focus on theory is, in my view, really just a special case of the need for a broader array of research strategies. But it is a very special case that deserves special pleading.

Behavioral scientists who have a strong preference for an empirical approach to research often talk about "grounded theory." That phrase sometimes turns out to mean "theory" that starts at—and largely remains at—the raw empirical level. It is one thing to "ground" theory in empirical evidence, as in Davis and Kerr's use of extant evidence as the base for their thought experiments. It is quite another matter to keep our research information permanently "grounded" because we are unwilling to go beyond empirical description to bring useful theoretical concepts into our interpretations. The latter seems to be, too often, the implicit posture of the behavioral science work on groups in organizations.

Substantive theory has many functions, among them a screening or filtering function and a focusing function. Furthermore, as I have argued elsewhere (for example, Brinberg and McGrath, 1985; McGrath and Brinberg, 1984), an emphasis on substantive theory early in the research process is one route by which the basic researcher and applied researcher can approach the same problems from a common ground, rather than in seeming conflict with each other. Such a rapprochement of applied and basic research is badly needed in research on organizations.

Conceptual Requirements

The central conceptual issues revolve around our need to deal with our units of study with more conceptual clarity. In the present context, that means that we must study work groups in organizations as intact social systems, and do so at a group level of analysis. This need, in turn, implies that we have some means for conceptualizing different classes of groups and different types of tasks in which those groups may be engaged. It also implies that we need to deal with the behavior of those groups with respect to a much broader array of content than just simple task performance outcomes. *Rather than identifying our focus as the study of work groups, perhaps we should identify it as the study of groups at work.*

Studying Groups at a Group Level of Analysis. We need to study work groups as if they were semiautonomous, intact social systems that are partially independent of, though also interdependent with, other parts of the work organization. We need to approach the group as a unit, not as a collection of members or even a collection of dyadic relations. We need to study groups as concrete systems and to recognize that groups are full-fledged social systems, not just vehicles for task performance.

Closely related to the need to deal with groups as intact social systems is the need to do our group research at a group level of analysis. We need to get beyond the idea that a group is a forum for shaping members. It is that, but it is also much more than that. We also need to get beyond the idea that the group is to be construed as the simple sum of its members, and the group's behavior as the simple sum of its members' behaviors. We need to ask, "What goes on at the *group level?*"

A group level of analysis is especially important, I think, for those interested in organizations. When researchers try to work without some level of analysis between the organization as a whole and the individuals who are its members, they burden themselves with an incredibly complex set of interconnections. Much of this complexity can be organized, so to speak, by attending to patterns of interrelation among individuals at intermediate levels and construing those patterns as systems in themselves. It is perhaps analogous to the biologist trying to work only with the level of cells and the level of organisms, refusing to take seriously such intermediate levels as organs and functional subsystems (cardiovascular, neural, and so on). It might be possible to do so, but it certainly would be more complex. So it is with organization research that ignores intermediate levels—such as the level of work groups as intact systems.

These themes arose at several points in the conference on which this book is built. Several of the contributors, most notably Hackman and Walton, emphasized the importance of regarding the units of study as intact and complex social systems—not just as a set of people with a common task and a common supervisor, not just as a set of dyads who work together, not just as a task performance vehicle within a subsystem of an organization, but as an intact social system, a concrete social unit, worthy of study in and of itself.

Goodman's approach (Chapter Four) carries this theme to its most extreme form. His is a modified form of a *sociotechnical* approach, as I understand it; and in any such approach the focus needs to be on the intact social system. But in such a sociotechnical view, the focal system includes the hardware, the location, the work procedures, and the situational factors, as well as the people and their relationships. I am urging just such a sociotechnical view of work groups—namely, a view that focuses on the operating system itself.

Goodman uses this approach to argue for a much more idiographic approach to the study of work groups in organizations than has been the habit of behavioral scientists working on these problems. He believes that we have tried to generalize too much, too far, and too soon. In Goodman's view, I infer, we have tried to generalize across groups and types of groups far too broadly and have done so far too early in our knowledge accrual process. He seems to argue that we should immerse ourselves thoroughly in the particularities of content and process of the specific groups we are studying (in his case, specific mine sites of particular coal-mining companies); we should understand those processes in relatively complete detail before we attempt to generalize that understanding to a broader array of groups—even to other operations of that same mining company or to other similar mining companies, much less to other work organizations that assemble cars or sell insurance or ship cargo overseas. Furthermore, from his work on such groups, he reaches conclusions that suggest that a major part of the variance in work group productivity is associated with "individual differences," not among the members of such work groups as individual human beings but rather among the specific work groups (the "system" composed of workers, their supervisors, their machinery, their work site, and combinations of all of those contributing sources) as unique, concrete systems that operate as intact social units.

I do not agree with Goodman's idiographic prescription.[1] I do not think it a necessary consequence of an attempt to study work groups as intact social systems at a group level of analysis. If he were right, then we should each set about developing a "science of mine shaft 32," or mine shaft 46, or assembly plant G, or whatever our personal piece of the grand pie is to be. Further, we would hope that meanwhile someone else is developing an equivalent intimate knowledge of all the other specific instances of mine shafts and offices and field stations and warehouses to which we might ultimately want to generalize our understandings.

I hope Goodman is not right on this issue, for two reasons. One is a matter of personal preference; I really don't want to get to know most "intact social systems" at the level of intimacy that would be necessary to carry off that totally particularistic approach. I just don't want to be the world's leading student of mine shaft 32! To paraphrase Will Rogers, I have never met a group I liked that much!

The other reason, a much more important one, is a matter of the logic of our enterprise. If Goodman were right, then

1. Actually, Goodman probably does not agree with it in the extreme form in which I have presented it (and in which he presented it at the conference). He offered it in extreme form to stir controversy and make a point. I respond to his extreme formulation, here, in the same spirit.

we would be out of the science business altogether and in the history business—as some social psychologists (for example, Gergen, 1973) have argued that we are. By the time we could study each specific system in its full particularity and digest and communicate what we had learned, *that* concrete system would be a thing of the past. This statement is more than just a version of the Heraclitean saying that we cannot step in the same river twice. The kind of particularistic and idiographic immersion in the focal system reflected in Goodman's work involves not just a stepping into the river, so to speak, but a concentrated splashing around in it. Two consequences of that intense immersion are pertinent here: First, the very thrashing around—the research process itself—changes the river, often in dramatic ways. In the behavioral sciences, research activities themselves disturb the phenomena being studied. Second, surely even the most nondynamic views of such systems would expect substantial changes to occur during the considerable period of time it would take to carry out such a total immersion strategy. So the system we are studying will change *while* we are studying it and *because* we are studying it. If we followed this prescription, we would each mount an enormous research effort to learn about one particular concrete system in all its particularistic and idiosyncratic glory, only to find at the end of that effort that the system we presumably know all about no longer exists. And, by this rationale, our information is not to be generalized, even to another copy of that same kind of system, much less to systems of other kinds. Such a resource-consuming enterprise could serve no purpose other than satisfying the curiosity and fattening the vita of the individual researcher! If Goodman is right, in the extreme form of his antigeneralization argument, we are out of the knowledge accrual business and in the business of being social system raconteurs (and raconteuses)!

Nevertheless, I think we must take seriously Goodman's evidence that a very large part of the variance in work group productivity is "between specific groups" variance. Evidence on the same point exists elsewhere. For example, Kent and McGrath (1969) studied groups of various gender compositions working on tasks of three types and found "among groups" variance to

be a major component of the variation on task product characteristics, along with task type, whereas very little of the variation
was associated with gender composition or with the higher-order
interactions of those factors. Furthermore, in their integration
of small group research information, McGrath and Altman
(1966) found that one of the most consistently significant relations in the small group research literature was for (unspecified)
between group differences on a variety of dependent variables.

Such evidence, along with Goodman's, means at least that
the groups we study (in both field and lab) differ from one another in a variety of important ways that are not taken into
account in our experimental designs. I find this less an argument against generalization than a challenge to do it better—and
another strong indication of our fundamental need for more
and better theory. I agree with Goodman that we need to study
work groups in more detail. But I think we need to do so, not as
an alternative to generalization across groups, but as an aid to it.

Classifying Variations in the Groups We Study. One reason for this discrepancy in views, perhaps, is that the matter has
been posed in dichotomous terms. Thus far, the discussion has
seemed to pose the choice between believing that every group is
unique and not comparable to others *or* that all groups are
alike and information about any one of them applies to all others. Actually, of course, neither of those two positions is even
sensible, let alone likely to be true. Instead, groups come (or
are constructed) in a variety of shapes and sizes, colors and
kinds. One of the ways in which we can resolve some of the
issues already discussed is to try to specify, much more carefully than is often done, just what kinds of groups are to be the
subject of any given inquiry.

In short, we need some form of classification of types of
groups if we are to clarify how the behavior of different types
of groups may vary. In fact, an effective classification of groups,
into subclasses that are *homogeneous* in regard to key system
features (including technology), would provide a resolution of
the dilemma of generalization versus specificity that was discussed in the preceding section and thereby dissolve the disagreement between Goodman's idiographic view and my own.

It is remarkable how little effort has been given, in the group research field, to what would seem to be a fundamental definitional task for any field of study: the development of a meaningful classification of major varieties of its units of study. I have reviewed some of those efforts elsewhere (McGrath, 1984). The tendency to ignore what types of groups were involved in a given study, when we try to generalize over studies, does not seem to be any less prevalent in studies of work groups in organizations than it has been in the past in group research in general.

Elsewhere (McGrath, 1984), I have presented a classification of types of social units that have been, or could be, the focus of study in work regarded as group research. Some features of that classification are relevant to the present context. In that classification system, the entities that researchers have used as their focal units for study, in work that gets regarded as research on groups, are divided into three main categories, each with a number of subdivisions. Some studies of groups (many would say too few) deal with entities that could reasonably be called *natural groups*. I regard as *natural groups* those social units whose existence and behavior is independent of any ongoing research project to which they might (knowingly or unwittingly) be contributing evidence. Such groups are not created by the investigator. Their composition, structure, and process is not determined by the investigator. The tasks on which they work are not chosen by the investigator. They are not behaving so as to attain goals set by that investigator.

Other studies of groups—a far larger set than the first—deal with entities that I call *concocted groups*. I consider concocted groups to be social units that exist, or have the particular form they do, because they are part of some ongoing research activity. Such units are created, or modified in their composition, structure, task, goals, or process, by researchers and for research purposes.

The distinction between natural and concocted groups is not a distinction between groups that are "real" and "not real." Concocted groups are real, in the sense that individual behavior and group processes operate in context. But they are not natural groups, in that such behavior and processes are not an integral part of the lives of the group and its members. Concocted groups are doing what they are doing because they are part of a research endeavor. Natural groups are doing what they are doing because they are living their lives.

Still other studies of groups—by far the most numerous category—involve entities that I call *quasi-groups*. These studies use social units whose social and/or task processes are so highly constrained that we would not be likely to consider them as real, let alone natural. (These quasi-groups, however numerous in the small group research literature, are less pertinent to this chapter and will be given very little further consideration here.) These three categories of units of study for research on groups are not totally distinct. The units of study used in certain kinds of group studies really fit into two of the categories, and thereby the three categories are tied to one another. (See McGrath, 1984, chapter 4, for a more complete presentation of this classification system.)

Furthermore, social units included in the category of natural groups are not all alike. There are at least four main forms, each occuring in "nature" at relatively high base rates but each quite different from one another in terms of their relation to group research. One form of natural group functions more or less as total *embedding systems* for the individuals who are members of the group. In these groups, the individual carries out a very broad band of his or her activities as part of that group and remains a member of that group for a relatively long time. An example is the family, especially for young children.

Another form of natural group is what I call the *expedition*. These function as embedding systems for a broad band of the individual's activities, but only for a delimited period of time that is more or less predictable. Exemplars of this form of group would be such social units as an arctic wintering-over party, the crew of a spaceship or a submarine on a very extended mission, and a child's living group in summer camp.

Still another form of natural group is the *standing crew*. Such groups engage only in certain types of activities—often a certain set of tasks in a work setting. But such groups often persist for (or recur repeatedly during) a relatively long period of time, with more or less the same membership, tasks, and goals. A standing crew would be any case in which the same set of members do the same set of activities for the same organizational goals in a recurring pattern. Exemplars of this form of group would include athletic teams, work crews, and standing committees of a legislature or a college.

The fourth form of natural group in my classification system is the *task force*. Task forces are groups that are created by natural circumstances (as opposed to experimental purposes) for a one-time performance of a delimited task. Such groups exist for and deal with only a sharply delimited band of activities—a specific task or mission—and they exist only for the period of time needed to carry out that mission. Any ad hoc committee is an example. So is a jury.

In practice, the distinctions between these four forms of natural groups are often far less clear-cut than this classification schema implies. The differentiation between embedding systems and expeditions is a matter of how soon, and how predictably, the group will end. The distinction between embedding systems and standing crews is a matter of how broadband the set of activities are that define the group's purposes and behaviors. The distinction between task forces and the other three forms depend both on the *anticipated* duration of the group as a major locus of action for its members and on the bandwidth of member activities that are encompassed within the group's purview.

Frequently, natural groups that would seem to fit one of these forms actually end up fitting another. Some athletic teams, for example, deliberately try to become more like a family, broadening the scope of activities that members do together. Conversely, some families seem to migrate toward becoming more like standing crews, sharply delimiting the bandwidth of (recurrent) activities that members carry out with one another. One could postulate, too, that the developing adolescent comes to view his or her family of orientation as an expedition, with its totally embedding nature soon to end as the child gains maturity and independence and develops other relationships that compete for his or her time. But at any given time, natural groups can be characterized, more or less, as being one of these four forms; and that characterization is indicative of the centrality, extensiveness, and intensity of the group's role in its members' lives.

In principle, work groups in organizations include social units that fit all four of these types of natural groups: the embedding system that functions like a family; the expedition that serves as total context but for a predetermined period of time; the standing crew that does its tasks recurrently; and the ad hoc task force that does a job just once. In practice, though, the first type—embedding systems—probably have a low base rate as naturally occurring work groups in organizations. Yet, in a sense, this form is the most natural type of group, and it is such groups that we often have in mind when we talk about how important it is to study "real" or "natural" groups rather than artificial ones. When we set out to study natural groups in work settings, we intend to study social units that encompass a broad band of member activities over a relatively long period of time. But we seldom end up studying work groups that are as broadband and time enduring as families.

Hence, much of the actual interest in natural work groups in organizations focuses on groups of the other three types. Expeditions are a form of work group of relatively high frequency and importance in certain kinds of organizations such as military forces. Task forces (such as ad hoc committees) are even more frequent in many kinds of organizations and often carry out very important functions. Standing crews are the core of the work force in most work contexts.

These four types of natural groups are all quite different from one another, and we have no reason to suppose that the pattern of relations among their structures, processes, tasks, goals, members' abilities and attitudes, and so forth are similar from one type to another. The matter is more complex still if we consider a variety of types of social units called concocted groups in my group classification schema (McGrath, 1984). Concocted groups depart from "naturalness" in group composition, in group task, or in both. The task forces discussed under natural groups, although limited in bandwidth of group activities and in expected duration of the group's existence, are nevertheless "natural" in composition and are engaged in tasks endogenous to the organizational settings in which they exist. That is, the people who are members of such task forces are drawn from the organization within which those task forces are to operate, and their composition occurs by the operation of processes natural to that setting. Furthermore, those task forces are created to do tasks that are a part of the work of the embedding organization.

There is overlap between natural groups of the fourth type, task forces, and certain kinds of concocted groups—ad hoc groups created for the purpose of a research study. By definition, task forces as natural groups are created in forms and for purposes that are natural or endogenous to the context in which they occur. In contrast, similar but concocted groups are often created in forms and for purposes related to some research activity.

The overlap can be shown by a hypothetical example. Suppose a department of an organization decided to form a set of committees to do certain important tasks. They would choose members from the pool of eligible members and assign them to specific committees by the "natural" processes routinely used by that part of the organization. In contrast, suppose that for some reason a research activity intervened just when the committees were to be established. Hence, a set of committees designed to do the same set of tasks would be assigned, from the same pool of eligibles, by the "unnatural" process of having researchers allocate members to committees using a randomizing procedure. The tasks of the two committees would be the same under the two sets of conditions. The actual composition of any one committee might in fact be the same under the two conditions. The composition of all committees would be, in a sense, the same. The distinction between natural and concocted forms of these social units is, at this limit, quite arbitrary; it inheres mainly in what the members know about the assignment process.

But sometimes it is useful to study social units for which one or the other of those two major facets of "naturalness"— composition procedures and tasks—are constrained. There are many cases in which groups doing tasks natural to (endogenous to) the organization are composed in much more "unnatural" ways than just a randomization of the allocation procedure. For example, I have discussed (McGrath, 1984) a category of studies called *system tests,* involving a completely arbitrary set of participants but an actual set of system tasks. Conversely, there are many cases in which actual group members may be studied while doing relatively "unnatural" tasks—either tasks that are simulations or representations of actual group tasks or tasks that are purely artificial. There is a category of such tasks that I refer to as *training tasks;* it would include both military training exercises and practice games or scrimmages of athletic teams. Here, the group's composition is natural, and the group's task is a simulation of its endogenous tasks.

When we modify both task naturalness as in the training tasks category and the naturalness of the group's composition as in the system test category, we have a type of study that I call *mock studies.* I chose the term to suggest one major example of that type of study, the so-called mock jury study. But many simulations (for example, aircraft flight simulations, automobile driving simulations, games simulating international conflict, "in-basket tests," and the like), when used with groups that are not composed naturally from the organization's own membership and processes, would fit this category.

If we restrict still further the naturalness of task—giving up any attempt to simulate tasks endogenous to the organizational setting and using, instead, "artificial" tasks designed to maximize the precision of certain kinds of performance information—we have a category of studies that I refer to as *crew tests.* Suppose, for example, that a basketball coach conducts sprinting drills or dribbling and rebounding drills, or that a play director holds dance drills, with members of his or her team or chorus line. The composition of such groups is as natural as it can be. The tasks, however, are not natural, nor are they attempts to simulate the group's natural tasks. Rather, they reflect abilities and skills contained in and/or underlying performance of the endogenous tasks. Why would these not generate data of interest to the researcher who cares about task performance of work groups in organizations?

When we combine the use of artificial tasks with the use of artificial composition procedures, we have the final type of concocted group. I call this type, quite unelegantly, *ad hoc laboratory groups with artificial tasks.* These are the prototypical "artificial laboratory groups" that so often serve as the whipping boys for critics of experimental approaches: groups composed of an arbitrary combination of individuals, previously unacquainted, who interact with one another only while working on tasks arbitrarily assigned by the experimenter. They are the most restricted of the types of concocted groups. On the other hand, they also can be viewed as the most unconstrained of the types of *quasi-groups* that have been used in group research. (See McGrath, 1984, chapter 4, for further discussion of quasi-groups.) Such groups are, far and away, the most frequently used type of unit of study for the group research field.

Why study unnatural groups? Among the conference participants and among researchers in general, the people who seem most committed to the development of a field of study focusing on task performance of work groups in organizations are also the people who seem to have the strongest preference for studying natural groups—and studying *only* natural groups. However, there are many powerful reasons why group researchers often choose to study social units that do not fit my category of natural groups but rather are what I have termed concocted groups. I have presented some of those reasons elsewhere (for example, McGrath, 1984; Runkel and McGrath, 1972) and will deal with them here only briefly to make my central point.

Take, for example, the case of jury studies. It is, in fact, illegal to study juries in their ongoing natural state. Some researchers interested in the problem have chosen to study *jurors,* retroactively—attending to the naturalness of membership but at the same time accepting artificiality in many other features of the "natural" jury situation. Other researchers have chosen to study what I would call mock juries—simulations of the presentation of evidence from a given case or cases. These mock jury studies are of two kinds: studies that use individuals drawn from jury rolls and studies that use jurors drawn from an arbitrary but accessible population (such as college students). Both of these are "artificial" in composition, but in different ways;

and both are "artificial" in the tasks being done, but with the degree of that artificiality being a function of how thoroughly they attempt to simulate the endogenous tasks of actual juries. But we really cannot consider any of these kinds of jury research as dealing with *natural groups* as here defined. Should we therefore gainsay all opportunity to acquire empirical evidence about juries and their operations?

Furthermore, if it were not illegal or otherwise impractical to study actual juries as naturally occurring groups and if that were the *only* kind of study we did on the topic, those studies would not be very informative. After all, each jury is unique—it deals only with one case, under one judge in one particular legal jurisdiction, and with one set of attorneys, witnesses, and surrounding conditions. A study of the specific jury that heard case 632 in courtroom B of the Muskogee county courthouse on June 17th, 1956, would be even more particularistic, more idiographic, than the studies of the hypothetical "mine shaft 32" that I conjured up earlier in the chapter.

Generally, we do not want to get into the courtroom equivalent of the "mine shaft 32" bind but rather want to learn about a more general topic than that. To do so, we must somehow get information on lots of cases that are somehow "the same" (that is, comparable) and combine that information over cases. In that intellectual enterprise we call science, we have no way to use single-case information to gain "intellectual leverage" on a topic that is not totally particularized to that case.

If we worked solely with "naturally occurring" juries, even if we got evidence from a lot of cases, we would have no logical basis on which to combine that information over cases. Each case is a specific jury hearing a specific legal case under a specific judge in a specific jurisdiction, and so forth. We cannot combine information from their results unless we are willing to assume that all juries (and all jurors) are alike, that all types of cases (murder, fraud, rape, and so on) are alike, that all judges are alike, and/or that all jurisdictions are alike. Those assumptions are highly dubious (if not downright silly) to anyone who is a substantive system expert in the legal system. Even if we assume merely that at least all rape cases in a given jurisdiction heard by the same judge are "the same," we would be unlikely to collect data on enough instances of that kind of legal case to gain much inferential leverage from their aggregate results.

Mock jury studies let us replicate the hearing of a given legal case with multiple juries and potentially with alternative judges, attorneys, and jurisdictional peculiarities. Mock studies certainly have their limitations, used alone. But they also offer lots of intellectual leverage on otherwise intractable questions about juries and jurors, if they are used in sensible combinations with studies of other types.

I will not belabor further the many good methodological and conceptual reasons that one might want to study such "unnatural" units, along with rather than instead of studies of such natural groups. Instead, I will argue that, if we want to build a systematic body of knowledge about task performance of work groups in organizations, we had better not reject, out of hand, any opportunities to gain major methodological leverage on that relatively intractable topic. Our Humean logic and positivistic methods are, at best, relatively blunt instruments for acquiring knowledge and increasing our confidence in that knowledge. If we want to study anything at all complex, and we begin that effort by restricting ourselves both to a very limited set of positivistic tools *and* to using only naturally occurring instances of the phenomena to be studied, we are burdening ourselves with an unnecessary, perhaps fatal, handicap. The topic is tough in any case. We will need all the help we can get.

Classifying Variations in Group Tasks. Cutting across these distinctions about the group's status as a natural or concocted group is the matter of what the group *does*: its tasks or goals or span of activities. When we set up a work crew or a task force, we set it up to do something—and, by implication, *not* to do many other things that such a group could do. The research literature on groups reflects a bewildering array of tasks that have been the focus of such studies. At the same time, that literature reflects surprisingly little consideration of how group task performance depends on variations in the tasks that are performed.

There have been surprisingly few attempts to develop systematic ways to classify group tasks. I have tried to build a task typology based on the best of those past efforts (McGrath, 1984). That task classification schema specifies four related task performance processes: to generate, to choose, to resolve, and to execute. Each of those performance processes embodies two related subtypes:

1. Generating plans (planning tasks)
2. Generating ideas (creativity tasks)
3. Choosing correct answers (problem-solving or intellective tasks)
4. Choosing preferred answers (decision-making tasks)
5. Resolving conflicts of viewpoint (cognitive conflict tasks)
6. Resolving conflicts of interest (mixed-motive or negotiating tasks)
7. Executing tasks requiring competition against another group (contests or battles)
8. Executing tasks requiring competition against standards of excellence (performances)

Those eight task types are related to one another in a form that resembles a circumplex. Furthermore, I believe, the operating rules by which groups do business vary systematically across that circumplex, and these four task performance processes are systematically related to socioemotional stages of group development. If so, then this task circumplex (or some improved version of it, perhaps) can serve as another template (along with the group typology already discussed) for framing our questions and qualifying our generalizations about groups. (See McGrath, 1984, especially chapter 5, for a more detailed presentation of this task typology).

Work groups in organizations do tasks of all eight types but not with equal frequency. One way in which this task typology may help us plan for the systematic study of groups at work is to highlight how the frequency distribution of these types of tasks for naturally occurring groups is quite different than the frequency distribution for types of tasks included in our studies. Research on group task performance has dealt mainly with problem-solving and decision-making tasks (types 3 and 4) and to a lesser extent, with the resolution of conflicting interests and the allocation of rewards (type 6). There was a flurry of work, a few years back, on so-called creativity tasks (type 2). But in the workaday world of groups at work, I wonder how often most workers do anything that they would regard as problem solving or decision making or bargaining or allocation of payoffs? That world, I think, is much more densely filled with tasks of quite different types: tasks that involve performances and competitions (types 7 and 8) and planning tasks (type 1). These types of tasks are strikingly absent from the group research literature.

A second way in which we might use this task typology to help our study of groups at work is by building on the idea that group performance is a function of different rules of combination of member inputs for different types of tasks. There are strong tendencies for results of problem-solving groups (type 3) to reflect a "truth wins" or a "truth supported wins" combination rule, for decision-making groups such as (mock) juries (type 4) to reflect a "strong majority" rule, and for groups engaged in coalition-forming and allocation tasks (type 6) to reflect use of some form of minimum-winning-coalition rule (Davis, Laughlin, and Komorita, 1976). I have conjectured (McGrath, 1984) that groups engaged in intergroup competitions (type 7) reflect a conjunctive combinatorial rule, to wit: that the team with the "strongest weakest link" will win. If these or other specific operating rules are accurate descriptions for task performance of groups doing tasks of different types, then people interested in research on task performance of work groups in organizations had better take task type into account in all their empirical and theoretical activities. Otherwise, they will be faced with the same kind of dichotomous choice posed earlier in the discussion about generalization versus particularity across variations in groups. Without some conception of task type differences, we must choose either *to be willing* to generalize across all groups regardless of task or *not to be willing* to generalize at all across groups that have even very minor differences in tasks. We must avoid confronting ourselves with such choices of "to be . . . or not to be . . . ."

Inclusion of a Broad Band of Content. One further implication of the diversity of tasks in the group area and of the high
level of variation that is accounted for by yet unspecified features of groups is that we need to bring to our study of groups a
broadband conception of what the relevant phenomena are. We
need a study of groups that is broader than just task performance; broader, too, than just cognition; broader, indeed, than
any single process currently in fashion in the supporting behavioral sciences. If we are to study work groups in organizations as
intact social systems, we must study *all* of the processes that go
on in that "system"—not only cognitive and decision-making
processes but also motivational, behavioral, and conative processes, as well as affective, evaluative, and emotional processes,
plus whatever else goes on in those systems. Much of the tone
of the conference on which this book is based seemed to imply
that the study of work groups in organizations ought to study
only task performance processes. I think that is a misguided ex-
clusivity. A successful field of study dealing with work groups
in organizations certainly must treat the group's task performances as of special interest. At the same time, we would
undercut that enterprise, I believe, if we insisted that task performance be the only set of processes of interest within those
intact social systems. *If we are to study, successfully, work
groups in organizations, we must do it not by studying the work
of groups but by studying groups at work.*

Substantive Requirements

The central substantive issues in any topical area revolve
around what the important phenomena are and how they are to
be construed. In the present case, if work groups in organizations are to be viewed as intact social systems, interdependent
with their surroundings, then we need to study such groups in
ways that allow us to learn about group behavior in relation to
that context.

One crucial feature of the context is its temporal structure. Furthermore, one crucial aspect of group behavior is its
temporal patterning. Hence, we need to study work groups dy-

namically; that is, we need to take into account temporal features of the group's context, as well as temporal patterns in the group's behavior. Furthermore, the phenomena of most central concern are the *processes* by which groups do what they do, not the inputs to those performances and not the products or outcomes of them.

Group Behavior in Context. The need to study group behavior as it occurs within the group's time/place/thing context has methodological and conceptual implications as well as substantive ones. On the methodological side, we must reckon with the potential distortion, as well as the massive reduction in potential information gain, that can result from cutting our phenomena out of their context. That issue has been raised obliquely in earlier sections; it is a far more complex question than the simple argument about whether to study groups in the lab or the field.

The context question is also a matter of conceptual strategy. If we are to take a view of groups that stresses their status as intact social systems, we need to think of group behavior as action within a complex context with which the focal system (the group) is intricately interdependent. This is true for the study of groups in general, I would argue. It is even more the case for the study of work groups within organizations. The embedding organization is a crucial part of any work group's context, and the pattern of mutual interdependence between the group and the surrounding organization is a crucial part of the pattern of substantive phenomena to be explored.

A number of the contributors to this volume made indirect reference to these contextual issues. One would certainly infer from Schwartzman's (Chapter Seven) general point of view that she would insist on a full treatment of group context. Hackman and Walton (Chapters Three and Five) also seem to assume the importance of context; it is an inevitable consequence of their concern with groups as intact social systems. Davis and Kerr (Chapter Nine) recognize contextual problems as particularly intractible in specific empirical instances and see this intractibility as adding urgency to the use of powerful formal models that let us transcend those particulars. Goodman

(Chapter Four) treats contextual complexity as a critical feature of our field that prevents us from generalizing and requires us to follow the ideographic approach he advocates.

Temporal Patterns. One important facet of that critical contextual fabric is its temporal structure, and here perhaps more than anywhere else we have simply failed to deal with it. We have long talked about group dynamics, which originally had a time-based meaning, but we have certainly been sparing in our practice of it. Moreover, there are at least two sides to the temporal question. One is more or less a methodological issue: We must take seriously the idea of studying groups over time and of paying attention to the ways in which they change over time quite apart from our experimental activities. We have long recognized the need for longitudinal studies—and recognized some of their major limitations and difficulties. But we have not practiced them much. And when we have, it has most often been in the form of a simple before-after design that leaves much of the causal process to the imagination of the researcher. (The group research area is not especially notable in its lack of attention to these temporal matters. Virtually all of the behavioral sciences have given short shrift to time. See McGrath and Kelly, forthcoming.)

The other face of the temporal issue is that there is much temporal patterning in the group's behavior, and we need to deal more adequately with such temporal factors that are a part of the phenomena themselves. This is one area in which group research has been making some progress in recent years. There have been several major efforts to study the temporal flow of interpersonal interaction. Some of these (Jaffe and Feldstein, 1970; Dabbs, 1983; Warner, 1979) have concentrated on the temporal pattern of sounds and silences. Others (Gottman, 1979a, 1979b) have also been concerned with the content of that interaction and with patterns of mutual influence. Both of those sets of work have drawn on sophisticated data collection systems involving complex computer-aided audio-visual recording systems, and sophisticated data analysis methods such as Fourier analyses. Still others (for example, Kelly and McGrath, 1985; McGrath and Kelly, forthcoming; McGrath, Kelly, and

Machatka, 1984; Warner, 1979, 1984) have developed conceptual models of temporal processes ("social entrainment") by
which group members influence one another, and by which
they are collectively influenced by outside forces. The latter
work has also shown such entrainment effects for group task
performance processes, effects that are manifested in interaction patterns, in productivity rate and in aspects of product
quality. This, of course, is at the heart of the study of groups at
work.

Focus on Group Process. That we have given so little attention to temporal factors in the study of groups is closely related to our emphasis on structure rather than process. In spite
of considerable lip service to the idea of group dynamics, mainly what we have studied has been group statics, and we have
used relatively simple input-output models to do so. We have
talked about process to a moderate extent, but, as with multiple
methods and use of theory, there has been at best a very loose
coupling of talk to action.

As with dynamics, we must begin to take seriously the
idea of *process.* We often try to finesse the process issue by assuming that all important aspects of process can be captured
in a "series of states," if only that series is just fine grained
enough. We seldom obtain a very fine-grained set of measures in
any case; most often we have only a "snapshot"or two. But, I
am arguing here, even if we did have data from a series of occasions that offered a very fine-grained picture of a time-ordered
"series of states," we would probably still miss much of the essence of the underlying process(es) because we continue to
think about ongoing process as if it were *nothing but* (that is,
merely) a succession of states.

That kind of interpretation in the group area is analogous
to viewing the growth process as *nothing but* a series of measurements of height and weight. Such a series of "states" is not
a good representation of process, however accurate those measurements and however small the time interval between successive measures. Growth is more than that. The current and recurrent status of a set of processes (a system or subsystem) can be
assessed by such measures. Differences from one measure to the

next represent an assessment of change in the status of the system. Number of inches and number of pounds reflect the state of the system at the time of those measurements. Change in inches per day and change in pounds per day are *indexes of growth* of that system. But they do not provide a description, much less an explanation, of the growth process itself.

The results of the studies of temporal patterning noted above, particularly the work on "social entrainment" noted there, point up one major reason why we often fail to study process even when we get a fine-grained time-ordered series of measures of the phenomena in question. Much of group behavior is *cyclical rather than linear.* Those cycles indicate underlying periodicities or rhythms that themselves are a function of a variety of factors (group size, task type, verbal proclivities of members, past history, and so forth). If we regard our observations as involving a temporally ordered series of "states," even if that series is relatively fine grained temporally, we are not likely to interpret those observations as involving recurrent cycles. Instead, such data are likely to be analyzed in terms of differences between successive measures (that is, as before-after changes) or perhaps as an early-middle-late sequence. If the underlying processes are really recurrent cycles (for example, sine waves), the pattern of such *differences* will be chaotic, even if the recurrent cycles are quite regular. Such chaotic values would be likely unless we just happened to use the period of the cycle as the interval between our measures. If we did the latter, we would find no differences at all. If behavior is rhythmic, we will not find out about it in designs geared to assessing only linear changes over time.

Some of the work that shows promise in this domain begins with the premise that many features of behavior of individuals and groups are periodic; those studies search for the phase, periodicity, and intensity of those temporal patterns. (See, for example, Dabbs, 1983; Kelly and McGrath, 1985; Jaffe and Feldstein, 1970; McGrath and Kelly, forthcoming; Warner, 1979, 1984). A next step in that chain of logic, after temporal patterns have been identified and verified, is to try to manipulate conditions (of composition, structure, situation, and the like) so as to modulate those rhythms in predictable ways. From results of those activities, one may be able to infer the pattern of periodicities underlying the behaviors, the nature of the underlying processes that are driving those behavioral rhythms, and the nature of the processes by which those rhythms can be modified. Such an approach, it seems to me, is a way to study group processes within a dynamic, contextual framework.

Concluding Comments

The past fifty-some years of intensive study of small-group processes and structure has yielded much valuable research information. But there has been much chaff among the wheat. Furthermore, the recent annual yield of information has been far below the bumper crops of some years of the past. However, those recent smaller crops may have a higher-quality product; we may be better positioned, nowadays, to assess and use the information that we gain from small-group research.

From a far less informed position, I would venture that the situation is very much the same in the study of work in organizations. We have gained much from the past, and we currently are generating research information at a reduced rate but perhaps of a higher quality.

If we are going to take seriously the idea of a field of study that is, more or less, the intersection of those two areas —small group research and research on work in organizations— then we should also be concerned with how researchers in that "new" area of study—*research on the task performance of work groups in organizations*—can best gain from the past research efforts of those two underlying areas while at the same time avoiding their most serious pitfalls. This chapter has been addressed to those concerns and has dealt with them by postulating a series of requirements, or critical needs, for building such a field of study.

I have argued for ten such critical needs. Some of those requirements are methodological: We need to develop better data collection tools and use broader research strategies, including a stronger focus on theory. Some of those requirements are conceptual: We need to study groups as intact systems at a group level, to deal with the variation in types of groups and types of tasks, and to include a broader range of content as part of the phenomena of interest. Some of the critical requirements are substantive: We need to study groups in context, to give much more attention to temporal features of both the context and the group's behavior, and to focus on group process rather than group structure or outcomes.

If we give only lip service to those critical needs—as has too often been the case in many areas of the behavioral sciences in the past—then we will surely not get to harvest a bumper crop of high-grade information. On the other hand, if we take all ten critical needs seriously, and do our best to meet them, we still may not get a good crop. In research, there is no guarantee that a whole field will not turn out to be barren.

References

Brinberg, D., and McGrath, J. E. *Validity and the Research Process*. Beverly Hills, Calif.: Sage, 1985.

Dabbs, J. "Fourier Analysis and the Rhythm of Conversation." (ED 222 959) 1983.

Davis, J. H., Laughlin, P. R., and Komorita, S. S. "The Social Psychology of Small Groups: Cooperative and Mixed-Motive Interaction." *Annual Review of Psychology*, 1976, *27*, 501-541.

Gergen, K. J. "Social Psychology as History." *Journal of Personality and Social Psychology*, 1973, *26*, 309-320.

Gottman, J. M. "Detecting Cyclicality in Social Interaction." *Psychological Bulletin*, 1979a, *86*, 81-88.

Gottman, J. M. *Marital Interaction: Experimental Investigations*. Orlando, Fla.: Academic Press, 1979b.

Jaffe, J., and Feldstein, S. *Rhythms of Dialogue*. Orlando, Fla.: Academic Press, 1970.

Kelly, J. R., and McGrath, J. E. "Effects of Time Limits and Task Types on Task Performance and Interaction of Four-Person Groups." *Journal of Personality and Social Psychology*, 1985, *49*, 408-419.

Kent, R. N., and McGrath, J. E. "Task and Group Characteristics as Factors Influencing Group Performance." *Journal of Experimental Social Psychology,* 1969, *5* (4), 429–440.

McGrath, J. E. *Groups: Interaction and Performance.* Englewood Cliffs, N.J.: Prentice-Hall, 1984.

McGrath, J. E., and Altman, I. *Small Group Research.* New York: Holt, Rinehart & Winston, 1966.

McGrath, J. E., and Brinberg, D. "Alternative Paths for Research: Another View of the Basic vs. Applied Distinction." In S. Oskamp (ed.), *Applied Social Psychology Annual.* Vol. 5. Beverly Hills, Calif.: Sage, 1984.

McGrath, J. E., and Kelly, J. R. *Time and Human Interaction: Toward a Social Psychology of Time.* New York: Guilford Publications, forthcoming.

McGrath, J. E., Kelly, J. R., and Machatka, D. E. "The Social Psychology of Time: Entrainment of Behavior in Social and Organizational Settings." In S. Lskamp (ed.), *Applied Social Psychology Annual.* Vol. 5. Beverly Hills, Calif.: Sage, 1984.

McGrath, J. E., Martin, J., and Kulka, R. A. *Judgment Calls in Research.* Beverly Hills, Calif.: Sage, 1982.

Runkel, P. J., and McGrath, J. E. *Research on Human Behavior: A Systematic Guide to Method.* New York: Holt, Rinehart & Winston, 1972.

Warner, R. M. "Periodic Rhythms in Conversational Speech." *Language and Speech,* 1979, *22,* 381–396.

Warner, R. M. "Rhythm as an Organizing Principle in Social Interaction: Evidence of Cycles in Behavior and Physiology." Unpublished manuscript, Department of Psychology, University of New Hampshire, 1984.

Webb, E. J., and others. *Nonreactive Measures in the Social Science.* (2nd ed.) Boston, Mass.: Houghton Mifflin, 1981.

Name Index

Subject Index